Equity Ownership and Performance

Contributions to Economics

www.springer.com/series/1262

Further volumes of this series can be found at our homepage.

Sardar M. N. Islam
Empirical Finance
2004. ISBN 978-3-7908-1551-1

Jan-Egbert Sturm/Timo Wollmershäuser (Eds.)
Ifo Survey Data in Business Cycle and Monetary Policy Analysis
2005. ISBN 978-3-7908-0174-3

Bernard Michael Gilroy/Thomas Gries/ Willem A. Naudé (Eds.)
Multinational Enterprises, Foreign Direct Investment and Growth in Africa
2005. ISBN 978-3-7908-0276-4

Günter S. Heiduk/Kar-yiu Wong (Eds.)
WTO and World Trade
2005. ISBN 978-3-7908-1579-5

Emilio Colombo/Luca Stanca
Financial Market Imperfections and Corporate Decisions
2006. ISBN 978-3-7908-1581-8

Birgit Mattil
Pension Systems
2006. ISBN 978-3-7908-1675-4

Francesco C. Billari/Thomas Fent/ Alexia Prskawetz/Jürgen Scheffran (Eds.)
Agent-Based Computational Modelling
2006. ISBN 978-3-7908-1640-2

Kerstin Press
A Life Cycle for Clusters?
2006. ISBN 978-3-7908-1710-2

Russel Cooper/Gary Madden/ Ashley Lloyd/Michael Schipp (Eds.)
The Economics of Online Markets and ICT Networks
2006. ISBN 978-3-7908-1706-5

Renato Giannetti/Michelangelo Vasta (Eds.)
Evolution of Italian Enterprises in the 20th Century
2006. ISBN 978-3-7908-1711-9

Ralph Setzer
The Politics of Exchange Rates in Developing Countries
2006. ISBN 978-3-7908-1715-7

Dora Borbély
Trade Specialization in the Enlarged European Union
2006. ISBN 978-3-7908-1704-1

Iris A. Hauswirth
Effective and Efficient Organisations?
2006. ISBN 978-3-7908-1730-0

Marco Neuhaus
The Impact of FDI on Economic Growth
2006. ISBN 978-3-7908-1734-8

Nicola Jentzsch
The Economics and Regulation of Financial Privacy
2006. ISBN 978-3-7908-1737-9

Klaus Winkler
Negotiations with Asymmetrical Distribution of Power
2006. ISBN 978-3-7908-1743-0

Sasha Tsenkova, Zorica Nedović-Budić (Eds.)
The Urban Mosaic of Post-Socialist Europe
2006. ISBN 978-3-7908-1726-3

Brigitte Preissl/Jürgen Müller (Eds.)
Governance of Communication Networks
2006. ISBN 978-3-7908-1745-4

Lei Delsen/Derek Bosworth/Hermann Groß/ Rafael Muñoz de Bustillo y Llorente (Eds.)
Operating Hours and Working Times
2006. ISBN 978-3-7908-1759-1

Pablo Coto-Millán; Vicente Inglada (Eds.)
Essays on Transport Economics
2006. ISBN 978-3-7908-1764-5

Christian H. Fahrholz
New Political Economy of Exchange Rate Policies and the Enlargement of the Eurozone
2006. ISBN 978-3-7908-1761-4

Sandra Gruescu
Population Ageing and Economic Growth
2007. ISBN 978-3-7908-1905-2

Patrick S. Renz
Project Governance
2007. ISBN 978-3-7908-1926-7

Christian Schabbel
The Value Chain of Foreign Aid
2007. ISBN 978-3-7908-1931-1

Martina Eckardt
Insurance Intermediation
2007. ISBN 978-3-7908-1939-7

George M. Korres (Ed.)
Regionalisation, Growth, and Economic Integration
2007. ISBN 978-3-7908-1924-3

Kerstin Groß

Equity Ownership and Performance

An Empirical Study of German Traded Companies

With 42 Figures and 116 Tables

Physica-Verlag
A Springer Company

Series Editors
Werner A. Müller
Martina Bihn

Author
Kerstin Groß
gross.ker@web.de

Library of Congress Control Number: 2007925250

ISBN 978-3-7908-1933-5 Physica-Verlag Heidelberg New York

This work is subject to copyright. All rights are reserved, whether the whole or part of the material is concerned, specifically the rights of translation, reprinting, reuse of illustrations, recitation, broadcasting, reproduction on microfilm or in any other way, and storage in data banks. Duplication of this publication or parts thereof is permitted only under the provisions of the German Copyright Law of September 9, 1965, in its current version, and permission for use must always be obtained from Physica-Verlag. Violations are liable to prosecution under the German Copyright Law.

Physica-Verlag is a part of Springer Science+Business Media

springer.com

© Physica-Verlag Heidelberg 2007

The use of general descriptive names, registered names, trademarks, etc. in this publication does not imply, even in the absence of a specific statement, that such names are exempt from the relevant protective laws and regulations and therefore free for general use.

Production: LE-TEX Jelonek, Schmidt & Vöckler GbR, Leipzig
Cover-design: WMX Design GmbH, Heidelberg

SPIN 11949541   134/3100YL - 5 4 3 2 1 0   Printed on acid-free paper

To my family

Foreword

Corporate governance has been at the center of interest in the corporate finance literature for the past decade. The discussion has continuously intensified due to the occurrence of multiple corporate governance failures which have triggered the introduction or further refinement of national and international corporate governance codes. The necessity of regulatory action however rests on the need for a sound understanding of potentially negative effects of ownership structure on financial performance.

Unfortunately, the empirical literature so far has not delivered consistent evidence leaving the overall effects still somewhat in the open. This inconsistency is argued to stem from different biases in the statistical analysis, where the most important ones are the endogeneity and simultaneity bias. The objective of this dissertation is to provide less distorted results by modelling various ownership aspects and performance simultaneously.

The study sets out with a simultaneous equations analysis of the relationship between general ownership concentration and performance. This is followed by an examination of more specific ownership effects with a follow-up model focusing on managerial ownership and another one on institutional ownership. Subsequently, the author combines the three previous models in a final comprehensive analysis which allows for the simultaneous assessment and separation of the different ownership and performance effects.

With its state-of-the-art analysis, the dissertation contributes substantially to the existing international empirical literature on the relationship between corporate ownership and performance.

I wish for this dissertation to give impetus to and become widely accepted by corporate governance researchers and practitioners alike.

Oestrich-Winkel,
November 2006

Professor Ulrich Hommel, Ph.D.

Preface

This dissertation was written during my time as a doctoral candidate at the Endowed Chair for Corporate Finance and Capital Markets at the European Business School, Oestrich-Winkel. Throughout the dissertation process, I was supported by several people and institutions. At this point, I would like to express my sincere thanks.

I owe special thanks to my academic supervisor Professor Ulrich Hommel, Ph.D, who continually facilitated my research project and academic development, and to my second advisor Professor Onno Lint, Ph.D. I am also grateful to the team members and alumni of the Endowed Chair for the friendly and cooperative working atmosphere and the support provide for my dissertation.

I extended my statistical background within the ICPSR Summer School in Quantitative Methods in Ann Arbor, Michigan. This stay was financially supported by the European Business School (ebs), whom I thankful to.

Most of all, I would like to express my deepest gratitude to my parents and my sister. This dissertation is dedicated to them.

Frankfurt,
November 2006 *Kerstin Groß*

Contents

1 Introduction 1
   1.1 Motivation 1
   1.2 Objectives 3
   1.3 Outline 5

2 Basic Aspects of Ownership Structure and Performance ... 9
   2.1 Introduction 9
   2.2 Ownership Structure and its Measures 9
       2.2.1 General Aspects of Ownership Structure and its Measures 10
       2.2.2 Non-metric Measures 13
       2.2.3 Metric Measures 17
       2.2.4 Summary 19
   2.3 Ownership Characteristics in Germany and Around the World 19
   2.4 Forms of Financial Performance Measures 23
       2.4.1 Introduction 23
       2.4.2 Market-based Performance Measures 23
       2.4.3 Accounting-based Performance Measures 26
       2.4.4 Hybrid Performance Measures 28
       2.4.5 Summary 33

3 Theoretical Background and Hypotheses 35
   3.1 General Remarks 35
   3.2 Theoretical Background 36
   3.3 Ownership Concentration and Performance 41
       3.3.1 Effect of Ownership Concentration on Performance ... 41
       3.3.2 Effect of Performance on Ownership Concentration ... 45
       3.3.3 Summary of Hypotheses on Ownership Concentration .. 47
   3.4 Insider Ownership and Performance 48
       3.4.1 Effect of Insider Ownership on Performance 48
       3.4.2 Effect of Performance on Insider Ownership 53

		3.4.3	Summary of Hypotheses on Insider Ownership	55
	3.5	Institutional Ownership and Performance		56
		3.5.1	Effect of Institutional Ownership on Performance	57
		3.5.2	Effect of Performance on Institutional Ownership	61
		3.5.3	Summary of Hypotheses on Institutional Ownership	62
	3.6	Ownership Concentration, Insider and Institutional Ownership		63
		3.6.1	General Discussion	63
		3.6.2	Effect of Ownership Concentration on Insider Ownership	64
		3.6.3	Effect of Institutional Ownership on Insider Ownership	65
		3.6.4	Summary of Hypotheses of Ownership Concentration, Institutional Ownership and Insider Ownership	66
	3.7	Summary of Hypotheses		67

4 Model, Methodology and Data ... 69
  4.1 Introduction ... 69
  4.2 Model Specifications ... 69
    4.2.1 Linearity and Monotonousness ... 69
    4.2.2 Timing of Effects ... 74
    4.2.3 Endogeneity, Simultaneousness and Causation ... 75
    4.2.4 Summary ... 78
  4.3 Methodology ... 78
    4.3.1 General Aspects of Simultaneous Equations Systems ... 78
    4.3.2 Estimation of Simultaneous Equations Systems ... 81
    4.3.3 Effect Decomposition after Simultaneous Equations Estimation ... 83
  4.4 Sample Selection and Variables Used ... 85
    4.4.1 Sample Selection ... 85
    4.4.2 Ownership Variables ... 89
    4.4.3 Financial Performance Variables ... 91
    4.4.4 Further Control Variables ... 93
    4.4.5 Descriptives Statistics ... 103

5 Empirical Analyses ... 109
  5.1 Analysis Procedure ... 109
  5.2 General Ownership Concentration ... 111
    5.2.1 Endogeneity Tests ... 111
    5.2.2 Model Specification ... 113
    5.2.3 Results ... 116
    5.2.4 Robustness Checks ... 129
    5.2.5 Summary ... 133
  5.3 Insider Ownership ... 134
    5.3.1 Endogeneity Tests ... 134
    5.3.2 Model Specification ... 135
    5.3.3 Results ... 137
    5.3.4 Robustness Concerning the Insider Definition ... 139

	5.3.5	Further Robustness Checks 146
	5.3.6	Summary 148
5.4	Institutional Ownership 149
	5.4.1	Endogeneity Tests 150
	5.4.2	Model Specification 151
	5.4.3	Results 151
	5.4.4	Robustness Checks 157
	5.4.5	Summary 160
5.5	Combined Model 160
	5.5.1	Results 162
	5.5.2	Robustness Checks 171
	5.5.3	Summary 171
5.6	Comparison and Summary of Results 175

6 Conclusion 183

List of Abbreviations 187

List of Symbols 189

References 191

Appendices 217
- A.1 Results of "Global Investor Opinion Survey 2002" by McKinsey 217
- A.2 Detailed Data on National Ownership Structures 220
- A.3 Example on Argument of Constant Market Return 223
- A.4 Historic Tobin's Qs 225
- A.5 Overview over Selected Studies 229
- A.6 Decomposition of Effects in Simultaneous Equation Models ... 312
  - A.6.1 Decomposition of Total Association in Causal and Noncausal Effects 312
  - A.6.2 Decomposition into Direct and Indirect Effects 312
- A.7 Detailed Skewness and Kurtosis 314
- A.8 Detailed and Additional Results of Empirical Analyses 315
  - A.8.1 Simultaneous Equations Model of General Ownership .. 315
  - A.8.2 Simultaneous Equations Model of Insider Ownership ... 333
  - A.8.3 Simultaneous Equations Model of Institutional Ownership 345
  - A.8.4 Combined Simultaneous Equations Model 357

1
Introduction

1.1 Motivation

Lately the corporate governance practices of contemporary corporations have met with considerable interest. The corporate governance research and discussion have their origin in the 1930s, when Berle/Means [1932] observed and addressed the increasing separation of ownership and control of firms. This development was caused by significant corporate law reforms taking hold around the turn of the 19th century.[1] The reforms enhanced the rights of corporate boards to govern without unanimous consent of shareholders in exchange for statutory benefits like appraisal rights.[2] Although the aim of the reforms was to make corporate governance more efficient, they were and still are also causing problems. They have watered down shareholder inspection rights,[3] which lead Cook [1894] to the drastic statement that these corporate law changes allow managers to turn firms into "efficient instruments of fraud, speculation, plunder and illegal gain."[4] Consequently, in the following years researchers have argued over the positive and negative effects of the separation of ownership and control on the firm and its performance.

A significant advance in the discussion was the development of the new institutional economics and the financial agency theory by Jensen/Meckling [1976] and Fama [1980], which allowed an institutional approach of the issue. These theoretical frameworks raised a multitude of arguments for different, even contradicting effects of the corporate governance structure on the firm. The empirical evidence on the separation's effect as well as that on the corporate governance mechanisms have not reached a consensus. Thus more and more studies have tried to achieve an explanation by further developing the research question from the simple separation to a precise consideration

---

[1] See Winkler [2004, p. 112].
[2] See Horwitz [1985, pp. 200-202].
[3] See Machen Jr. [1908, pp. 892-894].
[4] Cook [1894, p. 894].

of ownership and control structure. Aspects of the ownership structure like the owner's identity have become important. Especially management or institutional investors have attracted attention as owner types, since they are directly involved in the agency conflict and their special characteristics and utility functions are assumed to cause different effects.

The increasing academic discussion has also found recognition in the business world. The agency problems caused by the control loss of the shareholders led to the development and implementation of corporate governance systems to protect the rights and the equitable treatment of shareholders. The corporate governance structure defines the rules and procedures for making decisions on corporate affairs. It also provides the structure through which the company objectives are set, as well as the means of attaining and monitoring the performance of those objectives. Thus corporate governance systems increase the transparency and diminish the information asymmetry. This reduces the agency costs by limiting the space for opportunistic behavior and easing monitoring actions. Another way to reduce the agency conflict is the alignment of interest impacting especially the managerial remuneration systems, for example in form of performance-based managerial remuneration or stock option plans.

In the last decade corporate governance has been even receiving greater attention in both, developed and developing countries, as a result of the increasing recognition of its positive effect on both, the firm's economic performance and its access to capital. In the "Global Investor Opinion Survey" of over 200 institutional investors, first undertaken in 2000 and updated in 2002, McKinsey & Company (ed.) [2002] found that the majority of respondents still put corporate governance on a par with or above financial indicators when evaluating investment decisions.[5] 77% of the respondents would pay a premium for well-governed companies, which varies from 13% for North America up to even 30% for Eastern Europe or Africa.[6]

Furthermore, numerous high-profile cases of corporate governance failure as that of Enron Corporation have focused the minds of governments, companies, investors and the general public on the threat posed to the integrity of financial markets. Corporate governance practices may serve as a prevention of business failures or frauds. In response many countries have implemented governance-related reforms that have been welcomed by investors. The most prominent example is the Organisation for Economic Co-operation and Development (OECD) who revised its Principles of Corporate Governance in 2004.

---

[5] For more detailed information see Figure A.1 in Appendix A.1, p. 217. More than 60% of investors state that governance considerations might lead them to avoid individual companies with poor governance and with a third avoiding even whole countries. See Figure A.2 in Appendix A.1, p. 218.

[6] For more detailed information see Figure A.3 and Figure A.4 in Appendix A.1, pp. 218 and 219.

Also the German Minister of Justice reacted on this trend and the criticism on the German system, especially from the international community, by appointing a Government Commission in 2001. It adopted the German Corporate Governance Code on February 26, 2002, which entered into force on July 26, 2002. The German Corporate Governance Code aims at making Germany's corporate governance practises transparent for investors, hence it strengthens confidence in the management of German corporations.[7]

All these resulting activities in corporate governance are based on the assumed effects of ownership and performance. However, since the academic discussion formulates different, contradicting effects, it requires empirical evidence to clarify the relations of ownership and performance. Yet, the multiple attempts to reach a consistent picture of the relation of ownership and performance by empirical studies have let to even more contradicting results. Consequently, the adequacy of the corporate governance mechanisms and the deduction of general corporate governance rules becomes questionable as long as their basis, the effects of ownership and performance, maintains unclear.

Multiple forms of biases are often argued to distort empirical analyses. While biases as reasons for inconsistent empirical results are not new to the discussion, they are rarely considered in the existing literature. This leaves room for further research by improving the study approach and its results.

1.2 Objectives

This work aims at clarifying the relation between ownership structure and company performance by incorporating several sources of biases. It conducts a study on the basis of annual data on German listed companies with several advantages over other comparable studies. These should yield in consistent and undistorted empirical results shedding light on the relation of ownership and performance.

A possible source of bias is the assumed direction of causation. An effect may not only run the other direction than assumed yielding a reverse-causation problem,[8] but there maybe even a multidirectional causation. The resulting endogeneity or simultaneous equations bias is very likely to exist in analyses of ownership and performance. As theory contains effects for both directions, from ownership on performance and vice versa, it supports the assumption of simultaneous reciprocal determination of ownership and performance. Although the endogeneity was already addressed by Demsetz/Lehn in 1985 and is widely accepted by researchers, it is rarely modelled in empirical studies. The author knows only five studies that model ownership and

---

[7] Information is taken from the official web page of the commission of the German Corporate Governance Code (www.corporate-governance-code.de).

[8] In a reverse-causation problem the real causation runs in the opposite direction of the assumed one. This might yield significant results, but gives a wrong picture of the relation. See Holderness [2003, p. 58].

performance simultaneously.[9] Since the ignorance of an existing endogeneity bias results in inconsistent estimates and confused directions of causation, the results of these five studies partly differ drastically from those of studies without modelled endogeneity.[10] Therefore, the consideration of the simultaneous causation estimated by the simultaneous equations method is seen as the main advantage of this study.

A further improvement in the quality of findings will stem from the consideration of multiple ownership forms. Ownership structure combines a multiplicity of different aspects with the owner type being a major dimension. While many studies consider only one single form of ownership, this study applies three different ownership variables to mirror the ownership structure. Besides the general ownership concentration, shareholdings by management and institutional investors are considered as ownership types. As the management is an important party in agency relations, managerial ownership is the earliest and most often considered identity in the academic field. The institutional investors have gained importance in research as the size of institutional investments increased over time. Following the OECD (ed.) [2001] the financial assets of institutional investors in Germany reached only € 151.75 billions in 1980 and augmented to € 1,677.54 billions in 2001. Also the portion of national shares as financial assets enlarged from only 6% to 24%, which equals 20% of the German gross domestic product at this time. Many researchers argued that the special characteristics of institutional investors justify a consideration as a separate identity.[11] Following this view institutional investors are selected as a second owner type.

The consideration of multiple aspects of ownership structure in a simultaneous model is also supported by an agency theoretic point of view. Jensen/Meckling [1976] and Jensen [1986] introduced the hypothesis of the substitution effect of agency devices, implying that agency devices influence each others' cost-efficiency and hence the extend of their usage. Different types of ownership, such as institutional and managerial ownership, are argued to be agency devices and therefore to interact. Thus the simultaneous model has to be extended to the different devices and ownership aspects. While some studies included agency devices in a simultaneous setting, none is known to the author that analyzed the several ownership forms simultaneously with performance as endogenous variable, as it will be done in the following study. Hence, this work does not only eliminate the endogeneity bias between ownership and performance, but also that between ownership aspects themselves.

---

[9] See Agrawal/Knoeber [1996], Bøhren/Ødegaard [2003], Cho [1998], Demsetz/Villalonga [2001], and Loderer/Martin [1997].
[10] See Mathiesen [2002, p. 47].
[11] See Barclay et al. [1993], Bathala/Moon [1994], Brickley et al. [1988], Brown/Brooke [1993], Chaganti/Damanpour [1991], Chowdhury/Geringer [2001], Dahya et al. [1998], Duggal/Millar [1999], Gillan/Starks [2000], Jones/Morse [1997], McConnell/Servaes [1995], Moyer et al. [1992], and Nyman/Silberstan [1978].

Another problematic issue of most studies is the origin of their data, which is mainly the USA and the UK. The ownership structure in these two countries differs drastically from those in continental Europe or Asia.[12] Apart from a generally low applicability of the results to other countries, both US and UK data have two further shortcomings. First, since both countries show the lowest ownership concentration worldwide, they provide little data of highly concentrated companies. Consequently, those studies yield good results for low concentrated firms, but fail in significance for higher concentration, since they cannot provide a large enough sample of those firms. Second, with the evolution of stock markets, shareholdings become increasingly complex through multiple control chains, pyramiding, and crossholdings. These complex ownership structures have a strong impact on the separation of ownership and control and the resulting agency conflicts. While these structures are prominent for most countries, they are little found in the USA and the UK. In contrast, German shareholders use these structures extensively,[13] making the German ownership structure again more similar to the international average and a more promising research object.

Combining the improved methodological design with the advantageous data source leads to a more precise and realistic picture of the relations between performance, ownership concentration, managerial ownership and institutional ownership. The results give new insights contradicting some widely assumed ownership effects. While general ownership concentration above a certain level has a positive effect on the firm's performance, institutional and managerial ownership have a negative effect. These effects shed a different light on the relation and question some corporate governance practices. For example, as managerial ownership has a negative effect, managerial stock remunerations appear as counterproductive. In contrast, higher general ownership concentration grants a better corporate governance. Following the implications of these results, shareholders have to fear more agency conflicts with the management or institutional investors and less value losses through blockholders. Therefore, the frequent call for an increased protection of minority shareholders is not justified by the results of this study, while a stronger control of the impact of institutional investors on the investment behavior and preservation of the efficiency of management disciplining actions appears necessary.

1.3 Outline

After motivation, objectives and outline of the work have been clarified in this section, the analytical approach of this dissertation is structured as shown in Figure 1.1.

---

[12] For detailed information on national differences in the ownership structure see Section 2.3, p. 19.
[13] See Beyer [1996, pp. 89-91].

Chapter 2: Basic Aspects of Ownership Structure and Performance
- 2.2 Ownership Structures and its Measures
- 2.3 Ownership Characteristics in Germany and Around the World
- 2.4 Forms of Financial Performance Measures

Literature review and basis for variable selection

Chapter 3: Theoretical Background and Hypotheses
- 3.2 Theoretical Background
- 3.3 Ownership Concentration and Performance
- 3.4 Insider Ownership and Performance
- 3.5 Institutional Ownership and Performance
- 3.6 Ownership Concentration, Insider and Institutional Ownership

Literature review and basis for effect interpretation

Chapter 4: Model, Methodology and Data
- 4.2 Model Specification
- 4.3 Methodology
- 4.4 Sample Selection and Variables Used

Literature review and basis for model selection

Chapter 5: Empirical Analyses

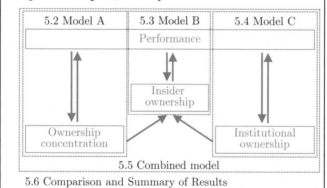

5.6 Comparison and Summary of Results

Chapter 6: Conclusion

Fig. 1.1: Analytical approach of the dissertation

This work consists of four main parts: Chapter 2 explaining basic aspects and measures of ownership structure and financial performance, followed by a theoretical chapter elaborating the assumed effects. Chapter 4 prepares the analyses later conducted by specifying the model, explaining the applied methodology and introducing the data set used. Chapter 5 conducts the empirical studies and discusses their results. The literature is not reviewed separately but discussed within these chapters along the dimensions "used measures", "theory and assumed effects", and "used model specifications". The major studies reviewed are also summarized in a table of more than 170 papers in Appendix A.5, pp. 231-311.

As mentioned above Chapter 2 examines the basic aspects of ownership structure and financial performance. This is achieved by presenting the universe of possible measures and their usage in the relevant literature. To show the advantages related to the German data set, the national differences in ownership structure are stated afterwards. Finally, the counterpart of ownership, financial performance, is examined. Possible forms of measures are explained and compared. These three parts give not only an introduction to the research field and the relevant literature, they also form the basis for the later selection of the ownership and performance variables.

The third chapter explains the most important hypotheses applied in the model and reviews the corresponding literature. The theoretical foundation is given by an elaboration on the principal-agent theory. The following sections explain the hypotheses on the relation of ownership and performance, starting with ownership concentration, followed by managerial ownership and institutional ownership. Finally, Section 3.6 states hypotheses on interactions of the different ownership variables.

The empirical analyses are defined in Chapter 4. In the first step different model specification issues are presented. This discussion in combination with the relevant literature is used to deduct further model aspects and to justify the usage of simultaneous equations as estimation method. Subsequently, Section 4.3 elaborates on the used methodology by explaining the estimation method. Then the data set is constructed, starting with the sample selection. After the ownership and performance variables have been chosen on the basis of Chapter 2, the control variables are specified. The data section closes with the presentation of the descriptive statistics.

Chapter 5 performs the empirical analyses and discusses their results. The constructed model is first analyzed by the separate relationships of the three ownership variables to performance. Afterwards, the models on ownership concentration, institutional ownership, and managerial ownership are combined to a large four-equations model also including ownership interactions. Section 5.6 recapitulates and compares the results of the different models.

Finally, Chapter 6 concludes the dissertation and gives an outlook on further research opportunities.

2

Basic Aspects of Ownership Structure and Performance

2.1 Introduction

To introduce the subject, the following chapter starts by taking a closer look on the concept and the different aspects of ownership structure. This is implemented by an elaboration on the different measures and their development in literature. The section will make clear that ownership is not summarizable in one single or a few variables, but that it constitutes rather a large spectrum of measures due to its different aspects and dimensions. Therefore, ownership variables can always mirror only a part of the real ownership structure, which makes the variable selection an important issue in the ownership and performance literature.

Next Section 2.3 states some statistics on the ownership structure of different countries and compares them to the characteristics of the German market. This will verify the advantageousness of German corporations as research objects.

Finally, the literature also uses varying forms of performance measures. They can be distinguished by the applied data type, market-based, accounting-based and hybrid measures. Each type raises different problems. The measures of financial performance and their appropriateness in the ownership literature are discussed in the Section 2.4.[1]

2.2 Ownership Structure and its Measures

The following section introduces the reader to the concept of ownership structure. This is done by an elaboration on the different aspects of ownership structure and the resulting measures. The discussion of the various forms of

---

[1] For an overview of selected studies and the used measures see Table A.9 in Appendix A.5, p. 231.

measures and the way they are mirroring the ownership structure is of further importance for the later variable selection.

After assessing some general issues of ownership information, different forms of ownership measures are explained. They are examined by their classification into non-metric and metric measures. Finally, some concluding remarks summarize the topic.

2.2.1 General Aspects of Ownership Structure and its Measures

Ownership structure is a multidimensional construct which therefore cannot be mirrored by a single variable. Two major dimensions structuring ownership information are ownership concentration and owner type.

The ownership concentration renders quantitative information on ownership, representing a share size or the sum of shares or a concentration index, e.g., Herfindahl coefficient. The second dimension, the owner's identity, is the qualitative information about the type of shareholder. This information is important since different owner types have different incentives, utility functions and means of control.[2] Widely researched identities are management insiders, with the subgroups of officers and directors, and institutional investors. These also constitute the main focus of this work. Further identities like families, company founders, strategic investors and governmental organizations have also gained importance, but are not considered in the course of the dissertation.

Apart from these two key ownership dimensions there are also other aspect that form many shades of measures. One common issue is the general definition of shareholding. Many studies do not use the direct share, but the cohesive ownership, which includes indirect shareholdings.[3] These shares are not personally hold by the individual, but controlled by him. They could be shares legally belonging to family members or close friends.[4]

Another distinguishing aspect is the level at which the ownership is measured. Early studies only examined the shareholdings on the first level, i.e., only the direct ownership of the shares of the considered company. However, with the evolution of stock markets shareholdings became increasingly complex through multiple control chains, pyramiding, and crossholdings.[5] Figure 2.1 gives examples of the complex ownership structures. Firms form a control chain if Firm A directly controls Firm B which in turn controls Firm C or a sequence of firms leading to Firm C, each of which has control over the next one. In a multiple control chain the control over a company is exe-

---

[2] For an explanation of the different characteristics see Chapter 3, p. 35.
[3] See Demsetz/Lehn [1985], Kamerschen [1968], Leech/Leahy [1991], McConnell/-Servaes [1990], McEachern/Romeo [1978], Mørck et al. [1988], and Palmer [1973b].
[4] See Holderness et al. [1999, p. 438] and Mathiesen [2002, pp. 87-88].
[5] See Claessens et al. [2000, p. 92], Faccio/Lang [2002, p. 366], and La Porta et al. [1999, pp. 23-25].

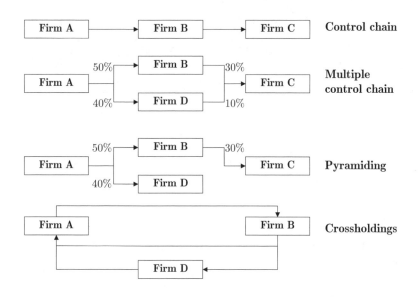

Fig. 2.1: Examples of complex ownership structures

cuted via a multitude of parallel control chains.[6] Pyramiding is a subform of control chains, where every share in the chain has to present a minimum of control, e.g., 20 or 25%.[7] Crossholding means a company directly or indirectly controls its own stocks, e.g., Firm A holds shares of Firm B owning in turn shares of Firm A.[8] Due to this complex ownership structures, the incorporation of the further levels of ownership and thus the ownership structure of the shareholding companies became important.[9]

The consideration of complex ownership structures raises the further question of the measured object: control rights or cash flow rights. Control rights measure the degree of control given by a share or control chain, cash flow rights measure the cash flow entitled through the share. Both the size of the rights themselves as well as the degree of their separation matter for shareholders' incentive and behavior.[10] Control rights can be separated from cash

---

[6] See Bertrand/Mullainathan [2001, p. 478] and La Porta et al. [1999, pp. 23-25].
[7] See Bertrand/Mullainathan [2001, p. 478], Beyer [1996, p. 84], and Grant/-Kirchmaier [2005, p. 66].
[8] See Beyer [1996, pp. 82-83], Claessens et al. [2000, p. 91], Faccio/Lang [2002, p. 366], and La Porta et al. [1999, p. 10].
[9] See Becht [1999, p. 1073], Claessens et al. [2000, p. 91], Faccio/Lang [2002, p. 366], Franks/Mayer [2001, p. 961], and La Porta et al. [1999, pp. 23-25].
[10] See Becht [1999, p. 1073] and Faccio/Lang [2002, pp. 391-393]. This will be shown in detail in Chapter 3.

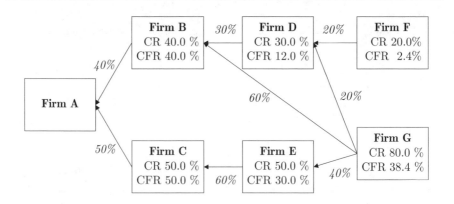

Fig. 2.2: Example of separation and calculation of control and cash flow rights CR for control rights concerning Firm A, CFR for cash flow rights concerning Firm A. Control rights correspond to the weakest link in the control chain. Cash flow rights are calculated as follows: $CFR_{FirmD} = 40\% * 30\%$, $CFR_{FirmE} = 50\% * 60\%$, $CFR_{FirmF} = 40\% * 30\% * 20\%$, $CFR_{FirmG} = 50\% * 60\% * 40\% + (20\% * 30\% + 60\%) * 40\%$

flow rights in two ways. First, the company can issue classes of shares that differ in terms of their relative proportion of voting rights and dividend entitlement, e.g., preferred stock or multiple-vote stock. Second, even in the absence of violations of the one-share-one-vote rule multiple control chains explain the divergence of control and cash flow rights.[11]

For the calculation of the size of control and cash flow rights La Porta et al. [1999] developed a now widely accepted standard methodology, which was followed by Claessens et al. [2002, 2000], Faccio/Lang [2002], and Barontini/Caprio [2005]. Cash flow rights equal the product of the share percentages of the control chain, whereas the voting right is represented by the lowest percentage in the control chain. Figure 2.2 gives an example for the calculation of cash flow and control rights.[12]

Edwards/Weichenrieder [1999] use a different definition. They measure the cash flow rights as fraction of total dividends paid and control rights as votes

---

[11] See Becht [1999, p. 1073], Claessens et al. [2000, p. 91], Edwards/Weichenrieder [1999, p. 2], Faccio/Lang [2002, p. 372], and Franks/Mayer [2001, p. 961]. For the special studies on dual-class equity see Bebchuk et al. [2000], Bergström/Rydqvist [1990b], DeAngelo/DeAngelo [1985], Grant/Kirchmaier [2005], Hanson/Song [1995], and Jarrell/Poulsen [1988].

[12] See Faccio/Lang [2002, p. 372], Franks/Mayer [2001, p. 950], and La Porta et al. [1999, pp. 9-12].

exercised at the last annual shareholder meeting.[13] This method may proxy the voting power better than the classical definition. However, it imposes also high data requirements. Furthermore, the question if and how to handle stock options, especially in case of managerial ownership, is still controversial and difficult to implement.[14]

With regard to owner identity, especially the definition of an insider varies in literature. Mørck et al. [1988], Agrawal/Mandelker [1990] and Loderer/- Martin [1997] define only management as insiders. Hermalin/Weisbach [1991] and Holderness et al. [1999] even just consider the Chief Executive Officer (CEO)'s shareholding, and Jensen/Murphy [1990] focus on the share size of the highest paid executive. However, most studies define both managers and directors as insiders.[15] Kole [1996] and Short/Keasey [1999] solve the problem by considering both board and manager shares, but separately.

A final classification of measures is referring to the type of variable: non-metric or metric, where the first is a nominal or cardinal variable, consisting of one or a set of dummy variables. Following this categorization the measures and their evolution in literature are further examined.

2.2.2 Non-metric Measures

Non-metric measures are categorial variables, returning only a dim picture of the ownership structure. However, their simplicity also eases their use; thus they were the first measures to be used in the ownership and performance literature. Table 2.1 gives an overview over most frequently used non-metric measures.

In earlier literature a single dummy variable which distinguishes only two groups of companies was used: those with a blockholder of a certain size and those without. Consequently, if the largest share owned by a shareholder or a group of cohesive shareholders is greater than a particular threshold of the stocks, the firm was classified as owner-controlled (OC). Due to the assumption that a dispersed ownership with no significant influence of the owner leaves the control to the management, the other group was labelled as management-controlled (MC). This appears misleading from a today's point of view, since the variable mirrors only general ownership concentration and not managerial ownership.

When using this measure, the share fraction needed to have control over a firm has to be defined. However, the control ability of a blockholder does not only depend on the share size, but also on other circumstances as for instance the dispersion of the remaining shares. As a consequence, the literature could

---

[13] See Edwards/Weichenrieder [1999, pp. 12-13].
[14] See Mehran [1995] for an assessment of stock options, control and cash flow rights.
[15] See Agrawal/Knoeber [1996], Agrawal/Mandelker [1990], Agrawal/Nagarajan [1990], Cho [1998], Holderness et al. [1999], Jarrell/Poulsen [1987], and McConnell/Servaes [1990].

Table 2.1: Non-metric ownership measures

Measured aspect	Examples	Representative Studies
Ownership concentration by share size	Separation of concentrated and dispersed firms by one threshold	Berle/Means [1932], Chevalier [1969], Holl [1977], Kamerschen [1968], Larner [1966], Villajero [1962]
	Separation of concentrated and dispersed firms by two threshold with unused middle range	Radice [1971], Sorensen [1974]
	Separation of concentrated and dispersed firms with a split condition considering active control	Boudreaux [1973], Elliott [1972], Monsen et al. [1968]
	Classification of different levels of ownership concentration by more than two categories	Bothwell [1980], Hindley [1970], Jacquemin/De Ghellinck [1980], Palmer [1973b], Stano [1976]
Ownership concentration by chance of winning majority vote	Separation of concentrated and dispersed firms by a probability threshold	Cubbin/Leech [1983], Leech/Leahy [1991], Nickell et al. [1997]
Ownership concentration with owner's identity	Differentiation of concentrated firms by the type of their owner	Levin/Levin [1982], McEachern [1975], Nyman/Silberstan [1978], Steer/Cable [1978], Ware [1975]
Ownership characteristics	Native categorial measures for ownership characteristics	Agrawal/Knoeber [1996], Cubbin/Leech [1986], Denis/Denis [1994], Denis et al. [1997], Johnson et al. [1985], Slovin/Sushka [1993], Steer/Cable [1978]

not agree on a consistent share fraction, thus the defined threshold varies through the different studies from 5% to 50%. Nevertheless since the stock dispersion rose with the development of stock markets, the early American studies show a trend of dropping thresholds since Berle/Means [1932]: from 20% to 10% by Larner [1966], Kamerschen [1968], and Holl [1977], reducing to 5% by Villajero [1962] and Chevalier [1969].[16] However, in later studies a general variance in definition is visible, e.g., 15% by Zeckhauser/Pound [1990] and 50% by Denis/Denis [1994].

A study that accounts for the dispersion effect on control is Thonet/Poensgen [1979] who used a classification at 25%, but only if no other shareholder holds 25%. Kania/McKean [1976] tried to include control capability by not using the sole fraction of share capital of the firm, but in relation to the total market. Three cohesive shareholders are defined as controlling if they own at least 10% of the 500 largest companies, 15% of the 500 second largest companies or 20% of the following 800 companies.

Other studies define two threshold thereby trying to circumvent the definition of one exact threshold and the resulting fuzziness of the classification around this threshold to improve their statistical results. The idea is that the resulting middle range contains the companies which cannot clearly be defined as OC or MC. Omitting the undefined middle range in the analysis would leave only correct classified companies within the sample.[17]

Apart from this consideration of the dispersion of shares, an improvement in the variable's ability to proxy actual control was achieved by accounting for active control by shareholders. This is achieved by splitting condition for the OC classification into two parts. The threshold lies at 10% if there is an evidence of active control by the shareholder and at 20% if not.[18]

A next step in the development of ownership measures was the incorporation of the unused but potentially valuable information of the omitted middle range of concentrations. For example Palmer [1973b] used all three ranges defined by the two thresholds and categorizes them as strong-owner-controlled (SOC), weak-owner-controlled (WOC), and management-controlled (MC) with the thresholds of 10% and 30%. This approach was copied by Stano [1976] and Bothwell [1980]. Jacquemin/De Ghellinck [1980] used the different labels of "internal control" if smaller than 5%, "minority control", and "majority control" if larger than 50%. Also Hindley [1970] uses the deviating nomenclature "intermediate" for ownership concentration between 20% and 40%.

The concept of the classification into OC and MC was brought further forward by Cubbin/Leech [1983] who developed a statistical definition of ownership control. It is not based on the size of the largest share, but on the chance of

---

[16] See McEachern/Romeo [1978, p. 354].
[17] See Radice [1971] and Sorensen [1974], who define MC for share size below 5% and OC for a share bigger than 15% and 20% respectively.
[18] See Boudreaux [1973], Elliott [1972], and Monsen et al. [1968]. The limit for MC is located at 5%.

winning a majority vote and therefore might enhance the variable's adequacy for control over the firm. A company is owner-controlled if the probability of winning the vote lies above a defined threshold.[19] Leech/Leahy [1991] and Nickell et al. [1997] are further examples of the implementation of measures on the concept of the winning probability.

As mentioned above, these variables measure the ownership concentration and do not include owner's identity information. However, the identity has high influence on the possibility of control over the firm, which becomes obvious in the case of the unity of management and owner.[20] An owner who is at the same time CEO of the company, obviously has higher ability of control over the company as a non-management owner. Therefore, studies started to incorporate the identity of the owner into their considerations. Ware [1975] altered the threshold for OC; it is 15% if the owner is part of the management and 25% else.[21] In contrast, McEachern [1975] modified the classic categorization by adding the group "externally controlled (EC)". Firms with the largest share below 4% are MC. If the share is bigger than the threshold and the owner is a management representative, it is classified as OC otherwise as EC. By a similar approach Levin/Levin [1982] distinguish institutional ownership, defining a firm with a share above 10% only as OC if the shareholder is no financial institution, otherwise it is labelled as "financially controlled (FC)". Nyman/Silberstan [1978] even introduce eight types of identity, with the most important being management, financial institutions and government.[22]

A further method to delineate the identity of the controlling shareholder is adding dummy variables. Most variables describe management, outside blockholders, family, and institutional investors.[23] These dummy variables present a special form of non-metric variables, the native categorial measures. The variables presented before converted the underlying metric information into non-metric dummies, which implies a loss of potentially valuable information. In contrast, native categorial measures differ in the way that the data is natively non-metric. The study by Johnson et al. [1985] gives a further example by considering the stock price effects caused by the sudden death of an insider.[24] They use a dummy to indicate whether the deceased was the founder.

---

[19] Cubbin/Leech's measure is calculated as $P^* = Z_\alpha * \sqrt{\Pi \sum_{i=1}^{N} P_i^2}$ where P^* is the share size needed for control, Π the probability of exercising the vote, P_i the fraction of share hold by the individual i, N the number of shareholder excluding the largest. Z_α is the critical value resulting of the standardization of $Z = Y/\sigma_y$ and $Y = \sum_{i=1}^{N} X_i$ where X_i is the sum votes by the shareholder i in favor of the largest shareholder (contra votes counting negative). See Cubbin/Leech [1983, pp. 357-358].

[20] See Jensen [1986] and Jensen/Meckling [1976].

[21] Similar, Steer/Cable [1978] changed the threshold to 3% with management representation and 15% without.

[22] For the full description of the groups see Nyman/Silberstan [1978, p. 85].

[23] See Cubbin/Leech [1986], Denis/Denis [1994], and Steer/Cable [1978].

[24] Slovin/Sushka [1993] performed an akin and more detailed study of this scenario.

Similarly, Agrawal/Knoeber [1996] and Denis et al. [1997] apply a dummy to reflect whether the founder is the top manager or not. However, these variables are mainly used as additional control variables.

2.2.3 Metric Measures

As shown in Table 2.2 metric ownership measures can be distinguished in two general groups: Concentration indices, such as the Herfindahl coefficient, and concentration ratios. The first are measures for the symmetry of share size over all shareholders and may not say anything about the control ability of the largest shareholder. Therefore, they are rarely used in literature with the exceptions of Demsetz/Lehn [1985] and Leech/Leahy [1991].[25] This leaves the concentration ratios as alternative to the non-metric OC and MC measures, which focus on the concentration of controlling shareholders.

Table 2.2: Metric ownership measures

Measures type	Examples	Representative Studies
Ownership distribution	Herfindahl index	Demsetz/Lehn [1985], Leech/Leahy [1991]
Ownership ratios		
- Differentiation by degree of cumulation	largest shareholder vs. three largest shareholder	Agrawal/Knoeber [1996], Agrawal/Mandelker [1990], Cho [1998], Demsetz/Lehn [1985], Jarrell/Poulsen [1987], Leech/Leahy [1991], Loderer/Martin [1997], McConnell/Servaes [1990], Mørck et al. [1988], Pedersen/Thomsen [1999]
- Differentiation by owner type	insider vs. institutional investors	
- Differentiation by unit	share fraction vs. monetary value	

Ownership concentration ratios are defined as percentage of stock ownership, voting rights or cash flow rights by the largest or a group of largest shareholders. The ratio is not converted into non-metric classifications, but used for analysis as it is. The number of shareholders consolidated in the ratio varies with the most important ones being the largest, the three largest, the five largest or the twenty largest shareholders. The chosen value often reflects the average national stock dispersion, since in high dispersed firms an alliance of shareholders might be needed to exploit possible benefits from blockholdings. Therefore, the large sum of twenty shareholders is only used in studies

---

[25] However, both studies use the Herfindahl index only as additional measure.

on USA or UK, where the ownership is very diluted. The application of such high sums to continental European countries does not appear reasonable considering that the median of the sum of the twenty largest shareholders is at 37.7% for the USA and at 60.5% for the UK,[26] and at the same time the continental European median of largest share is eight times higher than the US one and four times higher than the UK one.[27] However, the studies using such high sums of shareholding often employ several variables to avoid a proxy bias. For example Demsetz/Lehn [1985] use ratios of the largest, five largest and twenty largest shareholdings. Leech/Leahy [1991] even use additionally the ten largest shareholders. In contrast, Pedersen/Thomsen [1999], analyzing the European continental countries, use only the largest share.

These concentration measures can also be extended by the additional information of the owner's identity. By doing so, the concentration of the different sharcholder types is reflected. These measures do not substitute measures of general ownership concentration, instead they represent a different, additional aspect of the ownership structure.

Most studies using special identity measures, such as insider and institutional ownership, employ the total sum of shares held by one identity group.[28] Contrarily, Demsetz/Lehn [1985] and Agrawal/Mandelker [1990] use the sum of the five largest shares or the Herfindahl index of ownership.

A further dimension distinguishing the metric measures is the unit used. For example, measures of insider ownership are mainly notated in percentage of shares.[29] In contrast, Kaplan [1989] and Holderness et al. [1999] also use the dollar value of shares as basic unit.

Furthermore, a qualifying minimum share may be imposed, e.g., Mcconnel/Servaes [1990] and Loderer/Martin [1997] consider outside shareholders under the condition of a minimum share of 5%.[30]

Some unconventional metric measures are treated by Wruck [1989] and Himmelberg et al. [1999]. Wruck [1989] runs an event study on the changes in ownership concentration in percentage. Himmelberg et al. [1999] employ in addition to the standard total sum of managerial shareholding also the average share per top-level manager. Their main argument for doing so is that "[...] theoretical models generally emphasize managerial ownership levels relative to the managers' wealth and not simply the fraction of firm equity held by

---

[26] See Demsetz/Lehn [1985] for the USA and Leech/Leahy [1991] for the UK.
[27] The median of the largest share lies below 5% for US firms and at 9.9% for UK firms compared to a European median of 39.1%. For further information on the ownership structure for different countries see Section 2.3, p. 19.
[28] See Agrawal/Mandelker [1990], Jarrell/Poulsen [1987], Loderer/Martin [1997], McConnell/Servaes [1990, 1995], Short/Keasey [1999], and Slovin/Sushka [1993].
[29] See Agrawal/Knoeber [1996], Agrawal/Mandelker [1990], Cho [1998], Jarrell/Poulsen [1987], Loderer/Martin [1997], McConnell/Servaes [1990], and Mørck et al. [1988].
[30] For further studies see Agrawal/Knoeber [1996], Mehran [1995], and Short/Keasey [1999].

managers."[31] Unfortunately, they only integrate this measure in the regression analyzing the determinants of managerial ownership and eliminate it in their further analysis.

2.2.4 Summary

Ownership measures can be characterized by the two dimensions: Ownership concentration, giving the quantitative information of share size, and ownership identity, representing qualitative identity information, such as management, board or institutionals investors.

Several aspects distinguish the variables. Shareholding can be defined as direct or cohesive shares and measured at different levels of the control chains. In addition, it can refer to control or cash flow rights. Also the identity definition differs, especially in the case of insider ownership, where the inclusion of board shares is questionable.

A final aspect is the statistical type of the variables, the differentiation into dummy and metric variables. The ownership measures in early contributions are non-metric variables, which are easy to use, but lose potentially valuable information. Later studies mainly use different forms of metric measures.

2.3 Ownership Characteristics in Germany and Around the World

After ownership measures are elaborated on, they are used to depict the different national ownership structures and their key characteristics. This section will show the higher adequacy of German data as research object compared to data sets based on US and UK data. This constitutes a further advantage of this study over previously performed ones of the USA and UK.

Most research was conducted using US or UK data. However, the ownership structure of these two countries are not representative for other countries terms of ownership structure of the average country. While in the USA the median of the largest share lies below 5%, the German market features an almost symmetrical distribution with a median largest share of 52.1%. This is demonstrated by Figure 2.3 based on the data of Becht/Röell [1999].[32] The US median as well as that of the UK of 9.9% are not only drastically deviating from the ownership concentration in Germany but also those in most European countries, where the average median lies at 39.14%.[33]

La Porta et al. [1999] extended the analysis to the 27 wealthiest economies. They find that in contrast to Berle/Means [1932]'s image of the modern corporation relatively few firms are widely held. An exception are the economies

---

[31] Himmelberg et al. [1999, p. 370].
[32] For the detailed data see Table A.1 in Appendix A.2, p. 220.
[33] See Becht/Röell [1999, p. 1052]. For an overview over the medians of selected European countries see Table A.1 in Appendix A.2, p. 220.

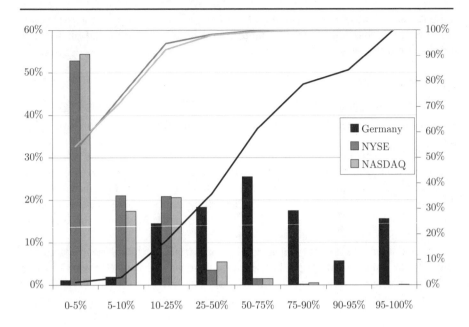

Fig. 2.3: Distribution of the largest voting stock in Germany and the USA

The bar chart states the percentage of companies in the range, the lines the cumulated density functions. *Source: Becht/Röell [1999]*.

with very good shareholder protection as the USA and UK. La Porta et al. [1999] further determined the corporations' ultimate controlling shareholders. Their results for the USA, UK, Germany and the sample average are shown in Figure 2.4.[34]

Following La Porta et al. [1999] most firms in the USA (80%) and UK (90%) have no dominant owner with a control right share of over 10%. The controlled firms are held by families or in the UK also by financial institutions. In contrast, only about a third of the German firms (35%) are widely held and also the amount of family-owned, traded companies is fairly small with 10%. The remaining firms are almost equally controlled by the state and financial institutions. The distribution of the sample average is more concentrated and resembles more the German structure than the structures typical for the USA or the UK.

While the differences in ownership concentration may partially result from legal and fiscal differences, Dyck/Zingales [2004] also state the existence of private benefits of control as a reason for these differences, making the block ownership advantageous. Private benefits are caused by block ownership, which

---

[34] For a comprehensive list of countries see Table A.3 in Appendix A.2, p. 221.

2.3 Ownership Characteristics in Germany and Around the World

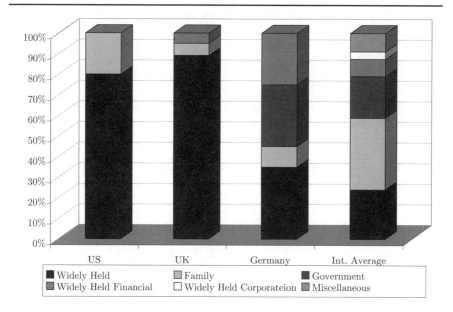

Fig. 2.4: Distribution of shareholders by identity type
Widely held if no combined share exceeds 10% of the control rights, else classification by the largest owner. *Source: La Porta et al. [1999].*

can be at the expense of minority shareholders.[35] While being low in countries with very good shareholder protection as the USA and UK, private benefits have a highly significant effect in Germany. The study analyzed block sales, yielding a premium of 10% of firm's equity in Germany. In contrast, it did not find a significant premium in the UK and only a weakly significant one of 1% in the USA.[36]

La Porta et al. [1999] further find that the controlling shareholders typically have power over the firms in significant excess of their cash flow rights.[37] To measure the divergence, they calculated the minimum percent of the book value of common equity required to control 20% of the votes. While 20% are needed in the UK and 19.19% in the USA, the percentage is significantly lower for the total sample (18.56%) and Germany (18.61%). This result is also supported by Faccio/Lang [2002], who surveyed the ownership structure

---

[35] For an explanation of private benefits of control see Section 3.3.1, p. 41.
[36] See Dyck/Zingales [2004, pp. 555-556].
[37] See La Porta et al. [1999, p. 551].

of Western European corporations. Besides control rights they also considered the concentration of cash flow rights and a divergence ratio.[38]

Both sources find that the divergence is primarily achieved through the use of pyramids, multiple control chains, and dual-class shares.[39] As shown in Table 2.3, especially Germany features these control-enhancing devices. Beyer [1996] finds even stronger results in his German sample with 50% and more of the companies being connected by pyramids.[40] Comparative data by La Porta et al. [1999] state no crossholdings and pyramiding for the USA.[41]

Table 2.3: Existence of complex ownership structures by country

Dual-class shares give the percentage of dual-call shares on total equities. *Source: Faccio/Lang [2002].*

	Pyramids	Multiple control chains	Crossholdings	Dual-class shares
Austria	20.78	6.49	1.14	23.23
Belgium	25.00	2.38	0.00	0.00
France	15.67	2.87	0.00	2.64
Germany	22.89	7.22	2.69	17.61
Italy	20.27	8.78	1.13	41.35
Norway	33.90	20.34	2.04	13.16
Portugal	10.91	0.00	0.00	0.00
Spain	16.00	5.43	0.22	0.16
Sweden	15.91	0.00	0.67	66.07
Switzerland	10.91	0.91	0.00	51.17
UK	21.13	4.93	0.00	23.91
Total	19.13	5.52	0.73	19.91

Following this data, the corporate ownership structure of Germany more resembles the global or European average ownership structure than the USA and UK data do. Consequently, to achieve generally applicable and transferable results, the German ownership structure may be the preferable research object. Especially the higher ownership concentration could give new insights to the effect of and on more concentrated firms.

---

[38] For a table of the cash flow and control rights of the largest owner and their ratio see Table A.4 in Appendix A.2, p. 222.
[39] See Faccio/Lang [2002, pp. 389-391] and La Porta et al. [1999, p. 551].
[40] See Beyer [1996, pp. 89-91].
[41] See La Porta et al. [1999, p. 499].

2.4 Forms of Financial Performance Measures

2.4.1 Introduction

Since economic performance is the basic goal of every firm, its measurement is one of the most interesting and challenging areas of inquiry.[42] Due to the complexity of the issue it is unlikely to ever measure performance perfectly. Given the multitude of concepts in literature the objective of discussion presented in the following section is not to give a comprehensive picture of the literature but to focus on the performance measures common for the ownership literature.

The performance measures discussed in this section are divided into two general groups, market-based and accounting-based measures, with the first relying on market data and the latter on accounting information. A third group are hybrid measures using both types of data. The three groups and the measures most relevant for the ownership literature are shown in Table 2.4.

The following section is structured in three parts. After market-based measures are briefly discussed in the next section. Chapter 2.4.3 and Chapter 2.4.4 elaborate on accounting-based and hybrid measures respectively. A concluding chapter summarizes the introduced performance measures.

2.4.2 Market-based Performance Measures

Market-based measures find their main usage in event studies. Their characteristic of fast adaption to information and their daily availability qualifies them for this methodology.

The typical measure is the cumulated abnormal return (CAR) with the idea to measure potential abnormal market returns related to a particular event. First, the Capital Asset Pricing Model (CAPM) is applied to estimate a function of the daily stock return of each stock in relation to the return of the market portfolio.[43] This estimation typically uses a period of 100 to 200 days. As next step, the estimated stock returns are compared to the ones actually observed for a short period around the particular event:

$$AR_{jt} = R_{jt} - (\hat{a}_j + \hat{b}_j R_{mt})$$

with AR_{jt} as the abnormal return of company j at day t, R_{jt} as the observed stock return of company j at day t, $\hat{a}_j$ and $\hat{b}_j$ as estimated parameters from the CAPM and R_{mt} as the stock return of the market portfolio. Subsequently, the abnormal returns of the considered period are summed up to the CAR:

$$CAR_j = \sum_{t=d_{j1}}^{d_{j2}} AR_{jt}$$

---

[42] For a discussion on performance measures by research discipline see Hofer [1983].
[43] For information on the CAPM see Lintner [1965], and Sharpe [1963, 1964].

Table 2.4: Selection of measures of financial performance

Measure	Definition	Representative Studies
Market-based measures		
Cumulated abnormal returns (CAR)	Cumulated abnormal stock returns from a single unexpected event	Eckbo/Smith [1998], Lewellen et al. [1985], Loderer/Martin [1997], Seyhun [1986], Slovin/Sushka [1993]
Market returns (MR)	Growth in stock value over a specific period assuming that dividends are reinvested	Chaganti/Damanpour [1991], Holl [1977], Kim et al. [1988], Stano [1976]
Accounting-based measures		
Return on equity (ROE)	Net earnings after interest expenses and taxes divided by shareholders' equity	Demsetz/Lehn [1985], Kamerschen [1968], Monsen et al. [1968], Palmer [1973b], Short/Keasey [1999]
Return on assets (ROA)	Earnings before interest expenses and taxes (EBIT) divided by total assets	Denis/Denis [1994], Himmelberg et al. [1999], Kole [1996], Mehran [1995], Oswald/Jahera Jr. [1991]
Return on investment (ROI)	Earnings divided by value of equity plus long-term debt	Gugler et al. [2003a, 2004], Schellenger et al. [1989]
Earnings per share (EPS)	Earnings divided by number of outstanding shares	Kesner [1987], Kim et al. [1988]
Hybrid measures		
Market-to-book ratio (M/B)	Market values of liabilities divided by book values of assets that represent these liabilities	Hindley [1970], Holderness et al. [1999]
Tobin's Q ratio (Q)	Market values of liabilities divided by replacement costs of the assets that represent these liabilities	Bøhren/Ødegaard [2003], Cho [1998], Demsetz/Villalonga [2001], Himmelberg et al. [1999], Loderer/Martin [1997], McConnell/Servaes [1995], Monsen et al. [1968], Mørck et al. [1988]

where d_{j1} and d_{j2} are the starting and ending dates of the considered period around the event regarding company j. Finally, the CARs of the different firms are consolidated to an average cumulative abnormal return, which is tested for statistical significance.[44] Since the event study approach is not relevant for the following empirical analysis and the CAR is not usable for a one year period, further issues concerning this measure are neglected.

In contrast to the commonly used CAR, the second market-based measure, market return, is rarely applied in the performance and ownership literature. It equals the growth in stock value over a specific period assuming that dividends are reinvested and thereby captures the income of shareholders in form of dividends and capital gains from stock price changes.[45]

One reason for its rare usage is given by Demsetz/Lehn [1985], who note that the stock market rates of return presumably adjust for the ownership structure and its effects on performance. Stock prices incorporates changes in expectations about future cash flows and the cost of capital. Consequently, a preferable ownership structure leads to a higher stock price. However, capital gains due to stock price changes do not reflect a preferable ownership structure, as soon as the ownership information is reflected in the stock price. Market returns should be equal for all firms with equal risks in periods when expectations are constant. Hence, they give only valuable information about the relationship of ownership and performance in the case of an unexpected event.[46]

Nevertheless, this does not have to be the case for very long time periods as ten years or more. For example, if it were possible to measure the market return of the entire lifetime of a company, the market return would also cover the stock price changes due to the ownership structure and then could be regressed on the average ownership over the lifetime. However, such an approach would provoke problems caused by missing data, the controlling of other effects and the ambiguity of calculating averages. Furthermore, it is impossible to include the implied theoretical causation and timing issues into the model.[47]

Despite the disadvantages of market return as a financial performance measure in performance and ownership studies, a few studies apply it. Yet, militating in their favor is their use of long-term averages and the additional use of an accounting-based or hybrid measure.[48]

---

[44] See Mathiesen [2002, pp. 118-119]. For detailed calculation methods and an assessment of different types of CAR see Mathiesen [2002, pp. 120-131].

[45] See Chaganti/Damanpour [1991, p. 484], Holl [1977, p. 263], and Stano [1976, p. 672].

[46] For a detailed example see Appendix A.3, p. 223.

[47] See Mathiesen [2002, pp. 103-104]. For information on the causation and timing issues in the ownership performance relationship see Chapter 4.2.2, p. 74, and Chapter 4.2.3, p. 75.

[48] Elliott [1972] uses a three-years-average, Stano [1976] a six-years-average; Holl [1977], Levin/Levin [1982], McEachern [1975], and Thonet/Poensgen [1979] ex-

2.4.3 Accounting-based Performance Measures

One significant advantage of accounting-based performance measures is that they are not requiring an exchange listing; thus, also private and small firms may be examined. Furthermore, they are easy to interpret.

The accounting-based performance measures most common in the ownership literature are return on equity (ROE) and return on assets (ROA).[49] They are defined as:

$$ROE = \frac{\text{Earnings after interest expenses and taxes}}{\text{Shareholders' equity}}$$

$$ROA = \frac{\text{Earnings before interest expenses and taxes}}{\text{Total assets}}$$

The ROE measures only the return on assets of the equity owners, whereas the ROA aggregates the return of equityholders and debtholders. This fact leads to three arguments militating in favor for a preference of ROE over ROA in equity ownership and performance studies. First, generally financial performance is based on the shareholder value concept, which is stronger reflected in the pure equity focus of the ROE than by the diluted equity returns of the ROA. Second, regarding the effect of performance on equity ownership the pecuniary benefits of shareholders play an important role. These depend stronger on the ROE than on the ROA also including the debtholders' return. Consequently, the ROE should lead to a more significant relationship of ownership and performance improving the results. Finally, also other benefits gained by shareholders through their control rights can only be derived from residual profits. However, the rents for corporate debt are paid according to predetermined contracts and therefore not part of the residual profits. Thus again the ROE should better proxy the financial performance and its effect on ownership. The inclusion of the return of debtholders would again dilute the performance measure and its relation to ownership. However, the discussion of ROE or ROA appears irrelevant when taking a look at the seven studies that used both

---

tend the time period to ten years and Sorensen [1974] even uses 18 years. Chaganti/Damanpour [1991], Levin/Levin [1982], Sorensen [1974] and Thonet/Poensgen [1979] use return on equity, return on assets and/or the market-to-book ratio as additional performance measures.

[49] For studies using the ROE see Boudreaux [1973], Demsetz/Lehn [1985], Demsetz/Villalonga [2001], Gugler et al. [2004], Jarrell/Poulsen [1988], Kamerschen [1968], Leech/Leahy [1991], Mak/Li [2001], Monsen et al. [1968], Mudambi/Nicosia [1998], Palmer [1973a,b], Pedersen/Thomsen [1999], and Short/Keasey [1999]; for those using ROA see Bøhren/Ødegaard [2003], Gedajlovic/Shapiro [2002], Himmelberg et al. [1999], Kole [1996], McConnell/Servaes [1990], and Mehran [1995]. For studies applying both measures see Chaganti/Damanpour [1991], Denis/Denis [1994], Kesner [1987], Lehmann/Weigand [2000], Murali/Welch [1989], Oswald/Jahera Jr. [1991], Schellenger et al. [1989], and Steer/Cable [1978].

2.4 Forms of Financial Performance Measures 27

measures.[50] They obtain similar coefficients for both. But as predicted by the arguments above, the ROA sometimes appears insignificant in contrast to the highly significant ROE as in the study of Chaganti/Damanpour [1991].

Further accounting-based performance measures, as the return on investment or the earnings per share, are rarely used and will be neglected in the further conduct.[51]

When calculating accounting-based variables the return measure or the kind of income to be used, has to be carefully defined. Book return can be disaggregated into three components:

1. income from ordinary operating activities,
2. income from extraordinary activities, and
3. non-operating income.

The latter stems from non-operating activities, such as rents and patents but also from return on non-operating financial assets. It could be argued that these returns are arbitrary and mainly elude from the management's influence and are therefore not related to ownership structure. The inclusion of non-operating results would bias the actual performance measure. An objection is that managers decide on the assets creating non-operating income. For example, the selection of financial assets is part of the responsibilities of the Chief Financial Officer (CFO). Nevertheless, the maximization of non-operating income is normally not the function of the CFO.

The second income component originates from extraordinary activities. These are infrequent and unusual events, e.g., restructuring activities or changes in accounting principles. The inclusion of the income of extraordinary activities may also cause potential problems. It distorts the given picture of regular performance and hence diminishes the comparability of companies. Yet, this is only the case for small samples. Due to the Central Limit Theorem large samples are not affected by these one-time effects.[52] Therefore, the exclusion of extraordinary income from large samples studies would only result in a loss of information.

---

[50] See Chaganti/Damanpour [1991], Denis/Denis [1994], Kesner [1987], Murali/-Welch [1989], Oswald/Jahera Jr. [1991], Schellenger et al. [1989], and Steer/Cable [1978].

[51] For studies applying the return on investment see Gugler et al. [2003a, 2004] and Schellenger et al. [1989], for studies applying the earnings per share ratio see Kesner [1987] and Kim et al. [1988].

[52] The Central Limit Theorem states: Given a population with *any* distribution and taking random samples of size n from that population, the sample means ($\bar{x}$) will be approximately *normally distributed* with a mean equal to the mean of the population and a variance equal to the variance of the population divided by n. The higher n, the closer the distribution will be to normal, i.e., for a population with the mean μ and the variance σ^2, the mean of a drawn sample is $\lim_{n \to N} \bar{x} = N(\mu, \frac{\sigma^2}{n})$.

A further problem of accounting-based measures is the accounting bias. The comparability of accounting variables may suffer from different accounting standards applied by the companies. In addition, the reporting entities are incentivized to distort the data. However, the incentive error should not be too pronounced in Germany, since companies are required to charter an external accountant to verify and sign their statements.

2.4.4 Hybrid Performance Measures

While the two previous parts discussed measures that purely rely on either market or accounting data, the following measures, the market-to-book ratio (M/B) and the Tobin's Q (Q), use both, market and accounting data.[53]

The M/B is defined as market value of the firm's liabilities divided by the accounting value of these liabilities. It measures how much market value is generated by the stock of invested capital. There are two ways to calculate the M/B:

- market value of stock divided by the shareholders' equity (market-to-equity), or
- market value of stock and debt divided by total assets (market-to-assets).

These definitions resemble the accounting-based measures ROE and ROA; they apply the same denominator and instead of the accounting earnings they use the market values of liabilities in the nominator. Hence, the discussion, whether one of the two methods of calculation is preferable, takes an analogous course to the discussion of ROE and ROA in Chapter 2.4.3. As a result the market-to-equity ratio seems to be advantageous over the market-to-assets ratio.

The usage of market value of liabilities yields in two advantages of the M/B over the accounting-based measures. First, the inclusion of extraordinary items is no issue in the case of the M/B. Second, market data cannot be manipulated by management, as accounting data can. Nevertheless, as the M/B includes book values, it is not completely free of the accounting bias. Furthermore, the reliance on market data creates also a disadvantage of the M/B. Sudden outburst and speculative market movements that are not motivated by changes in the expectations can make it less representative as performance measure.

The advantages and disadvantages do not only apply to the M/B but also to the second hybrid measure, the Tobin's Q. Tobin [1969] introduced the concept of the Tobin's Q as the ratio of market value to replacement values of a firm's assets.[54] Since then it has been frequently used as performance

---

[53] In principle, the Tobin's Q should be categorized as a market-based measure. However, the ideal composition of pure market data is mostly replaced by an approximation including accounting data.
[54] See Tobin [1978].

measure in the ownership literature.[55] The original definition of Tobin makes the Tobin's Q theoretically a market-based measure. However, since it is often estimated on the basis of accounting and market data, it is here categorized as a hybrid.[56]

The Tobin's Q is closely related to the M/B. However, in contrast to the M/B using the book value of the total assets as denominator, the Tobin's Q applies the replacement values of assets. Consequently, instead of measuring the financial performance of the existing assets, the Tobin's Q measures the financial performance of a new investment assuming the possibility to reproduce the entire existing production capacity. It is profitable to invest in the reproduction of the production capacity as long as the Tobin's Q is above one. As a consequence, while the M/B and other performance measures are present and past oriented and state if it were profitable to have invested in a company, the Tobin's Q has a future orientation and is therefore rather an investment profitability measure. This difference in explanatory power creates a potential problem: The Tobin's Q is no direct measure of financial performance but a proxy. This may cause a proxy error in the variables, which results in lower significance levels if it is used as endogenous variable, and in inconsistent variables if it is used as explanatory variable.[57]

The quality of a proxy and therefore the strength of the proxy error depends on its correlation with direct measures. Fortunately, in the case of Tobin's Q there are several arguments for a high correlation with financial performance and consequently for an adequacy as performance measure. Companies with a high Tobin's Q find it easier to expand their capacity and hence to make higher returns. This does not mean that a firm with a low Tobin's Q cannot achieve the same, but it is more difficult and may take longer. Consequently, a high correlation exists especially for shorter time horizons. Furthermore, high book and market returns should condition high market values and thus a high Tobin's Q. Additionally, the issue of measurement errors is not a problem limited to the Tobin's Q, but seems to apply to all financial performance measures. Finally, Chung/Pruitt [1994] state its similarity to the concepts of economic and market value added and forecast even a gain in importance of the Tobin's Q by virtue its advantages as standardized measure.[58] Regarding the ownership literature, the probably most important, but practical reason for its usage is that it produces next to the M/B the most significant estimates in regressions.

---

[55] The following studies use the Tobin's Q: Barnhart/Rosenstein [1998], Bøhren/-Ødegaard [2003], Chang [2003], Chen et al. [1993], Cho [1998], Cui/Mak [2002], DaDalt et al. [2003], Demsetz/Villalonga [2001], Gugler et al. [2004], Hermalin/-Weisbach [1991], Himmelberg et al. [1999], Loderer/Martin [1997], Mak/Li [2001], McConnell/Servaes [1990, 1995], Monsen et al. [1968], Mørck et al. [1988], Palia/-Lichtenberg [1999], and Weber/Dudney [2003].
[56] For information on the estimation of Tobin's Q see p. 29.
[57] For detailed information see Maddala [1992, Chapter 11].
[58] See Chung/Pruitt [1994, p. 74].

Unfortunately, the calculation of the Tobin's Q can be very complicated and complex, especially for continental European countries. Their accounting standards allow companies to report historic purchase values, in contrast to Anglo-American accounting standards which require a reporting of current values. This complicates the estimation of the replacement values. To cope with this problem different approaches evolved which can be classified into two general competing groups.

The first approach is a computationally costly and complex algorithm, which demands sophisticated programming. It uses an extensive set of financial statement information as estimation basis for both market and replacement values. The data is then adjusted for factors that call for a systematic divergence between market and accounting values. This effort yields extremely accurate estimates.[59] Several variants of the approach are currently in use. They all base on the first calculation method of Lindenberg/Ross [1981], with the most commonly used enhancements developed by Hall [1999], Lewellen/-Badrinath [1997], Lee/Tompkins [1999], and Perfect/Wiles [1994]. Exemplarily, the calculation formula of the Lindenberg/Ross [1981] approach omitting the adjustment procedure will be explained:[60]

$$Q_{LR} = \frac{MV_t}{RC_t} \approx \frac{MVD_t + MVCS_t + MVPS_t}{BVTA_t + (RCFA_t - BVFA_t) + (RCINV_t - BVINV_t)}$$

where
Q_{LR} = Tobin's Q estimate by Lindenberg/Ross [1981],
MV_t = year-end market value of outstanding financial claims,
RC_t = year-end replacement costs of production capacity,
MVD_t = year-end market value of outstanding debt,
$MVCS_t$ = year-end market value of outstanding common stock,
$MVPS_t$ = year-end market value of outstanding preferred stock,
$BVTA_t$ = year-end book value of total assets,
$RCFA_t$ = year-end replacement costs of fixed assets,
$BVFA_t$ = year-end book value of fixed assets,
$RCINV_t$ = year-end replacement costs of inventories, and
$BVINV_t$ = year-end book value of inventories.

By this formula the complexity and high data needs of the Perfect/Wiles's Tobin's Q become obvious.[61] As a result, the costly approaches suffer from a sample-selection bias and may cause a loss of up to 20% in sample size.[62]

On this account and due to the high effort, researchers developed a more simple group of approximations for the Tobin's Q to circumvent the complex

---

[59] See DaDalt et al. [2003, p. 537].
[60] See Lindenberg/Ross [1981, pp. 10-17].
[61] The other techniques as the ones of Lindenberg/Ross [1981] and Hall [1999] have even higher data requirements, making it hard to implement them.
[62] See DaDalt et al. [2003, p. 551].

2.4 Forms of Financial Performance Measures

accurate calculation. Hence, competing estimation approaches evolved using a comparatively small set of financial statement information with minimal adjustments. An important representative is the approximation by Chung/Pruitt [1994]. It estimates the Tobin's Q as follows:[63]

$$Q_{CP} = \frac{MVE_t + PS_t + BVINV_t + LTDEBT_t + CL_t - CA_t}{TA_t}$$

where
Q_{CP} = Tobin's Q estimate by Chung/Pruitt [1994],
MVE = year-end value of common stock,
PS = liquidation value of preferred stock,
$BVINV$ = year-end book value of inventory,
$LTDEBT$ = year-end book value of long-term debt,
CL = year-end book value of current liabilities,
CA = year-end book value of current assets, and
TA = book value of total assets.

The liquidation value of preferred stock is used due to difficulties in obtaining price quotes for preferred stock. It can be calculated by aggregating the preferred stock market value and dividing it by Standard & Poor's preferred stock yield index.[64]

These approximations, of course, do not yield as accurate results as the original calculations do. However, Chung/Pruitt [1994] also verify the good approximation quality of their approach by comparing their measure to the Tobin's Q of Lindenberg/Ross [1981] where they find an $\overline{R}^2$ of at least 96%.[65] Furthermore, DaDalt et al. [2003] also analyzed the quality of the Tobin's Q of Chung/Pruitt [1994] by benchmarking it against the calculation method of Perfect/Wiles [1994].[66] They concluded that the simple technique is preferable, except for cases where extremely precise estimates are needed and a sample-selection bias is no issue.[67] In addition, DaDalt et al. [2003] further found both approaches are significantly related to a wide range of financial performance measures.

Theoretically the value of the Tobin's Q is one if the firm is traded at the exact replacement costs of its assets. A Tobin's Q above one implies that market value is greater than replacement value of the company's recorded assets. These high values can result from some unmeasured or unrecorded assets of the company or positive earnings expectations reflected in the market value. Contrary, if the Tobin's Q is less than one, the market value is less than replacement value of the assets. This equals an undervaluation which makes the company a possible takeover target, since it is traded at a value less than

---

[63] See Chung/Pruitt [1994, p. 71].
[64] See Lindenberg/Ross [1981, pp. 10-11].
[65] See Chung/Pruitt [1994, pp. 71-74].
[66] For the calculation of the Tobin's Q of Perfect/Wiles [1994] see Perfect/Wiles [1994, p. 322].
[67] See DaDalt et al. [2003, pp. 550-551].

the value of its parts. Both over- and undervaluation should be regulated by the market in the long run, thus the company is priced at its reproduction costs. Hence, on an aggregate basis the Tobin's Q should tend to be mean reverting, converging at one.[68]

However, since the Tobin's Q reflects the over- and undervaluation and markets can be over- or undervaluated as total, the Tobin's Q in practice also depends on the general market valuation and therefore the economic situation. Due to this sensitivity to the general economic environment the Tobin's Q is often far from one and varying strongly over time, as shown in Figure 2.5. In the period from 1900 to 2004 the average Tobin's Q for the United States tended to revert to .63 instead of one as predicted by Tobin.[69]

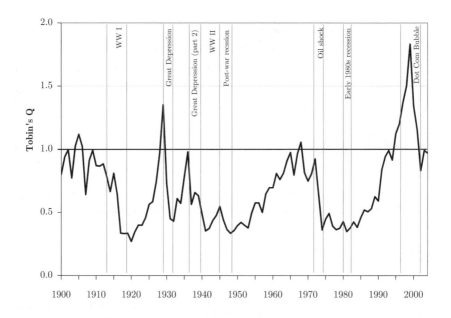

Fig. 2.5: Historic values of Tobin's Q in the USA

Data source: Smithers/Wright [2000] and the Flow of Funds Accounts of the Federal Reserve of the United States.

---

[68] See Tobin [1978, p. 422].
[69] It varied in values between low .27 in 1920 and 1.83 in 1999. See Smithers/Wright [2000]. For more information and a detailed list of the Tobin's Q over this time period see Appendix A.4, p. 225.

2.4.5 Summary

Recapitulating, the previous subsections show that the characteristics of market-based measures account for their advantages in event studies, but at the same time prove their low adequacy for other studies.

Accounting-based measures as ROE and ROA have the advantage that they can be applied to non-listed companies, but they have also shortcomings, such as the question of the earnings definition and a potential accounting-bias. Comparing both measures, the ROE is preferable to ROA in ownership studies.

The hybrid measures result in the most significant estimates in ownership studies. The M/B avoids the disadvantages of accounting-based measures, but might be distorted by abnormal market returns at the point of observation. Similar to the ROE versus ROA discussion, the market-to-equity ratio seems advantageous.

Apart from the benefits and shortcomings of the M/B, the Tobin's Q may feature a further disadvantage; it is an indirect measure of financial performance. Nevertheless, the proxy error should be low. An advantage of the Tobin's Q over the M/B consists in its frequent use in literature and the higher significance achieved by its results.

Regarding the two calculation approaches, the estimates of the computationally costly approach are more theoretically defensible. However, they also demand sophisticated programming and are associated with high efforts. Furthermore, they suffer from a sample-selection bias. Thus the simple approach of Chung/Pruitt [1994] is preferable, as long as no extreme accurate estimates are necessary.

3

Theoretical Background and Hypotheses

3.1 General Remarks

Already the origin of the separation of ownership and control, the legal reforms, was controversially judged. While their aim was to increase the efficiency in corporate governance, many critics already saw the potential problems caused by the loss of control by shareholders. The following academic discussion also broached the issue of these potential problems and the resulting effects of ownership and performance. However, the discussion has yielded in controversial and partially contradicting effects and reached no consensus on the relation of ownership and performance.

The following chapter introduces the key hypotheses of this academic discussion.[1] After introducing to the chapter and adding some general remarks, the second section briefly explains the agency theory and the shareholder-management conflict as the theoretical background of the hypotheses. Subsequently, the hypotheses of the relation of performance and ownership concentration, of performance and insider ownership and finally of performance and institutional ownership are explained. Each section consists of three subsections, with the first considering the assumed effects of the ownership variable on performance and the second the reverse effect. The last subsection summarizes the hypotheses and their effects. After the examination of the relation of ownership and performance Section 3.6 addresses the interactions of the three ownership variables. Finally, the chapter is recapitulated by Section 3.7.

All effects explained in the following are assumed to be monotonous, i.e., having a constantly positive or negative effect.[2] This, however, does not necessarily imply linearity, the stability of the effect strength. Actually many

---

[1] For an overview of selected studies and their findings see Table A.9 in Appendix A.5, p. 231.

[2] Exceptions are the combined effect by Mørck et al. [1988] and the integrated argument by Stulz [1988]. These are combinations of before explained effects and are mentioned due to their importance and frequent use in literature.

studies assume nonlinear effects with increasing marginal values.[3] Furthermore, based on the general concept of decreasing marginal values, it is likely that the function saturates for higher values. For example, a 1% increase in ownership will have a stronger effect at an ownership level of 5% than at 80%. Considering both increasing marginal values and a later saturation of the effect results in a function with the shape of a logit distribution:[4]

$$f(x) = \frac{e^{x\beta}}{(e^{x\beta} + \alpha)} \ .$$

However, since α and β are not fixed to a value of one as they are in the simple logit distribution of $f(x) = e^x/(e^x + 1)$, the function can form a wide range of shapes. Table 3.1 shows the function after adjustments of α and/or β.[5] The consideration of these potentially different shapes of the effect is important, since then a combination of effects must not yield in a constant dominance of one effect but the prevalence of the effect can change at different levels of the exogenous variable. An example of such a combination with changing dominance is also given in Table 3.1.

The studies performed later distinguish control and cash flow rights, where the control rights are used as the main ownership variable and the regressions are controlled by a ratio of voting and cash flow rights.[6] Hence, also a separate consideration of their theoretic effects is necessary. Accordingly, the effects are explained on the basis of the control rights. Furthermore, a possible effect mediation through the divergence of control and cash flow rights is examined.

3.2 Theoretical Background

Most of the hypotheses formulated in the following are based on the economic principal-agent theory, where a positive effect stems from the amelioration of the shareholder-management conflict, e.g., by disciplining the management. Analogously, an aggravation of the conflict results in a negative effect.

The principal-agent theory is part of the new institutional economics, which developed as extension of the neoclassicism. It abandons the assumption of a complete market by allowing informational asymmetries and trans-

---

[3] See Chen et al. [1993], Cho [1998], Cleary [2000], Cui/Mak [2002], Gugler et al. [2003b], Hermalin/Weisbach [1991], Holderness et al. [1999], Hubbard/Palia [1995], Kole [1996], McConnell/Servaes [1990, 1995], Monsen et al. [1968], Mørck et al. [1988], Short/Keasey [1999], Short et al. [2002a, 1994], Stulz [1988], Welch [2003], and Wruck [1989].
[4] Such functions were already found by Mørck et al. [1988] and Stulz [1988]. See Figure 3.3 and Figure 3.4, p. 51 and p. 53.
[5] A change in α moves the graph to the left or right and hence alters the saturation point and the increase of the gradient for low values. β adjusts the gradient and its difference in the course of the function.
[6] See Section 4.4.2, p. 89.

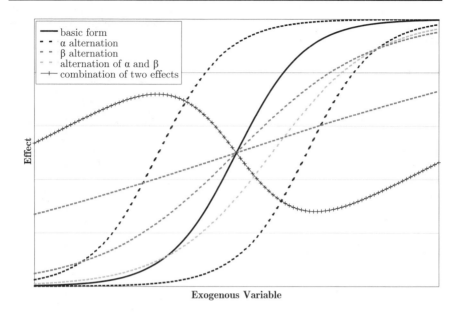

Fig. 3.1: Effect as logit function and its alternations

action costs to cause incomplete contracts.[7] This leads to a methodological individualism, which does no longer consider institutions as profit maximizing collectives, but as a "nexus for a complex set of explicit and implicit contracts of individuals".[8] Consequently, the economic focus on markets is shifted to man-made institutions, incorporating the individual into economic theory.

The agency theory in particular analyzes the contractual conflicts arising from informational asymmetry.[9] An agency relation is based on an explicit or implicit contract between the agent and the principal delegating decision power to the agent.[10] Due to the contract the agent's actions influence the utility of both contractual partners.[11] However, the agent behaves opportunistically maximizing his profit regardless of the principal's interests. In the case of incomplete informational structures for the benefit of the agent the principal cannot prevent those harming actions.[12] Consequently, an agency conflict requires two conditions, a conflict of interest through diverging utility func-

---

[7] See Barnea et al. [1981, p. 8] and Richter/Furubotn [1999, p. 137].
[8] Jensen/Meckling [1976, p. 310]. See Richter/Furubotn [1999, p. 5].
[9] See Barnea et al. [1981, pp. 25-26] and Richter/Furubotn [1999, p. 3].
[10] See Jensen/Smith [1985, p. 96] and Richter/Furubotn [1999, p. 163].
[11] See Jensen/Meckling [1976, p. 308] and Richter/Furubotn [1999, p. 25].
[12] See Jensen/Meckling [1976, p. 305] and Richter/Furubotn [1999, p. 163].

tions of the principal and the agent as well as the existence of informational asymmetries.[13] These informational asymmetries are classified into different forms shown in Figure 3.2.

Time of appearance	Informational asymmetry	Object of asymmetry	Agency problem
Before contract conclusion	Hidden characteristics	Characteristics of agent	Adverse selection
	Hidden intention	Intention of agent	Hold-up
After contract conclusion	Hidden action	Actions of agent (quantity uncertainty)	Moral hazard
	Hidden information	Dependency of output on actions of agent (quality uncertainty)	

Fig. 3.2: Forms of informational asymmetries in agency theory

Hidden characteristics are important features of the agent unknown to the principal before contract conclusion. The uncertainty over the agent's quality may lead to an adverse selection in the agent's engagement.[14] Since this work deals with already existing contracts, this form is not further considered.

The *hidden intention* of the agent to harm the principal can result in a problem before and after the contract conclusion. Besides problems of adverse selection it can cause a hold-up problem, where the principal recognizes the opportunistic actions of the agent, but cannot sanction him or prevent his actions. Consequently, the agent will not change his behavior.[15]

If after the contract conclusion the result of the agent's actions is also influenced by other exogenous factors, the problem of moral hazard can arise. One information asymmetry conditioning this problem is the *hidden action*, where the principal can observe the results, but cannot draw conclusions on the effort of the agent.[16] The second informational asymmetry is *hidden information*. The principal knows both the result and the agent's effort. However, he lacks information on the input-output relation and thus cannot assess the work of

---

[13] See Richter/Furubotn [1999, p. 163].
[14] See Richter/Furubotn [1999, pp. 144-145 and p. 509].
[15] See Breid [1995, pp. 823-824].
[16] See Darrough/Stoughton [1986, p. 501] and Spremann [1987, p. 343].

3.2 Theoretical Background   39

the agent.[17] Kleine [1995] compares the situation with a production. In the case of hidden action the principal does not know the input by the agent. At the occurrence of hidden information he sees the input and output, but does not know the parameters of the production or transformation function.[18]

These conflicts, however, hurt the welfare of both the principal and the agent, since the principal anticipates the reduced utility given rational expectations and partially passes it on to the agent. Consequently, it is often in the interest of both parties to reduce the conflict.[19]

The principal can reduce the conflict by controlling the agent or by reducing the information asymmetry. These efforts are called *monitoring*, where explicit monitoring consists of governance activities and implicit monitoring summarizes forms of information gathering.[20] The conflict can also be reduced by trust building actions by the management that are called *bonding*.[21] However, as both efforts also create costs, only a second-best solution is achieved.[22] The difference between the first-best and second-best solution is called agency costs. They are distinguished on the basis of their origin into monitoring or control costs, bonding costs, and residual loss.[23]

The economic principal-agent theory knows two major conflicts: the shareholder-management conflict and the debtholder-shareholder conflict. However, since this work focusses on the relation of equity ownership and performance where already Cook [1894] state the loss of control over the management as the key critical issue, only the first conflict is further considered. The shareholder-management conflict is based on the separation of ownership and control by Berle/Means [1932]. It assumes informational asymmetries in favor of the management due to their daily professional occupation with the company and the market.[24] Furthermore, a conflict of interest exists through differing utility functions. While the shareholder's utility consists of the two monetary elements dividends and changes in stock price, the manager features a more complex utility function. It is composed by the monetary effect of the fixed and variable remuneration and considerations of personal risk, career prospects, prestige, and other personal interests.[25] The quality and quantity

---

[17] See Hartmann-Wendels [1989, p. 715] and Richter/Furubotn [1999, pp. 215-217].
[18] See Kleine [1995, p. 31].
[19] See Jensen/Meckling [1976, p. 309] and Jensen/Smith [1985, p. 97].
[20] See Bushee [1998, p. 309] and Jensen/Smith [1985, p. 97].
[21] In the shareholder-management conflict these might include the application of certain accounting standards [Jensen/Smith 1985, p. 126], the creation of a positive reputation [Spremann 1988, p. 619] or the fulfillment of the German Corporate Governance Code [Bassen et al. 2000].
[22] See Coase [1937, pp. 390-391], Jensen/Meckling [1976, p. 308], and Jensen/Smith [1985, p. 97].
[23] See Jensen/Meckling [1976, p. 308].
[24] See Barnea et al. [1981, p. 15], Jensen/Meckling [1976, p. 308], and Swoboda [1982, p. 710].
[25] See Rappaport [1995, pp. 6-7].

of work performed by the management has a direct negative effect on its utility, but a positive one on shareholders' gain. However, it might have a positive indirect effect on management incentive through performance-based compensation, prestige, and career prospects.[26] The conflict of interest together with the informational asymmetry causes the problem of moral hazard.

Table 3.1: Types of agency problems in the shareholder-management conflict

Problem	Definition
Effort	Managers have an incentive to exert less effort than the shareholders expect them to.
Asset Use	Managers have an incentive to misuse corporate assets or to consume excessive perks, since they do not bear the full costs of these actions.
Over-Investment	Subform of the asset use problem: Managers execute also unprofitable investments to increase corporate size.
Horizon / Time Preference	Managers tend to have shorter time horizons to achieve investment results than shareholders.
Risk Preference	Managers tend to be more risk averse than shareholders, since more of their wealth is tied up in the ongoing business.

The conflict manifests itself through a set of a different problems listed in Table 3.1. In the case of the *effort problem* managers optimize their utility by reducing their effort and its direct negative effect. This is assumed to also decrease the performance of the firm and thus the shareholder value. Furthermore, managers might misuse corporate assets, therefore *asset use problem*, or consume excessive perquisites which harm the company value. A special form of an asset use problem is *over-investment*, where the manager performs unprofitable investments to increase the firm size, as this empire building often has a positive effect on manager's prestige. The *horizon or time preference problem* is based on differing time horizons of management and shareholders. While the shareholder is long-term oriented under the assumption of going concern, the short-term focus of the management stems from the limited duration of its working contracts with the shareholders. Especially shortly before the expiration of the contract the management might neglect profitable and important long-term investments in favor of short-term results. Finally, the *risk preference problem* accounts for the fact that the manager's personal risk is strongly linked to the firm's risk. His inclination to be risk averse leads to

---

[26] See Achleitner/Wichels [2000, p. 7] and Barnea et al. [1981, p. 8].

suboptimal investment decisions that are not in the interest of the risk neutral shareholder.[27]

Apart from debt or compensation design ownership structure is argued to influence the shareholder-management conflict. These potential effects of ownership structure are explained together with not agency-related effects in the following sections.

3.3 Ownership Concentration and Performance

Ownership concentration, i.e., the existence or degree of blockholdings, is the most often examined form of ownership measure.[28]

The following section examines its effect on performance, before the reverse effect is considered in Section 3.3.2. Finally, the hypotheses considered in the further analysis and their effects are summarized.

3.3.1 Effect of Ownership Concentration on Performance

Table 3.2 gives a brief overview over the different hypothesized effects explained in this section and the theories, they are based on.

The argument for a positive effect of ownership concentration on performance is given by the shareholder-management agency conflict. The benefits of monitoring are increasing with share size, while the occurred costs do not augment with the ownership concentration. A larger share size thus increases the cost-efficiency of monitoring and due to this higher incentive enhances its usage.[29] Furthermore, a larger share size might even raise the shareholders' capability of control, since blockholders are assumed to be better informed than average investors. In addition, this higher insight to the company also reduces the costs for explicit monitoring, which further increases its cost-efficiency. Thus high ownership concentration leaves the shareholder not only highly motivated to monitor the management but also more capable in controlling them.[30]

---

[27] See Achleitner/Wichels [2000, p. 7], Barnea et al. [1981, p. 31], Byrd et al. [1998, p. 15-18], and La Porta et al. [2000, p. 4].

[28] See Section 2.2.2, p. 13. For an overview over studies on ownership concentration and its effect on corporate control see Holderness [2003] and Short [1994].

[29] See Shleifer/Vishny [1986, p. 463].

[30] See Bøhren/Ødegaard [2003, pp. 4-5], Bushee [1998, p. 309], Holderness [2003, p. 56], Shleifer/Vishny [1997, p. 754], and Shleifer/Vishny [1986]. This hypothesis is theoretically proven by the models of Grossman [1976], Grossman/Hart [1980], Shleifer/Vishny [1986] and others as Bolton/von Thadden [1998], Burkart et al. [1997], Huddart [1993], Leech [2001], and Maug [1998]. Empirical evidence supporting this hypothesis is found by several studies as Agrawal/Knoeber [1996], Agrawal/Mandelker [1990], Bebchuk/Fried [2003], Bertrand/Mullainathan [2000], Brailsford et al. [2002], Carney/Gedajlovic [2002], Denis/Serrano [1996],

Table 3.2: Hypotheses for an effect of ownership concentration on performance

Hypothesis	Theory	Explanation
$\frac{\partial Perf}{\partial OC} > 0$	Monitoring argument	Large owners are more capable of monitoring and controlling the management, thereby contributing to corporate performance.
$\frac{\partial Perf}{\partial OC} < 0$	Over-monitoring argument	Managers may be discouraged from making costly firm specific investments.
	Private benefits of control	The blockholder gains private benefits of control, possibilities for certain actions (e.g., insider contracts) which can be against shareholder's interest.
	Cost-of-capital argument	Ownership concentration reduces market liquidity or decreases portfolio diversification; thus the cost of capital rises.
$\frac{\partial Perf}{\partial OC} = 0$	Natural selection argument	Any kind of ownership structure is determined by financial performance in the sense that corporations with inefficient (ownership) structures will fail to survive in the long run.
	Mutual neutralization argument	Performance effects from various incentive mechanisms matter, but cancel each other out.

While the ability to control the actions of the management rests on the control rights of the share, the incentive for monitoring depends on the degree of alignment between the cash flow function of the shareholder and the performance of the cooperation. Therefore, it depends on the cash flow rights held by the shareholder. Recapitulating, the monitoring activity by the shareholder is determined by the incentive through cash flow rights and the control capability represented through the control rights. Hence, it is a conjoint effect, which can be viewed as a product of the control and cash flow rights. For example, if the shareholder holds only a small cash flow entitlement, he will not put much effort in monitoring activities, no matter how high his control ability is.

Edwards/Weichenrieder [1999, 2004], Franks et al. [1997], Gedajlovic/Shapiro [2002], Hill/Snell [1989], Hindley [1970], Kaplan [1989], Monsen et al. [1968], Mørck et al. [1988], Pedersen/Thomsen [1998, 1999], Renneboog [2000], Short et al. [2002a], Wruck [1989], Yafeh/Yosha [1995], and Zeckhauser/Pound [1990].

3.3 Ownership Concentration and Performance

Consequently, an increasing divergence of control and cash flow rights causes a mitigation of the monitoring effect.

The second group of hypotheses supports a negative effect of ownership concentration on performance.[31] An argument closely linked to the monitoring argument is the *over-monitoring*. It was introduced and model theoretically proven by Burkart et al. [1997] and Pagano/Röell [1998]. They assume that the increased control reduces the space for self-realization of the management and hence discourages the managers. This demotivation renders the management less active. The reduced managerial effort and space for initiative diminishes the firm performance.[32] Fee [2002] proves the importance of the over-monitoring argument by using the artistic stakes in the film industry, where self-realization and motivation have a high impact. Similar to the monitoring argument, the over-monitoring effect is conjointly determined by control and cash flow rights. Accordingly, a high divergence reduces its strength.

A further negative effect based on agency theory is the theory of *private benefits of control*.[33] While the higher information base and influence of a large shareholder is advantageous in reducing the shareholder-management agency conflict, it also generates an additional conflict. Since the large shareholder is better informed and has more control rights than minority shareholders, he might use this to exploit possibilities for beneficial actions, which may endanger for shareholder value.[34] Apart from theoretical arguments by the models of Burkart et al. [1997] and Zwiebel [1995] the existence of such benefits is empirically supported by several studies as Barclay et al. [1993], Dyck/Zingales [2004], Zingales [1994], ?, and Wruck [1989]. They prove higher premiums for block trades, which have to stem from benefits only accessible for blockholders. Prominent examples for such private benefits are self-trading or insider contracts.[35] Furthermore, blockholders and minority shareholders may also have different preferences regarding time horizon and investment goals. An example is given by Fama/Jensen [1985] who prove different investment rules for companies with large shareholders and a stronger retention of dividends.[36]

Minority shareholders cannot prevent those damages given the large share and influence of the blockholder which creates a hold up problem.[37] With

---

[31] Such a relation was found by several studies as Hindley [1970], Lehmann/Weigand [2000], and Pedersen/Thomsen [1999].
[32] See Burkart et al. [1997, p. 674] and Pagano/Röell [1998, pp. 187-190].
[33] See Aggarwal/Samwick [2003], Barclay/Holderness [1989], Dyck/Zingales [2004], Zingales [1994], and Zwiebel [1995].
[34] See Barclay/Holderness [1989, p. 372] and Holderness [2003, pp. 55-56].
[35] See Bebchuk [1999], Bebchuk et al. [2000], Burkart et al. [1997], Goshen [2003], Zingales [1994], and Zwiebel [1995].
[36] See also Anderson/Reeb [2003, p. 1304], Becht [1999], and Lemmon/Lins [2003, pp. 1445-1446 and p. 1466].
[37] See Barclay/Holderness [1989] and La Porta et al. [2002, p. 1148]. This problem is similar to the general entrenchment argument of insider ownership. See Chapter 3.4.1, p. 48.

the increase of control rights the blockholder has more power to influence the company decisions and is more entrenched against the sanctions of other shareholders; thus the possibility of a successful execution of harmful actions rises. The cash flow rights indicate the degree to which the damage of the company's performance is carried by the blockholder and determine the opportunity costs of the exploitation of the private benefits. Consequently, the increase of cash flow rights reduces the incentive for a harmful action and a high divergence of control and cash flow rights strengthens the negative effect of ownership concentration on performance.

An argument not linked to the agency theory is the *cost-of-capital argument* introduced by Fama/Jensen [1983a]. Their assumption of a negative effect is based on the liquidity reduction as result of the increased ownership concentration. Setting up a block of shareholding reduces the number of shareholders who can participate in the trading of the stock. This equals effectively a reduction of liquidity.[38] The decreased liquidity makes the stock more risky and increases the firm's beta.[39] With beta as a driving factor the cost of equity and consequently the cost of capital rise. Finally, this increase in costs causes a reduction in performance.[40] However, in models controlled for risk this effect is hard to detect and to separate from the general risk effect. Furthermore, the ownership measure needed for the analysis of the cost-of-capital argument is the share concentration at the first level. However, as explained in Section 4.4.2, the following studies extend to multiple level ownership. Consequently, the cost-of-capital argument cannot be considered in the further conduct.

The last hypothesis predicts no observable effect. One of those theories is the *natural selection argument*. The idea stems from a more general theory called "economies of natural selection" of Alchian [1950] and Friedman [1953]. It states that all kinds of economic organizations and structures, among those also the ownership structure, are equally efficient and thus perform equally well.[41] This hypothesis is based on the concept of competition that sorts out all inefficient forms in the long run. Demsetz/Ricardo-Campbell [1983], Demsetz/Lehn [1985], and Kole/Lehn [1997] apply this theory on ownership structure, claiming that corporations with inefficient ownership structures will fail to survive in the long run. This hypothesis is supported by the models of Huddart [1993] and Bolton/von Thadden [1998]. The latter shows that both dispersed and concentrated ownership can be optimal depending on the company environment. There is also empirical evidence by Witte [1981],

---

[38] See Bolton/von Thadden [1998, p. 3] and furthermore Barclay/Holderness [1989] and Becht [1999].
[39] See Elton/Gruber [1995, p. 149-151] and for empirical evidence see Beaver et al. [1970], Hartzell/Starks [2003], Rosenberg/Guy [1976], and Thompson II [1976].
[40] See Bolton/von Thadden [1998, pp. 2-3], Fama/Jensen [1983a, p. 329], and Thomsen [2005, p. 4].
[41] See Alchian [1950], Becker [1962], Friedman [1953, p. 22], and Williamson [1985, p. 22].

Gedajlovic [1993], Demsetz/Villalonga [2001], Dilling-Hansen et al. [2003] and Edwards/Weichenrieder [2004] suiting the assumption of no relation between ownership and performance. However, a shortcoming of this theory is the definition of "in the long run". Consequently, it becomes hard to differentiate an efficient firm from an inefficient one which may just have not existed long enough to be already sorted out. Furthermore, the theory assumes a perfect selection which is unrealistic. Structures are eliminated only if their inefficiencies are not outbalanced by other mechanisms, i.e., if it is not set off by superiority in other areas such as an optimal financing structure.[42] Consequently, only completely inefficient firms will be sorted out by the market.

The *mutual neutralization* theory also argues for no observable effect of ownership on performance, however, it does not assume absence of effects. In contrast, it believes that the effects of the different incentive mechanisms, such as contractual designs or institutions, countervail each other. In addition, a neutralization is also possible within the effects of ownership concentration. For example, the monitoring argument might outbalance the cost-of-capital argument. Bahng [2002], Eckbo/Smith [1998], and Himmelberg et al. [1999] apply this theory as explanation to their empirical results.

3.3.2 Effect of Performance on Ownership Concentration

While many studies support the effect of ownership concentration on performance, Demsetz/Lehn [1985] argue for the endogeneity of ownership and a reverse effect of performance on ownership concentration. The hypotheses on this effect direction are summarized in Table 3.3.

The most known hypothesis is the *insider-investment argument* which assumes a positive effect of performance on ownership concentration. As already indicated in the previous section, a large shareholder is better informed than minority shareholders or potential investors. He uses his knowledge about the firm's prospects to maximize his wealth. He capitalizes on his insights and increases his ownership when expecting good financial performance and decreases his share when expecting the deterioration of financial performance. As a result, well performing firms should be higher concentrated than bad ones.[43] The models by Grossman/Stiglitz [1976], Grossman [1976, 1995], and Grossman/Hart [1980] provide a detailed rationale on how an informed investor is able to generate higher returns on his investments than the average investor.

A further argument for the positive effect of performance on ownership concentration is the *profit-debt-ownership argument*.[44] It combines two effects:

---

[42] See Mathiesen [2002, pp. 23-24].
[43] See Anderson/Reeb [2003, p. 1303], Chang [2003], Demsetz/Lehn [1985], Lemmon/Lins [2003, p. 1446], Loderer/Martin [1997, p. 237], and Thompson II [1976, p. 2].
[44] See Jensen et al. [1992, p. 250].

Table 3.3: Hypotheses for an effect of performance on ownership concentration

Hypothesis	Theory	Explanation
$\frac{\partial OC}{\partial Perf} > 0$	Insider-investment argument	Blockholders have insider knowledge and may capitalize on their insights by adapting their ownership position.
	Profit-debt-ownership argument	The modified pecking order hypothesis combined with the substitution effect of agency devices: performance decreases debt and lower leverage increases ownership concentration.
$\frac{\partial OC}{\partial Perf} = 0$	Natural selection argument	Any kind of ownership structure is determined by financial performance in the sense that corporations with inefficient (ownership) structures will fail to survive in the long run.

the modified pecking order hypothesis and the substitution effect of agency devices. The modified pecking order hypothesis by Myers/Majluf [1984] assumes a negative relation of performance on debt, since profitable firms have more internal funds to finance their investments.[45] The second element by Jensen/Meckling [1976] claims that financial leverage has a negative effect on ownership concentration. Since leverage controls the agency conflicts between shareholders and managers, the need for external capital to mediate the conflict decreases.[46] Consequently, performance decreases the leverage, which increases the ownership concentration. However, the studies performed in the following include leverage as a control variable. Consequently, the effect of leverage on ownership concentration will be represented in its coefficient and not be detectable in the direct effect of performance on ownership. Hence, this hypothesis is not further considered in this work.

A hypothesis predicting no effect is again the *natural selection argument* based on Friedman's economies of natural selection. Since all firms perform equally well in the long run, there is no pattern to derive a systematic effect from. Thus no relation will be found.[47]

---

[45] The pecking order theory was first proposed by Donaldson [1961] to explain observed financial behavior of firms. Myers/Majluf [1984] and Myers [1984] introduced a modified version with informational asymmetries and bankruptcy costs to also influence capital structure policy. It states that, as far as firms can choose, they prefer internal over equity financing and equity over debt financing.
[46] See Jensen [1986, pp. 323-329].
[47] For a more detailed explanation see Chapter 3.3.1, p. 44.

3.3.3 Summary of Hypotheses on Ownership Concentration

The hypotheses considered in the following conduct of this work are summarized in Table 3.4. The cost-of-capital hypothesis and the profit-debt-ownership argument are excluded since the mediating variables "risk" and "debt" are included as control variables.[48] Apart from the general effects of the control rights, Table 3.4 states the effect of the divergence ratio of control and cash flow rights on performance in the third column. In the case of the monitoring argument, for example, the cash flow rights have a positive effect on performance. Accordingly, the divergence, calculated as control rights (CR) by cash flow rights (CFR), has a negative effect on performance.

Table 3.4: Summary of assumed hypotheses on ownership concentration

Hypothesis	Theory	$\frac{\partial Perf}{\partial (CR/CFR)}$
$\frac{\partial Perf}{\partial OC} > 0$	Monitoring argument	< 0
$\frac{\partial Perf}{\partial OC} < 0$	Over-monitoring argument	> 0
	Private benefits of control	< 0
$\frac{\partial Perf}{\partial OC} = 0$	Natural selection argument	$= 0$
	Mutual neutralization argument	$= 0$

Hypothesis	Theory	
$\frac{\partial OC}{\partial Perf} > 0$	Insider-investment argument	
$\frac{\partial OC}{\partial Perf} = 0$	Natural selection argument	

The effect of general ownership concentration on performance is unclear due to the contradicting hypotheses. While the concentration could lead to better monitoring and consequently to better performance, it could also trigger managerial demotivation with a negative effect on performance. Furthermore, the blockholder could use control to consume private benefits at the expense of other shareholders and firm performance.

However, performance can also determine ownership concentration. Large shareholders use their better company knowledge to increase their share if they assume good performance or to sell it in the case of a bad firm's prospect.

Finally, the natural selection argument assumes the absence of any relation of ownership concentration and performance.

---

[48] The cost-of-capital argument is mediated by risk and the profit-debt-ownership argument by leverage. For a list of the included control variables see Table 4.5, p. 94.

3.4 Insider Ownership and Performance

The effect of managerial ownership on performance has been intensively discussed since Jensen/Meckling [1976], who introduced the management-shareholder agency conflict. Accordingly, the most extensive research was done on this relation.[49] However, as mentioned in Chapter 2.2 the definition used for managerial or insider ownership varies in literature. In the following explanations the denotations "insider ownership" and "managerial ownership" are used synonymously and refer to cohesive shareholdings of management (and board) neglecting the definition differences. Other forms of insiders such as company founders and families are not considered. Nevertheless, the latter may be considered indirectly in the indirect shareholdings of the management or board.

The sections are structured analogously to the previous chapters. First, the effects of insider ownership and then the reverse effects by performance are examined. Finally both sections are summarized.

3.4.1 Effect of Insider Ownership on Performance

Given the early discussion of the effect of insider ownership on performance, its main arguments stem from 1976 and 1980. These arguments also have been combined to non-monotonous effects. The two best known combinations are stated together with the simple hypothesized effects in Table 3.5.

The earliest argument was brought on by Jensen/Meckling [1976] and is based on the principal-agent theory. It assumes a positive effect of managerial stock ownership, since it adds a factor depending on shareholder value to the utility function of the management. Thus the managerial utility function becomes more similar to that of the shareholders. Consequently, the opportunity costs of harming actions rise and diminish their advantage for the management.[50] Due to the assimilation of the utility functions the hypothesis is called *interest* or *incentive alignment argument*.[51] Since the effect depends on the degree of loss due to harming actions, it depends on the cash flow rights. Accordingly, the divergence of ownership and control reduces the strength of the effect and has a negative effect on performance.

---

[49] For a literature review on insider ownership and performance see Short [1994] and Holderness [2003].

[50] See Benston [1985], Brandhoff [1999, p. 223], Byrd et al. [1998, pp. 18-19], Cebenoyan et al. [2000, p. 23], Cui/Mak [2002, p. 315], and Jensen/Meckling [1976, p. 312-313]. Next to simple stock ownership similar amelioration of the agency conflict can be achieved through different compensation designs. See Byrd et al. [1998, pp. 19-21], Huddart [1993], and Jensen/Murphy [1990].

[51] See Achleitner/Wichels [2000, pp. 7 and 10], Bøhren/Ødegaard [2003, p. 5], and Cebenoyan et al. [2000, p. 23]. For an overview over selected studies assuming the incentive alignment argument and their results see Table A.7 in Appendix A.5, p. 229.

3.4 Insider Ownership and Performance

Table 3.5: Hypotheses for an effect of insider ownership on performance

Hypothesis	Theory	Explanation
$\frac{\partial Perf}{\partial MO} > 0$	Incentive alignment argument (IAA)	Managerial ownership reduces conflict of interest between shareholder and manager.
$\frac{\partial Perf}{\partial MO} < 0$	Entrenchment argument (EA)	Managerial ownership increases power of manager creating a hold-up problem.
Dep. on MO: $\frac{\partial Perf}{\partial MO} > 0$ $\frac{\partial Perf}{\partial MO} < 0$ $\frac{\partial Perf}{\partial MO} > 0$	Mørck et al.'s combined argument - IAA - EA	Non-monotonous relationship: IAA dominates EA for low managerial ownership, then the relation reverses for medium level and reverses again for high level of managerial ownership.
Dep. on MO: $\frac{\partial Perf}{\partial MO} > 0$ $\frac{\partial Perf}{\partial MO} = 0$ $\frac{\partial Perf}{\partial MO} < 0$	Stulz's integrated argument - Takeover premium argument (TPA) - EA	Takeover premium argument: Managerial ownership increases the opposition to takeovers. Raiders have to pay higher premiums thus stock price rises. Combined argument is roof-shaped: TPA prevails at low levels of managerial ownership, then TPA and EA equalize and for high managerial ownership EA dominates.
$\frac{\partial Perf}{\partial MO} = 0$	Natural selection argument	Any kind of ownership structure is determined by financial performance in the sense that corporations with inefficient (ownership) structures will fail to survive in the long run.
	Mutual neutralization argument	Performance effects from various incentive mechanisms matter, but cancel each other out.

While many studies support the incentive alignment argument, many other studies find no or even a negative relation, as for instance Ware [1975]. These contradicting results are explained by a further hypothesis, implying a negative effect of insider ownership on performance. This argument is called *entrenchment argument* and was developed by Fama [1980], Fama/Jensen [1983b], and Demsetz/Ricardo-Campbell [1983].[52] It is also based on the

---

[52] For an overview over selected studies assuming the general entrenchment argument and their results see Table A.8 in Appendix A.5, p. 230.

principal-agent theory. Instead of reducing the conflict through an interest alignment, insider ownership is argued to create a hold-up problem.[53] Due to its share the management can protect itself against disciplining actions, the so-called managerial entrenchment.[54] It averts punishment or reduces the degree of possible punishment and thus allows the management to conduct firm-harming actions at lower opportunity costs and risk.[55] A rise in control rights strengthens the entrenchment, while the cash flow rights increase the opportunity costs and reduce the incentive for harming actions. Consequently, a high divergence of both worsens the performance loss.

One could argue that due to the incentive alignment the manager will not harm shareholder value. However, his utility function does not only consist of monetary aspects, but also includes factors such as power, prestige, and career prospects. Following the principle of diminishing marginal rates of substitution these aspects gain relatively more importance the wealthier a manager is. If a manager holds a large share, he is probably wealthy and therefore less motivated by money than by intrinsic factors.

Mørck et al. [1988] indicate that the entrenchment works through several channels:[56]

- impeding owner's and creditor's control,
- impeding control through the market for managerial labor,
- impeding control through the market for corporate control, and
- impeding control through product markets.

Next to the shareholder the creditor has also a monitoring function. For firms with high managerial ownership the control through other owners and creditors becomes inefficient, since the other shareholders and creditors are relatively too weak to impose a sanction.[57]

Additionally Fama [1980] assumes a disciplining effect of the market for managerial labor. However, he argues that highly concentrated managerial ownership would prevent any competition for the managerial position.

Furthermore, the market of corporate control has a sanctioning function on opportunistic behavior. A poorly performing company is more likely to become the object of a hostile takeover, after which the management might be replaced. But with rising managerial ownership the management can more easily oppose the takeover.[58] This was already supported by Weston [1979],

---

[53] The shareholder recognizes the opportunistic behavior of the management, but cannot prevent it. See Grossman/Hart [1986], and Williamson [1975].
[54] The notation "entrenchment hypothesis" was first introduced by Mørck et al. [1988, p. 294].
[55] See Mørck et al. [1988, pp. 293-294], Shleifer/Vishny [1989, pp. 123-124], and Stulz [1988, pp. 27-28].
[56] See Mørck et al. [1988, p. 294].
[57] See Demsetz/Ricardo-Campbell [1983] and Fama/Jensen [1983b].
[58] See Jensen/Ruback [1983], Mørck et al. [1988, p. 294], Stulz [1988, p. 50], and Walkling/Long [1984].

who found no hostile takeovers in the case of a managerial ownership above 30%.

Finally, Machlup [1967] argues that in the case of efficient product markets supernormal profits do not exist. Therefore, if managers do not maximize profits, the company will fail. Yet, the model by Hart [1983] proves that managerial ownership can cause even an entrenchment against the control of product markets.

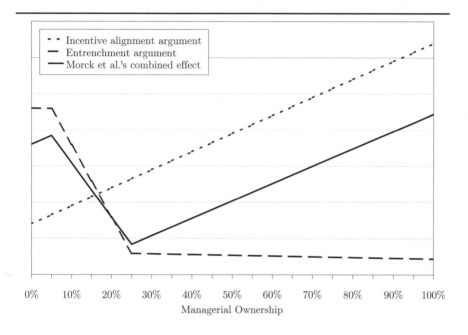

Fig. 3.3: Mørck et al.'s combined argument

Many studies combine those two contradicting hypotheses resulting in a non-monotonous effect. The most famous example is Mørck et al. [1988], whose combination is graphically demonstrated in Figure 3.3. They assume the incentive alignment argument to be linear, while the general entrenchment argument is a monotonous, nonlinear effect with a large gradient for medium managerial ownership. In *Mørck et al.'s combined argument* the incentive alignment dominates the combined effect for low managerial ownership. For medium levels the general entrenchment forces a negative effect. The combined effect again turns positive for high managerial ownership.[59]

---

[59] The N-shape was often applied as for instance by Brailsford et al. [2002], Chen et al. [1993], Chen/Ho [2000], Cho [1998], Cleary [2000], Cui/Mak [2002], Gu-

The entrenchment channel of impeding the market of corporate control gained individual importance in the takeover event studies. They analyze the importance of managerial ownership in the case of a takeover threat. Although these studies do not lie in the focus of this work, an important hypothesis of them is stated in the following. The reasons are its importance in literature and completeness but also its use used for the elaboration on different model specifications in Chapter 4.2.

As already explained for the general entrenchment argument, the probability of a successful takeover bid decreases with rising managerial ownership. However, the raiders try to overcome the managerial resistance by increasing the takeover premium. This increases share price and thus market performance. The effect is called *takeover premium argument* due to its causation by the premium increase and was first introduced by Stulz [1988].[60] He combines the takeover premium argument with the entrenchment effect in his event studies to the so called *Stulz's integrated argument* that is a roof- or bell-shaped relation in the range from zero to 50%. The range is determined by the fact that the management only needs the majority to obviate the takeover. Additional shares do not alter the outcome. As shown in Table 3.4 the takeover premium effect outweighs the entrenchment effect in the first part. Both outbalance each other at a medium level of managerial ownership. With further increasing ownership the management becomes increasingly entrenched.[61] However, since the event study approach has not been chosen for this work, the argument has no importance for the further conduct.

Similar to ownership concentration, the *natural selection argument* by Demsetz/Lehn [1985] can be applied as argument for the absence of effects.[62] Furthermore, the *mutual neutralization* argument as a combination of effects assumes a total balance of negative and positive effects. Therefore, no relation can be found.[63] One example, only based on managerial ownership, is that the incentive alignment and the general entrenchment effect simply cancel out. However, other factors such as capital structure effects can neutralize the effects as shown in a second example: Managers minimize their personal risk. Due to their strong relation to the firm, they can reduce the firm risk by reducing the leverage. The probability of success for such a manipulation of corporate finance decisions rises with the level of managerial ownership. However, following the free cash flow argument of Jensen [1986]

---

gler et al. [2003b], Hermalin/Weisbach [1991], Hubbard/Palia [1995], Kole [1996], Mudambi/Nicosia [1998], Short/Keasey [1999], Short et al. [2002a, 1994], and Welch [2003]. However, the thresholds of 5% and 25% were often altered.

[60] See McConnell/Servaes [1990], McConnell/Servaes [1995], and Stulz et al. [1990].

[61] Stulz's argument was also applied by Holderness et al. [1999], McConnell/Muscarella [1985], McConnell/Servaes [1990, 1995], Slovin/Sushka [1993], Song/Walkling [1993], Stulz [1990], and Stulz et al. [1990].

[62] For an explanation see Section 3.3.1, p. 44.

[63] This hypothesis is assumed by Bahng [2002], Eckbo/Smith [1998], and Himmelberg et al. [1999].

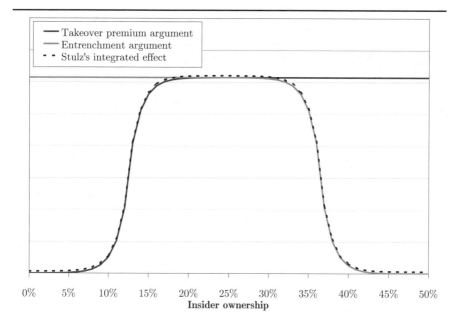

Fig. 3.4: Stulz's integrated argument

a decreased debt ratio leaves more free cash flow for inefficient investments by the management.[64] This reduces the performance and may neutralize the positive incentive alignment effect due to the initial increase in managerial ownership.[65]

3.4.2 Effect of Performance on Insider Ownership

Apart from the many studies on the effect of insider ownership on performance, some researchers analyze whether the direction of causality is assumed right. The literature knows two main hypotheses stating a positive or no effect of performance on insider ownership. These are given in Table 3.6.

The first argument for a positive effect is the *reward argument*.[66] Shareholders try to use the incentive alignment effect to ameliorate the firm's performance. Next to performance-based salaries they also use stock grants or options as remuneration.[67] Managers of a well performing company receive

---

[64] See Jensen [1986, p. 324].

[65] See Mathiesen [2002, pp. 22-23]. The capital structure neutralizing effect was also mentioned by McEachern [1975, p. 48].

[66] See Kole [1996, p. 16].

[67] See Byrd et al. [1998, pp. 18-21], Huddart [1993], and Jensen/Murphy [1990]. For studies on the effect of the salary level and management turnover see Baker et al.

Table 3.6: Hypotheses for an effect of performance on insider ownership

Hypothesis	Theory	Explanation
$\frac{\partial MO}{\partial Perf} > 0$	Reward argument	Firms reward their managers for good past financial performance by giving them equity ownership; therefore, better financial performance causes more management ownership.
	Insider-reward argument	Managers prefer equity compensation when they expect their firm to perform well. Consequently, firms with high corporate values have higher levels of insider ownership.
	Insider-investment argument	Insiders may capitalize on their insights by increasing their ownership when they expect the financial performance to improve and decrease their ownership.
$\frac{\partial MO}{\partial Perf} = 0$	Natural selection argument	Any kind of ownership structure is determined by financial performance in the sense that corporations with inefficient (ownership) structures will fail to survive in the long run.

shares or options that will be executed in the case of high performance. Consequently, the insider ownership rises with performance.[68] However, there is no consensus on the time period the performance data should be taken from. While some take the previous year's performance, others rely on the same year's performance.[69]

The second effect, the *insider-reward argument*, is introduced by Cho [1998]. He hypothesizes that managers will choose or accept equity compensation if they expect the firm to perform well. They anticipate bad performance by trying to decrease the equity-based component of their remuneration. As a result, insider ownership increases when insiders expect good performance. If

---

[1988], Dahya et al. [1998], Denis/Serrano [1996], and Warner et al. [1988]. For performance based boni see Baker et al. [1988], Bushman et al. [1996], Gilson [1989], Kaplan [1994], Lambert/Larcker [1987], Murphy/Zimmerman [1993], and Sloan [1993]; for accounting based boni see Banker et al. [1996] and Kole/Lehn [1997] and for market-based boni see Yermack [1995] and Mehran [1995].

[68] See Lorie/Niederhoffer [1968], Masson [1971, p. 1291], and McEachern [1975, pp. 92-93].

[69] For a detailed consideration of the timing issues see Section 4.2.2.

their expectations hold true, which is likely due to the inside knowledge, high performance correlates with high managerial ownership.[70]

The third explanation does not originate from the research field of managerial remuneration. The *insider-investment argument* states that managers might capitalize on their insider knowledge regarding the firm's prospect. When they expect the financial performance to improve, they increase their share and decrease it in the case of performance deterioration.[71] Most countries circumscribe the possibility for insider investment. But even if insider trading immediately before announcements is forbidden by insider legislation, opportunities for capitalizing on the insight in periods without announcements still exists.[72]

Besides the fact that, compared to the reward arguments, literature deals more often with the insider-investment argument, its importance is further supported by statistical data. Forbes (ed.) [1991] names a sum of $0.6 million as average stock grants for the CEOs of the 800 largest US corporations in 1991. In comparison Holderness et al. [1999] report for a sample of 4,200 publicly listed US companies in 1995 combined holdings by officer and directors of $73.0 million. The simple adjustment for the sample size difference results in a comparative value of $3.15 million of CEO stock grants. This equals 4% of the total managerial ownership in 1995. It seems very unlikely that 96% of the insider holdings belong to other insiders than CEO or that the values changed that dramatically in four years.[73] This indicates that a large part of managerial ownership arises from personal investments rather than from equity remuneration.

Finally, an argument for no relation is again given by the *natural selection argument* of Demsetz/Lehn [1985].[74]

3.4.3 Summary of Hypotheses on Insider Ownership

The hypotheses considered in the following are summarized in Table 3.7. The combined arguments are not mentioned due to their implicit inclusion.

---

[70] See Cho [1998, p. 115] and Yermack [1997].
[71] Lorie/Niederhoffer [1968] started a whole series of papers examining if insider can outperform other investors by using their inside knowledge. See Ahuja et al. [2005], Beneish/Vargus [2002], Burton et al. [2003], Bushman et al. [2005], Chalmers et al. [2002], Gombola et al. [1999], Hanson/Song [1995], Hu/H. [2001], Lee [2002], Pescatrice et al. [1992], and Zhang [2005].
[72] See Mußler [2005], Loderer/Martin [1997, p. 237], and Mathiesen [2002, p. 20]. Studies analyzing the insider-investment argument are Demsetz [1986], Eckbo/-Smith [1998], Hermalin/Weisbach [1991], Jaffe [1974], Loderer/Martin [1997], Rozeff/Zaman [1988], and Seyhun [1986].
[73] Especially if considering the probably higher stock remuneration for CEOs compared to other insiders and for CEOs of the largest 800 companies compared the market.
[74] For an explanation see Chapter 3.3.1, p. 41.

Table 3.7: Summary of assumed hypotheses on insider ownership

Hypothesis	Theory	$\frac{\partial Perf}{\partial (CR/CFR)}$
$\frac{\partial Perf}{\partial MO} > 0$	Incentive alignment argument	< 0
$\frac{\partial Perf}{\partial MO} < 0$	General entrenchment argument	< 0
$\frac{\partial Perf}{\partial MO} = 0$	Natural selection argument	$= 0$
	Mutual neutralization argument	$= 0$

Hypothesis	Theory
$\frac{\partial MO}{\partial Perf} > 0$	Reward argument
	Insider-reward argument
	Insider-investment argument
$\frac{\partial MO}{\partial Perf} = 0$	Natural selection argument

For the effect of insider ownership on performance two contradicting arguments exist. While the managerial ownership aligns the managers' incentive with shareholders' interest, it can also entrench the management against controlling and sanctioning actions. The divergence of control and cash flow rights has a negative effect on performance, since the cash flow rights form opportunity costs of opportunistic behavior and benefits for shareholder-value-oriented actions. Furthermore, the natural selection and the mutual neutralization arguments support the absence of an observable effect.

The effect of performance on insider ownership is assumed, if existent, as positive. The first argument is that shareholders try to use managerial stock ownership or option plans as incentive alignment; thus they reward the management for good performance with stocks. Second, the management of well performing companies favors stock remuneration and is more likely to accept or to promote those compensation designs. Finally, the managers use their insider knowledge to perform legal forms of insider trading. They increase their share if the company is perceived as well-performing and reduce it in the case of bad firm prospects.

3.5 Institutional Ownership and Performance

With increasing importance of institutional investors as equityholders the discussion of the relation between ownership and performance started to include institutional investors. While in 1950 only 8% of the US equity was held by institutional investors, the percentage of institutional ownership rose to 33%

in 1980 and 45% in 1990.[75] Furthermore, Coffee Jr. [1991] found a change in the behavior of institutional investors. He showed a trend towards rising activism and thus an increased investors' influence on the firm.

This chapter examines the theoretical relation of institutional ownership and performance. First the hypothesized effects of institutional ownership on performance are explained. Then the arguments for a reverse effect are discussed. The last section recapitulates all arguments and their effects.

3.5.1 Effect of Institutional Ownership on Performance

Prior to explaining the arguments an overview of all considered hypotheses is given in Table 3.8.

Table 3.8: Hypotheses for an effect of institutional ownership on performance

Hypothesis	Theory	Explanation
$\frac{\partial Perf}{\partial IO} > 0$	Active monitoring	Institutional investors are more capable of monitoring and controlling the management due to their business and industry knowledge, thereby contributing to corporate performance.
$\frac{\partial Perf}{\partial IO} < 0$	Institutional myopia	Institutional investors might prefer short-term returns and use their control to support myopic investment behavior.
	Strategic alignment-conflict-of-interest	Institutional investors may have business relationships with the company and actions against management may harm those relations.
$\frac{\partial Perf}{\partial IO} = 0$	Natural selection argument	Any kind of ownership structure is determined by financial performance in the sense that corporations with inefficient (ownership) structures will fail to survive in the long run.

The *active monitoring* argument for a positive relation of institutional ownership on performance resembles the monitoring hypothesis of general ownership concentration in Section 3.3.1. However, the monitoring effect should be stronger in the case of institutional investors than average shareholders. Given their professional occupation with capital markets, industries

---

[75] See Taylor [1990, p. 70].

and businesses, institutional investors are better informed and more sophisticated.[76] Business insight and industry knowledge reduce the cost of acquiring information. Thus the monitoring by institutional investors is more effective and less costly.[77] Similar to the monitoring argument of block ownership the ability of monitoring depends on the control rights, while the incentive to monitor depends on the cash flow rights. Thus the divergence of control and cash flow rights diminishes the strength of the monitoring effect and has a negative effect on performance.

A special interest in literature is given to the time preference agency problem in relation with institutional ownership.[78] Stein [1988, 1989] identified two conditions for myopic investment behavior of the management. First, the management must believe that current earnings create a potential for misvaluation. This might be either through overreaction to earning declines related to long-term investments or market underreactions to cuts in valuable R&D expenses that temporarily increases the earnings. While Bernard et al. [1993] give evidence to this condition through several cases of market overreaction on earnings news, Holthausen et al. [1995a], Francis/Smith [1995], and Palia/Lichtenberg [1999] find further support in their empirical studies.[79]

The second condition states that the management fears temporary misvaluation. These concerns about the current stock price could be driven by several reasons:

- ending of employment contracts of the management,
- stock-based compensation,
- near-term equity funding requirements,
- the threat of a raider, and
- an expected short time horizon of influential investors.

The first item is the classical example of the horizon problem. A temporary misvaluation could endanger for the prolongation of the employment contracts of the managers and harm their career prospects. Since the further

---

[76] Hand [1990] uses institutional ownership even as proxy for sophisticated investors.
[77] See Becht et al. [2002, pp. 38-41], Byrd et al. [1998, pp. 23-25], Jensen/Warner [1988, pp. 27-28], Maug [1998], and Moyer et al. [1992, p. 32]. The monitoring effect is proven positive by several studies like Agrawal/Knoeber [1996], Agrawal/Mandelker [1990], Bethel et al. [1997], Brickley et al. [1988], Chaganti/Damanpour [1991], Chowdhury/Geringer [2001], Dahya et al. [1998], Elston [2004], Elston et al. [2002], Gugler et al. [2003b], Holderness/Sheehan [1985], Huson [1997], Jones/Morse [1997], McConnell/Servaes [1990], Mikkelson/Ruback [1985], Nesbitt [1994], Nickell et al. [1997], Nyman/Silberstan [1978], Opler/Sokobin [1997], Pound [1988a], Ryan/Schneider [2002], Shome/Singh [1995], Short/Keasey [1999], Smith [1996], and Strickland et al. [1996].
[78] For an explanation of the time preference or horizon problem see Table 3.1 in Appendix A.5, p. 40.
[79] See also Jensen/Warner [1988, pp. 25-27], Bushee [1998, p. 308], and Dechow/Sloan [1991].

employment of the management is unclear and it is unsure if they will be given the credit for the long-term company results, the managers might prefer short-term profits. A second reason is that stock-based compensation does not only reduce the agency problems by incentive alignment,[80] but also reinforces the preference divergence of time horizons of management and shareholder at the point of remuneration fixing.[81] Furthermore, firm-based arguments, such as the cost of equity in the case of near-term equity funding, or a possible takeover threat can force the management to focus on the current stock price. Finally, the time horizon assumed by influential investors is an important concern.[82] If investors do not perceive the stock price as a misvaluation or prefer short-term over long-term results, an earning disappointment could trigger large-scale selling and the stock price would drop.[83] Consequently, the management will try to avoid this stock price decline and adapt its investment behavior.

On this last point of concern bases the hypothesis of *institutional myopia*. If institutional investors, who have nowadays an important share in most companies, are myopic, the management will try to avoid their negative reactions on earnings disappointment. Hence, the management will adopt the short-term investment focus of the institutional investors and thereby aggravating the time preference problem. The sacrifice of long-term profits for short-term gains reduces the performance, which forms the negative relation of institutional ownership and performance. Increasing control rights induce institutional investors to increase their support of myopic behavior. With regard to the effect of cash flow rights no clear prediction can be made, since a high cash flow entitlement enhances both, the gain on short- and long-term earnings.

Concerning the degree of myopia of institutional investors, Schipper [1989] argues that sophistication of institutional investors diminishes the potential of misvaluation of the company stock.[84] His argumentation is empirically supported by studies of Hand [1990] and Bushee [1998, 2001].[85] However, Gillan/Starks [1997] and Wahal [1996] find only a positive effect of institutional ownership on short-term performance, but no long-term gains to stockholders. Furthermore, Lang/McNichols [1997] show that institutional investors are sensitive to earnings news. Brown/Brooke [1993], Kim et al. [1997], and Potter [1992] prove higher trading volume and stock return volatility around quarterly earnings reports for firms with higher institutional ownership. These

---

[80] For an explanation of the incentive alignment argument see Section 3.4.1, p. 48.
[81] See Bebchuk/Fried [2003].
[82] See Froot et al. [1992a, pp. 50-55].
[83] See Graves/Waddock [1990, pp. 76-77], Jacobs [1991, pp. 37-38], and Porter [1992, pp. 43-46].
[84] See also Monks/Minow [1995, Chapter 2].
[85] Furthermore, Eames [1997] reports no changes in the earnings response coefficients for changes in institutional ownership.

studies indicate an institutional myopia and a consequent increase of potential misvaluation.

Literature states different possible reasons for the short-term focus. First, due to fiduciary responsibilities institutionals sell stocks with declining earnings, since fund sponsors and courts use earnings as criterion for judgement of prudence.[86] Second, institutional investors might use current earnings as proxy in the case of information asymmetry especially with regard to R&D quality.[87] This asymmetry could be caused by a short-term focus of institutional investors themselves reducing insight and knowledge of the firm due to the only short-term occupation with the company.[88] Another reason might be that the institutional investor has too many firms with small stakes in his portfolio; thus a monitoring of all firms is not cost-efficient.[89]

The two contradicting views of the time horizon of institutionals are reconciled by the differentiation of institutional investor groups based on their investment behavior.[90] The most famous classification is made by Porter [1992], who distinguishes between:[91] transient investors, dedicated investors, and quasi-indexer. Transient institutional investors focus on value proxies such as current earnings. Therefore, they behave myopic and show high portfolio turnovers. In contrast, dedicated investors, who Porter [1992] assigns mainly to Germany and Japan, focus on long-term performance and attenuate the pressures for myopic investment behavior. Dedicated institutional owners have thus a positive monitoring effect. The quasi-indexers have very fragmented shareholdings and thus gather little information. This renders them passive and causes them to abdicate their power to other shareholders. Apart from a general company investment policy the type of investment behavior of institutional investors is also influenced by other factors such as national legal or fiduciary regulations.

A second argument for a negative relation between institutional ownership and performance is given by the *strategic alignment-conflict-of-interest* by Pound [1988a]. Institutional investors may have business relationships with the company they own shares of. Monitoring and controlling actions against management could harm these business relations. Hence, the utility function of the institutional investors changes: The gain by effective monitoring faces a opportunity loss on the business relation, which might avert the monitoring incentive of the institutional investors.[92] The studies of Brickley et al. [1988], Borokhovich et al. [1997], and Duggal/Millar [1999] give empirical evidence to this hypothesis.

---

[86] See Badrinath et al. [1989].
[87] See Froot et al. [1992a, pp. 55-56] and Porter [1992, p. 43].
[88] This view is also supported by Froot et al. [1992b] and Porter [1992, p. 43].
[89] See Coffee Jr. [1991], Froot et al. [1992a, p. 56], and Porter [1992, p. 43].
[90] See Anand [1991], Elgin [1992], Gugler et al. [2003b], and Lang/McNichols [1997].
[91] See Bushee [1998, pp. 310-311] and Porter [1992, p. 46-49].
[92] See Pound [1988a].

The strength of the effect depends on the amount of non-executed control and therefore on the control rights. If institutional ownership rises, less control rights remain for other shareholders to enforce the monitoring and control of the management. The cash flow rights held by institutional investors represent the degree to which the investor has to carry the shareholder value loss due to managerial opportunistic behavior. Consequently, high cash flow rights might outweigh the loss on the business relation and weakens the strategic alignment-conflict-of-interest. Accordingly, the divergence of control and cash flow rights has a positive effect on performance.

The hypothesis of the *natural selection argument* is also present for institutional ownership and is supported by the results of Karpoff et al. [1996], who do not find a relation.[93]

3.5.2 Effect of Performance on Institutional Ownership

The investment behavior of institutional investors does not only play a role in the case of the monitoring and myopia argument, but also in the effects of performance on institutional ownership. The hypotheses on this effect are stated in Table 3.9.

Table 3.9: Hypotheses for an effect of performance on institutional ownership

Hypothesis	Theory	Explanation
$\frac{\partial IO}{\partial Perf} > 0$	Wall Street Rule	Institutional investors either vote with management or sell their stocks.
	Insider-investment argument	Institutional investors have insider knowledge and may capitalize on their insights by adapting their ownership position.
$\frac{\partial IO}{\partial Perf} = 0$	Natural selection argument	Any kind of ownership structure is determined by financial performance in the sense that corporations with inefficient (ownership) structures will fail to survive in the long run.

Brickley et al. [1988] and Pound [1988a] predict a positive effect of performance on institutional ownership, which they call *Wall Street Rule*. Institutional investors elude the costs of monitoring and activism. They either vote with the management or sell their stocks.[94] Hence, bad firms have a

---
[93] The results of Duggal/Millar [1999] and Edwards/Nibler [2000] support their evidence further.
[94] Agrawal/Mandelker [1990, pp. 143-144] call it also "passive voting hypothesis".

lower level of institutional ownership. This argument prevails especially in the case of small shareholdings as found by quasi-indexers, since the monitoring costs are relatively high. Given the low cost-efficiency of monitoring investors rather sell the shares than bear the costs. A similar behavior will be found with transient institutional investors. Their short-term focus makes the information gathering and monitoring costly. Similar to the quasi-indexers, they have too many firms in their portfolio, actually not at one point of time, but over a time period. Hence, they will not benefit from the long-term performance increase through monitoring. Consequently, they rather sell the stock than try to increase the firm's performance.[95]

A further argument for a positive relation is the *insider-investment argument*. This argument resembles that of ownership concentration. Institutional investors capitalize on their knowledge due to their professional occupation with the company and the market. According to their knowledge they evaluate the firm's prospects more precisely than the average investor and consequently adjust their share sizes. If the company is perceived as a good investment, institutional investors increase their share. If the firm does not perform well, they reduce their share.[96] The higher knowledge of institutional investors is especially pronounced with dedicated investors. Both other groups will not be as successful in the investment, since they have less knowledge on their portfolio firms.

Finally, the positive effect of performance on institutional ownership holds for all three classes of institutional investors. However, if the firms are distinguished by low, medium and high performance, a difference might be seen. Following this argument the quasi-indexers and transient investors will be found in medium- and high-performing firms, but not in low-performing ones. Whereas the dedicated investor will be found in low-performing firms, trying to improve performance and will be found at a higher rate in medium firms and in good firms.

Finally, the natural selection arguments appears also for this effect.[97]

3.5.3 Summary of Hypotheses on Institutional Ownership

The hypothesized effects of the relation of institutional ownership and performance are summarized in Table 3.10.

With the exception of the omnipresent argument of natural selection, the increased importance of institutional investors and the existence of their influence on the firm is widely accepted. Nevertheless, the direction of the effect is unclear. Some argue that the insider knowledge of institutional investors allows a more efficient monitoring and increases the performance. Others argue that institutional investors have a short-term horizon and thus tempt the

---

[95] Especially, since they intended to keep the stock only for a short period in the first place.
[96] See Loderer/Martin [1997, p. 237] and Demsetz/Lehn [1985].
[97] For an explanation of the effect see Section 3.3.1, p. 44.

Table 3.10: Summary of assumed hypotheses on institutional ownership

Hypothesis	Theory	$\frac{\partial Perf}{\partial (CR/CFR)}$
$\frac{\partial Perf}{\partial IO} > 0$	Active monitoring	?
$\frac{\partial Perf}{\partial IO} < 0$	Institutional myopia	< 0
	Strategic alignment-conflict-of-interest	< 0
$\frac{\partial Perf}{\partial IO} = 0$	Natural selection argument	$= 0$

Hypothesis	Theory
$\frac{\partial IO}{\partial Perf} > 0$	Wall Street Rule
	Insider-investment argument
$\frac{\partial IO}{\partial Perf} = 0$	Natural selection argument

management to also act myopic. These two contradicting effects are reconciled by Porter [1992] classifying institutional investors by their investment behavior. Applying his classification both arguments hold true and the effect direction depends on the investor group. For Germany Porter predicts mainly dedicated investors which yields in the assumption of active monitoring for Germany.

The reverse effect, if existent, is assumed as positive, since bad investments are sold and insider knowledge is used to identify good investments.

3.6 Ownership Concentration, Insider and Institutional Ownership

3.6.1 General Discussion

Apart from the effects between ownership and performance, assumed in literature, several studies also arguing for effects within the ownership structure itself.

Already the early discussion on the principal-agent theory by Jensen/Meckling [1976] and Jensen [1986] formed an important effect hypothesis on interactions within the ownership structure. The substitution effect of different agency devices states that monitoring mechanisms, such as insider ownership, leverage, board composition and dividend policy, influence each other's cost-efficiency and therefore the usage of the devices.[98] Since all three ownership

---

[98] See Agrawal/Knoeber [1996], Bathala/Moon [1994], Chen/Steiner [1999], Crutchley/Hansen [1989], Hermalin/Weisbach [1991], Holthausen/Larcker [1993], Jensen et al. [1992], and Moyer et al. [1992].

variables are argued to have a monitoring effect or a negative impact on the agency conflict, they should also underly the substitution effect and hence be interdependent.

The monitoring mechanisms can be classified into two groups according to the interference through shareholders. Mechanisms sensible to the influence of other shareholders' decision or company policy are based on internal decisions. Agency devices, such as dividend policy, capital structure policy, or equity-based managerial remuneration, are part of this internally determined group. They are likely to be endogenous. In contrast, the shareholdings of other owners and therefore blockholdings and institutional investments are hard to influence by a shareholder and rather based on external decisions.[99] Since they are not subject of corporate decision and direct influence, they are assumed to be exogenous. Accordingly no direct effect of insider ownership on ownership concentration and institutional shareholdings is assumed. Nevertheless, both exogenous ownership aspects have an effect on the internal decision of managerial remuneration and thus on managerial ownership. Consequently, their effect on insider ownership must be considered.

The following two subsections give the effect of ownership concentration and institutional ownership on insider ownership, respectively. A final section will summarize the effects.

3.6.2 Effect of Ownership Concentration on Insider Ownership

Table 3.11 states the two hypothesized effects of ownership concentration on insider ownership and their arguments.

Table 3.11: Hypotheses for an effect of ownership concentration on insider ownership

Hypothesis	Theory	Explanation
$\frac{\partial MO}{\partial OC} > 0$	Stock-based compensation preference	Stockholders perceive stock-based compensation to be in their interest and actively promote their adoption.
$\frac{\partial MO}{\partial OC} > 0$ or $\frac{\partial MO}{\partial OC} < 0$	Substitution-monitoring effect argument	Ownership concentration reduces the shareholder-manager conflict through improved monitoring or worsens it by hampering the market of corporate control. The utility of insider ownership as control mechanism decreases or increases.

---

[99] See Agrawal/Knoeber [1996, p. 381].

3.6 Ownership Concentration, Insider and Institutional Ownership

Hill/Snell [1989] hypothesize a positive effect of ownership concentration on insider ownership. They assume that stockholders seek an alignment of the managers' interest by increasing the managerial ownership. Stockholders will therefore push stock-based compensation and the probability of success of their promotion rises with their shareholding and power. Hence, concentrated firms are more likely to accept stock-based remuneration and thus have a higher level of insider ownership. Consequently, the argument is called *stock-based compensation preference*.[100]

An effect with unclear direction is the *substitution-monitoring effect argument*. It is based on the substitution effect of agency devices stating that one monitoring device can be replaced by another. Agency devices substitute each other and are chosen by their cost-efficiency.[101] Following this argument the improved monitoring capability of a large shareholder and its reduced costs, will reduce the utility of equity-based compensation as agency device. Accordingly, the shareholders will promote less stock-based compensation and insider ownership decreases for concentrated firms.

Chen/Steiner [1999] oppose that in the case of concentrated ownership shareholders will stress the necessity of alignment. A high ownership concentration hampers the acquisition of large share sizes and reduces the threat of a takeover. However, the market of corporate control has a monitoring function for opportunistic managerial behavior.[102] Accordingly, a high ownership concentration equals an impediment to the market of corporate control and paves the way for more opportunistic and firm-harming actions. To substitute the lost monitoring through the market of corporate control, other control mechanisms such as managerial ownership have to be increased.[103]

Furthermore, the substitution effect is based on the expectations of the effect on performance. If shareholders expect blockholdings to have a negative effect on performance, e.g., due to private benefits, they might increase the managerial ownership with rising share concentration to limit possible negative effects. Consequently, a positive effect of ownership concentration on insider ownership may stem from the impediment of the market of corporate control or the expectation of a negative effect of blockholdings on performance.

3.6.3 Effect of Institutional Ownership on Insider Ownership

Insider ownership is also sensitive to institutional ownership with its effect shown in Table 3.12.

---

[100] See Hill/Snell [1989, pp. 28-29] and Holderness [2003, p. 56].
[101] The substitution effect of agency devices was introduced by Jensen/Meckling [1976] and Jensen [1986] and especially pronounced on the relation of managerial ownership and debt.
[102] See Jensen/Ruback [1983] and Walkling/Long [1984]. For a more detailed explanation see Section 3.4.1, p. 50.
[103] See Chen/Steiner [1999, p. 123].

Table 3.12: Hypotheses for an effect of institutional ownership on insider ownership

Hypothesis	Theory	Explanation
$\frac{\partial MO}{\partial IO} > 0$ or $\frac{\partial MO}{\partial IO} < 0$	Substitution-monitoring effect argument	Institutional ownership reduces the shareholder-manager conflict through improved monitoring or worsens it by hampering the market of corporate control. The utility of insider ownership as control mechanism decreases or increases.

The *substitution effect of agency devices*, introduced in the previous section, can also be used to explain the assumed negative effect of institutional ownership on managerial ownership. Since institutional investors are argued to increase the monitoring of the management,[104] the adoption of stock remuneration for the management is less advantageous and will be pushed less by the shareholders. Consequently, institutional ownership has a negative effect on insider ownership.[105]

The impediment of the market of corporate control claimed by Chen/Steiner [1999] may also cause a reverse effect. However, the effect should be lower than for ownership concentration, since the efficiency of monitoring stems also from the professional occupation with the company and not only from share size. Furthermore, the substitution effect of institutional shareholdings is also based on the expectations of its effect on performance. Similar to ownership concentration, shareholders will increase the managerial ownership with rising institutional investments to limit its effect on performance if expected to be negative. Consequently, a positive effect of institutional ownership on insider ownership may stem from the impediment of the market of corporate control or the expectation of a negative effect of institutional ownership on performance.

3.6.4 Summary of Hypotheses of Ownership Concentration, Institutional Ownership and Insider Ownership

An overview of the effects of the ownership on insider ownership is given by Table 3.13.

An argument for a positive effect of the ownership concentration on insider ownership is the preference of stock-based compensation by the shareholders. The direction of the substitution-monitoring effect is questionable for both

---

[104] See Section 3.5.1, p. 57.
[105] See Bathala/Moon [1994, pp. 40-41], Chen/Steiner [1999, pp. 122-123], Jensen/Meckling [1976], and Jensen [1986]. The argument found empirical support by Bathala/Moon [1994]

Table 3.13: Summary of assumed effects of ownership on insider ownership

Hypothesis	Theory
$\frac{\partial MO}{\partial OC} > 0$	Stock-based compensation preference
$\frac{\partial MO}{\partial OC} > 0$ or $\frac{\partial MO}{\partial OC} < 0$	Substitution-monitoring effect argument

Hypothesis	Theory
$\frac{\partial MO}{\partial IO} > 0$ or $\frac{\partial MO}{\partial IO} < 0$	Substitution-monitoring effect argument

ownership concentration and institutional ownership. While the monitoring increases with a rising ownership, it also always implies a reduction of monitoring through the market of corporate control. Furthermore, the expectation of a negative effect of the exogenous ownership aspects on performance may also turn the substitution effect positive. Consequently, it is not clear if managerial ownership shrinks due to improved monitoring or if increases to compensate for monitoring losses.

3.7 Summary of Hypotheses

All the potential effects introduced above are graphically illustrated in Figure 3.5. The effects themselves are monotonous, but not necessarily linear. While the effect of performance is always positive or non-existent, all ownership variables have contradicting arguments. Accordingly, the observed ownership effects can be non-monotonous, formed by a combination of contradicting effects. Furthermore, all ownership-performance relations may be subject to the natural selection argument of Demsetz/Lehn [1985], giving an explanation for insignificant results.

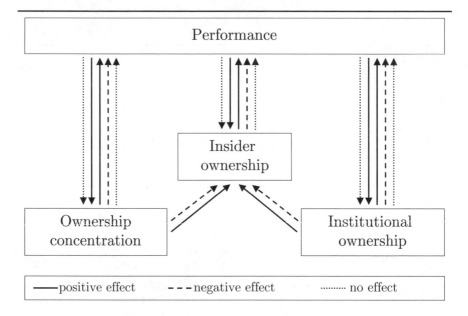

Fig. 3.5: Summary of hypothesized effects

4

Model, Methodology and Data

4.1 Introduction

Prior to the performance of the empirical analyses, the following chapter specifies the applied model and estimation method. To deduct the model specifications, the following section first elaborates on crucial model issues in the ownership performance literature. Especially the endogeneity discussion in Chapter 4.2.3, gives also justification of the estimation method used, the simultaneous equations methodology, which is explained in the Section 4.3. It gives an overview over the statistical method itself as well as over important aspects of its estimation.

After Chapter 4.2 and Chapter 4.3 yielded the model and its estimation methodology, the used data set is the final part to be introduced prior to the analyses. The section starts with the introduction of the used variables, followed by the explanation of the sample selection and a presentation of the descriptive statistics of the data set.

4.2 Model Specifications

4.2.1 Linearity and Monotonousness

One bias always present in economic literature is the model specification error. In the ownership and performance literature there are several issues to be considered to minimize the potential model specification error and subsequent bias of results. This section elaborates on the treatment of different model specification issues in literature. Based on these discussions the models analyzed in this work are deducted.

This section states and compares different alternatives for the assumed shape of the analyzed relationship. Section 4.2.2 elaborates on the timing within the relation. Chapter 4.2.3 broaches the issue of endogeneity, simultaneousness and causation, justifying the appliance of simultaneous equation models. Finally, the section closes with a summary of the chosen model specifications.

In the ownership literature a severe model specification error may lie in the assumed shape of the relationship. From the early studies in the 1960s until today many studies have supposed a linear effect.[1] This surprises considering that a multitude of studies result in a nonlinear and even non-monotonous relation of ownership and performance, with the first indication given by Monsen et al. [1968].[2] Furthermore, the variety of contradicting effects argues also for a potential nonlinear relation. However, given the contradicting empirical evidence the exact shape is still unclear.

A frequently modelled shape of the effect of managerial ownership is given by Mørck et al. [1988].[3] They use a piecewise regression with two turning points of 5% and 25%, cutting the function in three parts. Many studies copy this approach and find a significantly positive relation of ownership and performance in the first range from zero to 5%.[4] Other adjust the range size such as Chen et al. [1993] and Cho [1998], who use a range from zero to 7%. Nevertheless, they still find evidence for a positive effect. The second part of the function is also proven significant by the majority of studies indicating a negative relation.[5] Chen et al. [1993] also alters the second turning point to 12% and Cho [1998] to 38%. Yet, both find a negative relation for their definition of the second piece of the function. However, for the last range of the function ending at 100% none of the studies finds significant evidence for an effect.

Figure 4.1 shows that the result is a two parted function with a maximum potentially approximating a bell-shaped relation. If so, the results would concur with Stulz [1988]'s hypothesis, that assumes a parabolic relation.[6] Stulz ranges the shape from zero to 50%, since the probability of a takeover vanishes at an insider ownership of theoretically 50% or higher. This high threshold may be exaggerated, since already a smaller share might guarantee the control over a firm. This holds especially under the condition of other entrenchment

---

[1] See Demsetz/Lehn [1985], Jacquemin/De Ghellinck [1980], Kamerschen [1968], Kamerschen/Paul [1971], Larner [1966], Leech/Leahy [1991], McEachern [1975], Mehran [1995], Murali/Welch [1989], Pedersen/Thomsen [1999], Radice [1971], Round [1976], Stano [1976], Steer/Cable [1978], and Thonet/Poensgen [1979].

[2] See Chen et al. [1993], Cho [1998], Cleary [2000], Cui/Mak [2002], Gugler et al. [2003b], Hermalin/Weisbach [1991], Holderness et al. [1999], Hubbard/Palia [1995], Kole [1996], McConnell/Servaes [1990, 1995], Monsen et al. [1968], Mørck et al. [1988], Short/Keasey [1999], Short et al. [2002a, 1994], Stulz [1988], Welch [2003], and Wruck [1989].

[3] For an explanation of the assumed combined effect see Chapter 3.4.1, p. 48.

[4] See Holderness et al. [1999], Hubbard/Palia [1995], Kole [1996], McConnell/Servaes [1990], Mørck et al. [1988], and Wruck [1989].

[5] See Hubbard/Palia [1995], Mørck et al. [1988], Wruck [1989] and Holderness et al. [1999] with their 1935 sample.

[6] For an explanation of the assumed combined effect see Chapter 3.4.1, p. 48

activities reducing the threshold. For example, Weston [1979] supports Mørck et al. [1988]'s lower threshold. He finds evidence that no hostile takeover has been observed with an insider ownership over 30%.

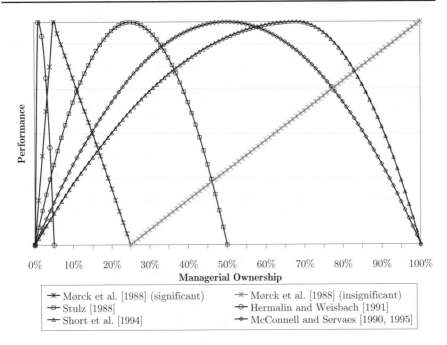

Fig. 4.1: Comparison of different shapes of the managerial ownership-performance relation in literature; only considering the effect direction not the strength

Besides the studies by Chen et al. [1993] and Cho [1998],[7] five further studies present significantly different turning points. Hermalin/Weisbach [1991] document a bell shape from zero to 5% with a maximum at 1%. In contrast, Short et al. [1994] observe a positive effect from zero to 68% and a weakly significant and negative effect from 68% to 100%. The two studies by McConnell/Servaes [1990, 1995] produce similar results of a bell shape peaking at 50%. Finally, Short/Keasey [1999] use a third degree polynomial with a maximum at 16% and a minimum at 42%. Except for the latter, the assumed effect shapes are illustrated in Figure 4.1.

One explanation for the different thresholds is given by Mathiesen [2002]. He argues that larger firms have a bell closer to zero.[8] The dispersion of

---

[7] Chen et al. [1993] and Cho [1998] change the threshold to 7% and 12% or 7% and 38% respectively.

[8] See Mathiesen [2002, p. 33] and Kole [1995].

shareholdings is higher for large firms; thus only a small share is needed for controlling the firm. The studies support this hypothesis. Hermalin/Weisbach [1991] consider a small sample of very large firms. In contrast, Short et al. [1994] use small firms and McConnell/Servaes [1990, 1995] use a large sample including both small and large companies. Furthermore, Kole [1995] analyzes the studies of Mørck et al. [1988] and McConnell/Servaes [1990], which are based on the same model, and concludes that the differences in the results are caused by such a size effect.

Short/Keasey [1999] explain their deviating evidence by the scope of their study on the United Kingdom. The institutional differences cause a nation effect on the shape of the relation. In particular, they argue that US managers become more easily entrenched than UK managers do. The importance of national differences and their effect on the ownership structure and the corporate governance are also shown in comparative studies by La Porta et al. [1999] and Faccio/Lang [2002].[9]

Another explanation for the differing results is the estimation method used. Studies using a squared ownership measure or a third degree polynomial assume that the shape fully ranges from zero to 100%.[10] In contrast, a piecewise modelled function is flexible in its range and turning points. Due to its flexibility and its simple application the piecewise approach can not only proxy a third-degree polynomial but also more complex functions. Furthermore, high collinearity between simple and, for example, squared measures could cause a multicollinearity bias in polynomial functions reducing significance of coefficients. However, in the case of an exact polynomial relationship in reality the fit of a piecewise model could be worse, since it assumes linear pieces and no curves. Yet, this case is not very likely regarding the multitude of possible functions. Therefore, the piecewise approach is preferable to complex polynomials.

Based on this argumentation, the analyses performed in the following apply a piecewise approach and discard a third-degree polynomial in its favor. Besides different amounts and locations of turning points within the piecewise estimation, the later analyses also test simple linear and squared functions to identify the best shape.

The piecewise approach creates dummy variables for each measure with constant percentages as break points of the estimated function.[11] The calculation of three piecewise variables for ownership (O) with the thresholds τ_1 and τ_2 is explained below and graphically illustrated by Figure 4.2.

---

[9] For some information on the national differences in ownership structure see Chapter 2.3, p. 19.

[10] Examples for a squared variable are McConnell/Servaes [1990, 1995], and Short et al. [1994]. The third-degree polynomial is applied by Short/Keasey [1999, p. 86].

[11] See Cho [1998, p. 111], Hermalin/Weisbach [1991, p. 107], Hubbard/Palia [1995, p. 788], Mørck et al. [1988, p. 298], and Wruck [1989, pp. 18-19].

$$O_a = \begin{cases} O & \text{if } O < \tau_1, \\ \tau_1 & \text{if } O \leq \tau_1; \end{cases}$$

$$O_b = \begin{cases} 0 & \text{if } O < \tau_1, \\ O - \tau_1 & \text{if } \tau_1 \leq O < \tau_2, \\ \tau_2 - \tau_1 & \text{if } O \geq \tau_2; \end{cases}$$

$$O_c = \begin{cases} 0 & \text{if } O < \tau_2, \\ O - \tau_2 & \text{if } O \geq \tau_2. \end{cases}$$

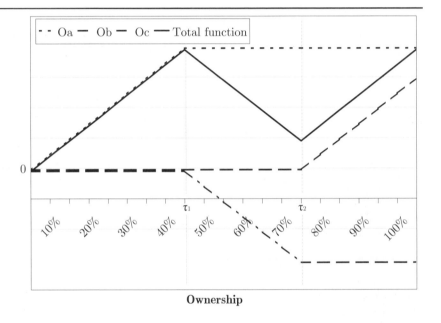

Fig. 4.2: Graphic example for the creation of a nonlinear function through piecewise regression with the thresholds of 45% and 75%

Each dummy variable forms a function of ownership and performance. Nevertheless, the value of the variables only deviates from zero or a constant calculated on the thresholds in the according parts of the function, i.e., O_b for ownership between the thresholds τ_1 and τ_2. Consequently, the formed functions only show a gradient deviating from zero for the according ownership values. This results in the fact that each function has a non-zero gradient only in its part. When considering all ownership dummies together as done in the estimation, the resulting function equals the sum of the individual functions and shows the gradients of individual functions in its different pieces.

74   4 Model, Methodology and Data

In contrast to Hubbard/Palia [1995], Mørck et al. [1988], and Wruck [1989], who used fixed thresholds of 5% and 25%,[12] a grid search and iteration technique is used to identify the turning points for the piecewise model. This allows the incorporation of possible size and nation effects. Similar approaches are used by Hermalin/Weisbach [1991] and Cho [1998]. They use the following model to estimate the thresholds assuming two changes in the slope:

$$\text{Perf} = \beta_0 + \beta_1\, O_a + \beta_2\, O_b + \beta_3\, O_c\ ,$$

where Perf is a performance measure, and O_a, O_b and O_c are the piecewise ownership measures at the thresholds of τ_1 and τ_2. To find the breakpoints a simple grid search technique is applied: First, τ_1 is changed, starting with zero, until it produces the most significant slope coefficient on the first variable O_a. Then the level is fixed and τ_2 is altered, starting at τ_1. Thus the second and third coefficients become most significant. Finally, by simultaneous iteration around the two levels the ultimate thresholds are estimated.[13] This simple approach of a grid search is preferred over other nonlinear optimization methods such as gradient methods. Most of those need an approximately squared relation e.g., Newton's iteration or are very complicated and do not promise more precise results for nonlinearity exceeding a third degree polynomial.[14] This thesis applies a similar approach, but uses the simultaneous equation model for the simultaneous iteration of the thresholds. In addition, according to the iteration results the number of threshold is varied from one up to three breakpoints.

4.2.2 Timing of Effects

Another model specification issue is the timing of the different effects on ownership. Some hypotheses explicitly incorporate certain timing effects. One example is the reward argument for managerial ownership by Kole [1996]. The management is rewarded with shares for past times' performance. Thus it is likely that the effect is lagging for one period.[15] Also the natural selection hypothesis by Demsetz/Lehn [1985] implies that past performance determines

---

[12] Mørck et al. [1988] arrived at that turning points as a result of examining a variety of piecewise formulations. Their regression including the turning points of 5% and 25% provided the lowest sum of squared errors. Nevertheless, they note that the choice of 5% is motivated by the fact that this is the mandatory disclosure level of ownership interest (mandated by the SEC for their US sample) and also Herman [1981] presents a share of 5% as a non-negligible stake. The choice of the second turning point is motivated by the suggestion of Weston [1979] that directors' ownership of 20%–30% prohibits a successful hostile takeover bid.
[13] See Cho [1998, p. 109].
[14] See Greene [1990, pp. 363-377].
[15] See Kole [1996, p. 16].

ownership due to the failure of firms with a non-optimal ownership structure. However, the effect works "in the long run" and hence probably includes several periods.

Another argument for potential timing misspecifications is based on the stickiness of ownership variables, which is sometimes assumed.[16] This implies that ownership is not changing significantly over a limited period of time, i.e., it is only slowly adapting to changes. This may especially be the case for large shares which cannot be sold in a short term. The sale of a large share by insiders such as managers, founder, or family owners would probably originate a severe stock price drop dramatically harming the company and is therefore avoided. To protect against such a possible error some studies, for instance by Cho [1998] and Edwards/Nibler [2000], test both the relationship of ownership to the current and the previous year's performance.

Table 4.1: Correlation of the ownership data of 2000 and 2003

	Ownership concentration	Institutional ownership	Managerial ownership	Man. & board ownership
Correlation$_{2000/2003}$	0.63	0.36	0.65	0.71

Table 4.1 shows the correlations of the ownership data of 2000 with that of 2003. Even for the lagged period of three years the measures for general ownership concentration and insider ownership lie conspicuously above .5. While this could stem from the absence of changes to adapt to, it could also indicate the stickiness of the variable. Thus the stickiness over a one-year period would be very probable for those variables. In contrast, the institutional ownership shows only a small correlation. Possible explanations are a low average share size making a sale easier and/or the Wall Street Rule by Brickley et al. [1988] and Pound [1988b] assuming that institutional investors are more likely to sell their share than other blockholders.[17] As for the empirical analyses performed in the following the stickiness of ownership variables cannot be excluded, they will test lagged effects of performance on ownership in form of robustness tests.

4.2.3 Endogeneity, Simultaneousness and Causation

A further modelling aspect argued in the ownership performance literature is the issue of endogeneity and the direction of causation. Already the existence of hypotheses of effects in both directions argues for endogeneity and simultaneity within the ownership and performance relation and requires the

---

[16] See Mikkelson/Partch [1989, p. 287].
[17] For an explanation of the Wall Street Rule see Section 3.5.2, p. 61.

incorporation of these effects. Bøhren/Ødegaard [2003] use the assumed mechanisms and the modelled causations to classify the existing research by the two-by-two matrix shown in Figure 4.3.[18]

	One-way causation	Two-way causation
Exogenous mechanisms	**First generation** *McConnell/Servaes [1990], Mørck et al. [1988], and for the other direction Baesel/Stein [1979], Kole [1996], Murphy [1985]*	**Third generation** *not feasible*
Endogenous mechanisms	**Second generation** *Demsetz/Lehn [1985], Himmelberg et al. [1999]*	**Fourth generation** *Agrawal/Knoeber [1996], Bøhren/Ødegaard [2003], Cho [1998], Demsetz/Villalonga [2001], Loderer/Martin [1997]*

Fig. 4.3: Classification of studies based on endogeneity and causation

Most of the studies belong to the first cell. They assume that ownership is exogenous and causation runs only in one way. Examples are Mørck et al. [1988] and McConnell/Servaes [1990], who analyze the effect of ownership on performance. Other studies prove the reverse direction of causation, from performance to ownership.[19]

Demsetz/Lehn [1985] founded the second generation, as they were the first to argue that in equilibrium the ownership structure is endogenously determined. Although ownership is viewed as endogenous, only one way of causation is modelled. Himmelberg et al. [1999] support the argumentation, but also does not consider both effect directions.

As a two-way causation model always implies the endogeneity of at least one mechanism, the third cell is not feasible.

The last generation of studies models the endogeneity and two-way causation resulting in a simultaneous equations model. Only five studies of the fourth generation are known to the author: Agrawal/Knoeber [1996], Bøhren/Ødegaard [2003], Cho [1998], Demsetz/Villalonga [2001], and Loderer/Martin [1997]. While Agrawal/Knoeber [1996] do not give information about the cau-

---

[18] See Bøhren/Ødegaard [2003, pp. 7-8].
[19] See Baesel/Stein [1979], Demsetz [1986], Jaffe [1974], Kole [1996], Murphy [1985], Pope et al. [1990], Rozeff/Zaman [1988], Seyhun [1986], and Yermack [1996].

sation, the others find interesting new evidence. The approaches of the first and fourth generation applied on the same data produce tremendously different results. For example, Cho [1998] finds an effect of ownership on performance in the ordinary least squares (OLS) model. In contrast, the simultaneous equation model indicates the reverse causation running from performance to ownership and leaving the traditional effect of ownership on performance insignificant.

This example illustrates the bias resulting from lacking consideration of existing endogeneity. The so-called simultaneous equations bias yields in confused directions of causation and/or inconsistent estimates. Consequently, the results of the studies of the first and second generation have to be questioned.[20] To further demonstrate the bias due to endogeneity and feedback effects, Table A.12 of Appendix A.8.1 compares the results of an OLS estimation, abstracting from endogeneity, to the results of the simultaneous equations estimation. The coefficients do not only show strong differences in their magnitude but also in their signs and significance.[21]

Consequently, a test for simultaneity of effect, such as a Hausman test, appears necessary to exclude the possibility of an endogeneity bias. This test is conducted by only two studies: Hermalin/Weisbach [1991] reject the hypothesis of simultaneity justifying its neglect.[22] In contrast, Himmelberg et al. [1999] find simultaneity, but do not reflect it in their model leaving their results questionable.[23] Consequently, due to the different facts arguing for simultaneity of ownership and performance endogeneity should not only be tested but it should further be incorporated in the resulting model, if statistically proven.

Furthermore, not only performance and ownership may suffer from the simultaneity bias, but also the different ownership types themselves as indicated by their interaction stated by theory.[24] Especially the substitution effect of agency devices by Jensen/Meckling [1976] and Jensen [1986] argues for an interdependence of the ownership aspects, such as block ownership, institutional ownership, and managerial ownership. Since these ownership types are theoretically agency devices, they influence each others' cost-efficiency and hence the extend of their usage. Thus the simultaneous model has to be extended to the different agency devices and ownership aspects.

Hermalin/Weisbach [1991] examine the interactions of managerial ownership and board composition, while Crutchley/Hansen [1989] and Jensen et al. [1992] simultaneously consider the effects of managerial ownership, debt, and dividend policy. Moyer et al. [1992] consider even more monitoring mechanisms: board composition, insider and institutional ownership, analyst following as well as debt and dividend policy. Yet, they do not study them in

---

[20] See Mathiesen [2002, p. 47].
[21] See Table A.12 of Appendix A.8.1, p. 315.
[22] See Hermalin/Weisbach [1991, p. 106].
[23] See Himmelberg et al. [1999, p. 373].
[24] For detailed information on possible interactions between the different ownership types see Chapter 3.6, p. 63.

a simultaneous setting. Holthausen/Larcker [1993] are the first to introduce performance as further endogenous variable analyzing the effects of managerial ownership, capital structure policy, and performance. Agrawal/Knoeber [1996] combine the approaches of Moyer et al. [1992] and Holthausen/Larcker [1993] by first modelling insider and institutional ownership, blockholding, debt policy, board composition, and CEO tenure simultaneously. In a second step they analyze the effects on firm performance. Yet, they do not study the several ownership forms simultaneously with performance as endogenous variable in order to consider both the endogeneity between ownership and performance and that of ownership itself.

A simultaneous equations model assuming the performance as well as the different ownership forms as exogenous allows the consideration of ownership interactions and the clear separation of their effects on performance. Consequently, the model applied in this work picks up this thought by forming a four-equations system with both performance and the different ownership aspects as exogenous, interdependent variables.

4.2.4 Summary

On the basis of the evidence given by the ownership and performance literature, the model of this work is specified as follows.

Since the literature does not find clear results with regard to the effect shape, the following empirical analyses will use linear, squared, and piecewise relations. The thresholds for the piecewise approach are iterated following an approach similar to that by Cho [1998].

The possibility of a lagged relation cannot be excluded and therefore robustness tests are run on the performance of the previous year.

The literature discusses the issue of endogeneity and the direction of causation. The rare evidence argues for the assumption of endogeneity. Consequently, the following empirical analyses apply a Hausman test to ensure the simultaneity. If statistically proven, the model will be set up as a simultaneous equations systems. This model will include performance and the different ownership forms as exogenous, interdependent variables.

4.3 Methodology

4.3.1 General Aspects of Simultaneous Equations Systems

To explain the analysis structure of the performed analyses this section introduces to general aspects of simultaneous equations systems, followed by a discussion on the different estimation methods and their efficiency. Finally, Section 4.3.3 gives a short excursion on the decomposition and the calculation of the different effects in a simultaneous equations system.

In general a simultaneous equations system is stated as:

$$Y = \beta Y + \Gamma X + U$$
$$(m \times 1) \quad (m \times m)(m \times 1) \quad (m \times k)(k \times 1) \quad (m \times 1)$$

where Y is the matrix of endogenous variables $(m \times 1)$, for m being the number of endogenous variables. Analogously, X is the matrix of exogenous variables $(k \times 1)$, for k being the number of exogenous variables and U is the matrix of disturbance terms $(m \times 1)$. β is the matrix of coefficients or direct effects of endogenous variables on each other $(m \times m)$, with β_{ij} as the effect of y_j on y_i. Per definition there is no causal effect of an exogenous variable on itself, i.e., β_{ii} equals zero. Γ is the matrix of coefficients or direct effects of exogenous on endogenous variables $(m \times k)$, with γ_{ij} effect of x_j on y_i.

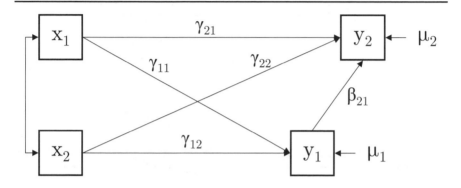

Fig. 4.4: Example of a recursive simultaneous equations system

For example the model stated in Figure 4.4 results in the following equations:

$$y_1 = \gamma_{11}x_1 + \gamma_{12}x_2 + \mu_1$$
$$y_2 = \beta_{21}y_1 + \gamma_{21}x_1 + \gamma_{22}x_2 + \mu_2$$

Since both, m and k, equal two, the following matrices are formed:

$$\begin{pmatrix} y_1 \\ y_2 \end{pmatrix} = \begin{pmatrix} \beta_{11} & \beta_{12} \\ \beta_{21} & \beta_{22} \end{pmatrix} \begin{pmatrix} y_1 \\ y_2 \end{pmatrix} + \begin{pmatrix} \gamma_{11} & \gamma_{12} \\ \gamma_{21} & \gamma_{22} \end{pmatrix} \begin{pmatrix} x_1 \\ x_2 \end{pmatrix} + \begin{pmatrix} \mu_1 \\ \mu_2 \end{pmatrix}$$

$$\begin{pmatrix} y_1 \\ y_2 \end{pmatrix} = \begin{pmatrix} 0 & 0 \\ \beta_{21} & 0 \end{pmatrix} \begin{pmatrix} y_1 \\ y_2 \end{pmatrix} + \begin{pmatrix} \gamma_{11} & \gamma_{12} \\ \gamma_{21} & \gamma_{22} \end{pmatrix} \begin{pmatrix} x_1 \\ x_2 \end{pmatrix} + \begin{pmatrix} \mu_1 \\ \mu_2 \end{pmatrix}$$

Simultaneous equations systems are classified in two general groups: recursive and non-recursive models. Recursive models, as the example in Figure 4.4, consist of a chain of relations and do not contain feedback loops. This chain of functions can be estimated by subsequent OLS regressions. In contrast, non-recursive models contain reciprocal causation, feedback loops and/or have correlated disturbances.²⁵ The example of Figure 4.4 can be converted to a non-recursive model by adding a direct effect from y_2 to y_1 (β_{12}) as shown in Figure 4.5. y_1 does not only influence y_2 by β_{21} but also itself through the subsequent effect of y_2 on y_1 (β_{12}). Consequently, a feedback loop is created. Hence, subsequent estimation of such a non-recursive system by OLS estimations produces inconsistent estimates, since the reciprocal effects and their feed-back loops are omitted.²⁶

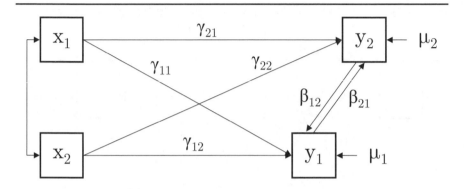

Fig. 4.5: Example of a non-recursive simultaneous equations system

However, this is not the only aspect making the estimation of non-recursive models more problematic. It is also possible that the non-recursive model is not even identified, i.e., it does not have a unique and discernable true solution. To avoid the under-identification and thus the insolvability of a linear system of m simultaneous equations, two conditions have to be met. The first condition allows the construction of a matrix of the order $(m-1) \times (m-1)$, the *order condition*. The second condition, the *rank condition*, assures that the matrix can be solved by being of a particular rank.²⁷

The *order condition* is applied to each equation and states that an equation is identified if it excludes at least $m-1$ variables of the system, regardless if they are endogenous or exogenous. Equivalently, an identification by the order condition can be achieved if the number of excluded predetermined variables is equal or greater than the number of endogenous variables m. The state tested by the order condition refers to the distinction of the equation to the remaining equations in the system. If two endogenous variables are impacted by the same

---

[25] Equation systems that only have correlated disturbances are a subgroup of non-recursive models and are called not fully recursive or seemingly unrelated. They are mostly estimated by Generalized Least Squares regressions.
[26] See Greene [1990, p. 613].
[27] See Greene [1990, pp. 600-606].

variables, the effects are not separable, since the estimation method lacks a distinguishing information.

Even if all equations within a system meet the order condition, the system does not have to be identified as a total and thus to be solvable. The variables still could be dependent. In that case again the estimation is not capable of distinguishing the equations and yields no results. To assure the interdependence of equations, the *rank condition* is needed. It guarantees identification if at least one non-zero determinant of the order $(m-1) \times (m-1)$ can be constructed from the coefficients of the variables excluded from the equation but included in other equations.

While under-identification leaves the equations system unsolvable, also over-identification, i.e., the existence of too much distinguishing information, may cause a problem. The estimation uses only as much information as needed for an exact identification. Information that is not included in the estimation, is acting as a restriction on the estimation results. If the information contradicts itself, the remaining information will not only restrict the results but eliminate them completely. Hence, estimated results do not have to suit the model in case of over-identification. Yet, there are estimation methods yielding consistent results for over-identified models.

Furthermore, over-identified models are not very reasonable, since influencing factors to add always exist. Liu [1960] states that strictly speaking all models are under-identified, since further variables have to be included until the whole world is modelled. However, the consideration of all influencing variables is obviously impossible and even if possible, would lead to a system of unreasonable magnitude.[28] Already systems with a size larger than five equations struggle with the growing complexity. They suffer from vanishing degrees of freedom and from severe identification problems. This requires to focus on a "small piece of a potential bigger puzzle."[29] To do so, the model considered in the following analysis is limited to a maximum of four equations.

4.3.2 Estimation of Simultaneous Equations Systems

After the identification of the simultaneous equations system is assured, it can be estimated through different methods explained in the following section.

While recursive models allow an estimation by subsequent OLS regressions, the appliance of this method on non-recursive models yields inconsistent results.[30] For the estimation of non-recursive systems two types of methods exist: limited information methods (LIM) and full information methods (FIM). They differ in the scope of information used for estimation. Limited information methods use only the information of one equation at a time. In contrast, full information methods take advantage of the information from all equations. This makes full information methods more efficient. However, in the

---

[28] See Liu [1960, p. 858].
[29] Loderer/Martin [1997, p. 236].
[30] See Greene [1990, p. 613].

case of a model specification error they are also potentially more biased by it. In the limited information methods the error is limited only to the equation carrying the misspecification, whereas the coefficients of the remaining equations stay consistent. In contrast, the full information methods transfer the model specification error also to the other equations; thus all coefficients become inconsistent.[31]

Limited information methods comprise two estimators. The method of indirect least squares (ILS) works only for exactly identified equations but yields several estimates per parameter in an over-identified setting.[32] In contrast, the alternative, two-stage least squares (2SLS) estimator, provides results equal to those of the ILS in exactly identified equations and only one estimate per parameter in an over-identified setting. To yield consistent estimates, the 2SLS needs a large data set. Nevertheless, for small samples it still suffers under the endogeneity bias, which is fortunately not as severe as in the case of OLS methods.[33]

In the case of uncorrelated structural disturbances the results of limited information methods are equivalent to those of full information methods. Also for an exactly identified equation, the coefficients of both estimation types are identical, since the exactly identified equation does not add new information to the system. Yet, the results of over-identified equations within the system may differ due to the incorporation of the full data of the system.[34] The full information methods use the full information maximum likelihood (FIML) and the three-stage least squares (3SLS) as estimators. Both are equivalent in efficiency and potential bias. Unfortunately, their results for small data sets are inconsistent due the endogeneity bias, which is only eliminate in larger samples. Nevertheless, even in that case their bias is lower than that of OLS methods and of 2SLS estimations in equally small samples. For large samples both full information methods are consistent and asymptotically efficient.[35]

The efficiency consideration even gains importance in the case of nonlinear simultaneous equations models. Due to the additional nonlinear variables, more correlations exists for a constant number of endogenous variables. This eases the identification,[36] but may cause forms of over-identification and estimation inefficiencies. Goldfeld/Quandt [1968] analyze the efficiency of the parameter estimates for nonlinear models. They conclude that generally full information methods are preferable. However, for small samples, i.e., with less than 60 observations, the limited information methods may yield better results.[37]

---

[31] See Greene [1990, pp. 636-638].
[32] See Greene [1990, p. 619].
[33] See Greene [1990, pp. 619-621].
[34] See Greene [1990, p. 632].
[35] For a detailed comparison of the methods see Greene [1990, pp. 636-638]. See Zellner/Theil [1962] for a detailed explanation of the 3SLS method.
[36] See Goldfeld/Quandt [1968, p. 118].
[37] See Goldfeld/Quandt [1968, pp. 130-132].

While some tried to reduce the shortcomings of the limited information methods, such as Amemiya [1985] developing a nonlinear two-stage least squares method,[38] others ameliorated the full information methods through adaptations to the nonlinear setting. One of these improvements is the iterated three-stage least squares (I3SLS), which is an asymptotically full-information maximum likelihood based on 3SLS. Instead of a one-step estimation, the disturbance covariance matrix is estimated in the second step by simultaneous iteration.[39] Nevertheless, the the iteration might not yield results due to a singular disturbances matrix leaving the model with no solution. In those cases non-iterated estimation techniques may result in a solution but the estimates would be inconsistent and questionable.

A final critique on simultaneous equations methodologies is the assumption of independent parameters to changes in exogenous variables. This problem is often referred to as "Lucas' critique", since it was first elaborated on by Lucas [1976]. He argues that if economic agents gain knowledge about the behavioral structure of the economic system, they will adjust their behavior based on this knowledge. But on the same time this alters the system behavior. Consequently, the gained knowledge is out of date and value. However, this problem is not limited to the simultaneous equations system but applies to most econometric models.

Since the following empirical analyses estimate a nonlinear equations system for a sample larger than 60 observations, a full information methods in the form of I3SLS will be used based on the elaborations above and following the advice of Goldfeld/Quandt [1968].

4.3.3 Effect Decomposition after Simultaneous Equations Estimation

The estimation of a simultaneous equations system $Y = \beta Y + \Gamma X + U$ yields the two matrices β and Γ. As shown in Figure 4.4 these matrices equal the direct effects on the endogenous variables. β equals the direct effect of the endogenous variables on each others, also stated as D_{yy}. In contrast, Γ repre-

---

[38] See Amemiya [1985, pp. 245-265]. In contrast, Hausman [1975] improved the instrumental variable approach. See Greene [1990, p. 630].

[39] See Savvides [1998, p. 816]. It is an iterative method that minimizes a distance function of the form $\varepsilon'[\Sigma^{-1} H(H'H)^{-1} H']$ where ε is the (stacked) vector of residuals, Σ is a consistent estimate of the residual variance-covariance matrix, and H is the Kronecker product of an identity matrix of the order of the number of the equations and the matrix of instruments. Thus, the criterion for estimation is the sum of squared transformed residuals. For each observation, fitted residuals are formed as the fitted values from regression on instrumental variables. These are transformed by multiplying by the square root of the covariance matrix of the residuals. The contribution of the observation to the criterion is the sum of squared values of the transformed fitted residuals.

sents the direct effects of the exogenous variables on the endogenous variables (D_{yx}).

In contrast to the direct effects, the indirect effects influence an endogenous variable through mediation by another endogenous variable. In the exemplary system given above the direct effect of x_1 on y_2 is symbolized through γ_{21}. However x_1 also indirectly effects y_2 through the combination of its effect on y_1 and the effect of y_1 on y_2. These indirect effects are labelled as I_{yy} for endogenous variables and as I_{yx} for those of exogenous variables.

While the direct effects are directly observable as coefficients of the system estimation, the indirect effects have to be calculated. One way to do this is by matrix algebra, which yields

$$I_{yy} = \sum_{i=2}^{m-1} \beta^i \quad \text{and} \quad I_{yx} = (\sum_{i=1}^{m-1} \beta^i)\Gamma$$
$$= (I - \beta)^{-1} - I - \beta \quad\quad\quad = (I - \beta)^{-1}\Gamma - \Gamma .$$

After the calculation of the indirect effect, the total effect of a variable on the endogenous variables (T_{yy} or T_{yx}) can be determined by adding the direct and indirect effects.[40] For non-recursive models, where the effect of the endogenous variables on each other includes a feed-back loop, the total effect can also be calculated by

$$T_{y_2\,y_1} = \beta_{21} + \beta_{21}\beta_{12}\beta_{21} + \beta_{21}(\beta_{12})^2(\beta_{21})^2 + \ldots \beta_{21}(\beta_{12})^i(\beta_{21})^i ,$$
$$\lim_{i \to \infty} T_{y_2\,y_1} = \frac{\beta_{21}}{1 - \beta_{12}\beta_{21}} .$$

Apart from direct and indirect effects, the simultaneous equations method distinguishes further noncausal effects. Consideration of the entire impact of one variable on another yields their covariance, the total association of the two variables. The covariance not only includes causal effects but also noncausal effects. Consequently, the difference between the covariance of two variables and their total causal effect represents the existing noncausal effects (N_{yy} and N_{yx}). These noncausal effects do not stem from a causation but may result from not analyzed associations among exogenous variables through correlations or due to the joint dependence on a single or correlated variable. In the example in Figure 4.4 a noncausal effect of x_1 on y_1 is given through the covariance of x_1 with x_2.

Recapitulating, the total association of two variables splits up as follows:

---

[40] The total effect can also be determined directly by $T_{yy} = (I - \beta)^{-1} - I$ and $T_{yx} = (I - \beta)^{-1}\Gamma$.

total association = total causal effects   + noncausal effects
               = direct effects + indirect effects + noncausal effects

yielding for endogenous variables in
$$cov(y,y) = T_{yy} \qquad\qquad\qquad + N_{yy}$$
$$= D_{yy} \quad + I_{yy} \qquad\quad + N_{yy}$$

and for exogenous variables in
$$cov(y,x) = T_{yx} \qquad\qquad\qquad + N_{yx}$$
$$= D_{yx} \quad + I_{yx} \qquad\quad + N_{yx}.$$

The decomposition of effects can be demonstrated by covariance algebra, as done on the example of Figure 4.4 in the Appendix A.6, where the Section A.6.1 clarifies the separation of causal and noncausal effects and Appendix A.6.2 clarifies the breakup of direct and indirect effects.[41]

4.4 Sample Selection and Variables Used

This chapter elaborates on the variables and the data set applied in the studies. First, Section 4.4.1 elaborates on the data sources and the applied sample selection. In the next section the variables are specified starting with the endogenous variables. Accordingly, Section 4.4.2 defines the applied ownership variables on basis of Section 4.4.2. Next the used performance variables are presented in Section 4.4.3. Section 4.4.4 continues the variable definition by the examination of further control variables. Apart from their calculation, their theoretical effect on the endogenous variables are hypothesized and finally summarized in Section 4.4.4. Finally, the descriptive statistics of the data conclude the section.

4.4.1 Sample Selection

Data Needs and Data Sources

The following chapter states and reasons the selected data sources. In general three types of data are needed: ownership, market and accounting data.

The construction of the ownership variables requires information consisting of the quantitative share information and the qualitative information of shareholder's identity. Both information is needed for multiple ownership levels. The share information enables the calculation of control and cash flow rights. Apart from the size of voting shares also the shareholdings of preferred stock is required to analyze the divergence of control and cash flow rights by dual-class shares. To calculate the ratio of cash flow rights the nominal value and the number of shares issued of both share types is needed.

---

[41] See Appendix A.6.1, p. 312 and Appendix A.6.2, p. 312.

With regard to the shareholder information the information for classification into these identities is further needed, since institutional ownership and insider ownership in form of management and board shareholdings are considered in this work. In the case of a company as shareholder its industry classification is needed to identify institutional investors. In contrast, private shareholders require knowledge of management and board composition to peg them as insiders. In addition, their relation to other shareholders is also important to calculate the cohesive shareholdings.

Unfortunately, for German cooperations ownership information, especially historical data, is hard to obtain. Three sources are the Hoppenstedt databases "Aktienführer", "Großunternehmen" and "Mittelständische Unternehmen". As most databases, they store only the present information referring to the closure date of the last accounting statements; thus current versions could only provide data for 2003. The Hoppenstedt databases serve also as a source for industry classification on the basis of the standard industrial classification (SIC) codes and for the share information.

A further source for ownership information is published by the Commerzbank, the reports "Wer gehört zu wem?" and "Wem gehört was?". The latest edition of those reports was published in 2000 and was included in the data set. In addition, a dummy variable is included to absorb differences in the data sources or the point of time.

A further source of ownership information is the database of the Bundesanstalt für Finanzdienstleistungsaufsicht (BAFIN), where the announcements regarding important voting shares are collected and the voting share is estimated. However, the BAFIN database contains only German companies of the Official and Regulated Market. The missing information for other companies leads to problems when regarding multi-level ownership, since not all companies appearing as shareholders are German firms of the Official and Regulated Market. In addition, the cash flow rights and the qualitative shareholder information are also missing. Due to these shortcomings the usage of the BAFIN data was discarded.

Market and accounting data in form of stock prices and annual statements is required to calculate the Tobin's Q as well as most of the control variables. Their collection is not as complicated since it can be extracted from Reuters and Datastream. In the case of this work the Reuters data is used as major data source and only complemented by data from Datastream.

Sample Restrictions

The need of market data automatically limits the sample to listed corporations. Further requirements restrict the sample. Their goal is to maximize the sample size under the constraint of a minimal bias. The criteria applied to the sample selection are:

1. the initial public offering has to be before 1999 and 2002 respectively;

2. the firms must be listed at the Frankfurt stock exchange;
3. the statement currency must be Euros or a currency part of the European Monetary Union;
4. annual reports, ownership and market data must be available;
5. the firms must be non-financial companies;
6. the firms have not become bankrupt for at least seven months after the required data points;
7. the annual reports refer to a 12-months period;
8. the closure of account is dated between October and March.

Table 4.2 shows the initial sample size, the eliminated cases and the resulting final sample size.

Table 4.2: Sample selection and eliminated cases

Restrictions		2000	2003
1. & 2.	Firms listed on the Frankfurt Stock Exchange	404	767
	less		
3.	Firms with statement currency not convertible to Euros	0	-4
	less		
4.a	Firms with no ownership data at Hoppenstedt	-11	-7
	less		
4.b	Firms not found at Reuters	-12	-16
	less		
4.c	Firms that did not have annual reports for both years	-20	-3
	less		
5.	Financial institutions	-117	-227
	less		
6.	Firms that did not file bankruptcy for the next six months	-38	-104
	less		
7.	Firms with annual reports that do not span 12 months	-7	-21
	less		
8.	Firms with a date of closure of account between April and September	-23	-40
Final subsample		176	345
Final sample		521	

To avoid biases due to liquidity differences between market places and conflicts between quotes at different exchanges, the sample is limited to listings at the Frankfurt Stock Exchange, the largest and most important stock exchange in Germany.[42]

---

[42] This limitation is quite common as many studies focus on one stock exchange, for example the New York Stock Exchange [McConnell/Servaes 1990], the Milan

As the possibility of a lagged relationship will be considered, the performance observations span the time period from 1999 to 2000 and 2002 to 2003 respectively. Therefore, the companies must have been listed before 1999 or 2002, which results in 414 firms in 2000 and 767 in 2003.[43]

To be able to harmonize the data without any bias caused by the currency conversion, the statements have to be in Euros or a currency that is part of the European Monetary Union. Four companies had to be excluded in the subsample of 2003, since they were nominated in American dollar. Due to varying exchange rates their conversion and inclusion could result in a recording error distorting the sample.

In addition, data availability reduces the data set to 348 in 2000 and 737 in 2003. For eleven and seven companies respectively no ownership data was available, twelve and 16 firms were not found in Reuters, and 20 and three companies do not have information for both of the two years needed.

Furthermore, as a result of legal requirements financial companies have a different capital structure and different income measuring rules governing the company. Their inclusion could lead to severe biases, especially in the calculation of the Tobin's Q. Thus they are excluded from the sample.[44] This causes a reduction by 117 and 227 companies.

To avoid a bias in the annual fiscal statements, Hüls [1995] and Baetge et al. [1996] define a minimum distance to the point of bankruptcy of seven month, because the bad company conditions would falsify the statements.[45] Therefore, cooperations that were filed bankrupt or were liquidated seven months after the required periods are also eliminated from the sample. This leaves a sample of 199 observations for 2000 and 510 for 2003.

Stub periods present a further data problem. They are caused by changes in the closure date of the fiscal period. For some companies interim statements were available that allowed a calculation of the 12-months fiscal statement. However, seven firms in 2000 and 21 in 2003 had to be excluded.

Finally, to be able to assign the accounting data to a certain year and thus to the ownership information, the end of the fiscal period has to be close to the dates 12.12.2000 and 12.12.2003.[46] Hence, firms must close the fiscal period between October and March, which leads to samples of 176 companies for 2000 and 345 for 2003. Consequently, the total final sample consists of 521 observations.

Stock Exchange [Zingales 1994] and the Stock Exchange of Singapore Main or Second Board [Mak/Li 2001].

[43] 14 non-German companies were excluded in 2000 and 44 in 2003 respectively since national legal differences may bias the sample. The influence of a national effect was analyzed in several studies, for instance by Dyck/Zingales [2004],La Porta et al. [1997], and Pedersen/Thomsen [1999].

[44] See Short/Keasey [1999, p. 88] with similar approach by Gugler et al. [2004].

[45] See Hüls [1995, pp. 70-71] and Baetge et al. [1996].

[46] See Mathiesen [2002, p. 37].

4.4.2 Ownership Variables

All ownership measures used in these analyses refer to cohesive shareholding, since both direct and indirect ownership influence the control ability and the incentive structure of the owner.

As shown in Chapter 2.3, the German ownership structure is molded by extensive usage of multiple control chains and crossholdings. This argues for a consideration of multiple levels of ownership to gain a fair picture of the ultimate owner. Therefore, ownership is backtracked up to three levels of owners, whereby totally owned companies are not included as an individual level.

Given the consideration of multi-level ownership the cash flow rights deviate from the control rights. In addition, 37 of the companies issued preferred stocks, which also results in a divergence of ownership and control. As shown before in Chapter 3, the divergence mediates the effects of ownership on performance advocating for the inclusion of a control variable of the divergence. The calculation of the control and cash flow rights follows the method of La Porta et al. [1999].[47]

Table 4.3 gives an overview over the used variables and their definition. Besides their linear measure, the squared measure (e.g., Ocr^2) and piecewise variables (e.g., Ocr_a, Ocr_b, etc.) are applied.[48]

As the measure of ownership concentration should reproduce the existence and power of a controlling shareholder, the control rights of the largest share are used in the variable *Ocr*. To account for the divergence of control and cash flow rights, the ratio of control rights divided by cash flow rights is included as the control variable *ORatio*.[49]

The extension of the concentration measure to further shareholders by using for example the share of the three largest shareholders is discarded for two reasons. First, the existence of concentration effects, such as private benefits, depends mainly on the largest shareholder. Indeed it is possible that large shareholders form alliances to conjointly exploit potential benefits. However, as explained in Chapter 2.2.3, the probability of shareholder coalitions and therefore the necessity of shareholder aggregation by concentration measures depends on the general level of concentration present in the market.[50] Since Germany is significantly higher concentrated than the USA and the UK, a lower shareholder aggregation appears reasonable. This is also supported by the majority of German studies using only the largest shareholder.[51]

---

[47] See La Porta et al. [1999, pp. 10-12]. For an example see Figure 2.2, p. 12.
[48] For information on the creation of the piecewise variables see Section 4.2.1, p. 72.
[49] A similar measure of the separation of ownership and control is used by Chapelle [2005].
[50] See Chapter 2.2.3, p. 17.
[51] Already Thonet/Poensgen [1979] use only the largest shareholder, also do Becht [1999], Becht/Röell [1999], Edwards/Nibler [2000], Edwards/Weichenrieder [2004], and Franks/Mayer [2001].

Table 4.3: Definition of ownership variables

Variable name	Definition
Ownership concentration	
Ocr	Control rights of the largest share (in percent)
ORatio	Ratio of the control rights of the largest share divided by its cash flow rights
OcST	Sum of the control rights of second and third largest share (in percent)
Institutional ownership	
Icr	Sum of the control rights of institutional investors (in percent)
IRatio	Ratio of the control rights of the institutional shares divided by their cash flow rights
Insider ownership	
Mcr	Sum of the control rights of management (in percent)
MRatio	Ratio of the control rights of the management shares divided by their cash flow rights
Mbcr	Sum of the control rights of management and board (in percent)
MbRatio	Ratio of the control rights of the management and board shares divided by their cash flow rights
Dcr	Sum of the control rights of the board (in percent)
DRatio	Ratio of the control rights of board shares divided by their cash flow rights

The second argument for the usage of only the largest shareholder is based on the fact that German shareholders are not only less likely to form coalitions but that the second and third largest shareholders are generally also argued to have a monitoring and controlling function. Accordingly, they might detain the controlling shareholder from exploiting his private benefits and harming the company value.[52] The aggregation of the three largest shareholders would not allow for such differing effects and might result in loss of significance of the estimate. Consequently, the largest share is preferred as measure basis. Nevertheless, the effects of other large shareholders is included as control variable *OcST* equalling the sum of the control rights of the second and third largest

---

[52] See Cubbin/Leech [1983, pp. 354-356], Leech [2001], and Boubaker [2003].

shareholders.[53] While its effect on performance is expected to be positive as indicated above, its relationship to ownership concentration and managerial ownership is assumed to be negative. Since the presence of other large shareholders reduces the possibilities of private benefits or moral hazard, it diminishes the advantages of large shareholdings and managerial shareholdings. Its effect on institutional ownership may also be positive as the improved monitoring triggers higher investments.

One could argue that the prediction of a negative relation of largest share and the OcST is also supported by a mathematical reason. Since OcST has a maximum of $(1 - Ocr)$, it reduces with increasing Ocr. However, this only holds strictly in the absence of other owners.[54] Also the later stated tolerance between the variables of .98 supports the informational value of OcST far from only replicating the largest share information.

In contrast, the effects of institutional and insider ownership are not based on their share size but on their identities. Accordingly, no difference is assumed in the utility function and the behavior of shareholders with different share sizes. Consequently, the entirety of shareholders is aggregated by the measures. The total sum of control rights of institutional investors is used as the variable *Icr*. Analogously to the ORatio, a control variable is included to count for the divergence of control and cash flow rights (*IRatio*).

Similarly, the total of insider shares is applied with *Mcr* being the sum of control rights owned by managers. To examine the effect of the insider definition, the combined ownership of management and board is introduced as *Mbcr*. In the robustness test also the pure ownership of directors is considered separately as *Dcr*. Furthermore, control variables for the difference of control and cash flow rights are created and named *MRatio*, *MbRatio* and *DRatio*.

Since the ownership variables were not extracted from an existing database but collected within the scope of this work and cross-checked, the probability of recording error is low. Therefore, no data processing is applied to avoid an information reduction.

4.4.3 Financial Performance Variables

Based on the discussion on financial performance measures in Section 2.4 the following empirical analyses use the Tobin's Q estimated through the Chung/-Pruitt [1994] approach as main performance variable.[55] The only change made is in the treatment of preferred stocks, where the liquidation value is replaced by the stock price.[56] Furthermore, robustness checks will test the effect of

---

[53] Edwards/Weichenrieder [2004] also use a dummy variable, whereas Cubbin/Leech [1983] implement the share sizes of other shareholders within their measure.
[54] The highest value of OcST occurs at an almost symmetrical distribution of ownership between the two owners, i.e., at 49,9%.
[55] For information on the calculation see Chapter 2.4.4, p. 29.
[56] This change was also made by Gugler et al. [2004, p. 18].

the usage of hybrid measures compared to the frequently used accounting-based variable. The ROE is used as alternative accounting-based performance measure, with the income definition including income from ordinary and extraordinary activities and excluding non-operating income.

Table 4.4 gives an overview over the variable definitions. Correspondingly to the ownership variables, squared and piecewise variables of the performance measures are considered to allow nonlinear effects of performance on ownership.[57]

Table 4.4: Definition and data processing of used performance variables

Variable name	Definition	Rule	Cases
Hybrid performance measures			
Q *Tobin's Q*	Sum of market value of stock, book value of inventories, long-term debt and current liabilities minus current assets divided by total assets	if < .000 if > 1.514	4 1% 0 0%
Accounting-based performance measures			
ROE *Return on equity*	Net earnings after interest expenses and taxes divided by shareholders equity	if <-2.664 if > 2.314	13 2% 26 5%

Furthermore, Table 4.4 states the applied rules for data processing. It serves as plausibility check reducing biases caused by measurement or reporting errors in the variables that might produce inconsistent estimates. The data processing rules are derived from natural boundaries or from the definition of highly suspect outliers by the interquartile range (IQR). The IQR is the range between the lower and upper quartiles. Values in the inner fences, located at a distance of 1.5 * IQR below the lower and above the upper quartiles, are not problematic. The outer fences at a distance of 3 * IQR distinguish values into suspect outliers, lying inside the fences, and highly suspect outliers outside the range.

A definition as highly suspect outlier results in a change of the affected value by setting it equal to the outer fence. This approach is called winsorizing and is based on the assumption that outliers are not completely false but exaggerated. The alternative of labelling them as missing values is problematic and a deletion of the observations could significantly reduce the sample size. Both results in a loss of potentially valuable information and could force a

---

[57] For the creation of the piecewise variables see Section 4.2.1 p. 72.

truncation error. Thus the concept of winsorizing is preferred over excluding affected values.[58]

The interval for acceptance for the Tobin's Q lies between zero and 1.514, and for the ROE between -2.664 and 2.314. Only four values of Tobin's Q fall below the limit. For the ROE, 13 cases (2%) are below and 26 cases (5%) above the limits. This high amount of cases could be due to reporting errors and accounting biases.

4.4.4 Further Control Variables

After the main variables have been introduced, further control variables are defined and their theoretical impact on the endogenous variables is discussed. Table 4.5 gives an overview over the control variables, the applied rule for data processing and the number of cases affected. The processing rules are derived similarly to those of the performance variables, namely natural boundaries and the definition of highly suspect outliers by the IQR. After giving this tabular overview, each variable is explained and its theoretical effects on the endogenous variable are discussed. Finally, Section 4.4.4 summarizes the hypothesized effects in Table 4.6.[59]

Firm Size

A commonly used control variable is size, mostly linked to sales or total assets.[60] The variable *Size* is defined as the logarithm of sales. The logarithmical transformation mirrors the assumption of a diminishing marginal size effect.[61] Additionally, the square variable of the logarithm of sales ($Size^2$) enables an analysis of nonlinear or contradicting size effects. A measurement error in the sales variable is presumed if size falls below 9.207 ($\simeq$ €9,967) or rises above 29.618 ($\simeq$ €7,293,466,000,000).[62] Only two values, 0% of the sample, exceed the upper limit.

The relation of size and ownership is ambiguous. Bathala [1996] and Pedersen/Thomsen [1999] state two reasons for a negative effect of size on

---

[58] This practice modifies outliers by making them no more extreme than the most extreme data that is believed to be relevant or accurately measured. This method is for example applied by Demsetz/Villalonga [2001].
[59] For Table 4.6 see p. 103.
[60] See Agrawal/Knoeber [1996], Bathala [1996], Bøhren/Ødegaard [2003], Chen/-Ho [2000], Crutchley/Hansen [1989], Cui/Mak [2002], Demsetz/Villalonga [2001], Edwards/Weichenrieder [2004], Gugler et al. [2004], Himmelberg et al. [1999], Leech/Leahy [1991], Loderer/Martin [1997], Mak/Li [2001], McConnell/-Muscarella [1985], McConnell/Servaes [1995], Mørck et al. [1988], Pedersen/-Thomsen [1999], Short/Keasey [1999], Weber/Dudney [2003], and Witte [1981].
[61] See Cui/Mak [2002], Himmelberg et al. [1999], Leech/Leahy [1991], and Mak/Li [2001].
[62] Mathiesen [2002] applies a rule cutting values below €100,000.

Table 4.5: Definition and data processing of used control variables

Variable name	Definition	Rule		Cases	
Size (and Size^2) *Size*	Logarithm of total sales	if < if >	9.207 29.618	0 2	0% 0%
Debt (and Debt^2) *Financial leverage*	Long-term debt divided by total assets	if < if >	.0% 71.4%	0 5	0% 1%
Inv (and Inv^2) *Investment level*	Capital expenditure divided by total assets	if < if >	−78.4% 90.8%	4 19	1% 4%
Nwc (and Nwc^2) *Liquidity*	Net working capital in thousands	if < if >	.000 .766	0 5	0% 1%
Eom (and Eom^2) *Ease of monitoring*	Fixed assets divided by total sales	if < if >	.000 1.642	0 30	0% 6%
Beta *Risk*	Beta calculated over the last five years	if < if >	−2.047 3.505	0 1	0% 0%
Gro *Growth*	This year's sales divided by previous year's sales	if > if >	.224 1.883	4 23	1% 4%
Div *Diversification*	Number of standard industrial classification codes of the firm	no modification			
Age *Firm age*	Logarithm of the years passed since foundation	no modification			
Ind$_i$ *Industry*	Industry dummies by the first digit of the SIC	no modification			
Time *Point of time*	Year dummy: zero if data refers to 2000 and one for 2003	no modification			

general ownership.[63] First, due to personal wealth constraints a large share is easier to hold in a small firm.[64] Second, non-diversification costs and liquidity costs increase with size; thus the disadvantages of blockholding increase.[65] In contrast, Himmelberg et al. [1999] argue that the private benefits and the scope of moral hazard are greater in large firms, resulting in an increased incentive to hold large shares. However, the authors are constraining the ar-

---

[63] This relation is empirically supported by Bathala [1996], Bergström/Rydqvist [1990a], Crutchley/Hansen [1989], Demsetz/Lehn [1985], and Pedersen/Thomsen [1999].
[64] See Bathala [1996, p. 133], Demsetz/Lehn [1985], Edwards/Weichenrieder [2004, p. 156], and Fama/Jensen [1983a].
[65] See Bathala [1996, p. 133] and Crutchley/Hansen [1989, p. 41].

gument with the possibility of economies of scale in monitoring, leading to a lower optimal share size.[66]

Besides these arguments concerning general ownership concentration, Agrawal/Knoeber [1996] predict a positive effect of size on institutional ownership, since they assume large firms to be more attractive to institutional investors.[67]

The hypotheses on general ownership concentration also apply to insider ownership. An additional reason for a positive relation of size and insider ownership is that larger firms are likely to employ a more skilled and probably wealthier management. Thus the wealth constraint argument is moderate.[68] In addition, Gugler et al. [2003b] note that the costly acquisition of a large share might not only reduce ownership concentration, but also increase the entrenchment effect of existing managerial ownership and therefore its advantages.[69] Consequently, the size effect on any kind of ownership is unclear.

As to the effect of firm size on performance, many studies use the relation between size and ownership as an argument. Yet, in the simultaneous equations setting such a mediating effect is not shown in the coefficient of size. It only states the direct effect leaving the indirect and total effect to be calculated.[70] But already Stekler [1964] states reasons for a positive direct effect of size on performance. These are economies of scale and synergies, such as potential reductions in production and distribution costs, lower costs by vertical integration or increased market power.[71] Consequently, while the sign of the size effect on ownership is doubtful, the coefficient in the performance equation is expected to be positive.

Financial Leverage

Another control variable often found in performance and ownership regressions is financial leverage.[72] Following Bøhren/Ødegaard [2003] and Chen/Ho [2000]

---

[66] See Himmelberg et al. [1999, p. 364].
[67] See Agrawal/Knoeber [1996, p. 383].
[68] See Himmelberg et al. [1999, p. 364].
[69] See Gugler et al. [2003b, p. 5].
[70] For the decomposition and calculation of the different effects see Section 4.3.3.
[71] See Jensen/Ruback [1983, p. 23], Gugler et al. [2003b, p. 6], and Pedersen/Thomsen [1998, pp. 391].
[72] See Agrawal/Knoeber [1996], Agrawal/Nagarajan [1990], Anderson/Reeb [2003], Bathala/Moon [1994], Bøhren/Ødegaard [2003], Boubaker [2003], Brailsford et al. [2002], Brau [2002], Chen/Ho [2000], Cho [1998], Chowdhury/Geringer [2001], Crutchley/Hansen [1989], Cui/Mak [2002], Edwards/Weichenrieder [2004], Gedajlovic [1993], Gedajlovic/Shapiro [2002], Jensen et al. [1992], Jensen/Meckling [1976], Jensen/Warner [1988], Kim/Sorensen [1986], Leech/Leahy [1991], Leland/Pyle [1977], Lins [2003], Mathiesen [2002], McConnell/Servaes [1995], Monsen et al. [1968], Mørck et al. [1988], Prowse [1990], Schulze et al. [2003], Short/Keasey [1999], Short et al. [2002a], and Zhang [1998].

the variable *Debt* is defined as long-term debt divided by total assets, where long-term debt are liabilities with a maturity over one year. Also the squared measure $Debt^2$ is included. Per definition the leverage ratio cannot fall below zero and, derived by the IQR, should not be higher than 71.4%. There are five violations for the upper rule, changing 1% of the data set.[73]

According to the free cash flow theory by Jensen [1986], high leverage reduces the free cash flow in the firm and therefore limits the consumption of private benefits.[74] This causes two negative effects on ownership concentration. First, it decreases the incentive to hold large shares. Second, following the substitution effect of agency devices less external capital is needed to moderate the shareholder-management conflict, since the higher leverage also controls the agency problems.[75] Furthermore, high debt implies higher bankruptcy risk. This increases the opportunity costs in form of non-diversification cost and further reduces the incentive for large shareholding.[76]

In contrast, Kim/Sorensen [1986] give three reasons for a positive relationship between ownership and leverage. One reason is the hypothesis that controlling shareholders want to protect their control and consequently prefer debt over equity. Furthermore, they want to avoid agency cost of other external minority shareholders, which arise due to the high ownership concentration and the possibility of private benefits on account of shareholder's return. Accordingly, they rather rely on debt than further equity. Finally, the agency costs of debt may be lower for high concentrated ownership. This is the case when strong owner control is preferred over a diffused ownership or when the high ownership concentration is perceived as signalling, as demonstrated by Leland/Pyle [1977] and Ross [1977]. The signalling reduces the uncertainty for debtholders and thus decreases the cost of debt.[77] Considering these contradicting arguments it is impossible to predict the sign of the leverage effect for general ownership concentration and institutional ownership.[78]

For insider ownership, agency conflicts are presumed to enlarge.[79] This strengthens the positive effect of agency cost avoidance and signalling. In addition, since higher leverage is used to control agency conflicts between shareholders and managers, the need for external capital to mediate the conflict decreases and the relative portion of insider ownership increases. Thus a positive relation between insider ownership and debt is predicted.[80] However, the

---

[73] If applying the rule by Mathiesen [2002] (95%), no cases are detected.
[74] See Bøhren/Ødegaard [2003, p. 5], Edwards/Weichenrieder [2004, p. 156], and Jensen [1986, p. 323].
[75] See Jensen/Meckling [1976, p. 340].
[76] See Bathala [1996, p. 131], Jensen/Meckling [1976, pp. 339-340], and Kim/-Sorensen [1986, p. 141].
[77] See Kim/Sorensen [1986, pp. 140-141].
[78] See Bathala [1996, p. 131].
[79] See Edwards/Weichenrieder [2004, pp. 155-156].
[80] See Bathala [1996, p. 130], Gugler et al. [2003b, p. 7], and Jensen/Meckling [1976, pp. 334-337].

substitution effect of agency devices reduces the cost-efficiency of managerial ownership and its appliance. Nevertheless, a positive effect of debt on insider ownership is expected.

With regard to performance, again only the direct effects of leverage are considered. The smaller agency costs pointed out by Kim/Sorensen [1986] and Jensen [1986] are implying a positive relationship of performance and debt.[81] However, Jensen et al. [1992] employ the pecking order theory by Myers/Majluf [1984] to claim that good firms avoid high leverage.[82] Following this theory, a negative relation of performance and leverage is assumed.

Investment Activities

A further financial control variable is the level of investment activities (Inv and Inv^2).[83] It is calculated as capital expenditure by total assets with the capital expenditure as total assets at the beginning of the year minus the year-end value plus depreciation.[84] The value is limited to the range from -78.4% to 90.8%, where four cases (1%) fall below and 19 (4%) cases exceed the range.

Pedersen/Thomsen [1998] and Carney/Gedajlovic [2002] state a negative relationship of ownership and investments. A high capital investment reduces the free cash flow and hence the possibility of private benefits. As a result large shareholdings become less advantageous.[85] In contrast, high investment activities are difficult to monitor; thus they allow an increased consumption of private benefits or have a positive prestige effect.[86] Nevertheless, a negative relation is expected for ownership concentration.

Assuming institutional investors to be long-term oriented, the effect of investments is predicted to be positive. But since institutional investors are also argued to show a myopic investment behavior, the effect is unclear.

---

[81] See Bathala [1996, p. 131], Byrd et al. [1998, p. 23], Edwards/Weichenrieder [2004, p. 156], Harris/Raviv [1991, p. 300], Jensen [1986, p. 323], and Kim/Sorensen [1986, pp. 140-141].

[82] As far as firms can choose, they prefer internal over equity financing and equity over debt financing. See Myers/Majluf [1984] and Myers [1984].

[83] Also included by Aggarwal/Samwick [2003], Amihud et al. [1990], Bathala [1996], Bøhren/Ødegaard [2003], Carney/Gedajlovic [2002], Chan et al. [1990], Cho [1998], Chowdhury/Geringer [2001], Demsetz/Lehn [1985], Farinha [2003], Fee [2002], Gugler et al. [2004], Hill/Snell [1989], Himmelberg et al. [1999], Jarrell/Poulsen [1988], Lang et al. [1991], Mathiesen [2002], McConnell/Muscarella [1985], Shin/Kim [2002], and Zhang [1998].

[84] See Himmelberg et al. [1999, p. 365].

[85] See Carney/Gedajlovic [2002, pp. 129-130] and Pedersen/Thomsen [1998, p. 392]. Similar results of a positive relation for Asian companies were found by Fukuyama [1995], Redding [1990, 1994], and Yoshihara [1988]. However, Hill [1995] and Redding [1994] originate this relation partly from the effect of weak appropriability regimes upon investment decisions.

[86] See Himmelberg et al. [1999, p. 365].

For insider ownership the free cash flow argument also applies and indicates a negative effect. However, the high investment level can also originate from empire building, which has a positive prestige effect on the manager's utility. Consequently, investments could have a positive effect on insider ownership.

The effect of investments on performance is regarded as positive. One reason are potential improvements in production or the exploration of valuable growth opportunities. Furthermore, firms with high investment levels have a long-term orientation and seem to be more efficient in investing.[87] Consequently, a positive sign of the investment level is expected. Very high investment levels might stem from over-investment and thus have a negative impact on performance.

Liquidity

The third financial variable Nwc (and Nwc^2) refers to the net working capital (NWC) in thousands as a liquidity measure. It is defined as current assets divided by current liabilities. The accepted data range lies between zero and .766. Five cases (1%) show values above the limit.[88]

From a purely economic viewpoint, high financial liquidity is interpreted as an inefficient use of assets and may render a firm vulnerable to takeovers.[89] But from the perspective of a large shareholder, who is exposed to large non-diversification costs, the maintenance of high balances in cash and other liquid investments limits his idiosyncratic risk.[90] This results in a positive relation between liquidity and ownership concentration. The effect on insider ownership is even stronger, since the insiders' personal risk is closer linked to the business risk. In contrast, institutional investors are assumed to have large portfolios, which enable them to diversify the risk. Hence, they regard high liquidity levels as wasted resources leading to a negative effect.

The consideration of high liquidity as a sign of unused resources and lacking investment opportunities influences also the relation of performance and liquidity and leads to a negative effect. Nevertheless Cleary [2000] states a positive effect of liquidity on the market-to-book ratio, which may also exist for the Tobin's Q.[91]

---

[87] See Bøhren/Ødegaard [2003, p. 11], Cho [1998, pp. 104-105], Chowdhury/Geringer [2001, p. 279], Demsetz/Lehn [1985, p. 1164], Hill/Snell [1989, p. 32], and Mathiesen [2002, 159]. Chan et al. [1990] and McConnell/Muscarella [1985] prove the positive effect by an increase in market value for announcements of increasing capital expenditures and decrease for reduction in capital expenditures.

[88] Used by Agrawal/Nagarajan [1990], Carney/Gedajlovic [2002], Cho [1998], Cleary [2000], Lang et al. [1991], and Mathiesen [2002].

[89] See Jensen [1988, p. 29 and p. 31].

[90] See Agrawal/Nagarajan [1990, p. 1326] and Carney/Gedajlovic [2002, p. 132].

[91] See Cleary [2000, pp. 221-222].

Ease of Monitoring

In the ownership literature the ratio of fixed assets to sales is used as a proxy for the ease of monitoring (Eom).[92] It is calculated as fixed assets divided by total sales and should range in this sample between zero and 1.642 as upper outer fence. 30 observations (6%) exceed this range. Similar to Himmelberg et al. [1999] the squared fixed assets ratio (Eom^2) is also used to allow for nonlinearity.

Himmelberg et al. [1999] note that investments in fixed assets are observable and more easily to be monitored. Following Gaver/Gaver [1993], Gertler/Hubbard [1993], and Smith/Watts [1992], this leads to a lower optimal level of ownership since the capture of private benefits is limited.[93] A further reason for a negative relation to ownership concentration is given by Carney/Gedajlovic [2002]. Highly concentrated firms are likely to be more active in disposing under-performing assets, whereas firms controlled by salaried managers will attempt a turnaround in order to not reduce their power by reducing the assets. This difference is reflected in a lower fixed asset ratio for concentrated ownership.[94]

This argument, however, also supports the assumption of a positive relation between managerial ownership and the ease of monitoring. Managers might use their power to promote turnarounds instead of reducing assets. Furthermore, a high ratio could also be a side effect of empire building actions. This makes the effect on managerial ownership ambiguous.

Following the argument of Cui/Mak [2002], the ratio represents better monitoring possibilities and hence improves the performance. Thus they predict a positive effect on performance.[95]

Risk

In addition, a measure of risk is included through $Beta$, representing the historic beta of the firm.[96] The value was extracted directly through Reuters database where it was calculated by 20 to 60 monthly historic observations. The test on measurement errors resulted in the range of -2.047 and 3.505 and yielded only one violation on the upper limit.

---

[92] See Carney/Gedajlovic [2002], Cui/Mak [2002], and Himmelberg et al. [1999].
[93] See Cui/Mak [2002, p. 323] and Himmelberg et al. [1999, p. 364].
[94] See Carney/Gedajlovic [2002, p. 131].
[95] See Cui/Mak [2002, p. 323].
[96] See Bøhren/Ødegaard [2003], Edwards/Weichenrieder [2004], and Mathiesen [2002]. Other studies use the volatility. See Aggarwal/Samwick [2003], Agrawal/Knoeber [1996], Bathala [1996], Bathala/Moon [1994], Bøhren/Ødegaard [2003], Chang [2003], Cho [1998], Crutchley/Hansen [1989], Demsetz/Lehn [1985], Demsetz/Villalonga [2001], Himmelberg et al. [1999], Leech/Leahy [1991], Loderer/Martin [1997], Mak/Li [2001], and Pedersen/Thomsen [1999]. However, the volatility is not only used as risk proxy but also to control the noisiness of stock.

An obvious effect of risk on ownership is the increase of the idiosyncratic risk, increasing the non-diversification cost of large shares or managerial ownership.[97] Consequently, a negative relation is implied for ownership concentration and insider ownership.[98] However, institutional investors are assumed to be risk neutral due to large portfolios and to react on the risk effect on performance.

Following the CAPM the cost of equity rises with increasing beta; thus costs of capital increase and the returns diminish.[99] Therefore, risk is assumed to impact performance negatively.

Growth

Following Short/Keasey [1999] growth is represented by sales growth (Gro), defined as this year's sales divided by previous year's sales.[100] Four values (1%) below .224 and 23 (4%) above 1.883 were replaced.

High growth results in high financing needs that may exceed internal financing capabilities. The possible equity financing increases the dispersion of equity.[101] Müller [1972] and Pedersen/Thomsen [1998] note that growth rates are also often found in early stages of the company life cycle, where ownership is more concentrated.[102] This effect should be moderate in the following empirical analyses, since firm age is also included as control variable.[103] Hence, a negative effect is predicted for ownership concentration and also for institutional ownership, since no special effects are assumed for the latter.

Considering managerial ownership, a valid argument for a positive effect of growth is given by Gugler et al. [2003b]. Growth may lead to empire building

---

[97] See Bathala [1996, p. 132], Pedersen/Thomsen [1998, p. 392], Pedersen/Thomsen [1999, p. 369], Mathiesen [2002, p. 164], Bøhren/Ødegaard [2003, pp. 10-11], Edwards/Weichenrieder [2004, p. 156].

[98] See Bathala [1996], Bergström/Rydqvist [1990a], Chang [2003], Cho [1998], Cui/Mak [2002], Demsetz/Lehn [1985], Himmelberg et al. [1999], Leech/Leahy [1991], Mak/Li [2001].

[99] The formula for the costs of equity is $R_i = R_f + \beta_i (R_M - R_f)$, with R_i as the expected return, R_f as risk-free rate of return and the risk premium $(R_M - R_f)$. See Elton/Gruber [1995, p. 298-302]. For further information on the Capital Asset Pricing Model see Elton/Gruber [1995, pp. 294-404].

[100] Further studies are Cubbin/Leech [1986], Cui/Mak [2002], Edwards/Weichenrieder [2004], McConnell/Servaes [1995], McEachern [1978], Nickell et al. [1997], Radice [1971], Schulze et al. [2003], Short/Keasey [1999], and Upton et al. [2003].

[101] See Bathala [1996, p. 132] and Pedersen/Thomsen [1998, p. 392].

[102] See Pedersen/Thomsen [1998, p. 392].

[103] See Chapter 4.4.4.

and thus positively influence prestige and career of managers.[104] Consequently, the effect of growth on insider ownership is indeterminable.

Regarding performance, growth has a positive effect on firm valuation and consequently the sign is expect to be positive.[105]

Diversification

To analyze the effect of diversification, *Div* is introduced as the number of different standard industrial classification (SIC) codes, which are reduced to two-digit groups.[106]

Since diversification reduces the idiosyncratic risk, it increases the incentive to hold large shares.[107] With regard to insider ownership, Aggarwal/Samwick [2003] state that a probably more important argument for a positive effect is the possible capture of private benefits:

- Managers may capture higher pecuniary benefits;[108]
- running a diversified firm may improve future career prospects;[109]
- diversification provides additional non-pecuniary private benefits, such as prestige, power, and perquisites;[110] and
- diversification may increase the entrenchment effect.[111]

However, Amihud/Lev [1981, 1999] and Crutchley/Hansen [1989] claim that the return loss of a diversified stock would offset the non-diversification costs, especially for general ownership.[112] Combining the arguments, a negative coefficient is expected for ownership concentration and institutional ownership and a positive one for insider ownership.

---

[104] See Gugler et al. [2003b, p. 7]. For studies of the influence of career prospectives on managerial ownership and behavior see Gibbons/Murphy [1992]; for prestige effects see Jensen [1986] and Stulz [1990].
[105] See Edwards/Weichenrieder [2004, p. 156].
[106] See Aggarwal/Samwick [2003], Amihud/Lev [1999], Anderson [2000], Bathala [1996], Carney/Gedajlovic [2002], Carter et al. [2003], Chen/Ho [2000], Denis et al. [1997, 1999], Fox/Hamilton [1994], Hill/Snell [1989], Hyland/Diltz [2002], Jensen/Murphy [1990], Lane et al. [1998, 1999], Leech/Leahy [1991], Mak/Li [2001], McEachern/Romeo [1978], and Zhang [1998].
[107] See Aggarwal/Samwick [2003, p. 74].
[108] See Bertrand/Mullainathan [2001] and Jensen/Murphy [1990].
[109] See Gibbons/Murphy [1992].
[110] See Jensen [1986] and Stulz [1990].
[111] See Shleifer/Vishny [1989].
[112] See Amihud/Lev [1999, p. 1063], Bathala [1996, p. 131], and Crutchley/Hansen [1989, pp. 40-41].

As indicated above, diversification can lead to a return loss but also has a positive effect on performance. Due to its direct negative impact on firm risk, it reduces the equity costs and causes return increases.[113]

Other Control Variables

Finally, variables are introduced to control for three further aspects: age, industry and point of time of the observation.

The logarithm of the years passed since foundation (*Age*) controls for life cycle effects. With increasing time the ownership concentration, especially managerial ownership, should decrease.[114] An effect on performance is not determinable on the basis of the life cycle theory, since for example old firms might have a good performance due to their size and established business, whereas they could also suffer from high competition and a saturated market.

As Pedersen/Thomsen [1998] prove in their study, industry effects exist and have a significant influence on ownership and performance. In order to avoid a bias industry dummies (Ind_i) are defined based on the first digit of the SIC code.[115]

Time effects are frequently assumed if the data set includes different point of time of observation. As later displayed in Section 4.4.1 the sample is based on two points of time. The dummy *Time* is included with the value of zero for 2000 and one for 2003.[116]

Summary of Hypothesized Effects

Table 4.6 gives an overview over the hypothesized signs of the effects of the different exogenous variables on performance and ownership.

---

[113] See Aggarwal/Samwick [2003, p. 93 and p. 111], Berger/Ofek [1995], Comment/Jarrell [1995], Denis et al. [1997, p. 135], Lang/Stulz [1994], Liebeskind/Opler [1994], and Servaes [1996]. For the effects of risk on performance see Chapter 4.4.4.

[114] See Chang [2003], Chen/Ho [2000], Mak/Li [2001], and Weber/Dudney [2003]. Other studies as Chang [2003], Leech/Leahy [1991], and Müller [1972] use the years passed since emission.

[115] See Demsetz/Lehn [1985, p. 1161], Holderness et al. [1999, p. 461], Lenz [1981, p. 142], and Pedersen/Thomsen [1998, p. 392]. Further studies including industry dummies are Bøhren/Ødegaard [2003], Chen/Ho [2000], Cho [1998], Cleary [2000], Demsetz/Villalonga [2001], Elston et al. [2002], Fee [2002], Gugler et al. [2003b], Mørck et al. [1988], Pedersen/Thomsen [1998], and Steer/Cable [1978].

[116] See Aggarwal/Samwick [2003], Ang/Cole [2000], Bøhren/Ødegaard [2003], Elston et al. [2002], Hermalin/Weisbach [1991], Himmelberg et al. [1999], Lehmann/Weigand [2000], Nickell et al. [1997], Palia/Lichtenberg [1999], and Short/Keasey [1999].

Table 4.6: Effects of exogenous variables on endogenous variables

	Ownership concentration	Institutional ownership	Insider ownership	Performance
OcST	−	+	−	+
Size	?	?	?	+
Debt	?	?	+	−
Inv	−	?	+	+
Nwc	+	−	+	−
Eom	−	−	?	+
Beta	−	−	−	−
Gro	−	−	?	+
Div	−	−	+	?
Age	−	−	−	?
Ind_i	────────── significant ──────────			
Time	────────── significant ──────────			

4.4.5 Descriptives Statistics

This chapter closes the variable and sample presentation by expounding the descriptive statistics. Table 4.7 states the mean and standard deviation, the divergency to the normal distribution by skewness and kurtosis, the data range by the minimum and maximum value, and the number of observations.

The ownership variables, with the exception of the divergence ratios, are bounded to the range of zero and one. The average ownership concentration lies around 44% with a standard deviation of about .25. Its average and also its maximum at 1.000 may appear unrealistically high at first glance. However, this is caused by the basis of the ownership concentration, the control rights. There are firms issuing dual-class shares and the common shares are held by one shareholder. Only their preferred shares are traded which is not reflected in the ownership measures but in the ownership ratios. The average ownership ratio lies at 1.151 with a standard deviation of .740, which indicates a relatively low divergence of control and cash flow rights. The second and third largest shares combine on average 17.7%. In the case of insider ownership the divergence between control and cash flow rights is even smaller with a value of 1.020. This is not astonishing since insiders hold their shares most times directly, leading to no divergence of control rights and cash flow rights by control chains. Also the averages and standard deviations of managerial and total insider ownership differ only by small values, ranging from

Table 4.7: Descriptive statistics of variables

	Mean	Std. Dev.	Skewness	Kurtosis	Min.	Max.	Obs.
Ownership Variables							
Ocr	0.444	0.248	0.409	2.406	0.004	1.000	521
ORatio	1.151	0.740	9.581	117.075	0.415	11.494	521
OcST	0.177	0.187	1.034	3.542	0.000	0.810	521
Mcr	0.231	0.305	1.007	2.736	0.000	1.000	521
MRatio	1.020	0.165	9.616	108.086	0.648	3.220	521
Mbcr	0.271	0.323	0.803	2.321	0.000	1.000	521
MbRatio	1.024	0.191	9.021	92.363	0.648	3.220	521
Icr	0.129	0.239	2.076	6.389	0.000	1.000	521
IRatio	2.719	7.158	8.752	99.001	0.521	100.647	521
Performance Variables							
Q	0.566	0.201	-0.659	3.053	0.000	0.979	521
Roe	-0.127	0.942	0.084	4.885	-2.664	2.314	521
Control Variables							
Size	19.466	2.317	0.534	3.933	13.143	29.618	521
Debt	0.123	0.137	1.610	6.069	0.000	0.714	521
Inv	0.076	0.293	0.526	4.868	-0.784	0.908	521
Nwc	0.373	0.272	0.551	1.580	0.026	0.766	521
Eom	0.475	0.430	1.613	4.702	0.010	1.642	521
Beta	0.770	0.590	0.946	4.258	-0.626	3.505	521
Gro	1.080	0.294	0.734	4.753	0.224	1.883	521
Div	1.996	1.108	1.061	3.473	1.000	6.000	521
Age	3.347	1.230	-0.232	1.974	0.000	5.541	521
Ind_1	0.025	0.156	-	-	0.000	1.000	521
Ind_2	0.165	0.372	-	-	0.000	1.000	521
Ind_3	0.361	0.481	-	-	0.000	1.000	521
Ind_4	0.079	0.270	-	-	0.000	1.000	521
Ind_5	0.094	0.292	-	-	0.000	1.000	521
Ind_7	0.209	0.407	-	-	0.000	1.000	521
Ind_8	0.067	0.251	-	-	0.000	1.000	521
Time	0.662	0.473	-	-	0.000	1.000	521

4.4 Sample Selection and Variables Used 105

23% to 27% with the standard deviation of approximately .3. The largest divergence of control and cash flow rights is found with institutional ownership with 2.719 and a standard deviation of 7.158. This is explained by the revers argument of the divergence of insider ownership; institutional investors hold their shares mainly through control chains. Also the standard deviation of the institutional ownership variable is relatively high. This might be explained by the fact that for bound variables the variance increases, the closer the mean is to the boundaries.

The average of Tobin's Q at .566 and the maximum value of .979 suggest a general undervaluation of the German stock market.[117] The mean of ROE is even negative with -.127. However, it has a very high standard deviation of .942.

The existence of boundaries also shows in the symmetry of distributions, the skewness. Positive values indicate left-skewed distributions, which is typical for downwards bounded variables. The lower bound causes a larger mean and thus an increase in the number of observations below it. The closer to the boundary the mean is, the larger is the skewness, as it is the case for institutional ownership, financial leverage, ease of monitoring, and diversification. It also shows that the divergence of control and cash flow rights is mostly in favor of the control rights which leads to more values above one and a high positive skewness.

Also the existence of an upper boundary can effect the skewness, as the upper boundary may enforce the same effect on the right tail as the lower limit does on the left tail. Consequently, the symmetry rises. This is an explanation for the relatively low skewness of the concentration measures. The only slightly right-skewed variables are Tobin's Q and age. This may be caused by the unlikeliness of values close to the lower boundary of zero. Together with the low mean and the unlimited upside this low probability results in a slightly heavier right tail.[118]

Furthermore, the boundaries effect the kurtosis. Since the observations are distributed over a limited, smaller range, the distribution is more likely to peak. Similar to the asymmetry, the kurtosis rises the closer the mean is to a boundary. In addition, high skewness may even enforce this effect. Thus it is not surprising that the strongly skewed variables also show high kurtosis values. Furthermore, the investment level has a sharp peak, probably caused by the low mean.

Table 4.8 presents the correlation matrix of the variables. As expected high correlations are found between the alternative measures of insider ownership. In addition, the share size of the second and third largest share has a medium correlation of .55 to the control rights of the institutional investors. This may

---

[117] In 2004 the average Q for the United States lies at .97, and is mean reverting to .63. For detailed information on historic values of Q see Appendix A.4, p. 225.

[118] For a more detailed presentation of the skewness by the percentiles of the variables see Appendix A.7, p. 314.

indicate that the second and third largest shareholders are often institutional investors.

Finally, the variables are tested for multicollinearity. This is important, since it may severely impact the estimation efficiency. In the case of multicollinearity an exogenous variable or a set of exogenous variables is a linear combination of a further exogenous variable, i.e., they are interdependent. This results in the problem, that the effects of those variables on the endogenous variable cannot be distinguished. This diminishes the efficiency of the estimates. The coefficients are unbiased in their sizes but since the variables share their explanatory power, their significance is reduced. To assure the absence of at least collinearity, the bivariate form of multicollinearity, a tolerance matrix of the variables is calculated and presented in Table 4.9. The tolerance is defined as $T_{ij} = (1 - \overline{R}^2_{ij})$, where $\overline{R}^2$ is the adjusted auxiliary R-square, i.e., the adjusted R-square of the regression of the variables on each other.[119] The lower the tolerance the higher is the collinearity and the bias of the variables. A low tolerance is shown in the alternative ownership measures, which is logical and has no effects on the models. A medium tolerance value of .48 exists for the Tobin's Q and the fixed asset ratio. However, this is not critical, since the Tobin's Q is an endogenous variable and its covariances are included in the model.

---

[119] Alternatively, the variance inflation factor (VIF) is often stated as measure of multicollinearity. It is calculated as $1/(1 - T_{ij})$.

Table 4.8: Correlation matrix of variables
Values over .5 are presented in bold and italic

	Ocr	ORa.	OcST	Mcr	MRa.	Mbcr	MbRa.	Icr	IRa.	Q
Ocr	1.00									
ORatio	-0.32	1.00								
OcST	-0.03	0.14	1.00							
Mcr	0.41	-0.13	0.18	1.00						
MRatio	-0.06	0.14	0.16	-0.05	1.00					
Mbcr	0.37	-0.08	0.10	***0.71***	-0.08	1.00				
MbRatio	-0.07	0.16	0.10	-0.17	***0.71***	0.39	1.00			
Icr	-0.13	***0.55***	0.28	-0.04	0.26	-0.11	0.46	1.00		
IRatio	-0.19	0.00	-0.03	-0.07	-0.04	-0.06	0.00	-0.20	1.00	
Q	0.04	0.12	0.13	0.46	0.21	-0.13	0.09	0.03	0.00	1.00
Roe	-0.06	-0.03	-0.05	0.25	0.46	-0.01	0.46	-0.03	0.24	-0.24
Size	-0.09	0.17	0.07	0.02	0.25	-0.24	0.22	0.23	0.18	0.17
Debt	0.02	-0.05	0.07	-0.07	0.25	0.02	0.11	-0.04	0.11	0.41
Inv	0.00	-0.06	-0.14	0.51	0.02	-0.05	-0.03	0.04	0.05	-0.10
Nwc	0.15	-0.05	-0.09	0.01	-0.07	0.02	-0.08	-0.02	-0.04	-0.09
Eom	0.02	0.07	0.03	-0.05	0.51	-0.08	0.28	-0.03	-0.03	0.45
Beta	-0.23	-0.01	-0.11	-0.15	-0.05	0.04	-0.05	-0.03	-0.09	-0.23
Gro	-0.03	-0.04	-0.02	0.12	-0.06	0.09	-0.06	-0.11	-0.10	-0.05
Div	-0.15	0.03	-0.06	0.17	-0.15	-0.12	-0.04	-0.01	0.16	-0.05
Age	0.17	0.08	0.13	-0.02	0.17	-0.03	0.07	0.17	0.10	0.15

	Roe	Size	Debt	Inv	Nwc	Eom	Beta	Gro	Div	Age
Roe	1.00									
Size	0.15	1.00								
Debt	-0.22	0.18	1.00							
Inv	-0.19	-0.11	-0.03	1.00						
Nwc	0.10	-0.18	-0.21	-0.02	1.00					
Eom	-0.07	-0.01	0.26	-0.15	-0.06	1.00				
Beta	-0.05	-0.19	-0.06	0.03	-0.20	0.09	1.00			
Gro	0.03	-0.10	-0.07	-0.51	0.00	0.14	0.23	1.00		
Div	-0.03	0.12	0.06	-0.07	0.02	-0.11	-0.10	-0.02	1.00	
Age	0.06	0.33	-0.04	0.05	0.04	-0.10	-0.49	-0.26	0.04	1.00

Table 4.9: Tolerance matrix of variables

Critical values below .5 are presented in bold and italic.

	Ocr	ORa.	OcST	Mcr	MRa.	Mbcr	MbRa.	Icr	IRa.	Q
Ocr	0.00									
ORatio	0.98	0.00								
OcST	0.94	0.91	0.00							
Mcr	0.83	0.85	0.99	0.00						
MRatio	0.96	0.88	0.99	0.74	0.00					
Mbcr	0.86	0.87	1.00	*0.22*	0.74	0.00				
MbRatio	0.94	0.84	1.00	0.85	0.83	0.72	0.00			
Icr	0.99	0.97	0.71	0.99	0.99	1.00	0.98	0.00		
IRatio	1.00	1.00	0.95	1.00	1.00	1.00	1.00	0.48	0.00	
Q	1.00	1.00	1.00	1.00	1.00	1.00	1.00	1.00	1.00	0.00
Roe	1.00	1.00	0.99	0.99	0.99	1.00	1.00	0.98	0.99	0.98
Size	1.00	1.00	0.97	0.95	0.95	0.95	0.95	0.96	0.96	0.98
Debt	1.00	1.00	1.00	0.99	0.99	1.00	1.00	1.00	1.00	0.83
Inv	1.00	1.00	1.00	1.00	1.00	1.00	1.00	1.00	1.00	0.94
Nwc	1.00	1.00	1.00	1.00	1.00	1.00	1.00	1.00	1.00	0.87
Eom	1.00	1.00	1.00	1.00	1.00	1.00	1.00	1.00	1.00	0.48
Beta	0.97	0.97	1.00	1.00	1.00	1.00	1.00	1.00	1.00	0.95
Gro	1.00	1.00	1.00	1.00	1.00	1.00	1.00	1.00	1.00	1.00
Div	0.96	0.96	1.00	1.00	0.99	0.99	0.99	1.00	1.00	1.00
Age	0.97	0.98	1.00	1.00	1.00	1.00	1.00	0.98	0.99	0.99
Ind_i	0.96	0.97	0.98	0.93	0.93	0.93	0.92	0.98	0.98	0.90

	Roe	Size	Debt	Inv	Nwc	Eom	Beta	Gro	Div	Age
Roe	0.00									
Size	0.97	0.00								
Debt	0.96	0.97	0.00							
Inv	0.99	1.00	1.00	0.00						
Nwc	0.97	0.96	0.91	1.00	0.00					
Eom	0.97	0.97	0.77	0.99	0.85	0.00				
Beta	1.00	0.95	1.00	0.99	1.00	1.00	0.00			
Gro	1.00	1.00	0.99	0.91	1.00	1.00	0.97	0.00		
Div	1.00	0.99	1.00	1.00	1.00	0.99	1.00	1.00	0.00	
Age	1.00	0.89	1.00	1.00	1.00	1.00	0.74	0.96	1.00	0.00
Ind_i	0.99	0.82	0.98	0.99	0.98	0.87	0.84	0.96	0.95	0.90

5
Empirical Analyses

5.1 Analysis Procedure

The following chapters present the empirical studies on ownership and performance. The analyzed equations system is aligned with the model of hypothesized effects.[1] To first analyze the relation of each ownership measure and performance separately, the model is decomposed in the three equations systems A, B and C as demonstrated in Figure 5.1. The first of the three models elaborates on ownership concentration; the second model focusses on insider ownership and the third on institutional ownership.

Each model contains the relation of performance to one of the ownership forms and thus includes two equations; one covering the effects of the ownership aspect on performance and a second with performance determining ownership:

$$\left| \begin{array}{l} Perf = O \quad\ \ + \text{control variables} \\ O = Perf + \text{control variables} \end{array} \right|$$

In the next step all three ownership dimensions and performance are combined to one four-equations system:

$$\left| \begin{array}{ll} Perf = \quad\ \ +OC +IO +MO + \text{control variables} \\ OC = Perf \qquad\qquad\qquad\quad + \text{control variables} \\ IO = Perf \qquad\qquad\qquad\quad + \text{control variables} \\ MO = Perf +OC +IO \qquad + \text{control variables} \end{array} \right|$$

All four model sections are similarly structured. To avoid a bias due to the misspecification as reciprocal system the Durbin-Wu-Hausman and the Wu-Hausman tests are applied to prove endogeneity. The null hypothesis of those tests states that an OLS estimator of the same equation would yield consistent estimates; i.e., any endogeneity among the regressors would not have deleterious effects on OLS estimates. A rejection of the null indicates that endogenous

---

[1] For an overview over the model see Figure 3.5, p. 68.

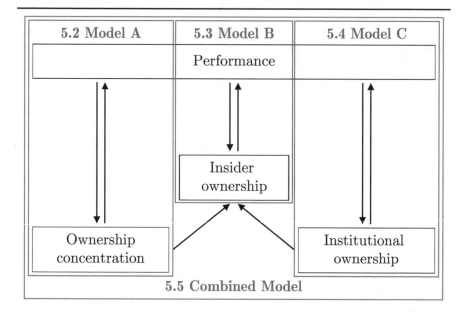

Fig. 5.1: Analyzed simultaneous equations models

regressors' effects on the estimates are meaningful and simultaneous equation techniques are required.

The two tests differ in the underlying distribution. The Durbin-Wu-Hausman test was first proposed by Durbin [1954] and by Wu [1973] and Hausman [1978]. Under the null, it is distributed χ^2 with m degrees of freedom, where m is the number of regressors specified as endogenous in the original regression. The Wu-Hausman test is often just termed Hausman test, but was first suggested by Wu [1973]. They showed that the test could be calculated straightforwardly through the use of auxiliary regressions. In contrast to the Durbin-Wu-Hausman test, the test statistic is distributed $F(m, N-k)$ under the null, where m is the number of regressors specified as endogenous in the original regression.[2]

After simultaneity is proven and the application of simultaneous equation methods justified, the relation shape is tested as further model specification. The forms of potential relations are compared by the model fit. The evaluation is based on the commonly used root mean square error of approximation (RMSEA). It is based on the population discrepancy and calculated as follows:

---

[2] For a more detailed elaboration on both tests see Davidson/MacKinnon [1993, Chapter 7.9, pp. 237-240] and Nakamura/Nakamura [1981]. Generally both methods test the OLS assumption of a zero correlation between explanatory variables and error terms.

$$\text{RMSEA} = \sqrt{\frac{(T_m - df_m)/(N-1)}{df_m}},$$

where T_m is the test statistic of equation m, df the degree of freedom of the equation and N the sample size.[3] Models with values below .1 are suggested to have a good fit, where a model fit below .05 is very good.[4]

With the selection of the modelled shape the model is finally specified. Since the following studies estimate a potentially nonlinear system for a large sample, the analysis uses a full information methods in the form of the I3SLS method, which is argued by Goldfeld/Quandt [1968] to be the most efficient in that case. Apart from the general results, the different effects are calculated and interpreted.

In a last step the estimates' robustness is tested. The tests include the impact of timing issues. Furthermore, the robustness with regard to the selection of the performance measures is assessed by the estimation with the ROE as alternative performance variable. Additionally, in the case of insider ownership a further robustness test is conducted on the insider definition as testing the combined ownership of management and board. Finally, the results of the model are summarized.

After the models are analyzed separately and combined, the results of all four models are recapitulated and discussed in Section 5.6.

5.2 General Ownership Concentration

As first ownership aspect general ownership concentration, i.e., the existence and strength of a controlling shareholder, is analyzed. The model contains two equations: The first displays the effect of ownership concentration on performance with the latter consequently as endogenous variable. The second equation examines the reverse effect, the influence of performance on ownership concentration:

$$\left| \begin{array}{l} Perf = OC\ + \text{control variables} \\ OC = Perf + \text{control variables} \end{array} \right|$$

5.2.1 Endogeneity Tests

In the equations system above both ownership concentration and performance are assumed as endogenous, which leads to the necessity of simultaneous estimation. To assure this assumption, the endogeneity of these variables is tested in this section by the Wu-Hausman F-test and Durbin-Wu-Hausman χ^2-test. As discussed in the Chapter 4.2 assessing the model specifications issues, both

---

[3] See Browne/Cudeck [1993, p. 144] and Steiger [1990].
[4] See Arbuckle [1999, pp. 409-411] and Hair et al. [1998, pp. 650-657].

ownership concentration and performance may have a linear, squared or non-monotonous effect. Accordingly, they should be modelled by simple linear measure, a combination of linear and squared measures, or piecewise measures. Those three potential effect shapes of both ownership concentration and performance result in nine alternative combinations. As the later applied model is still unclear at this point of the analysis, all alternative model structures are tested for endogeneity of both variables.

Table 5.1 presents the results of the Wu-Hausman F-test and Durbin-Wu-Hausman χ^2-test for each of the nine possible models. The first two columns specify the forms in which the variables are presented. The remaining columns state the results for the endogeneity test within the model for Tobin's Q and ownership concentration.

Table 5.1: Wu-Hausman F-test and Durbin-Wu-Hausman χ^2-test for different relationships of ownership concentration and Tobin's Q

Q	Ocr	Q value	Q distr.	Q p-value	Ocr value	Ocr distr.	Ocr p-value
Linear	Linear	0.937	$F(1, 499)$	(0.334)	1.240e^{1}3	$F(1, 496)$	(0.000)
		0.976	$\chi^2(1)$	(0.323)	521.000	$\chi^2(1)$	(0.000)
	Squared	0.926	$F(1, 499)$	(0.336)	1.19 e^{1}5	$F(2, 494)$	(0.000)
		0.965	$\chi^2(1)$	(0.326)	521.000	$\chi^2(2)$	(0.000)
	Piecewise	8.618	$F(1, 499)$	(0.003)	79.078	$F(3, 494)$	(0.000)
		8.845	$\chi^2(1)$	(0.003)	169.028	$\chi^2(3)$	(0.000)
Squared	Linear	3.074	$F(2, 497)$	(0.047)	132.423	$F(1, 496)$	(0.000)
		6.366	$\chi^2(2)$	(0.041)	109.786	$\chi^2(1)$	(0.000)
	Squared	2.588	$F(2, 497)$	(0.076)	87.485	$F(2, 494)$	(0.000)
		5.369	$\chi^2(2)$	(0.068)	136.269	$\chi^2(2)$	(0.000)
	Piecewise	7.121	$F(2, 497)$	(0.001)	39.412	$F(3, 494)$	(0.000)
		14.513	$\chi^2(2)$	(0.001)	100.617	$\chi^2(3)$	(0.000)
Piecewise	Linear	1140.000	$F(3, 495)$	(0.000)	321.133	$F(1, 496)$	(0.000)
		455.311	$\chi^2(3)$	(0.000)	204.753	$\chi^2(1)$	(0.000)
	Squared	419.092	$F(3, 495)$	(0.000)	27.742	$F(2, 494)$	(0.000)
		373.823	$\chi^2(3)$	(0.000)	52.607	$\chi^2(2)$	(0.000)
	Piecewise	66.348	$F(3, 495)$	(0.000)	2.699	$F(3, 494)$	(0.045)
		149.417	$\chi^2(3)$	(0.000)	8.403	$\chi^2(3)$	(0.038)

Overall, the results show endogeneity for both of the variables. Especially ownership concentration shows probability values constantly below 5% and is therefore strictly endogenous. In contrast, performance appears exogenous when using a linear performance effect in combination with linear or squared ownership concentration relation. In addition, the Tobin's Q shows only weak endogeneity if both effects are assumed as quadratic. This could be the case because the assumed relation is not fitting the true effects. Furthermore, the endogeneity tests were conducted with the ROE as performance measure. The results also show significant endogeneity and support the endogeneity of both variables as shown in Table A.11 of Appendix A.8.1.[5]

5.2.2 Model Specification

To further proceed with the analysis, the effect shapes and the according model structure has to be selected from the nine basic possibilities. For ownership concentration four alternatives of piecewise variables are applied increasing the number of presented models to 16. The model selection is based on the model fit in form of the RMSEA, assuming that the most realistic model yields the best fit. Table 5.2 presents the different shape combinations and their model fit. Also the table roughly states the coefficients by their significant effect direction, "+" or "-", or "insignificant".

Out of the displayed combinations of effects the three models containing a quadratic effect of ownership concentration on performance can be eliminated since their disturbance matrices do not converge. This results in insolvable equations systems. The best model fit for the ownership concentration equation is achieved when applying the piecewise performance variables. Since they show a constant, significant effect pattern over the different models, it is likely that they well approximate the performance effect. Accordingly, a non-monotonous performance effect is chosen for the model further analyzed.

With regard to the ownership effect on performance the shape selection is more complicated. Table 5.4 displays the ownership effect directions of the models which include the already selected non-monotonous performance effect. Both, the linear effect of ownership concentration and its piecewise variables, are significant. Since the piecewise coefficients have different effect directions and varying strength, it is likely that the relation is not simply constantly positive and linear. Therefore, the piecewise measures probably reflect the relationship more precisely.

All coefficients for an ownership concentration below 20% have a negative sign. Concentration values between 20% and 39% still have a negative effect, which is weaker though. This mitigation is also reflected in the weaker effect of the range from zero to 39% as a whole in Model 4. An ownership concentration above 39% yields positive coefficients. This effect is amplifying for share sizes exceeding 80%. Consequently, the relation seems to be a parabola with a minimum at 39% as presented in Model 5. The assumed turning point is supported by the results of Model 2, where the turning point is shifted to 51% and the medium range turns insignificant.

---

[5] For the results see Table A.11 of Appendix A.8.1, p. 315.

Table 5.2: Overview of the iterated three-stage least squares regression results for different relationships between ownership concentration and Tobin's Q (part 1)

piecewise$^1 \simeq \tau_1=.22$ and $\tau_2=.72$; piecewise$^2 \simeq \tau_1=20\%$ and $\tau_2=51\%$,
piecewise$^3 \simeq \tau_1=20\%$ and $\tau_2=39\%$, piecewise$^4 \simeq \tau_1=39\%$ and $\tau_2=80\%$,
piecewise$^5 \simeq \tau_1=20\%$, $\tau_2=39\%$ and $\tau_3=80\%$,

		Effect on Q		Effect on Ocr					RMSEA		χ^2	
		Ocr	Ocr²	Q	Q_a	Q^2	Q_b	Q_c	Q	Ocr	Q	Ocr
Linear	Linear	insignificant		insignificant					0.021	0.000	386.81	127.80
	Squared	−		insignificant	insignificant		+		0.000	0.032	116.24	462.88
	Piecewise¹	+			−		+	+	0.000	0.000	186.10	307.81
		Ocr	Ocr²	Q	Q_a	Q^2	Q_b	Q_c	Q	Ocr	Q	Ocr
Squared	Linear					non solvable						
	Squared					non solvable						
	Piecewise¹					non solvable						

Table 5.3: Overview of the iterated three-stage least squares regression results for different relationships between ownership concentration and Tobin's Q (part 2)

piecewise$^1 \simeq \tau_1=.22$ and $\tau_2=.72$, piecewise$^2 \simeq \tau_1=20\%$ and $\tau_2=51\%$,
piecewise$^3 \simeq \tau_1=20\%$ and $\tau_2=39\%$, piecewise$^4 \simeq \tau_1=39\%$ and $\tau_2=80\%$,
piecewise$^5 \simeq \tau_1=20\%$, $\tau_2=39\%$ and $\tau_3=80\%$,

Ocr		Q	Ocr$_a$	Ocr$_b$	Ocr$_c$	Ocr$_d$	Q	Q$_a$	Q^2	Q$_b$	Q$_c$	Q	Ocr	Q	Ocr
		Linear	insignificant	insignificant	−			insignificant				0.027	0.000	421.24	132.13
	2 Squared		−	insignificant	+			insignificant	insignificant			0.114	0.422	1876.96	21750.21
		Piecewise^1	−	insignificant	+					+		0.042	0.000	544.96	257.09
Piecewise		Linear	insignificant	insignificant	−			insignificant				0.029	0.000	435.67	131.36
	3 Squared		−	insignificant	+			insignificant	insignificant			0.095	0.519	1400.56	32740.88
		Piecewise^1	−	insignificant	+			−		+		0.036	0.000	490.40	232.96
		Linear	−	−	−			insignificant				0.029	0.000	431.27	128.80
	4 Squared		−	+	+			insignificant	insignificant			0.181	0.554	4237.42	37208.01
		Piecewise^1	−	+	+			−		+		0.071	0.000	937.14	321.99
	5 Piecewise^1		−	−	+	+		−		+	+	0.050	0.000	623.26	282.88

Table 5.4: Effects of general ownership concentration on Tobin's Q for different model specifications

	0%	20%	39%	51%	80%	100%
Linear	+ (spans all)					
Model 2	--		insignificant		+	
Model 3	--	-		+		
Model 4	-		+		++	
Model 5	--	-	+		++	

Table 5.5 reproduces the regression results of the third, fourth and fifth model.[6] The nonlinear estimation through four pieces appears to be the best at a first glance, since it can simulate the real relation in more detail. Yet, the RMSEA indicates that Model 4 is preferable. It also yields higher pseudo $\bar{R}^2$s of 46.3% and 18.2%. Consequently, Model 4 is chosen as further analyzed model, implying the thresholds for ownership concentration to lie at 39% and 80% and for the Tobin's Q at .22 and .72. This leads to the following equations system:

$$\left| \begin{array}{l} Q = Ocr_{Ocr \leq 39\%} + Ocr_{39\% < Ocr \leq 80\%} + Ocr_{Ocr > 80\%} + \text{control variables} \\ Ocr = Q_{Q \leq .22} + Q_{.22 < Q \leq .72} + Q_{Q > .72} \qquad\qquad\qquad\quad + \text{control variables} \end{array} \right|$$

For these relations the endogeneity is proven as highly probable.[7]

5.2.3 Results

Effect of Ownership Concentration

As explained in the methodology chapter,[8] the coefficients of Model 4 in Table 5.5 represent the direct effects of the variables on the endogenous variables. Apart from these direct effects, indirect effects are working through the endogenous variables. This does not only hold true for the exogenous variables but also for the endogenous variables themselves. In the case of a reciprocal effect of the endogenous variables, an endogenous variable y_1 does not only influence the second endogenous variable y_2 but also itself through the effect of y_2 on y_1. This feedback on y_1 again influences y_2; thus a feedback loop is created. Consequently, the total effect of an endogenous variable on a second one

---

[6] The complete results and the probability values of the coefficients are given in Table A.13 of Appendix A.8.1, p. 318.
[7] See Table 5.1, p. 112.
[8] See Chapter 4.3, p. 78.

5.2 General Ownership Concentration

Table 5.5: I3SLS estimates for ownership concentration and Tobin's Q
The values in brackets are the corresponding p-values
If not stated, *** implies a significance level of 1%, ** of 5% and * of 10%.

	Model 3		Model 4		Model 5	
	Q	Ocr	Q	Ocr	Q	Ocr
Ocr_a	−1.002	—			−0.907	
	(0.000)	—			(0.000)	
Ocr_b	−0.183		−0.192		−0.300	
	(0.143)		(0.002)		(0.028)	
Ocr_c	0.752		0.445		0.512	
	(0.000)		(0.000)		(0.000)	
Ocr_d	—		1.275		1.579	
	—		(0.000)		(0.000)	
$Q_{0 \leq x \leq .22}$		−1.944		−1.584		−2.134
		(0.000)		(0.000)		(0.000)
$Q_{.22 \leq x \leq .72}$		0.362		0.416		0.413
		(0.000)		(0.000)		(0.000)
$Q_{.72 \leq x}$		2.737		2.901		3.008
		(0.000)		(0.000)		(0.000)
ORatio	−0.015**		−0.015**		−0.016**	
OcST	0.355***	−0.395***	0.239***	−0.392***	0.267***	−0.394***
Size	0.045	0.026	0.186***	−0.010	0.094	−0.011
$Size^2$	−0.001	−0.001	−0.004***	0.000	−0.002	0.000
Debt	0.258**	−0.083	0.268***	−0.078	0.245**	−0.085
$Debt^2$	−0.201*		−0.234*		−0.173	
Inv	0.056	−0.038	0.060	−0.040	0.056	−0.040
Inv^2	−0.044*		−0.044*		−0.044*	
Nwc	−0.506***	0.046	−0.548***	0.044	−0.521***	0.044
Nwc^2	0.390***		0.443***		0.413***	
Eom	0.308***	−0.139*	0.315***	−0.151*	0.303***	−0.156*
Eom^2	−0.056**	0.008	−0.051***	0.009	−0.051**	0.009
Beta	0.011	−0.076***	−0.018	−0.067**	−0.008	−0.070***
Gro	0.026	−0.011	0.020	−0.008	0.024	−0.009
Div	0.017*	−0.034***	0.008	−0.034***	0.011	−0.034***
Age		0.009		0.020*		0.015*
Ind_i			partly significant			
Time	−0.013	0.006	−0.001	0.006	−0.004	0.007
constant	−0.302	0.476	−1.322**	0.804	−0.721	0.827
RMSE	0.186	0.230	0.144	0.231	0.160	0.232
pseudo $\bar{R}^2$	−0.093	0.172	0.463	0.182	0.200	0.151
$Prob._{\chi^2}$	(0.000)	(0.000)	(0.000)	(0.000)	(0.000)	(0.000)
RMSEA	0.073	0.000	0.036	0.000	0.050	0.000

depends not only on its direct effect but also on the reverse effect of the second variable and the thereby created feedback. Since the effects are modelled by a piecewise relation, the reverse effect and hence the total effect is depending on the level of the second endogenous variable. By applying the effect calculation methods stated in Chapter 4.3.3, the total effects of the endogenous variable on each other and the feedback on themselves can be identified.[9]

Table 5.6 presents the direct and total effects of ownership concentration on Tobin's Q and the feedback on itself. The first column shows the direct effects of the different piecewise variables, equivalent to the coefficients in the simultaneous equations model. Since the effects hypothesized in Section 3.3.1 are monotonous,[10] the non-monotonous direct relation must result from the interaction of at least two opposite effects. The only positively hypothesized effect is the increasing *monitoring capability* of large shareholders. In contrast, the *private benefits* and/or *over-monitoring argument* cause a negative effect.

Table 5.6: Feedback effects of ownership concentration on Tobin's Q and on itself

	$D_{Q\,Ocr}$	$T_{Q\,Ocr}$			$T_{Ocr\,Ocr}$		
		Q_a	Q_b	Q_c	Q_a	Q_b	Q_c
Ocr_a	−0.192	−0.214	−0.139	−0.104	1.443	0.942	0.700
Ocr_b	0.445	0.231	0.546	−1.529	0.520	1.227	−3.437
Ocr_c	1.275	0.350	2.715	−0.472	0.274	2.129	−0.371

For low ownership concentrations, the coefficient and direct effect equals -.192 and is highly significant. This indicates that the effects of *over-monitoring* and *private benefits* outweigh the positive *monitoring effect* resulting in this negative effect. Consequently, controlling shareholders with a share below 39% rather use their power to exploit private benefits. In addition, their increasing intervention may discourage the management in actions creating corporate value.

As soon as the share exceeds 39%, a higher share size creates shareholder value and therefore has a positive effect. The coefficient becomes even more positive for concentration values above 80%. This yields estimates of .445 and 1.275 for the second and third part of the slope. The controlling shareholder is now stronger aligned with corporate value. Consequently, the opportunity costs of private benefits rise. Furthermore, the gains of monitoring increase with higher shareholdings, while the monitoring costs diminish. As a result, the cost-efficiency of monitoring rises whereas that of the exploitation of pri-

---

[9] For an explanation of the decomposition of effects and their calculation see Chapter 4.3.3, p. 83.
[10] For an overview over the hypotheses see Table 3.2, p. 42.

vate benefits reduces. Accordingly, the controlling shareholder prefers to increase his utility rather by monitoring than by private benefits. Furthermore, the over-monitoring effect is probably loosing effectiveness for concentrations above 50%. The discouragement of the management depends on the intervention of shareholders. This again is strongly aligned with the possibility of control and thereby of intervention by shareholders. Since shareholdings below 100%, at most 50.1%, are sufficient to completely control a firm, the maximum of shareholders' capability of control should already be reached at these lower share sizes. Consequently, a further increase in share size has no effect anymore. In addition, the squeezed logit function leads to stronger and earlier decrease in marginal effects. Summarizing the decreasing negative effects of *over-monitoring* and *private benefits* face an increasing *monitoring effect* which leads in their combination to a positive and increasing effect beyond the threshold of 39%.

As mentioned before the total effects differ depending on the level of the second endogenous variable, the Tobin's Q. For low Tobin's Q firms ownership concentration below 39% has a negative effect of -.214 as shown in Table 5.6. After the first threshold the effect turns positive to .231 and even increases in the last part to .350. For firms with a Tobin's Q between .22 and .72 the effects are similar but generally more positive with gradients of -.139, .546 and 2.715. High Tobin's Q firms react akin for changes in ownership concentration below 39% with a weaker effect of -.104. But instead of an analogical positive effect, the gradient stays negative for higher concentration values. Above a concentration of 39%, the negative effect increases in strength to -1.529 and then diminishes to -.472 after the second threshold.

The feedback of ownership concentration on itself for a low Tobin's Q is positive and diminishing from 1.443 to .520 and .274. For medium Tobin's Q firms, it amplifies from .942 to 1.277 and 2.129. Only for companies with a high Tobin's Q, the feedback is non-monotonously changing from .700 to -3.437 and -.371.[11]

Figure 5.2 shows these different total effects of ownership concentration on Tobin's Q for the different levels of Tobin's Q and compares them to the direct effect. Considering the different relations for shares above 39%, it does not surprise that former studies were not able to find significant estimates for high concentrations. The different behavior of firms on different Tobin's Q levels in this area makes it difficult to produce one consistent estimate for all three groups.

The differences in the total effects may yield from two reasons: first, the feedback of the ownership concentration on itself and second, a mediation effect of the Tobin's Q on the direct effects of ownership concentration. The latter implies that the direct effects vary for different levels of Tobin's Q. Such a mediation is theoretically possible. Under the assumption that the potential

---

[11] Figure A.9 in Appendix A.8.1 graphically demonstrates the feedback effects, p. 320.

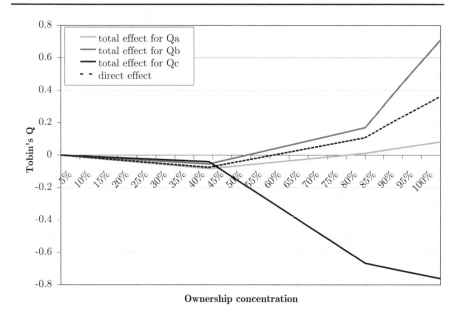

Fig. 5.2: Direct and total effects of ownership concentration on Tobin's Q

of improvement of firms with high Tobin's Qs is limited, the *monitoring effect* based on this improvement potential is weaker for these well performing firms than for poorer performing firms. Furthermore, since the potential damage on performance is higher for well performing firms, one could argue that the *over-monitoring effect* strengthens with an increase in Tobin's Q. The alternation of the *private benefits effect* by the Tobin's Q is ambiguous. Himmelberg et al. [1999] state that the size of potential private benefits is higher for larger and better performing firms.[12] This increases the utility of an adverse action. Also the opportunity costs of such an action rise. The cash flow entitlement generated by high Tobin's Q firms is higher than the same rights of companies with inferior performance. Accordingly, the loss by an action harming corporate value is higher for better performing companies. Given this counterbalance of a higher gain through the private benefits by the higher opportunity costs the mediation of the private benefits effects is unclear. In summary, the *monitoring effect* is hypothesized to weaken and the *over-monitoring* to strengthen for high Tobin's Qs. Both hypotheses cause a more negative effect on performance for higher Tobin's Q firms. The direction of mediation of the *private benefits effect* is unclear.

---

[12] See Himmelberg et al. [1999, p. 364].

5.2 General Ownership Concentration

To separate the feedback from the mediation effect, the equations are estimated separately for the three subsamples based on the Tobin's Q. The mediation effect is shown in the alternations in the coefficients. Since only 37 observations exist for a low Tobin's Q, the estimation with 25 parameters cannot be conducted efficiently for this subsample.[13] Table 5.7 and Figure 5.3 compare the estimates of the two remaining subsamples to the total sample's direct effects.

Table 5.7: Direct effects of ownership concentration on Tobin's Q for subsamples of Tobin's Q

	$D_{Q\,Ocr}$		
	total sample	subsample Q_b	subsample Q_c
Ocr_a	−0.192	−0.090	−0.306
Ocr_b	0.445	0.381	0.659
Ocr_c	1.275	1.003	2.016

The direct effect is constantly weaker for medium Tobin's Q firms and stronger for high-performing companies than that for the total sample. For low-concentrated firms the stronger negative effect for higher Tobin's Q firms suits the assumed mediation of *monitoring* and *over-monitoring effect*. For an ownership concentration above 39%, the mediation reverses resulting in a stronger positive effect for higher Tobin's Qs. Since the assumptions on monitoring and over-monitoring effects only explain a positive mediation, only the unclear alternation of the *private benefits effect* remains as an explanation. This indicates a negative effect of the performance level on the private benefits argument, at least for higher ownership concentrations. The concentration together with high performance increases opportunity costs of private benefits lowering the incentive for harming actions. For higher concentrated firms, this positive mediation outweighs the negative mediation of the other effects.

Since the direct effect of ownership concentration is only negative in the case of a largest owner with a share size below 39%, higher shares seem to align the controlling shareholder with the general shareholder, leaving him performance-oriented. Consequently, actions controlling the largest shareholder, i.e., minority shareholder protection, have only a positive effect for share sizes below 39%. As soon as ownership concentration passes this threshold, these actions lose their effectiveness. This is not implying that they have no effect at all, since the direct effect is a combination of the negative and positive effects of ownership. Only the cost-efficiency of the actions is proba-

---

[13] For a frequency table of the different ownership concentration and Tobin's Q categories see Table A.14 in Appendix A.8.1, p. 321.

122   5 Empirical Analyses

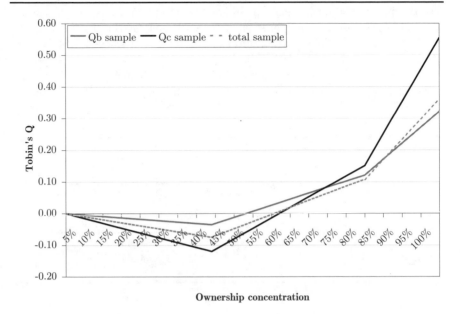

Fig. 5.3: Direct effects of ownership concentration on Tobin's Q for subsamples of Tobin's Q

bly overestimated, which can make them unprofitable. This is especially the case if the actions may also have a negative effect, such as boosting the over-monitoring problem.

Effect of Tobin's Q

Analogously to the previous analysis, Table 5.8 represents the effects of Tobin's Q on ownership concentration and on itself. Again the first column shows the direct effects of the different piecewise variables. They turn from negative -1.584 to .416 and amplify to 2.901 for the last part of the slope. While there is no assumed explanation for the negative gradient in the first part, the positive and increasing effect above the threshold of .22 suits the assumed *insider-investment hypothesis*.

An explanation for the negative effect might consist of the investor's incentive to sell stocks to realize the gain. This gain is obviously higher, the better the firm's performance is. The opportunity profit from selling stock and the reduction of non-diversification costs could outweigh the gain accrued from increasing the shareholding. Furthermore, for larger shares the sale does not have to imply a significant control loss, since also lower voting rights already

5.2 General Ownership Concentration

Table 5.8: Feedback effects of Tobin's Q on ownership concentration and on itself

	D_{OcrQ}	T_{OcrQ}			T_{QQ}		
		Ocr_a	Ocr_b	Ocr_c	Ocr_a	Ocr_b	Ocr_c
Q_a	−1.584	−1.584	−1.079	−0.569	1.443	0.520	0.274
Q_b	0.416	0.392	0.511	0.886	0.942	1.227	2.129
Q_c	2.901	2.030	−9.971	−1.075	0.700	−3.437	−0.371

grant high control over the firm. In addition, the sale could also be a planned exit option, executed as soon as a certain stock price has been reached.

For low ownership concentration, the total effects stay similar to the direct effects, changing from -1.584 to .392 and 2.030. In contrast, for firms with medium or high ownership concentration the effect shapes change; an increase of a Tobin's Q above .72 results in a decrease of share size. This induces an effect of Tobin's Q on ownership concentration with the gradients of -1.079, .511, and -9.971 for medium concentrations and -.569, .886, and -1.075 for highly concentrated firms. Figure 5.4 demonstrates and compares the different total effects of Tobin's Q on ownership concentration to the direct effects.

While the feedback of Tobin's Q on itself is constantly positive for low concentrated firms decreasing from 1.443 to .942 and .700, that of higher concentrated firms has a rising positive feedback for low and medium Tobin's Qs of .520 to 1.227 and .274 to 2.129 respectively. Nevertheless, for high Tobin's Q firms both turn negative with gradients of -3.437 and -.371.[14]

This change in the feedback might explain the changed total effect shape for medium and high concentrated firms. In addition, ownership concentration could influence the direct effects leading to a mediation. Theoretically, ownership concentration strengthens the assumed *insider-investment effect*. An increasing share size enhances the insight into the company and hence improves the quality of evaluation of the firm's prospect. Accordingly, a large shareholder should make better investment decisions, leading to a higher correlation of ownership concentration and performance. In the case that the negative effect is caused by the sale of stock to realize the gain, its mediation can also be hypothesized. The larger the share, the lower is the control loss by the partial sale and thus the opportunity costs of the sale. Accordingly, there should be more sales and thus a stronger effect for highly concentrated firms.

To find out how much of the indirect effect is brought about by the feedback and how much by an effect mediation of ownership concentration, subsamples based on ownership concentration are formed and estimated. In the case of mediation effects, the direct effects of the subsamples will vary from

---

[14] Figure A.10 in Appendix A.8.1 graphically demonstrates the feedback effects, p. 321.

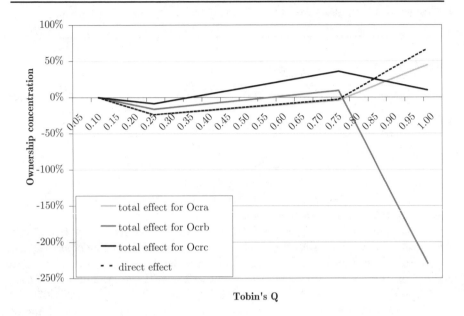

Fig. 5.4: Direct and total effects of Tobin's Q on ownership concentration

the total sample coefficients. Unfortunately, the matrices do not converge for the subsample of highly concentrated firms resulting in no solution.[15] This might be due to the relatively small sample size of 46 companies.[16] Table 5.9 and Figure 5.5 show the results for the total sample and the remaining two subsamples.

Table 5.9: Direct effects of Tobin's Q on ownership concentration for subsamples of ownership concentration

	$D_{Ocr\,Q}$		
	total sample	subsample Ocr_a	subsample Ocr_b
Q_a	−1.584	−0.104	0.189
Q_b	0.416	0.038	−0.028
Q_c	2.901	0.330	−0.219

---

[15] A number of 16,000 iterations was chosen as a maximum.
[16] For a frequency table of the different ownership concentration and Q categories see Table A.14 in Appendix A.8.1, p. 321.

5.2 General Ownership Concentration

The direct effects for the subsample of medium concentration are reversed in directions compared to dispersed firms and the total sample. This indicates that the changes in total effects for higher concentrated firms stems also partially from a mediating effect. The assumed positive mediation effect on the *insider-investment argument* is found for firms with a low Tobin's Q, where the amplification of the positive *insider-investment effect* reduces the unknown negative effect and even results in a positive total direct effect for firms with a concentration between 39% and 80%.

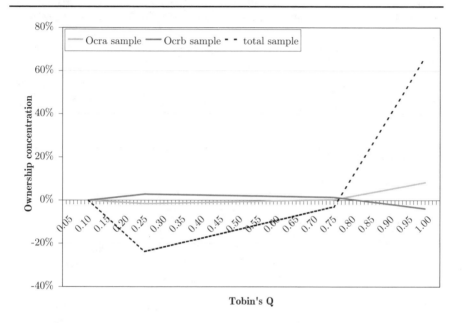

Fig. 5.5: Direct effects of Tobin's Q on ownership concentration for subsamples of ownership concentration

A Tobin's Q above .22 leads to a negative mediation effect reducing the direct effect of both subsamples. The mediation is even amplified for Tobin's Q above .72. Since this negative mediation does not suit the prediction for the *insider-investment argument*, it has to stem from the unknown negative effect. If this is really based on stock sales to realize a gain, the negative mediation fits the prediction. Coefficients imply that the mediation of this effect is stronger than that of the *insider-investment effect* for higher levels of Tobin's Q. This results in lower positive effects for dispersed firms, while higher concentrated companies display even negative effects for Tobin's Qs above .22.

Effect of Control Variables on Tobin's Q

Regarding the control variables, most of the significant effects carry the predicted signs in the direct effects.[17] Table 5.10 presents next to the direct effects on Tobin's Q also the indirect and total effects through the corresponding ownership levels. The influence by ownership concentration is mainly weakening the effect for low-concentrated companies and strengthening for medium and high ownership. This impact stems from two factors: First, the direct effect of the control variables on ownership concentration and its effect on performance and second, the feedback effect of performance changes on itself. Since all variables except for OcST and Eom have insignificant direct effects in at least one of the equations, their indirect effect through ownership concentration vanishes and their total effects are solely based on the remaining feedback effect. As this feedback loop is strengthening or weakening the effect without an interference by the indirect effect, the total effects stay constant in their basic shape and the location of their turning points. However, their gradients shrink for low concentration and rise for medium and high share sizes.

Table 5.10: Effects of the control variables on Tobin's Q

	D_{Qx}	Ocr_a		Ocr_b		Ocr_c	
		I_{Qx}	T_{Qx}	I_{Qx}	T_{Qx}	I_{Qx}	T_{Qx}
ORatio	−0.015	0.008	−0.007	−0.025	−0.040	−0.070	−0.085
OcST	0.239	0.263	0.502	−0.791	−0.552	−2.266	−2.027
Size	0.159	−0.086	0.073	0.260	0.419	0.744	0.903
Size^2	−0.004	0.002	−0.002	−0.007	−0.011	−0.019	−0.023
Debt	0.268	−0.146	0.122	0.438	0.706	1.255	1.523
Debt^2	−0.234	0.127	−0.107	−0.382	−0.616	−1.095	−1.329
Inv	0.000	0.000	0.000	0.000	0.000	0.000	0.000
Inv^2	−0.044	0.024	−0.020	−0.072	−0.116	−0.206	−0.250
Nwc	−0.548	0.298	−0.250	−0.895	−1.443	−2.565	−3.113
Nwc^2	0.443	−0.241	0.202	0.724	1.167	2.074	2.517
Eom	0.315	−0.020	0.295	0.060	0.375	0.171	0.486
Eom^2	−0.051	0.028	−0.023	−0.083	−0.134	−0.239	−0.290
Beta	0.000	0.067	0.067	−0.202	−0.202	−0.579	−0.579
Gro	0.000	0.000	0.000	0.000	0.000	0.000	0.000
Div	0.000	0.034	0.034	−0.102	−0.102	−0.294	−0.294
Age	0.000	−0.020	−0.020	0.060	0.060	0.173	0.173
Ind$_i$				partly significant			
Time	0.000	0.000	0.000	0.000	0.000	0.000	0.000

---

[17] For the hypothesized effects see Chapter 4.4.4, p. 93, and Table 4.6, p. 103.

5.2 General Ownership Concentration

The divergence ratio of control and cash flow rights has a negative effect on Tobin's Q in the direct effect. This was predicted by the *monitoring* and *private benefits argument*. However, this does not imply a dominance over the *over-monitoring hypothesis*, since it reflects only the effect of the divergence on performance. It solely shows that the mediating effect of the divergence on the over-monitoring effect is weaker than the sum of mediating effects on the other hypotheses. While the total divergence effect is weakening for low concentration levels, its magnitude increases for growing concentrations.

Furthermore, the direct effect of the share size of the second and third largest shareholder is positive as they monitor the controlling shareholder. Nevertheless, their total effect turns negative through the feedback loop for medium and high ownership concentration.

Size has a nonlinear effect on Tobin's Q. The effect is constantly positive suiting the hypothesized economies of scale. The marginal value starts decreasing for companies exceeding sales of € 428,000,000. The magnitude of the total impact increases with higher ownership concentration but maintains the same basic shape.

While the direct effect of debt on Tobin's Q was assumed to be negative, it is actually constantly positive. Consequently, the argument of reduced agency costs by Kim/Sorensen [1986] and Jensen [1986] prevails over the pecking order argument by Myers/Majluf [1984] and Jensen et al. [1992]. Again the effect strengthens with ownership concentration maintaining its basic shape and location constant.

The squared investment level variable is only significant at 10%, and the linear measure fails significance by 2.5%. While neglecting the linear measure results in a negative effect, its inclusion yields a positive relation which suits the predictions of potential improvements and long-term orientation.[18]

Furthermore, liquidity is significant in the linear and squared measure. The effect is monotonously negative supporting the potential negative effect of unused resources instead of productive investments.

As predicted, an increase in the ease of monitoring raises Tobin's Q. However, the shape of the total effects is not stable over the different ownership concentration levels. While the total effect of low and medium concentrated cooperations is monotonously positive,[19] the maximum of the effect reaches .84 for highly concentrated firms. Hence, the total effect turns negative for highly concentrated firms with an ease of monitoring above 1.60, which is only the case for 6% of the sample.

Beta, growth, diversification, and age appear insignificant but, except for growth, they all show indirect effects through ownership concentration. The effects of beta and diversification are turning from slightly positive to strongly negative.

---

[18] The function passes zero at 1.273 lying above the maximum.
[19] The maxima lie at at 6.40 and 1.40.

128   5 Empirical Analyses

All the industry groups Ind$_2$, Ind$_3$, and Ind$_5$ have a positive effect on Tobin's Q;[20] the others prove insignificant. The detailed effects of the different industry groups are stated in Table A.15 of Appendix A.8.1.[21] The point of time of the observations is insignificant in both equations.

Effect of Control Variables on Ownership Concentration

Table 5.11 presents the effects of the control variables on ownership concentration, again broken down into direct, indirect and total effects. Most direct effects are insignificant and the total effects stem from the effects on Tobin's Q. Only the ownership of the second and third largest shareholder, the linear measure of ease of monitoring, beta, diversification, and age show a direct effect.

Table 5.11: Effects of the control variables on ownership concentration

		Q_a		Q_b		Q_c	
	$D_{Ocr\,x}$	$I_{Ocr\,x}$	$T_{Ocr\,x}$	$I_{Ocr\,x}$	$T_{Ocr\,x}$	$I_{Ocr\,x}$	$T_{Ocr\,x}$
ORatio	0.000	0.211	0.211	−0.042	−0.042	−0.295	−0.295
OcST	−0.392	0.419	0.027	−0.084	−0.476	−0.585	−0.977
Size	0.000	−2.233	−2.233	0.448	0.448	3.124	3.124
Size^2	0.000	0.056	0.056	−0.011	−0.011	−0.079	−0.079
Debt	0.000	−3.764	−3.764	0.755	0.755	5.265	5.265
Debt^2	0.000	3.287	3.287	−0.659	−0.659	−4.597	−4.597
Inv	0.000	0.000	0.000	0.000	0.000	0.000	0.000
Inv^2	0.000	0.618	0.618	−0.124	−0.124	−0.864	−0.864
Nwc	0.000	7.697	7.697	−1.544	−1.544	−10.766	−10.766
Nwc^2	0.000	−6.222	−6.222	1.248	1.248	8.703	8.703
Eom	−0.151	−2.970	−3.121	0.596	0.445	4.154	4.003
Eom^2	0.000	0.716	0.716	−0.144	−0.144	−1.002	−1.002
Beta	−0.067	0.645	0.578	−0.129	−0.196	−0.903	−0.970
Gro	0.000	0.000	0.000	0.000	0.000	0.000	0.000
Div	−0.034	0.327	0.293	−0.066	−0.100	−0.458	−0.492
Age	0.020	−0.193	−0.173	0.039	0.059	0.269	0.289
Ind$_i$				insignificant			
Time	0.000	0.000	0.000	0.000	0.000	0.000	0.000

As predicted, the share size of the second and third largest owner is negative, since it limits the opportunities for private benefits. While for little concentrated firms its indirect positive effect through performance dominates

---

[20] The groups 2 and 3 comprise the manufacturing industry and group 5 the wholesale and retail trade.
[21] See Table A.15 of Appendix A.8.1, p. 322.

the total effect, it turns negative for other firms strengthening the negative direct effect.

The fixed assets to sales ratio confirms the assumption of lower private benefits by showing a negative sign. Similar to the results of Himmelberg et al. [1999], the squared measure is insignificant. However, a model using only a linear specification of ease of monitoring does not yield very different coefficients and probability values of the other variables. The coefficient of Eom rises to -.128 and becomes significant at a 1% level. However, the χ^2-value of the Tobin's Q equation worsens by twelve, while that of the ownership equations ameliorates only by two. Furthermore, the ownership equation has already a very good model fit. Thus the nonlinear Eom specification is maintained.[22] With rising Tobin's Q the total effect changes from negative to positive.

The direct risk effect shows the expected negative sign but its total effect switches from negative to positive for higher levels of Tobin's Q. Also diversification has a negative effect and behaves similar to the risk effect over the different Tobin's Q levels. Contradicting the hypothesis, age has a slightly positive direct impact on ownership. It could be that the assumed life cycle effects are only strong in the first years but decline with growing age and are substituted by other effects.

None of the industry groups shows a significant direct effect, but Ind_2, Ind_3, and Ind_5 have total effects due to the Tobin's Q equation. Again, the detailed effects of the different industry groups are stated in Table A.16 of Appendix A.8.1.[23] The point of time of the observations is insignificant.

For reasons of completeness, the noncausal effects of the control variables for both equations are given by Table A.18 and Table A.19 of Appendix A.8.1.[24] However, as their interpretation does not render any further insight, it is neglected.

5.2.4 Robustness Checks

After the estimation and discussion of the effects, this section examines the robustness of the results. Since some hypotheses argue for a lagged relationship and ownership is often viewed as sticky, the first robustness check analyzes the sensitivity to modelled *timing of the effects*. Therefore, two alternated models including previous year's data are considered. To both models the Tobin's Q of the previous year is added in form of piecewise variables with the thresholds of .3 and .6. The present year's measures of Tobin's Q are also included to reduce a possible bias through stickiness. To avoid problems due to multicollinearity, the tolerance of the present and previous year's measures is tested but does not result in any critical values.[25]

---

[22] For a comparison of the two models see Table A.17 of Appendix A.8.1, p. 323.
[23] See Table A.16 of Appendix A.8.1, p. 323.
[24] See Table A.18 and Table A.19 of Appendix A.8.1, p. 326 and p. 327.
[25] For the correlation and tolerance values see Table A.20 of Appendix A.8.1, p. 327.

Table 5.12 states the results for two alternations.[26] The first one includes only the Tobin's Q of the previous year. The second model additionally alters the other accounting variables by taking their previous year's equivalents.

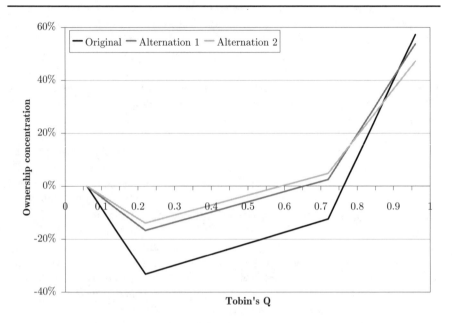

Fig. 5.6: Direct effects of Tobin's Q and previous year's Tobin's Q on ownership concentration

The estimates differ only slightly. The largest change is found in the Tobin's Q estimates, since fractions of their effect are now explained by the previous year's variables. Nevertheless, the basic shape of the relation stays constant but with weaker effects as shown in Figure 5.6. For the Tobin's Q variables of the previous year, only the low and high Tobin's Q estimates are significant with the first being negative and the latter positive. This effects resemble those of this year's Tobin's Q. It indicates that some of the performance effects in the original model actually stem from the performance of the previous year but with similar effects. Apart from the stickiness of variables, this might be explained by the fact that the effects already had an impact in the previous year and their results remained over the next period.

Furthermore, the robustness regarding the *type of performance measure* is tested with the ROE as alternative variable. The estimated thresholds for the piecewise variables are -.3 and zero. The results of the I3SLS are given in

---

[26] For the detailed results see Table A.21 of Appendix A.8.1, p. 328.

Table 5.12: Robustness checks on lagged measures of Tobin's Q for ownership concentration

	Alternation 1		Alternation 2		Original	
	Q	Ocr	Q	Ocr	Q	Ocr
Ocr_a	−0.117		−0.100		−0.148	
	(0.019)		(0.047)		(0.012)	
Ocr_b	0.573		0.564		0.445	
	(0.000)		(0.000)		(0.000)	
Ocr_c	1.581		1.526		1.275	
	(0.000)		(0.000)		(0.000)	
Q_a		−1.041		−0.868		−2.074
		(0.000)		(0.001)		(0.000)
Q_b		0.385		0.376		0.416
		(0.000)		(0.000)		(0.000)
Q_c		2.133		1.762		2.901
		(0.000)		(0.000)		(0.000)
Q_a^{t-1}		−0.301		−0.475		
		(0.050)		(0.002)		
Q_b^{t-1}		−0.086		0.080		
		(0.636)		(0.407)		
Q_c^{t-1}		0.514		0.864		
		(0.000)		(0.000)		
Oratio	−0.015**		−0.015**		−0.015**	
OcST	0.256***	−0.432***	0.246***	−0.423***	0.239***	−0.392***
Size	0.169***	0.070	0.190***	0.009	0.159***	−0.010
Size²	−0.004***	−0.002	−0.005***	0.000	−0.004***	0.000
Debt	0.352***	−0.218**	0.336***	−0.137*	0.268***	−0.078
Debt²	−0.289		−0.334*		−0.234*	
Inv	0.074**	−0.011	0.119***	0.015	0.060	−0.040
Inv²	−0.044		−0.077**		−0.044*	
Nwc	−0.774***	0.072*	−0.807***	0.079**	−0.548***	0.044
Nwc²	0.757***		0.791		0.443***	
Eom	0.531***	−0.314***	0.524***	−0.313***	0.315***	−0.151*
Eom²	−0.172***	0.106*	−0.166***	0.077	−0.051***	0.009
Beta	−0.014	−0.051**	−0.015	−0.056***	−0.018	−0.067**
⋮	⋮	⋮	⋮	⋮	⋮	⋮
constant	−1.485***	0.009	−1.678***	0.391	−1.322**	0.804
RMSE	0.156	0.239	0.155	0.237	0.144	0.231
pseudo $\bar{R}^2$	0.398	0.078	0.409	0.096	0.344	0.161
Prob.$_{\chi^2}$	(0.000)	(0.000)	(0.000)	(0.000)	0.000	0.000
RMSEA	0.037	0.000	0.039	0.000	0.036	0.000

Table 5.13: Robustness checks on ROE for ownership concentration

	ROE		Q	
	ROE	Ocr	Q	Ocr
Ocr_a	0.171		−0.148	
	(0.034)		(0.012)	
Ocr_b	−2.124		0.445	
	(0.000)		(0.000)	
Ocr_c	−5.832		1.275	
	(0.000)		(0.000)	
$Perf_a$		−0.588		−1.584
		(0.000)		(0.000)
$Perf_b$		0.133		0.416
		(0.051)		(0.000)
$Perf_c$		−0.652		2.901
		(0.000)		(0.000)
Oratio	0.029***		−0.015**	
OcST	−1.047***	−0.641***	0.239***	−0.392***
Size	−0.102	0.047	0.159***	−0.010
$Size^2$	0.003	−0.001	−0.004***	0.000
Debt	0.069	−0.016	0.268***	−0.078
$Debt^2$	−0.332		−0.234*	
Inv	−1.249***	−0.780***	0.060	−0.040
Inv^2	−0.139**		−0.044*	
Nwc	0.932***	0.368***	−0.548***	0.044
Nwc^2	−0.368*		0.443***	
Eom	−0.931**	−0.579**	0.315***	−0.151*
Eom^2	0.370*	0.254*	−0.051***	0.009
Beta	−0.236***	−0.182***	−0.018	−0.067
Gro	−0.054	−0.030	0.020	−0.008
Div	−0.100***	−0.069***	0.008	−0.034***
Age		−0.006		0.020*
Ind_i		partly significant		
Time	0.026	0.021	−0.001	0.006
constant	1.838	0.460	−1.322**	0.804
RMSE	0.864	0.545	0.144	0.231
pseudo $\bar{R}^2$	0.157	−3.793	0.344	0.161
$Prob._{\chi^2}$	(0.000)	(0.000)	(0.000)	(0.000)
RMSEA	0.066	0.194	0.036	0.000

Table 5.13.[27] The coefficients of both effect directions change partially in sign and size. The accounting-based measure alters the results of the endogenous variables effects as well as those of the control variables. Consequently, the estimates are not robust for the type of performance measures applied.

5.2.5 Summary

The empirical results of the relation of ownership concentration and performance indicate a non-monotonous effect in every direction.

Ownership concentration has a negative direct effect until an ownership level of 39%. From here on it has a positive impact on performance, which is even increasing for a share size above 80%. This implies that the negative effects of *private benefits* and *over-monitoring* prevail over the *monitoring effect* for low concentrations. Consequently, controlling shareholders with a share below 39% rather use their power to exploit private benefits. In addition, their increasing intervention may discourage the management in actions creating corporate value.

As soon as the share size exceeds 39%, a higher share size creates shareholder value. The controlling shareholder is now stronger aligned with corporate value. As a result the cost-efficiency of monitoring rises, whereas that of the exploitation of private benefits reduces. Accordingly, the controlling shareholder prefers to increase his utility rather by *monitoring* than by *private benefits*. Furthermore, the *over-monitoring effect* is probably loosing effectiveness for concentrations above 50%. The combination of these effects results in a positive and increasing effect beyond the threshold of 39%.

Since the direct effects of ownership concentration is only negative in the case of a largest owner with a share size below 39%, higher shares align the controlling shareholder with the general shareholder, leaving him performance-oriented. Consequently, actions controlling the largest shareholder, i.e., minority shareholder protection, have only a positive effect for share sizes below 39%. As soon as ownership concentration passes this threshold, its direct effect is positive leading to a reduced effectiveness of monitoring and controlling actions. They may even have a negative effect, such as boosting the over-monitoring problem.

The total effects of ownership concentration on performance depend on the level of Tobin's Q determining the feedback effect. They vary not only in their strength but also in their basic shape. The variation partially stems from a mediating effect of the Tobin's Q on the direct effects. It strengthens both the negative gradient in the first part as well as the following positive ones. The amplification of the negative effect by the Tobin's Q suits the prediction of a weakened *monitoring argument* and an enforced *over-monitoring effect*. The strengthening of the positive effect for ownership concentrations above 39% must origin from a mediation of the *private benefits argument*.

---

[27] For the detailed results see Table A.22 of Appendix A.8.1, p. 330.

The effect of performance on ownership is also non-monotonous. An increase of Tobin's Q below .22 has a negative direct effect, turning positive for higher levels and even strengthening when Tobin's Q exceeds .72. While the positive effect suits the *insider-investment argument*, there is no hypothesis explaining the negative impact. An explanation for the negative effect might consist of the investor's incentive to sell stocks realizing a gain by a relatively low loss in control. In addition, the sale could also be a planned exit option, executed as soon as a certain stock price has been reached.

The total effect depending on the concentration level does not vary in the strength of the gradients as well as in the effect's direction for the last part of the slope. It turns negative in the case of medium and highly concentrated firms. This partially stems from a mediation of the direct performance effects by ownership concentration. Since the found negative mediation does not suit the predictions on insider-investment, it probably originates from the unknown negative effect. In the case of a stock sale to realize a gain, the mediation is assumed to be negative and thus fits the observation.

The effect shape is robust for timing issues, but leads to weaker effects. In contrast, an alternation of the financial performance measure leads to significantly different estimates. Accordingly, the results are not robust for the performance definition.

5.3 Insider Ownership

After the effect of general ownership concentration was assessed, this section analyzes the first of the considered owner's identities, insider ownership. The definition of insider is first limited on managerial ownership. In a second analysis it is extended and compared to the estimates of the combined management and directors' ownership. The general equations system looks as follows:

$$\left| \begin{array}{l} Perf = MO \;\; + \text{control variables} \\ MO = Perf + \text{control variables} \end{array} \right|$$

5.3.1 Endogeneity Tests

As for the model before, the analysis starts with endogeneity tests to support the assumption of effect simultaneity. Table 5.14 shows the results of the Wu-Hausman F-test and Durbin-Wu-Hausman χ^2-test for the managerial ownership and performance variables.

Performance yields constant endogeneity. Similarly managerial ownership displays endogeneity at a significance level of 1%, except for the linear variable in combination with a piecewise performance effect. Nevertheless, endogeneity is still significant at a sufficient level of 5%. These results are also supported by the Wu-Hausman F-test and Durbin-Wu-Hausman χ^2-test for ROE. However,

Table 5.14: Wu-Hausman F-test and Durbin-Wu-Hausman χ^2-test for different relationships of managerial ownership and Tobin's Q

		Q			Mcr		
Q	Mcr	value	distr.	p-value	value	distr.	p-value
Linear	Linear	9.839	F(1, 499)	(0.002)	551.071	F(1, 496)	(0.000)
		10.074	$\chi^2(1)$	(0.002)	274.201	$\chi^2(1)$	(0.000)
	Squared	9.830	F(1, 499)	(0.002)	.	F(2, 494)	.
		10.065	$\chi^2(1)$	(0.002)	521.000	$\chi^2(2)$	(0.000)
	Piecewise	13.969	F(1, 499)	(0.000)	.	F(3, 493)	.
		14.188	$\chi^2(1)$	(0.000)	521.000	$\chi^2(3)$	(0.000)
Squared	Linear	56.492	F(2, 497)	(0.000)	103.495	F(1, 496)	(0.000)
		96.503	$\chi^2(2)$	(0.000)	89.944	$\chi^2(1)$	(0.000)
	Squared	46.714	F(2, 497)	(0.000)	52.579	F(2, 494)	(0.000)
		82.442	$\chi^2(2)$	(0.000)	91.441	$\chi^2(2)$	(0.000)
	Piecewise	48.828	F(2, 497)	(0.000)	188.858	F(3, 493)	(0.000)
		85.560	$\chi^2(2)$	(0.000)	278.588	$\chi^2(3)$	(0.000)
Piecewise	Linear	142.446	F(3, 495)	(0.000)	4.525	F(1, 496)	(0.034)
		241.390	$\chi^2(3)$	(0.000)	4.710	$\chi^2(1)$	(0.030)
	Squared	122.707	F(3, 495)	(0.000)	43.110	F(2, 494)	(0.000)
		222.207	$\chi^2(3)$	(0.000)	77.420	$\chi^2(2)$	(0.000)
	Piecewise	52.758	F(3, 495)	(0.000)	45.481	F(3, 493)	(0.000)
		126.228	$\chi^2(3)$	(0.000)	112.936	$\chi^2(3)$	(0.000)

the less significant variable for linear managerial ownership in combination with a piecewise ROE effect fails to prove endogeneity.[28]

5.3.2 Model Specification

Next, the best effect shapes are identified. Therefore, the model fits of different effect combinations are compared. Table 5.15 presents the results of the different model specifications for managerial ownership and performance. The quality of the model fit is also strongly varying, which explains the inconsistency of results.

The lowest RMSEA and χ^2 results are achieved by the squared-squared relation. However, the model fails the F-test for overall significance in both equations thus making its adequacy doubtful.[29] Also all three models with linear managerial ownership appear very well fitted in both equations, where the linear-squared relation is preferable according to the χ^2. Consequently,

---

[28] See Appendix A.8.2, Table A.23, p. 333.
[29] For the detailed results of Model 5 see Table A.24 in Appendix A.8.2, p. 333.

Table 5.15: Overview of the i3SLS regression results for different relationships between managerial ownership and Tobin's Q

piecewise[1] $\simeq \tau_1 = .73$,
piecewise[2] $\simeq \tau_1 = 10\%$, $\tau_2 = 20\%$, $\tau_3 = 30\%$ and $\tau_4 = 60\%$,
insign. = insignificant

Mcr	Q	Q equation							Mcr equation		RMSEA				χ^2
		Mcr	Mcr²	Mcr$_a$	Mcr$_b$	Mcr$_c$	Mcr$_d$	Mcr$_e$	Q / Q$_a$	Q² / Q$_b$	Q	Mcr	Q	Mcr	Mcr
Linear	Linear	insign.							insign.		0.000	0.000	459.130		55.260
	Squared	insign.							insign.	insign.	0.000	0.000	42.450		40.870
	Piecewise[1]	+							+	++	0.009	0.000	520.970		119.710
Squared	Linear								——— non solvable ———						
	Squared	−−	++						++	−−	0.000	0.000	24.710		20.460
	Piecewise[1]								——— non solvable ———						
Piecew.[2]	Linear			−−	++	+	−−	−−			0.120	0.000	4186.740		54.830
	Squared			+	insign.	insign.	+	++	insign.	insign.	0.136	0.785	5274.430		$1.606e^5$
	Piecewise[1]			+	−	insign.	+	++	+	++	0.031	0.000	735.890		132.700

Model 2 is chosen for further studies with a linear effect of managerial ownership and a squared performance effect:

$$\left| \begin{array}{l} Q = Mcr \quad + \text{control variables} \\ Mcr = Q^2 + Q + \text{control variables} \end{array} \right|$$

The Wu-Hausman F-test and Durbin-Wu-Hausman χ^2-test indicate endogeneity of both ownership and performance for this model.[30]

5.3.3 Results

Effect of Endogenous Variables

Table 5.16 gives the abbreviated I3SLS estimates for the selected model of managerial ownership.[31]

Managerial ownership fails weak significance only by .001 and has a strong negative coefficient which would support the *entrenchment argument*. Consequently, managerial ownership has no or a negative effect on performance and hence should not be promoted as agency device. Accordingly, managerial ownership enhancing activities, such as stock-based remuneration, harm the corporate value. Furthermore, both performance measures appear insignificant.

Effect of Control Variables

Since both endogenous variables are insignificant, there are no effects through endogenous variables. Consequently, there are also no feedback and indirect effects of the control variables. Hence, the direct effect matches the total effect. Generally, only a few control variables have a significant coefficient at a level of 5 or 10%. The effects are given in Table 5.17.

Only the squared size and the ease of monitoring show an effect on Tobin's Q. Increasing size has a negative effect on Tobin's Q and thus contradicts the assumed economies of scale. However, when including the linear variable with a significance level of 11%, the effect turns constantly positive and meets the prediction.[32] The ease of monitoring has the predicted positive effect, elevating performance by 1.282 through the improved monitoring.[33]

Regarding the effects on managerial ownership, again size and ease of monitoring are the only significant variables. However, this time both the linear and squared measures show an effect. The positive effect of size for all companies suits the hypotheses of Himmelberg et al. [1999] and Gugler

---

[30] See Table 5.14, p. 135.
[31] For the detailed results see Table A.24 in Appendix A.8.2, p. 333.
[32] The effect turns negative for firms exceeding € 2.036 e^{15} (35.25).
[33] For the detailed effects of the different industry groups see Table A.25 in Appendix A.8.2, p. 336.

Table 5.16: I3SLS estimates for managerial ownership and Tobin's Q

The values in brackets are the corresponding p-values
If not stated, *** implies a significance level of 1%, ** of 5% and * of 10%

	Model 2	
	Q	Mcr
Mcr	−5.484	
	(0.101)	
Q		−4.260
		(0.170)
Q^2		3.678
		(0.190)
MRatio	0.813	
OcST	−0.499	−0.142
Size	0.705	0.282*
$Size^2$	−0.020*	−0.007**
Debt	0.782	−0.101
$Debt^2$	−0.537	
Inv	−0.505	−0.005
Inv^2	0.494	
Nwc	−0.196	−0.021
Nwc^2	0.211	
Eom	1.282*	0.677*
Eom^2	−0.676	−0.348*
Beta	−0.094	−0.053
Gro	−0.007	0.034
Div	−0.046	−0.001
Age		−0.004
Ind_i	——— insignificant ———	
Time	−0.108	−0.036
constant	−5.570	−1.580
RMSE	1.517	0.348
adj. R^2	−55.909	−0.396
$Prob._{\chi^2}$	(0.008)	(0.006)
RMSEA	0.000	0.000

et al. [2003b] arguing for greater scope of moral hazard in large firms.[34] Also the ease of monitoring has a monotonously positive effect.[35] Consequently,

---

[34] The effect turns negative for firms exceeding € $3.132\ e^{17}$ (40.29).
[35] A firm had to have a Eom value above 1.945 to show a negative effect.

Table 5.17: Effects of the control variables on Tobin's Q and managerial ownership

	Q			Mcr		
	D_{Qx}	I_{Qx}	T_{Qx}	$D_{Mcr\,x}$	$I_{Mcr\,x}$	$T_{Mcr\,x}$
MRatio	0.000	0.000	0.000	0.000	0.000	0.000
OcST	0.000	0.000	0.000	0.000	0.000	0.000
Size	0.000	0.000	0.000	0.282	0.000	0.282
Size^2	−0.020	0.000	−0.020	−0.007	0.000	−0.007
Debt	0.000	0.000	0.000	0.000	0.000	0.000
Debt^2	0.000	0.000	0.000	0.000	0.000	0.000
Inv	0.000	0.000	0.000	0.000	0.000	0.000
Inv^2	0.000	0.000	0.000	0.000	0.000	0.000
Nwc	0.000	0.000	0.000	0.000	0.000	0.000
Nwc^2	0.000	0.000	0.000	0.000	0.000	0.000
Eom	1.282	0.000	1.282	0.677	0.000	0.677
Eom^2	0.000	0.000	0.000	−0.348	0.000	−0.348
Beta	0.000	0.000	0.000	0.000	0.000	0.000
Gro	0.000	0.000	0.000	0.000	0.000	0.000
Div	0.000	0.000	0.000	0.000	0.000	0.000
Age	0.000	0.000	0.000	0.000	0.000	0.000
Ind$_i$			insignificant			
Time	0.000	0.000	0.000	0.000	0.000	0.000
constant	0.000	0.000	0.000	0.000	0.000	0.000

Carney/Gedajlovic [2002]'s argument of diminished turnarounds or empire building outweighs the reduced benefits due to better monitoring.[36]

5.3.4 Robustness Concerning the Insider Definition

As shown in Chapter 2.2, there is no common definition for insider and managerial ownership. Since many studies also consider directors' shares as insider ownership, the sum of managerial and board ownership is examined as an alternative measure in the following.

The endogeneity is proven by the Wu-Hausman F-test and Durbin-Wu-Hausman χ^2-test for both variables, except for the models with piecewise performance measures where these measures appear exogenous.[37] These results are also supported by the tests on ROE.[38]

Table 5.18 gives an overview of the 13SLS results and the model fit. Again the results are not very consistent and do not indicate a clear relation. The

---

[36] For the detailed effects of the different industry groups see Table A.25 in Appendix A.8.2, p. 336. For the non-causal effects see Table A.26 in Appendix A.8.2, p. 337.
[37] For a table with the results see Table A.27 in Appendix A.8.2, p. 338.
[38] For a table with the results see Table A.28 in Appendix A.8.2, p. 338.

Table 5.18: Overview of the i3SLS regression results for different relationships between managerial and board ownership and Tobin's Q

piecewise^1 ≃ τ_1=.5 and τ_2=.8,
piecewise^2 ≃ τ_1=10%, τ_2=30% and τ_3=50%,
insign. = insignificant

Mbcr	Q	Q equation					Mbcr equation			RMSEA		χ^2	
		Mbcr	Mbcr²	Mbcr$_a$	Mbcr$_b$	Mbcr$_c$ Mbcr$_d$	Q / Q$_a$	Q² / Q$_b$	Q$_c$	Q	Mbcr	Q	Mbcr
Linear	Linear	insign.					insign.			0.000	0.000	457.370	55.180
	Squared	--					insign.	insign.		0.000	0.000	234.830	221.990
	Piecewise^1	-					-	-	--	0.000	0.032	111.430	766.310
Squared	Linear		insign.				--			0.000	0.000	199.360	60.360
	Squared		++				++	--		0.000	0.000	48.770	34.080
	Piecewise^1		insign.				-	-	--	0.331	0.023	28,951.550	642.170
Piecew.²	Linear			insign.	insign.	- --	--			0.200	0.000	10,804.970	90.330
	Squared			insign.	insign.	insign. --	++	--		0.036	0.000	836.890	841.430
	Piecewise^1			insign.	insign.	-- --	-	-	--	0.088	0.030	2,509.760	726.060

squared-squared model yields the best model fit and is hence chosen for the following analysis:

$$\begin{vmatrix} Q = Mbcr^2 + Mbcr & + \text{control variables} \\ Mbcr = Q^2 + Q & + \text{control variables} \end{vmatrix}$$

Endogeneity is proven for these effect shapes.

Table 5.19 compares the 13SLS estimates and their probability values for the combined insider ownership to those of the pure managerial ownership model.[39] The endogenous variables are weakly significant resulting in nonlinear effects in both direction. As demonstrated in Table 5.20, the strength of the direct effect of managerial and directors' ownership depends on the already existing level of ownership. The total effect and the feedback even depend on both endogenous variables.

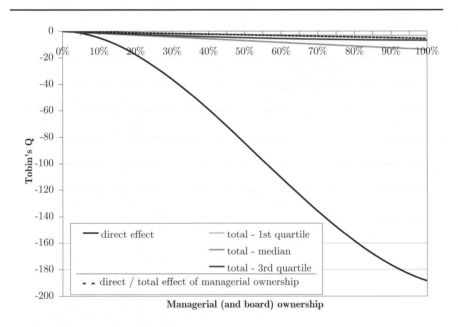

Fig. 5.7: Effects of managerial and board insider ownership on Tobin's Q for different performance levels

A closer examination of the direct effect function reveals that the effect is turning from negative to positive at 110% which obviously lies outside the natural boundary of ownership. Consequently, the effect of insider ownership

---

[39] For the detailed results see Table A.29 of Appendix A.8.2, p. 339.

Table 5.19: I3SLS estimates for managerial and board ownership and Tobin's Q

The values in brackets are the corresponding p-values
If not stated, *** implies a significance level of 1%, ** of 5% and * of 10%.

	Mbcr - Model 5		Mcr - Model 2	
	Q	Mbcr		Q	Mcr
Mbcr	−9.541	Mcr	−5.484	
	(0.057)		(0.101)	
Mbcr^2	8.671	Mcr^2		
	(0.087)			
Q		7.056		−4.260
		(0.082)		(0.170)
Q^2		−6.662		3.678
		(0.070)		(0.190)
MbRatio	−1.784*	MRatio	0.813	
OcST	−0.053	0.074	−0.499	−0.142
Size	0.145	−0.158	0.705	0.282*
Size^2	−0.007	0.003	−0.020*	−0.007**
Debt	0.717	0.451*	0.782	−0.101
Debt^2	−0.711		−0.537	
Inv	−0.162	−0.177*	−0.505	−0.005
Inv^2	−0.365		0.494	
Nwc	0.301	0.025	−0.196	−0.021
Nwc^2	−0.181		0.211	
Eom	0.787	−0.540	1.282*	0.677*
Eom^2	−0.426	0.281	−0.676	−0.348*
Beta	0.229	0.069	−0.094	−0.053
Gro	0.164	−0.040	−0.007	0.034
Div	−0.059	−0.032	−0.046	−0.001
Age		0.024		−0.004
Ind$_i$	———————	partly significant	———————	
Time	−0.092	−0.006	−0.108	−0.036
constant	2.224	0.546	−5.570	−1.580
RMSE	1.103	0.435	1.517	0.348
pseudo $\bar{R}^2$	−29.109	−0.930	−55.909	−0.396
Prob.$_{\chi^2}$	(0.002)	(0.036)	(0.008)	(0.006)
RMSEA	0.000	0.000	0.000	0.000

5.3 Insider Ownership

Table 5.20: Effects of managerial and board ownership on Tobin's Q

	Mbcr effects
$D_{Q\,Mbcr}$	$-9.541 + 8.671 * Mbcr$
$T_{Q\,Mbcr}$	$\dfrac{-9.541 + 8.671 * Mbcr}{68.321 + 63.562 * Q + 61.183 * Mbcr - 57.766 * Mbcr * Q}$
$T_{Mbcr\,Mbcr}$	$\dfrac{1}{68.321 + 63.562 * Q + 61.183 * Mbcr - 57.766 * Mbcr * Q}$

on performance is constantly negative and hence supports the *entrenchment argument*. Also the weakly significant divergence ratio fits the negative effect assumed by the entrenchment argument.

In Figure 5.7 the direct effect of combined insider ownership is graphically compared to the total effects on companies with a Tobin's Q equalling the first quartile, the median, and the third quartile. All total effects are much weaker than the direct effect. Due to the non-monotonous feedback of performance the Tobin's Q has no monotonous mediating effect. This leads to the strongest negative total effects for a median performance, followed by those for the third quartile and those for the first quartile.

If the slightly insignificant effect of managerial ownership is also included in Figure 5.7, the results seem to be more robust than assumed on first sight. Both direct effects show a negative sign. While the direct effects strongly differ in their strength, the total effects resemble each other even in the gradient. Given the similarity to the pure managerial ownership effect, these results lead to the same conclusion indicating a *managerial entrenchment*.

Table 5.21: Effects of Tobin's Q on managerial and board ownership

	Q effects
$D_{Mbcr\,Q}$	$7.056 - 6.662 * Q$
$T_{Mbcr\,Q}$	$\dfrac{7.056 - 6.662 * Q}{68.321 + 63.562 * Q + 61.183 * Mbcr - 57.766 * Mbcr * Q}$
$T_{Q\,Q}$	$\dfrac{1}{68.321 + 63.562 * Q + 61.183 * Mbcr - 57.766 * Mbcr * Q}$

As displayed in Table 5.21, the strength of the direct effect of performance on insider ownership depends on the performance level. Again a closer examination reveals a constant effect direction. The resulting direct effect suits the assumption of a positive influence through the *reward* and *investment hypothe-*

144   5 Empirical Analyses

ses.[40] The total effect are further determined by the corresponding ownership level. As demonstrated in Figure 5.8, again the feedback effect weakens total effect compared to the direct one. Nevertheless, this time the increasing ownership level has a constantly positive effect on the total effect of the Tobin's Q.

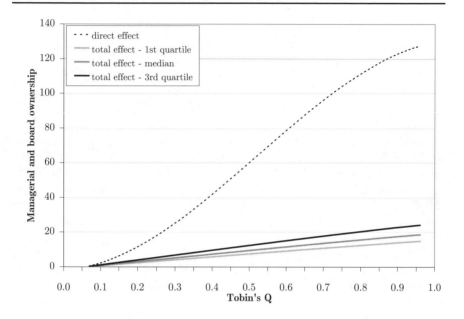

Fig. 5.8: Effects of Tobin's Q on management and board insider ownership for different ownership levels

The differing estimates of the two models and, thus, the missing robustness can stem from two major causes. First, the combined management and directors' ownership may proxy insider ownership better, since also directors have to be classified as insiders. Second, it could also indicate a dilution of the relation of pure managerial ownership and performance, if directors constitute a different type of insiders than the management does. The different utility functions and the degree of control would alienate the effects of pure managerial ownership.

The origins of the changes can be verified by running a model only with directors' ownership. Estimates similar to those of the management and board ownership model would indicate that the effects of directors' ownership proba-

---

[40] The function of the direct effect equals zero for 1.06, which is not achieved in this sample.

bly dominate and cover the effects of managerial ownership. The effects found in the combined insider model would originate only from the directors and consequently, management and directors would have to be modelled separately.

Table 5.22: I3SLS estimates for directors', management and combined ownership and Tobin's Q

	Dcr - Model 5		Mbcr - Model 5		Mcr - Model 2	
	Q	Dcr	Q	Mbcr	Q	Mcr
O	−35.904		−9.541		−5.484	
	(0.111)		(0.057)		(0.101)	
O^2	46.608		8.671			
	(0.116)		(0.087)			
Q		−8.585		7.056		−4.260
		(0.002)		(0.082)		(0.170)
Q^2		7.608		−6.662		3.678
		(0.003)		(0.070)		(0.190)
RMSE	1.660	0.407	1.103	0.435	1.517	0.348
pseudo $\bar{R}^2$	−67.149	−6.799	−29.109	−0.930	−55.909	−0.396
Prob.$_{\chi^2}$	(0.999)	(0.926)	(0.002)	(0.036)	(0.008)	(0.006)
RMSEA	0.000	0.000	0.000	0.000	0.000	0.000

Table 5.22 compares the basic results of a model only considering directors' shareholding to those of the two previous models covering pure managerial ownership and combined insider shareholding. The effect of board ownership on Tobin's Q is insignificant by less than 2% and passes zero at 77%. This value is not exceeded in the sample, which leads to a constantly negative effect. It indicates again an *entrenchment effect*, resembling the results of combined insider ownership. But since pure managerial ownership yields similar, only slightly insignificant results, the effect cannot be used to distinguish between an origination from management and from directors. The performance effect is constantly negative and resembles the estimates of management ownership and but contradicts the combined results. This does not support a dominance of the effects of directors altering the estimates of the combined insider model. Consequently, the results do not indicate a divergence in the identities, and hence, management and directors can be modelled together. Finally, the equations of the directors' model fail the χ^2-test of overall significance. Hence, this also does not support a dominant effect and indicate a similarity in the identities and their behavior.

5.3.5 Further Robustness Checks

In addition to the robustness regarding the insider definition, the effects of timing issues and the choice of performance measure are analyzed.

The *timing of effects* may play an important role considering that the reward and the insider-reward hypotheses argue for a lagged relation. Again two alternated models including previous year's data are considered. Table 5.23 states their results.[41] While the first alternation includes only the Tobin's Q of the previous year, the second also alters the other accounting variables by taking the previous year's equivalents.

The inclusion of the performance data of the previous year does not alter the sign of the ownership coefficient but even increases the significance. The shape of the performance effect of the first alternation resemble those of the original model. However, in both of these models the estimates are insignificant. In contrast, all four performance coefficients in the second alternation are highly significant. While the Tobin's Q variables of the previous year present a similar effect as the Tobin's Q coefficients in the original model, the variables of the current year show a reverted effect. The two effects are almost equally strong.

Since the first alternation shows no significance at all for the Tobin's Q variables, the interpretation of the results of the second alternation as indicators for a lagged effect becomes questionable. It could also be that there are two contradicting effects which not necessarily differ in their point of time. The this year's and previous year's Tobin's Q variables are strongly correlated and have only a tolerance of 28.84%.[42] Due to this high overlap in the variables, the two contradicting effects may just be randomly split up on the variables. If these contradicting effects are forced on the Tobin's Q variables of one year, they outbalance each other due to their similar strength. This would explain the insignificance of performance in the original model. Furthermore, the model fit of the second alternation is the lowest of all three models which does not support the superiority of the model specification.

Consequently, the estimates appear robust to timing issues up to a certain degree. While the ownership coefficients resemble each other, the robustness of the Tobin's Q effect is unclear.

Finally, the robustness regarding an *alternative performance measure*, the ROE, is tested. Table 5.24 displays the estimates, which differ from those of the Tobin's Q model.[43] The ownership variable is negative but insignificant and hence resembles that of the pure managerial ownership model. The ROE coefficients are both positive and significant and lead to a constant positive effect. A similar effect was found in the combined insider model. However, it is arguable if these resemblances to different models are sufficient to call the results robust.

---

[41] For the detailed results see Table A.30 of Appendix A.8.2, p. 341.
[42] The correlation between Q and Q^{t-1} is .844.
[43] For the detailed results see Table A.31 of Appendix A.8.2, p. 343.

5.3 Insider Ownership

Table 5.23: Robustness checks on lagged measures of Tobin's Q for insider ownership

	Alternation 1		Alternation 2		Original	
	Q	Mcr	Q	Mcr	Q	Mcr
Mcr	−2.973		−0.661		−5.484	
	(0.043)		(0.000)		(0.101)	
Q		−1.926		3.033		−4.260
		(0.373)		(0.001)		(0.170)
Q^2		1.437		−3.641		3.678
		(0.464)		(0.000)		(0.190)
Q^{t-1}		1.214		−3.527		
		(0.469)		(0.000)		
$Q^{2\,t-1}$		−1.111		2.873		
		(0.472)		(0.000)		
Mratio	0.061		−0.001		0.813	
OcST	−0.227	−0.078	−0.019	−0.041	−0.499	−0.142
Size	0.481**	0.188**	0.213***	0.231***	0.705	0.282*
$Size^2$	−0.014**	−0.005**	−0.005***	−0.006***	−0.020*	−0.007**
Debt	0.460	0.103	0.143	0.244***	0.782	−0.101
$Debt^2$	−0.185		−0.035		−0.537	
Inv	−0.210	−0.024	0.174***	−0.020	−0.505	−0.005
Inv^2	0.164		−0.156***		0.494	
Nwc	−0.287	−0.002	−0.091	−0.030	−0.196	−0.021
Nwc^2	0.275		0.090		0.211	
Eom	0.951**	0.415**	0.591***	0.646***	1.282*	0.677*
Eom^2	−0.445*	−0.189**	−0.222***	−0.237***	−0.676	−0.348*
Beta	−0.070	−0.034	−0.036	−0.021	−0.094	−0.053
Gro	0.011	0.023	0.087***	−0.043	−0.007	0.034
Div	−0.025	−0.008	−0.003	−0.006	−0.046	−0.001
Age		−0.002		0.004		−0.004
Ind_i			———— partly significant ————			
Time	−0.065	−0.029	−0.036	−0.042	−0.108	−0.036
constant	−3.488	−1.377	−1.803***	−1.799**	−5.570	−1.580
RMSE	0.837	0.290	0.229	0.347	1.517	0.348
pseudo $\bar{R}^2$	−16.329	0.032	−0.294	−0.384	−55.909	−0.396
Prob.$_{\chi^2}$	(0.000)	(0.000)	(0.000)	(0.000)	(0.008)	(0.006)
RMSEA	0.034	0.000	0.000	0.037	0.000	0.000

Table 5.24: Robustness checks on ROE for insider ownership

	ROE		Q	
	ROE	Icr	Q	Icr
Mcr	−2.538		−5.484	
	(0.370)		(0.101)	
ROE		0.128 Q		−4.260
		(0.006)		(0.170)
ROE^2		0.018 Q^2		3.678
		(0.022)		(0.190)
Mratio	1.824*		0.813	
OcST	−0.706*	−0.050	−0.499	−0.142
Size	−0.234	0.109	0.705	0.282*
Size^2	0.005	−0.004*	−0.020*	−0.007**
Debt	−2.684**	0.021	0.782	−0.101
Debt^2	5.852***		−0.537	
Inv	−1.282***	0.066	−0.505	−0.005
Inv^2	−0.664**		0.494	
Nwc	3.319***	−0.066	−0.196	−0.021
Nwc^2	−3.200***		0.211	
Eom	−0.133	0.276**	1.282*	0.677*
Eom^2	−0.110	−0.155**	−0.676	−0.348*
Beta	−0.126	0.014	−0.094	−0.053
Gro	−0.027	−0.001	−0.007	0.034
Div	−0.076	0.002	−0.046	−0.001
Age		0.004		−0.004
Ind$_i$		partly significant		
Time	−0.025	−0.028	−0.108	−0.036
constant	1.418	−0.767	−5.570	−1.580
RMSE	1.036	0.295	1.517	0.348
pseudo $\bar{R}^2$	−0.210	−0.001	−55.909	−0.396
Prob.$_{\chi^2}$	(0.000)	(0.000)	(0.008)	(0.006)
RMSEA	0.000	0.000	0.000	0.000

5.3.6 Summary

The estimates of the different models on managerial ownership do not yield consistent results and show many insignificant coefficients. In contrast to the frequent assumption of a nonlinear and non-monotonous ownership effect, the linear-squared relation of insider ownership and performance achieves the best model fit in the study.[44] The chosen model displays no significant estimates for the endogenous variables. However, the managerial ownership effect fails significance only slightly by .1%. Its negative coefficient indicates a dominance of the *entrenchment effect*.

The inclusion of board shares alters the results and shows the importance of the insider ownership definition. The best fitted relation combines the squared ownership effect with again the squared performance. All endogenous variables show weak significance. The nonlinear insider ownership effect is constantly negative, supporting the *entrenchment effect*. This result is similar and at the same time more significant than that of pure managerial ownership. The strength of the direct effect depends on the level of the endogenous variable itself, while the total effect is even determined by both, ownership and performance. All total effects are weaker than the direct effect. In addition, they strongly resemble the total effects of pure managerial ownership. The nonlinear positive effect of performance on insider ownership suits the hypotheses of the *insider-investment* and *reward arguments*.

While the increased significance and the effects, fulfilling the predictions, indicate an improved proxy quality for insider ownership, the alternation of the results could also originate by different identity characteristics of directors and managers. This was tested by a separate estimation of pure board ownership and performance. The results show that the effect of the model with combined insider ownership cannot stem from pure board ownership and that the estimation is not strictly robust with regard to the definition of insider ownership. The denotation of board and management as insiders seems to improve the model.

The robustness of the results with regard to timing issues and the selected performance measures is questionable in both cases.

5.4 Institutional Ownership

This section analyzes the second owner's identity, the institutional ownership. The considered equations system equals:

$$\left| \begin{array}{l} Perf = IO \quad + \text{control variables} \\ IO = Perf + \text{control variables} \end{array} \right|$$

Again the endogeneity is tested first to assure the applicability of simultaneous equations estimation. In a second step, the modelled shapes of effects are selected by a comparison of the model fits. The thereby specified model is

---

[44] For a non-monotonous relation see for example Brailsford et al. [2002], Chen et al. [1993], Chen/Ho [2000], Cho [1998], Cleary [2000], Cui/Mak [2002], Gugler et al. [2003b], Hermalin/Weisbach [1991], Hubbard/Palia [1995], Kole [1996], Mørck et al. [1988], Mudambi/Nicosia [1998], Short/Keasey [1999], Short et al. [2002a, 1994], Stulz [1988], and Welch [2003].

150   5 Empirical Analyses

then estimated and its results are discussed. Robustness checks finalize the analysis and its results are concluded.

5.4.1 Endogeneity Tests

Again general endogeneity tests by the Wu-Hausman F-test and Durbin-Wu-Hausman χ^2-test are performed for the different potential relationships to ensure the need of simultaneous estimations.

Table 5.25: Wu-Hausman F-test and Durbin-Wu-Hausman χ^2-test for different relationships of institutional ownership and Tobin's Q

			Icr			Q	
Icr	Q	value	distr.	p-value	value	distr.	p-value
Linear	Linear	3.647	F(1, 497)	(0.057)	0.106	F(1, 499)	(0.745)
		3.795	$\chi^2(1)$	(0.051)	0.111	$\chi^2(1)$	(0.739)
	Squared	1.525	F(1, 497)	(0.217)	71.191	F(2, 497)	(0.000)
		1.594	$\chi^2(1)$	(0.207)	116.020	$\chi^2(2)$	(0.000)
	Piecewise	140.764	F(1, 497)	(0.000)	455.486	F(3, 495)	(0.000)
		114.992	$\chi^2(1)$	(0.000)	382.455	$\chi^2(3)$	(0.000)
Squared	Linear	$1.190e^{14}$	F(2, 495)	(0.000)	0.105	F(1, 499)	(0.745)
		521.000	$\chi^2(2)$	(0.000)	0.110	$\chi^2(1)$	(0.740)
	Squared	80.068	F(2, 495)	(0.000)	64.406	F(2, 497)	(0.000)
		127.348	$\chi^2(2)$	(0.000)	107.239	$\chi^2(2)$	(0.000)
	Piecewise	96.856	F(2, 495)	(0.000)	38.292	F(3, 495)	(0.000)
		146.541	$\chi^2(2)$	(0.000)	98.136	$\chi^2(3)$	(0.000)
Piecewise	Linear	.	F(3, 494)	.	18.143	F(1, 499)	(0.000)
		521.000	$\chi^2(3)$	(0.000)	26.150	$\chi^2(1)$	(0.000)
	Squared	674.289	F(3, 494)	(0.000)	114.237	F(2, 497)	(0.000)
		418.740	$\chi^2(3)$	(0.000)	164.079	$\chi^2(2)$	(0.000)
	Piecewise	62.565	F(3, 494)	(0.000)	22.610	F(3, 495)	(0.000)
		143.449	$\chi^2(3)$	(0.000)	62.789	$\chi^2(3)$	(0.000)

The results in Table 5.25 show almost constant endogeneity for institutional ownership. Only the results for a linear measure with the linear and quadratic performance variables indicate exogeneity. Performance, too, yields no significance for linear and squared institutional ownership in combination with a linear performance variable.[45]

---

[45] The endogeneity assumption is also supported by the Wu-Hausman F-test and Durbin-Wu-Hausman χ^2-test for ROE implying high endogeneity. See Table A.32 in Appendix A.8.3, p. 345.

5.4.2 Model Specification

Table 5.26 gives an overview over the I3SLS regression results for the different model specifications.

The models show a generally good model fit. Therefore, not only the RMSEA but also the χ^2 is taken into consideration. A lower χ^2 indicates a better fit. The best model fit is achieved by the linear-squared, linear-piecewise and the squared-squared relations. Unfortunately, the models with squared performance effects fail the F-test for the overall significance of the equation and are consequently excluded from further considerations. Accordingly, in the remaining and further used model institutional ownership is displayed as linear and performance as piecewise variables with the turning points of .5 and .7:

$$\begin{vmatrix} Q = Icr & + \text{control variables} \\ Icr = Q_{Q \leq .5} + Q_{.5 < Q \leq .7} + Q_{Q > .7} + \text{control variables} \end{vmatrix}$$

Endogeneity is proven for these relations in the previous section.[46]

5.4.3 Results

Effects of Endogenous Variables

After the specification of the applied model, this section analyzes and decomposes the different effects. Table 5.27 presents the results of the I3SLS estimation.[47]

The coefficients represent the direct effects. These direct effects together with the feedback loop created by the non-recursive relation constitute the total effect. Table 5.28 presents both direct and total effects of institutional ownership on performance. The direct effect is -1.245 and supports the *strategic alignment-conflict of interest* and *institutional myopic behavior*. Accordingly, institutional investors do not improve corporate performance. Apart from omission of monitoring actions they even might impose myopic investment behavior at the expense of value-creating, long-term investments.

Table 5.28: Feedback effects of institutional ownership on Tobin's Q and itself

	$D_{Q\,Icr}$	$T_{Q\,Icr}$			$T_{Icr\,Icr}$		
		Q_a	Q_b	Q_c	Q_a	Q_b	Q_c
Icr	−1.245	−0.856	−1.995	2.111	0.688	1.603	−1.695

---

[46] See Table 5.25, p. 150.
[47] For the detailed estimates and p-values see Appendix A.8.3 Table A.33, p. 345.

Table 5.26: Overview of the iterated three-stage least squares regression results for different relationships between institutional ownership and Tobin's Q

piecewise$^1 \simeq \tau_1=.5$ and $\tau_2=.7$,
piecewise$^2 \simeq \tau_1=10\%$, $\tau_2=20\%$ and $\tau_3=40\%$,
insign. = insignificant

Icr: Linear

Q		Q equation		Icr equation			RMSEA		χ^2	
		Icr	Icr²	Q/Q$_a$	Q²/Q$_b$	Q$_c$	Q	Icr	Q	Icr
	Linear	insign.		insign.			0.010	0.000	526.430	237.300
	Squared	insign.		insign.	insign.		0.000	0.000	23.980	373.830
	Piecewise¹	−		+	−	−	0.000	0.000	128.170	381.990

Icr: Squared

Q		Q equation		Icr equation			RMSEA		χ^2	
		Icr	Icr²	Q/Q$_a$	Q²/Q$_b$	Q$_c$	Q	Icr	Q	Icr
	Linear	insign.	insign.	insign.			0.017	0.000	575.890	233.830
	Squared	insign.	insign.	++	− −		0.000	0.000	3.450	36.090
	Piecewise¹	insign.	insign.	+	−	−	0.076	0.004	1991.960	503.330

Icr: Piecew.²

Q		Q equation				Icr equation			RMSEA		χ^2	
		Icr$_a$	Icr$_b$	Icr$_c$	Icr$_d$	Q/Q$_a$	Q²/Q$_b$	Q$_c$	Q	Icr	Q	Icr
	Linear	−	−	insign.	−	insign.			0.037	0.000	842.170	235.800
	Squared	insign.	+	+	+	insign.	insign.		0.328	0.868	28254.420	196521.380
	Piecewise¹	−	−	−	−	+	−	−	0.087	0.005	2454.070	506.480

Table 5.27: Iterated three-stage least squares estimates for institutional ownership and Tobin's Q

The values in brackets are the corresponding p-values
If not stated, *** implies a significance level of 1%, ** of 5% and * of 10%.

	Q	Icr
Icr	−1.051	
	(0.001)	
$Q_{0 \leq x \leq .5}$		0.365
		(0.003)
$Q_{.5 \leq x \leq .7}$		−0.302
		(0.021)
$Q_{.7 \leq x}$		−1.277
		(0.000)
IRatio	0.000	
OcST	0.952***	0.831***
Size	0.509***	0.283**
Size^2	−0.012***	−0.006**
Debt	0.097	0.128
Debt^2	−0.003	
Inv	−0.054	−0.046
Inv^2	−0.252***	
Nwc	−0.389	0.154
Nwc^2	0.601*	
Eom	0.538**	0.160
Eom^2	−0.247	−0.065
Beta	−0.070	−0.023
Gro	−0.22*	−0.226**
Div	−0.06**	−0.049***
Age		0.010
Ind$_i$	— insignificant —	
Time	0.060	0.054
constant	−4.678***	−2.826**
RMSE	0.508	0.199
pseudo $\bar{R}^2$	−6.756	0.363
Prob.$_{\chi^2}$	(0.000)	(0.000)
RMSEA	0.000	0.000

154   5 Empirical Analyses

The total effect depends again on the feedback effect of the performance variables and therefore varies over the different levels of Tobin's Q. While for Tobin's Q values below .5 the total effect is weaker, the negative effect amplifies for firms with a medium performance level. In contrast, the feedback yields a positive total effect for very well performing companies. One origin for this change in the effect sign is the feedback of institutional ownership on itself. While for Tobin's Qs below .7 it reinforces itself, an increase finally causes a reduction in ownership for high Tobin's Q firms. Another reason could be a mediation effect of the Tobin's Q. This can be detected by a comparison of the direct effects of subsamples based on Tobin's Q levels with those of the total sample. However, the iterations within the 3SLS regressions of the subsamples do not yield results leaving the equations systems unsolvable; thus potential mediation is not analyzable.

Table 5.29 shows the direct and total effects of Tobin's Q on institutional ownership and the feedback effects on itself. The direct effect is positive (.365) for a Tobin's Qs below .5. This supports the *insider-investment argument* and the *Wall Street Rule*. However, passing this threshold the effect is -.302 and strengthens to -1.277 for Tobin's Qs exceeding .7. There are three potential explanations for the unpredicted negative effect. First, institutional investors of well performing firms might rather use the increase of Tobin's Q to realize a gain by selling parts of their share than to increase their shareholdings. This might especially be the case if they already hold relatively large shares and do not want to focus their risk by undiversified large shareholdings in one company. A second argument bases also on the diversification of the portfolio of the institutional investors. If the investors evaluate their diversification partially by market values, an increase in the Tobin's Q elevates the relative share of the company in the portfolio. Accordingly, the investors will reduce their share to balance the portfolio. Finally, some institutional investors might also have planned the sale at a certain Tobin's Q as an exit channel of an investment. In addition, the quasi $\bar{R}^2$ of the Tobin's Q equation indicates a low explanatory power of the equation. This raises the question of omitted important variables, which could also distort the estimates.

Table 5.29: Feedback effects of Tobin's Q on institutional ownership and itself

	D_{IcrQ}	T_{IcrQ}	T_{QQ}
Q_a	0.365	0.251	−0.454
Q_b	−0.302	−0.485	0.376
Q_c	−1.277	2.164	1.590

The gradients of the total effects are reduced for the first and second part of the slope, from .365 to .251 and from -.302 to -.485. However, for performance values above .7, the non-recursive relation has a very strong impact on the total effect, where it turns from -1.277 to a positive 2.164. Figure 5.9 demonstrates and compares the total effect to the direct effect. The feedback of Tobin's Q on itself changes for increasing values from negative -.454 to .376 and finally to 1.590.

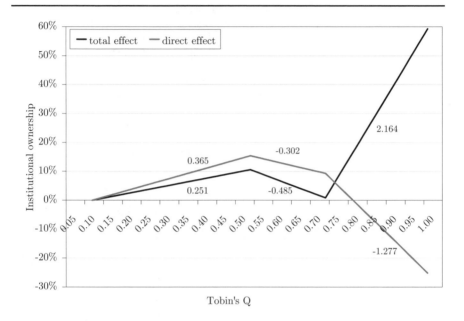

Fig. 5.9: Direct and total effects of Tobin's Q on institutional ownership

Effects of Control Variables

Most control variables are insignificant. Financial leverage, beta, all industry groups, and time are insignificant in even both equations. Table 5.30 presents the direct, indirect, and total effects of the control variables on Tobin's Q.[48] As before only the direct effects can be compared to the proposed hypotheses.[49]

The size of the second and third largest shareholders show the predicted positive effect with a coefficient of .952. Similar to the results of the ownership concentration equation, the size shows the assumed, constant positive

---

[48] The full information is given by Table A.34 in Appendix A.8.3, p. 348. Furthermore, the noncausal effects are shown in Table A.36, p. 350.
[49] For the hypothesized effects see Chapter 4.4.4, p. 93, and Table 4.6, p. 103.

Table 5.30: Effects of the control variables on Tobin's Q

	D_{Qx}	I_{Qx}	T_{Qx}
IRatio	0.000	0.000	0.000
OcST	0.952	−1.159	−0.207
Size	0.509	−0.116	0.393
Size^2	−0.012	0.001	−0.011
Debt	0.000	0.000	0.000
Debt^2	0.000	0.000	0.000
Inv	0.000	0.000	0.000
Inv^2	−0.252	−0.381	−0.633
Nwc	0.000	0.000	0.000
Nwc^2	0.601	0.908	1.509
Eom	0.538	0.813	1.351
Eom^2	0.000	0.000	0.000
Beta	0.000	0.000	0.000
Gro	−0.220	0.374	0.154
Div	−0.060	0.063	0.003
Age	0.000	0.000	0.000
Ind$_i$	———	insignificant	———
Time	0.000	0.000	0.000
constant	−4.678	1.766	−2.913

effect.[50] Debt appears insignificant in contrast to the significant estimates of the ownership concentration equation. This indicates the importance of control for ownership concentration, whose absence alters the results. Similar to the ownership concentration results, only the squared investment level is significant and shows a negative effect on Tobin's Q. One reason could be an over-investment increasing the investment level but decreasing the value of the firm. Furthermore, investment activities are probably linked to other variables such as the financial leverage. These mediation effects could also cause the negative effect. The NWC supports the hypothesis of a positive effect by a significant squared measure. The ease of monitoring shows the assumed positive effect on Tobin's Q through the linear variable. While beta marginally fails significance with a probability value of .118, it again shows the negative sign contradicting the assumption. Also the significant growth variable does not suit the hypothesis with a negative coefficient of -.220. This can be explained by no value-adding growth, e.g., due to empire building. In contrast, the coefficient of diversification supports the assumptions by a negative effect on Tobin's Q of -.060. Both firm age and time are insignificant.

Most of the direct effects of the control variables on institutional ownership are also insignificant with the exceptions of the share of the second and third

---

[50] The effect becomes zero at 42.42.

largest owners, size, growth, and diversification. The different effects are shown in Table 5.31.[51]

Table 5.31: Effects of the control variables on institutional ownership

		Q_a		Q_b		Q_c	
	$D_{Icr\,x}$	$I_{Icr\,x}$	$T_{Icr\,x}$	$I_{Icr\,x}$	$T_{Icr\,x}$	$I_{Icr\,x}$	$T_{Icr\,x}$
IRatio	0.000	0.000	0.000	0.000	0.000	0.000	0.000
OcST	0.831	0.495	1.326	−0.410	0.421	−1.732	−0.901
Size	0.283	0.338	0.621	−0.280	0.003	−1.182	−0.900
Size^2	−0.006	−0.008	−0.015	0.007	0.000	0.029	0.023
Debt	0.000	0.000	0.000	0.000	0.000	0.000	0.000
Debt^2	0.000	0.000	0.000	0.000	0.000	0.000	0.000
Inv	0.000	0.000	0.000	0.000	0.000	0.000	0.000
Inv^2	0.000	−0.231	−0.231	0.191	0.191	0.808	0.808
Nwc	0.000	0.000	0.000	0.000	0.000	0.000	0.000
Nwc^2	0.000	0.551	0.551	−0.456	−0.456	−1.927	−1.927
Eom	0.000	0.493	0.493	−0.408	−0.408	−1.725	−1.725
Eom^2	0.000	0.000	0.000	0.000	0.000	0.000	0.000
Beta	0.000	0.000	0.000	0.000	0.000	0.000	0.000
Gro	−0.226	−0.099	−0.325	0.082	−0.144	0.346	0.120
Div	−0.049	−0.033	−0.082	0.027	−0.022	0.115	0.065
Age	0.000	0.000	0.000	0.000	0.000	0.000	0.000
Ind$_i$	———————————————			insignificant		———————————————	
Time	0.000	0.000	0.000	0.000	0.000	0.000	0.000
constant	−2.826	−3.004	−5.830	2.485	−0.341	10.510	7.684

The share of the second and third largest owner has a positive impact on the size of institutional investors, as they perceive the risk of private benefits as reduced and good performance as more likely. Also the coefficient of size fulfills the positive effect predicted by Agrawal/Knoeber [1996].[52] Finally, both growth and diversification show the predicted negative sign.

5.4.4 Robustness Checks

Next, the results are tested for robustness. Although there are no specific arguments for lagged effects of institutional ownership, two general indicators for the potential existence of *timing issues* exist. On the one hand, the natural selection hypothesis implies a lagged relation. On the other hand, the ownership structure may adapt only slowly. Consequently, the effect is only

---

[51] The full information is given by Table A.35 in Appendix A.8.3, p. 349. Furthermore, the noncausal effects are shown in Table A.37, p. 351.
[52] Only if a company exceeded 47.16 (€ 3.05 e^{20}), the effect would be negative.

observable when considering more than one period. Therefore, the robustness regarding timing issues is tested in the following.

Again two alternated models including previous year's data are considered. Both alternations include the Tobin's Q of the previous year. The thresholds for the previous year's piecewise variables are adjusted to .45 and .6. The second alternation additionally substitutes the control variables of the current year by their equivalents of the previous year. To avoid multicollinearity problems through the inclusion of the Tobin's Q data of both years, the tolerance is tested in the first step. Multicollinearity appears slightly critical only for the high Tobin's Q variables of both years.[53] Table 5.32 states the results for the two alternations.[54]

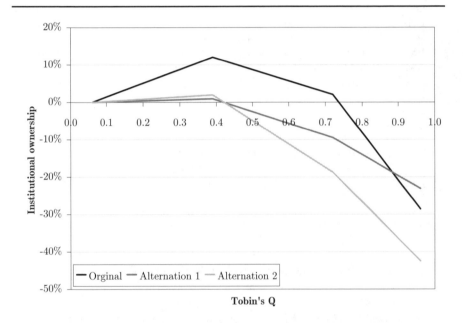

Fig. 5.10: Direct effects of Tobin's Q and previous year's Tobin's Q on institutional ownership

Comparing the different models, the inclusion of previous year's data alters the strength of the institutional ownership gradient, but keeps the basic direction of a negative effect. Furthermore, the coefficients of current year's Tobin's Q are reduced, since in the alternated models the effects are partially displayed by the Tobin's Q of the previous year. This is especially the case for

---

[53] For the correlation and tolerance values see Table A.38 of Appendix A.8.3, p. 351.
[54] For the detailed results see Table A.39 of Appendix A.8.3, p. 352.

Table 5.32: Robustness checks on lagged measures of Tobin's Q for institutional ownership

	Alternation 1		Alternation 2		Original	
	Q	Icr	Q	Icr	Q	Icr
Icr	−2.357		−0.861		−1.051	
	(0.010)		(0.000)		(0.001)	
Q_a		0.028		0.060		0.365
		(0.051)		(0.076)		(0.003)
Q_b		−0.315		−0.627		−0.302
		(0.000)		(0.000)		(0.021)
Q_c		−0.567		−0.988		−1.277
		(0.010)		(0.000)		(0.000)
Q_a^{t-1}		0.063		0.145		
		(0.001)		(0.000)		
Q_b^{t-1}		−0.100		−0.275		
		(0.402)		(0.053)		
Q_c^{t-1}		−0.168		−0.531		
		(0.011)		(0.000)		
Iratio	−0.001		−0.001		0.000	
OcST	1.433***	0.601***	0.559***	0.617***	0.952***	0.831***
Size	0.293**	0.060	0.246***	0.091*	0.509***	0.283**
Size^2	−0.006**	−0.001	−0.006***	−0.002	−0.012***	−0.006**
Debt	0.351*	0.088	0.304***	0.138***	0.097	0.128
Debt^2	−0.263		−0.328**		−0.003	
Inv	0.132	0.023	0.143***	−0.011	−0.054	−0.046
Inv^2	−0.073**		−0.120***		−0.252***	
Nwc	−0.292	0.026	−0.503***	−0.026	−0.389	0.154
Nwc^2	0.340		0.471***		0.601*	
Eom	0.609***	0.106	0.534***	0.196***	0.538**	0.160
Eom^2	−0.225*	−0.038	−0.184***	−0.056*	−0.247	−0.065
Beta	−0.003	0.007	−0.031*	−0.007	−0.070	−0.023
Gro	−0.026	−0.030	0.055**	−0.052***	−0.220	−0.226
Div	−0.018	−0.009	−0.003	−0.007	−0.060**	−0.049***
Age		0.002		0.004		0.010
Ind$_i$			partly significant			
Time	0.099	0.048**	0.029	0.039*	0.060	0.054
constant	−2.930**	−0.744	−2.221***	−0.974**	−4.678***	−2.826**
RMSE	0.474	0.194	0.213	0.206	0.508	0.199
pseudo $\bar{R}^2$	−4.554	0.302	−0.120	0.214	−6.756	0.363
Prob.$_{\chi^2}$	(0.000)	(0.000)	(0.000)	(0.000)	(0.000)	(0.000)
RMSEA	0.000	0.012	0.000	0.011	0.000	0.000

low and high Tobin's Q firms. However, the basic relations remain as shown in Figure 5.10. The effects of the Tobin's Q variables of the previous year resemble the relation of the present year's measures. Similar to those of ownership concentration, these results indicate that the effects already had an impact in the previous year and their results remained stable over the next period.

Unfortunately, as shown in Table 5.33, there is no robustness regarding the *type of performance measure*. The usage of ROE with estimated thresholds of -.2 and .1 drastically changes the estimates of both effects in sign, size, and significance.[55]

5.4.5 Summary

The specification tests lead to a model with a linear institutional ownership effect and a non-monotonous effect of performance on institutional ownership.

Institutional ownership has a negative direct effect on performance and therefore supports the *strategic-alignment-conflict of interest* and the *myopic investment behavior argument*. Accordingly, institutional ownership does not reduce agency conflicts through improved monitoring. In contrast, institutional ownership rather causes performance losses by neglecting the monitoring function or even enforcing myopic investment behavior. While the two total effects of Tobin's Q values below .7 are negative, the one for higher values turns positive due to the feedback of the performance effect.

The direct effect of Tobin's Q is non-monotonous. A Tobin's Q below .22 has a positive direct effect matching the assumed hypotheses of *insider-investment* or the *Wall Street Rule*. However, for Tobin's Q values above the threshold the effect turns negative and even strengthens for Tobin's Q exceeding .72. There are three potential reasons for the unpredicted negative effect and the consequent stock sale: First, realization of gains, especially in the case of large shareholdings, secondly, diversification considerations, and thirdly, a planned exit.

While the estimates are robust for timing issues, robustness again fails for a different measure of financial performance.

5.5 Combined Model

After the different ownership aspects have been considered separately, their models are combined to a non-recursive four-equations system. As basis for the model structure the model specifications of the previous chapters were taken and extended for the intra-ownership effects. For both, ownership concentration and institutional ownership, the squared measures yield the best results in the insider ownership equation. The only change made to the previous relations is the usage of the squared measure of institutional ownership

---

[55] For the detailed results see Table A.40 of Appendix A.8.3, p. 354.

Table 5.33: Robustness checks on ROE for institutional ownership

	ROE		Q	
	ROE	Icr	Q	Icr
Icr	−0.209		−1.051	
	(0.547)		(0.001)	
Perf$_a$		−0.022		0.365
		(0.177)		(0.003)
Perf$_b$		−0.068		−0.302
		(0.542)		(0.021)
Perf$_c$		0.024		−1.277
		(0.157)		(0.000)
Iratio	−0.001		0.000	
OcST	0.178	0.582***	0.952***	0.831***
Size	0.234***	0.017	0.509***	0.283**
Size^2	−0.006***	0.000	−0.012***	−0.006**
Debt	0.393***	−0.004	0.097	0.128
Debt^2	−0.440**		−0.003	
Inv	0.092***	−0.002	−0.054	−0.046
Inv^2	−0.089**		−0.252***	
Nwc	−0.938***	0.030	−0.389	0.154
Nwc^2	0.969***		0.601*	
Eom	0.524***	0.038	0.538	0.160
Eom^2	−0.168***	−0.032	−0.247	−0.065
Beta	−0.034***	0.021	−0.070	−0.023
Gro	0.028	−0.024	−0.220*	−0.226**
Div	0.002	−0.008	−0.060**	−0.049***
Age		0.010		0.010
Ind$_i$		partly significant		
Time	−0.002	0.048**	0.060	0.054
constant	−2.014***	−0.312	−4.678***	−2.826**
RMSE	0.135	0.192	0.508	0.199
pseudo $\bar{R}^2$	0.546	0.317	−6.756	0.363
Prob.$_{\chi^2}$	(0.000)	(0.000)	(0.000)	(0.000)
RMSEA	0.026	0.000	0.000	0.000

in the Tobin's Q equation, since it improves the model fit. These adaptations result in the following model:

$$\begin{vmatrix} Q = Ocr_{Ocr \leq 39\%} & +Ocr_{39\% < Ocr \leq 80\%} & +Ocr_{Ocr > 80\%} \\ & +Icr^2 & +Mcr & +\text{control var.} \\ Ocr = Q_{Q \leq .22} & +Q_{.22 < Q \leq .72} & +Q_{Q > .72} & +\text{control var.} \\ Icr = Q_{Q \leq .5} & +Q_{.5 < Q \leq .7} & +Q_{Q > .7} & +\text{control var.} \\ Mcr = Q & +Q^2 & +Ocr^2 \\ & +Icr^2 & & +\text{control var.} \end{vmatrix}$$

5.5.1 Results

The results of the combined model are stated in Table 5.34 and discussed in the following.[56]

Table 5.34: I3SLS estimates for ownership structure and Tobin's Q
The values in brackets are the corresponding p-values
If not stated, *** implies a significance level of 1%, ** of 5% and * of 10%.

	Q	Ocr	Icr	Mcr
Ocr $_{0 \leq x \leq 39\%}$	−0.089 (0.202)		Ocr^2	0.359 (0.000)
Ocr $_{39\% \leq x \leq 80\%}$	0.233 (0.012)			
Ocr $_{80\% \leq x}$	0.890 (0.000)			
Icr^2	−0.119 (0.014)			−0.165 (0.010)
Mcr	−0.613 (0.000)			
Q_a		0.043 (0.807)	−0.031 (0.621)	Q	−0.826 (0.000)
Q_b		0.011 (0.926)	−0.266 (0.117)	Q^2	−0.168 (0.388)
Q_c		0.010 (0.957)	−0.483 (0.044)	
Oratio	−0.002			

Table continues at the following page

---

[56] For the detailed results see Table A.41 in Appendix A.8.4, p. 357.

Table 5.34: I3SLS estimates for ownership structure and Q (continued)

	Q	Ocr	Icr	Mcr
Iratio	−0.001			
Mratio	0.006			
Oc2	0.154***	−0.433***	0.589***	0.208***
Size	0.251***	0.239***	0.040	0.239***
Size^2	−0.006***	−0.006***	−0.001	−0.006***
Debt	0.345***	−0.031	0.046	0.310***
Debt^2	−0.213			
Inv	0.033	0.011	0.020	−0.011
Inv^2	−0.043			
Nwc	−0.509***	0.028	0.034	−0.075*
Nwc^2	0.482***			
Eom	0.621***	−0.003	0.040	0.681***
Eom^2	−0.228***	0.035	−0.015	−0.270***
Beta	−0.030*	−0.071***	0.020	−0.017
Gro	0.029	0.003	−0.017	0.022
Div	0.000	−0.022**	−0.009	−0.003
Age		0.015	0.010	0.002
Ind$_i$		partly significant		
Time	−0.019	0.005	0.048**	−0.028
constant	−2.056***	−1.801***	−0.556	−1.985***
RMSE	0.202	0.214	0.192	0.288
pseudo $\bar{R}^2$	−0.009	0.259	0.318	0.042
Prob.$_{\chi^2}$	(0.000)	(0.000)	(0.000)	(0.000)
RMSEA	0.000	0.000	0.000	0.000

Effect of Ownership Structure on Tobin's Q

By matrix algebra the total effects can be deducted. Table 5.35 states the direct and total effects of the ownership structure on Tobin's Q, which are also graphically demonstrated in Figure 5.11. Ownership concentration does not show a significant effect for a concentration level below 39%. Values above this threshold have an increasingly positive effect. This indicates that the *monitoring argument* prevails for higher share sizes, which is caused by the alignment of the controlling owner's interest with shareholder value. The higher cash flow rights raise the opportunity costs of harming actions. The total effect of ownership concentration has a nonlinear component based on the indirect effect of the squared variable of ownership concentration in the managerial ownership equation. If the Tobin's Q lies above .7, the total effect additionally depends on the level of institutional ownership due to the feedback of the

Tobin's Q on itself through institutional ownership. This effect can turn the sign of the total effect from negative to positive.

Table 5.35: Direct and total effects of ownership on Tobin's Q

	$D_{Q\,x}$	$T_{Q\,x}$ for $Q < .7$	$T_{Q\,x}$ for $Q \geq .7$
Ocr_a	.000	$-.892 * Ocr$	$\frac{.174*Ocr+.103*Icr*Ocr}{1-.115*Icr}$
Ocr_b	.233	$.233 - .892 * Ocr$	$.233 + \frac{.174*Ocr+.103*Icr*Ocr}{1-.115*Icr}$
Ocr_c	.890	$.890 - .892 * Ocr$	$-.794 + \frac{.174*Ocr+.103*Icr*Ocr}{1-.115*Icr}$
Icr	$-.238 * Icr$	$.172 * Icr$	$\frac{.172*Icr-.047*Icr^2}{1-.115*Icr}$
Mcr	$-.613$	-1.242	$\frac{-.242+.143*Icr}{1-.115*Icr}$

Apart from the negative total effect under certain circumstances, a high ownership concentration is no cause for anxiety for a minority shareholder. When considering the negative total effect, one has to remember that it does not stem from a direct effect of the controlling shareholder. In contrast, he has a shareholder value orientation and hence does not cause an agency problem or value loss. He might even increase corporate value for ownership concentrations above 39%. Consequently, as there is no conflict between the controlling shareholder and minority shareholders, an increase in actions reducing the conflict is not effective in diminishing the negative total effect and probably does not lead to a performance augmentation.

Institutional ownership has a nonlinear, negative direct effect caused by its squared measure in the Tobin's Q equation. This resembles the results of the separate model and again supports the arguments of *strategic-alignment-conflict of interest* and *myopic investment behavior*. The total effect additionally includes the indirect effect through managerial ownership and in the case of a Tobin's Q above .7 also the feedback on itself.

Regardless of the complexity of the functions, the effects of institutional ownership just depend on the level of institutional ownership. In both cases the total effect is positive in contrast to the negative direct effect. Consequently, the direct effect proves the finding of the previous model that institutional shareholding does not improve the monitoring. However, the effect is positive in its total. Thus the negative direct effect of institutional ownership is outweighed by its indirect effects. Accordingly, shareholders should not try to limit institutional ownership, since it has a positive total effect on performance. Nevertheless, they can take actions controlling the behavior of institutional ownership.

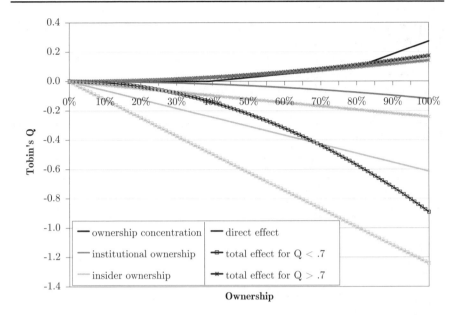

Fig. 5.11: Direct and total effects of ownership on Tobin's Q

Institutional ownership is assumed at its median of zero for the total effect of managerial ownership

Unlike the direct effect of the other ownership aspects, managerial ownership has a linear negative direct effect. This verifies the *entrenchment argument* which was already indicated by the previous models. The total effect is negative linear if the Tobin's Q is below .7. In contrast, for Tobin's Q values above .7 the feedback of Tobin's Q on insider ownership runs also through institutional ownership. Thus, the total effect also depends on the level of institutional shareholdings. All effects, direct and total ones, are negative and indicate a strong need for corporate governance mechanisms to enhance performance or, in more detail, to limit the performance loss caused by managerial entrenchment.

Effects of Tobin's Q on Ownership

The reverse effects of Tobin's Q on the ownership variables is stated in Table 5.36 and shown in Figure 5.12. Since there is no direct or indirect effect on ownership concentration, it is not displayed. Similarly, the coefficients of low and medium Tobin's Q on institutional ownership fail significance and do not lead to any effects. For Tobin's Q values above .7, however there is a negative direct effect. As in the institutional ownership model, this contradicts the hypothesized effects. Again potential explanations are the realization of a gain, diversification considerations and a planned sale as exit channel. Due to the feedback through the squared institutional ownership in the Tobin's Q equation, the strength of the total effect depends on the size of the institutional shareholdings and is monotonously negative.

Table 5.36: Direct and total effects of Tobin's Q on ownership

	D_{IcrQ}	T_{IcrQ}	D_{McrQ}	T_{McrQ}
$Q < .7$	.000	.000	$-.826$	-1.673
$Q \geq .7$	$-.483$	$\frac{-.483*Icr}{1-.115*Icr}$	$-.826$	$\frac{-.826+.095*Icr-.159*Icr^2}{1.506-.173*Icr+.097*Icr^2}$

The direct effect of Tobin's Q on managerial ownership is -.826. Even if the squared Tobin's Q measure was significant, the effect would still be monotonously negative. This contradicts the assumed insider investment and reward arguments. It could be that shareholders of well performing firms unlike those of companies with inferior performance do not perceive a necessity for managerial interest alignment and hence do not apply stock remuneration and reward plans. Hence, with rising performance the need and appliance of stock remuneration reduces. The total effect is also negative and depends on institutional ownership for Tobin's Q level above .7 due to the indirect effect of Q_c on institutional ownership and its effect on managerial ownership.

Interactions of Ownership

Figure 5.13 displays the direct effects of ownership concentration and institutional ownership on managerial ownership. Both are monotonous, but nonlinear. Ownership concentration has a positive effect meeting the assumption of the *stock-based compensation preference*. Consequently, the largest shareholder expects managerial ownership to align the interest rather than to rocket the danger of entrenchment. This expectation, however, is not verified in this study. If the *substitution effect of monitoring devices* is used as explanation, shareholder even have to have two spurious expectations. First, shareholders must expect ownership concentration to have a negative effect on corporate performance. Therefore, its increase would demand a substitution by a positive effect on performance. Second, shareholders have to assume managerial shareholding to align management with their interests to cover this demand. However, following these empirical results neither does ownership concentration have a negative effect on performance nor does managerial ownership has a positive one. Consequently, this argument needs an unsophisticated market with false expectations.

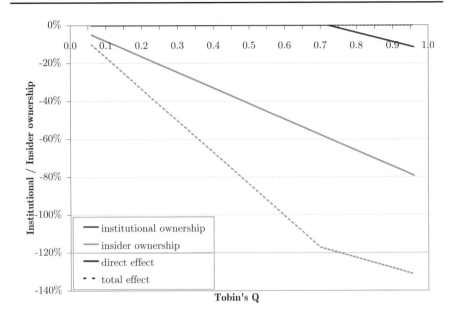

Fig. 5.12: Direct and total effects of Tobin's Q on ownership

Institutional ownership is assumed at its median of zero for the total effect of managerial ownership

The direct effect of institutional shareholdings on insider ownership is negative and supports the *substitution-monitoring effect*. Since institutional shareholding has a negative effect on performance and hence seems to hamper the market of corporate control, it increases the utility of insider ownership as agency control mechanism. Consequently, as the cost efficiency of managerial ownership rises, it is used more extensively. This effect is again based on the false expectation of an interest alignment by managerial ownership. It further has to be spuriously assumed that institutional ownership has a positive effect on performance. Another explanation of this effect is that institutional investors know about the entrenchment effect and thus do not promote stock-based remuneration.

The total effects are stated in Table 5.13. Their deduction for ownership concentration leads to two non-monotonous relations. They are not only non-linear through the piecewise sections of ownership concentration, but also within these three parts. The two formulas of total effect differ by the inclusion of the feedback loop through institutional ownership, which manifests in the case of a Tobin's Q above .7. Therefore, the relation considering this feedback not only depends on the level of ownership concentration but also on the institutional shareholding. Also for institutional ownership the threshold of

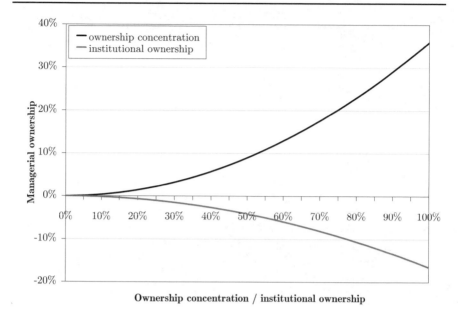

Fig. 5.13: Direct effects of ownership on managerial ownership

Tobin's Q of .7 distinguishes two cases. Total effects for Tobin's Q above this point incorporate a feedback by performance and therefore is more complex.

Table 5.37: Total effects of ownership on managerial ownership

	$Q < .7$	$Q \geq .7$
Ocr_a	$-.718 * Ocr$	$-.718 * Ocr$
Ocr_b	$-.718 * Ocr - .390$	$-.718 * Ocr + .890 * \frac{-.735+.085*Icr-.142*Icr^2}{1.506-.173*Icr+.097*Icr^2}$
Ocr_c	$-.718 * Ocr - 1.489$	$-.718 * Ocr + .890 * \frac{-.192+.022*Icr-.037*Icr^2}{1.506-.173*Icr+.097*Icr^2}$
Icr	$.068 * Icr$	$\frac{.068*Icr+.038*Icr^2}{1-.115*Icr}$

Effects of Control Variables

Table 5.38 states the direct effects of the control variables on the endogenous variables. Their total effects depend on the total effects between the endogenous variables and therefore form multiple cases. Given their complexity and the limited explanatory power of the total effect, they are omitted in this chapter.

Table 5.38: Direct effects of the control variables on Tobin's Q and ownership

	D_{Qx}	D_{Ocrx}	D_{Icrx}	D_{Mcrx}
ORatio	0.000	0.000	0.000	0.000
IRatio	0.000	0.000	0.000	0.000
MRatio	0.000	0.000	0.000	0.000
OcST	0.154	−0.433	0.589	0.208
Size	0.251	0.239	0.000	0.239
Size^2	−0.006	−0.006	0.000	−0.006
Debt	0.345	0.000	0.000	0.310
Debt^2	0.000	0.000	0.000	0.000
Inv	0.000	0.000	0.000	0.000
Inv^2	0.000	0.000	0.000	0.000
Nwc	−0.509	0.000	0.000	−0.075
Nwc^2	0.482	0.000	0.000	0.000
Eom	0.621	0.000	0.000	0.681
Eom^2	−0.228	0.000	0.000	−0.270
Beta	−0.030	−0.071	0.000	0.000
Gro	0.000	0.000	0.000	0.000
Div	0.000	−0.022	0.000	0.000
Age	0.000	0.000	0.000	0.000
Ind$_i$	———	partly significant		———
Time	0.000	0.000	0.048	0.000
constant	−2.056	−1.801	0.000	−1.985

All divergence ratios of the control and cash flow rights are insignificant in the four equations, indicating that the relation of cash flow rights to control rights does not significantly influence the effects of ownership on performance. In contrast, the size of the second and third largest shareholder is significant in all the equations. The coefficients fulfill the predictions with the exception of the effect on managerial ownership, where it shows a positive sign. This indicates that also the second and third largest shareholder prefer a stock-based remuneration and hence spuriously regard managerial ownership rather as an incentive alignment than as a danger of entrenchment.

As for the other control variables in the performance equation, most variables are significant with the exception of investment level, growth, and time. Both the linear and squared firm size variables are significant, leading to a monotonously positive effect on Tobin's Q as predicted by the economies of scale. Similarly, financial leverage has a constantly positive effect on performance, which remains even if the insignificant squared variable is taken into consideration. Consequently, the positive impact of reduced agency costs implied by Kim/Sorensen [1986] and Jensen [1986] outweighs the negative relation assumed by the pecking order theory. The negative effect of liquidity supports the assumption of unused assets and a lack of investment opportunities. The ease of monitoring shows the predicted positive effect through a significance in both variables. Also beta fulfills the predictions by a negative coefficient in the Tobin's Q equation. The industry groups are partly significant with a positive coefficient for the SIC groups 2, 3, 5, and 7. These comprise the manufacturing division, wholesale, and retail trade and services.[57]

In the ownership concentration equation less control variables appear significant. Firm size has a constant positive effect. This suits the argument of Himmelberg et al. [1999], who assume higher private benefits generated by larger firms. An increase in risk shows the predicted negative effect due to the increase of the idiosyncratic risk of the owner and of higher non-diversification costs. Similarly, diversification increases the risk and reduces the utility of large shareholding, displayed by its negative coefficient. None of the industry groups shows a significant effect.

For institutional ownership only time and the SIC division E, group 4, are significant. Time has a positive coefficient indicating higher institutional ownership in 2003, which mirrors the trend of rising institutional investments. Nevertheless, it can be argued if the trend is observable in the short period of three years. The fact that the time of observation only matters in the institutional ownership equation, could also indicate that institutional investors adapt their shareholdings faster to changes in the company or the market than other investors. This results in a lower stickiness of the ownership levels, which is also shown by the lower correlation of institutional ownership over time in Table 4.1.[58] Companies of the transportation, communications, electric, gas, and sanitary industry show less institutional shareholdings.

Finally, the control variables of the managerial ownership equation are considered. The size effect on managerial ownership is negative and supports the argument of larger opportunities for moral hazard and higher entrenchment of management, which was assumed by Himmelberg et al. [1999] and Gugler et al. [2003b]. In contrast, these opportunities are limited by a higher leverage, consequently showing a negative effect on managerial ownership. Both, NWC and ease of monitoring, however do not fulfill the hypotheses. High liquidity might reduce the idiosyncratic risk of the management, but is outweighed by the danger of a takeover threat. The positive effect of ease of monitoring may be caused by mediation effects or be due to the construction of the variable on the sales terms. Sales might have a positive relation with managerial owner-

---

[57] For the detailed effects of the different industry groups see Table A.42 in Appendix A.8.4, p. 360.
[58] See Table 4.1, p. 75.

ship, for example as a result of empire building activities. Again the industry groups 2, 3, 5 and 7 are significant with a positive coefficient.[59]

5.5.2 Robustness Checks

As shown in Table 5.39 the results are robust against changes in the *insider definition* with the exception of institutional ownership, which loses its significance in the performance and managerial ownership equation.[60] This may indicate that institutional ownership influences managerial ownership but not directors' shareholdings.

Table 5.39 also states the results of the model using ROE as *financial performance measure*.[61] The thresholds for ROE are taken from the previous studies and lie at .3 and .6 for ownership concentration and at .45 and .6 for institutional ownership respectively. As in the previous studies the results differ from those of the Tobin's Q model. Only the effects of ownership concentration and institutional ownership on managerial ownership appear robust, since the variables are not influenced by the performance measure.

Further robustness checks in Table 5.40 refer to *timing issues*. The coefficients of the ownership variables are mainly robust, while the Tobin's Q variables change in significance and size. However, this was expected since the variables of the different periods are strongly correlated and share the explanatory power.

5.5.3 Summary

The chapter combines the previous models to a four-equations system. In the performance equation, only ownership concentration above 39% has an effect. Its positive sign indicates an *increased monitoring*. Consequently, minority shareholders do not have to fear actions by the controlling shareholder harming corporate value. The positive impact is also reflected in most total effects. The coefficient of institutional ownership is negative and supports again the arguments of a *strategic-alignment conflict of interest* and *myopic investment behavior*. Unlike the direct effect, the total effects of institutional ownership turns positive. Managerial ownership has also a negative effect, suggesting a *managerial entrenchment* against disciplining actions. Its total effects stay negative. Consequently, corporate governance mechanisms should control institutional and managerial owners. The expectation of a positive effect on their basis cannot be verified. Also the typical assumption of a negative assumed effect of controlling shareholders does not hold true.

The reverse effects of performance on ownership are not as significant. While ownership concentration is not influenced by performance at all, only

---

[59] For the detailed effects of the different industry groups see Table A.42 in Appendix A.8.4, p. 360.
[60] For the detailed results see Table A.43 in Appendix A.8.4, p. 363.
[61] For the detailed results see Table A.44 in Appendix A.8.4, p. 366.

Table 5.39: Robustness checks on insider definition and ROE

The values in brackets are the corresponding p-values; if not stated, *** implies a significance level of 1%, ** of 5% and * of 10%

	Mbcr					ROE			
	Q	Ocr	Icr	Mbcr		ROE	Ocr	Icr	Mcr
Ocr_a	−0.040 (0.510)			Ocr^2 0.261 (0.000)	Ocr_a	−0.012 (0.863)			Ocr^2 0.394 (0.000)
Ocr_b	0.259 (0.004)				Ocr_b	−0.202 (0.037)			
Ocr_c	1.052 (0.000)				Ocr_c	−0.746 (0.004)			
Icr^2	−0.064 (0.372)		Icr^2	−0.077 (0.257)	Icr^2	0.032 (0.448)			Icr^2 −0.153 (0.017)
Mbcr	−0.982 (0.000)				Mcr	0.368 (0.004)			
Q_a		0.045 (0.798)	−0.032 Q (0.616)	−0.827 (0.000)	Roe_a		0.010 (0.599)	−0.024 Roe (0.142)	0.003 (0.793)
Q_b		0.016 (0.897)	−0.232 Q^2 (0.172)	−0.074 (0.545)	Roe_b		−0.011 (0.934)	−0.071 Roe^2 (0.560)	0.009 (0.148)
Q_c		0.031 (0.862)	−0.421 (0.079)		Roe_c		−0.030 (0.124)	0.016 (0.361)	
Ratios Oc2	0.144*	−0.434*** —insignificant—	0.588***	0.164**	Ratios Oc2	0.008	−0.436*** —insignificant—	0.580***	0.167**
RMSE	0.296	0.214	0.192 0.294	0.164		0.192	0.214	0.261	
Prob$_{\chi^2}$	(0.000)	(0.000)	(0.000)(0.000)	(0.000)		(0.000)	(0.000)	(0.000)	
RMSEA	0.000	0.000	0.000 0.000	0.022		0.000	0.000	0.000	

Table 5.40: Robustness checks on timing issues

*** implies a significance level of 1%, ** of 5% and * of 10%

	Alternation 1				Alternation 2			
	Q	Ocr	Icr	Mcr	Q	Ocr	Icr	Mcr
$Ocr_{0 \leq x \leq 39\%}$	−0.108							
$Ocr_{39\% \leq x \leq 80\%}$	0.216**							
$Ocr_{80\% \leq x}$	0.807***							
Ocr^2				0.370***				0.408***
Icr^2	−0.121***			−0.171***				
Mcr	−0.555***							−0.180***
Q					−0.129*			
Q^2				−0.723**	0.122			−0.006
Q^{t-1}				−0.232	0.509**			−0.504
$Q^{t-1\ 2}$				−0.113	−0.109**			−0.249
				0.090	−0.292***			0.237
Q_a		−0.017	−0.029			−0.062	−0.024	
Q_b		0.004	−0.211			0.038	−0.243	
Q_c		0.298	−0.403			0.491**	−0.602**	
Q_a^{t-1}		0.139	−0.028			0.100	−0.011	
Q_b^{t-1}		0.030	−0.245			0.012	−0.215	
Q_c^{t-1}		−0.344	−0.220			−0.422*	−0.034	
RMSE	0.190	0.214	0.192	0.287	0.164	0.215	0.192	0.270
pseudo $\bar{R}^2$	0.109	0.265	0.320	0.051	0.336	0.259	0.319	0.158
$Prob._{\chi^2}$	(0.000)	(0.000)	(0.000)	(0.000)	(0.000)	(0.000)	(0.000)	(0.000)
RMSEA	0.009	0.000	0.000	0.000	0.000	0.000	0.000	0.000

high Tobin's Qs above .7 have a negative effect on institutional shareholdings. Potential explanations are the realization of a gain, diversification considerations, and a planned sale as exit channel. Also the negative effect on managerial ownership is contradicting the assumptions. Its negative sign could originate from a perceived decreased utility of managerial ownership as agency devices, if the firm is already performing well. Accordingly, the reward and insider-reward arguments are not effective for higher values of Tobin's Q.

The effect of ownership concentration and institutional shareholdings on managerial ownership is ambiguous. Large owners seem to *prefer stock-based compensation* as managerial remuneration and hence the managerial share increases with their shareholding. This also implies that the controlling shareholder has a spurious expectation of management alignment by its shareholdings. If shareholders have an additional false expectation regarding the effect of controlling shareholders, also the *substitution effect of monitoring devices* might serve as explanation.

In contrast, the institutional shareholdings show a negative effect which suggests that they *substitute managerial ownership as agency device*. This is also based on the false expectations of the institutional and managerial ownership effects. Another explanation of this effect is that institutional investors know about the entrenchment effect and thus do not promote stock-based remuneration.

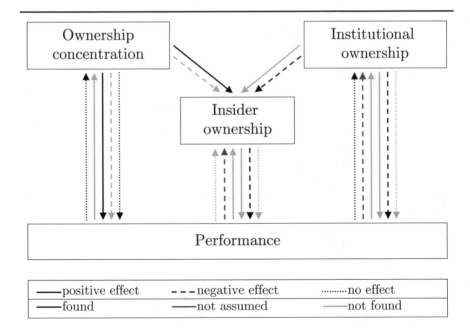

Fig. 5.14: Found and assumed relations of ownership and performance

Figure 5.14 demonstrates the results and compares them to the hypothesized effects displayed in Figure 3.5.[62] The results are mainly robust against changes in the insider ownership definition and timing issues. However, as in the previous studies, the measure of financial performance has an impact on the results.

5.6 Comparison and Summary of Results

After the models are analyzed, this section summarizes and compares the results of the four studies. Table 5.41 states the direct effects of all four models.

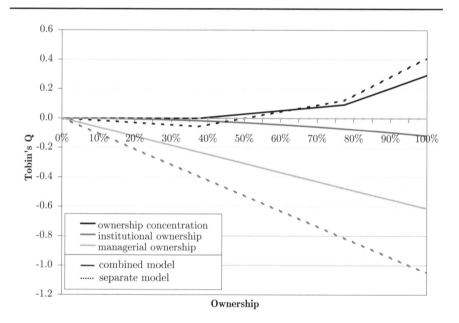

Fig. 5.15: Comparison of direct effects of ownership on Tobin's Q for separate and combined models

Figure 5.15 displays the direct effects of the ownership variables on performance, where the straight line shows the results of the combined model and the dotted graph those of the separate models. The basic shape of the effects is maintained in the combined model. Only the effects of managerial ownership seem to differ at first sight with a significant negative effect in the combined

---

[62] For Figure 3.5 see p. 68.

Table 5.41: Comparison of the direct effects of the four models

*** implies a significance level of 1%, ** of 5% and * of 10%

	Combined model				Ocr		Icr		Mcr	
	Q	Ocr	Icr	Mcr	Q	Ocr	Q	Icr	Q	Mcr
Ocr_a	−0.089 (0.202)				−0.148 (0.012)					
Ocr_b	0.233 (0.012)				0.445 (0.000)					
Ocr_c	0.890 (0.000)			Ocr^2 0.359 (0.000)	1.275 (0.000)					
Icr^2	−0.119 (0.014)			−0.165 (0.010)			Icr −1.051 (0.001)			
Mcr	−0.613 (0.000)								−5.484 (0.101)	
Q_a		0.043 (0.807)	−0.031 Q (0.621)	−0.826 (0.000)		−2.074 (0.000)		0.365 Q (0.003)		−4.260 (0.170)
Q_b		0.011 (0.926)	−0.266 Q^2 (0.117)	−0.168 (0.388)		0.416 (0.000)		−0.302 Q^2 (0.021)		3.678 (0.190)
Q_c		0.010 (0.957)	−0.483 (0.044)			2.901 (0.000)		−1.277 (0.000)		
Oratio	−0.002				−0.015**					
Iratio	−0.001									
Mratio	0.006									
OcST	0.154***	−0.433***	0.589***	0.208***	−0.433***	−0.392***	0.000	0.952***	0.813	−0.499 −0.142

model. However, in the separate model the coefficient fails significance only by .1% and carries also a negative sign.

Table 5.43 compares the verified hypotheses. The existence of a controlling shareholder does not imply the need for a stronger protection of the minority shareholders. For concentrations exceeding a share portion of 39%, the controlling shareholder even improves the performance by an *amelioration of monitoring*. For lower concentration no effect is found. The negative effect displayed in the separate model stems from the influence of ownership concentration on the not modelled managerial ownership. A high ownership concentration has a positive effect on performance and managerial ownership. However, the increase of managerial ownership has a negative effect on performance. Since this effect is not displayed in the separate model, it cannot be detached from the effect of ownership concentration which combine to a negative effect. Consequently, not the large shareholder, but the management should be controlled more intensively by corporate governance activities.

In contrast, both institutional ownership as well as managerial ownership have a negative effect. Thus, the institutional investors use their power and insight to impose their investment goals and horizons on the held firms. This leads to *myopic behavior* and inefficient corporate decisions. In addition, the possible improvement of monitoring by institutional investors can also be impeded by other business relations between the institutional investor and the firm. This might cause a conflict of interest preventing the institutionals to sanction actions harming shareholder value. These results were already found in the separate model.

Furthermore, the stock-based remuneration appears not to align the management with corporate value but rather provokes *management entrenchment* negatively affecting the performance of the company. In the separate model the effect slightly fails significance which can be explained by the relation of insider ownership and ownership concentration and their contradicting effect on performance. Again the effects of ownership concentration and insider ownership on performance cannot be distinguished in the separate model of managerial ownership. The effect of ownership concentration is not strong enough to change the coefficients but weakens its significance.

While the effects of ownership on performance are quite consistent over the different models and explained by the assumed hypotheses, the reverse effect is strongly affected by the combination of the models as shown in Figure 5.16. This is not astonishing since the Tobin's Q does not only explain one single ownership variable but three interdependent ones. As the indirect effects and feedbacks through the other ownership effects are not modelled, the separate models cannot distinguish them from the direct effect and only view their combination.

When comparing the results of the models, it shows that most effects indicated in the separate models yield from such indirect effects, since the direct effects in the combined model are mainly insignificant. Only managerial ownership and high values of institutional ownership show a significance. These

Table 5.42: Comparison of theoretic findings of the four models (effects of ownership)

*** implies a significance level of 1%, ** of 5% and * of 10%

	Combined model		Separate models	
Effects of ownership on Q				
Ocr < 39%	$\frac{\partial Q}{\partial Ocr} = 0$	Natural selection argument Mutual neutralization argument	$\frac{\partial Q}{\partial Ocr} < 0$	Over-monitoring argument Private benefits of control
39% ≤ Ocr < 80%	$\frac{\partial Q}{\partial Ocr} > 0$	Monitoring argument	$\frac{\partial Q}{\partial Ocr} > 0$	Monitoring argument
80% ≤ Ocr	$\frac{\partial Q}{\partial Ocr} > 0$	Monitoring argument		
Icr	$\frac{\partial Q}{\partial Icr} < 0$	Institutional myopia Strategic alignment-conflict-of-interest	$\frac{\partial Q}{\partial Icr} < 0$	Institutional myopia Strategic alignment-conflict-of-interest
Mcr	$\frac{\partial Q}{\partial Mcr} < 0$	General entrenchment argument	$\frac{\partial Q}{\partial Mcr} = 0$ $\left(\frac{\partial Q}{\partial Mcr} < 0\right.$	Natural selection argument Mutual neutralization argument *General entrenchment argument*)

Table 5.43: Comparison of theoretic findings of the four models (effects on ownership)

*** implies a significance level of 1%, ** of 5% and * of 10%

	Combined model		Separate models	
Effects of Q on ownership concentration				
$Q < .22$	$\frac{\partial Ocr}{\partial Q} = 0$	Natural selection argument	$\frac{\partial Ocr}{\partial Q} < 0$	?
$.22 \leq Q < .72$	$\frac{\partial Ocr}{\partial Q} = 0$	Natural selection argument	$\frac{\partial Ocr}{\partial Q} > 0$	Insider-investment argument
$.72 \leq Q$	$\frac{\partial Ocr}{\partial Q} = 0$	Natural selection argument	$\frac{\partial Ocr}{\partial Q} > 0$	Insider-investment argument
Effects of Q on institutional ownership				
$Q < .5$	$\frac{\partial Icr}{\partial Q} = 0$	Natural selection argument	$\frac{\partial Icr}{\partial Q} > 0$	Wall Street Rule / Insider-investment argument
$.5 \leq Q < .7$	$\frac{\partial Icr}{\partial Q} = 0$	Natural selection argument	$\frac{\partial Icr}{\partial Q} < 0$	?
$.7 \leq Q$	$\frac{\partial Icr}{\partial Q} < 0$	?	$\frac{\partial Icr}{\partial Q} < 0$	?
Effects of Q on managerial ownership				
Q	$\frac{\partial Mcr}{\partial Q} < 0$	?	$\frac{\partial Mcr}{\partial Q} = 0$	Natural selection argument

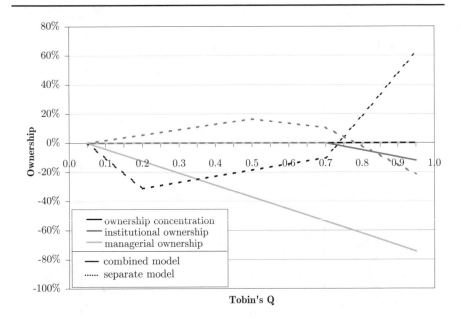

Fig. 5.16: Comparison of direct effects of Tobin's Q on ownership for separate and combined models

negative effects do not fit the assumed *insider-investment argument* or similar theories. For managerial ownership this effect can be caused by a reduced perceived utility of stock-based remuneration for well performing firms. In the case of institutional ownership potential explanations are the realization of a gain, diversification considerations, and a planned sale as exit channel.

In addition, ownership concentration and institutional shareholding have significant effects on managerial ownership. This fact shows the necessity of including those ownership interactions in the model. Table 5.44 displays the proven hypotheses and their directions. Whereas ownership concentration has a positive effect on managerial ownership, institutional ownership has a negative one.

The effect of ownership concentration could be caused by the controlling shareholder preferring stock-based compensation of the management given the false assumption of a positive interest alignment. If the substitution effect of monitoring devices is used as explanation, the shareholders must even have an additional false expectation, that of a negative effect of ownership concentration. However, following these empirical results neither does ownership concentration have a negative effect on performance nor does managerial ownership has a positive one.

5.6 Comparison and Summary of Results

Table 5.44: Effects of ownership on managerial ownership

	Effect of ownership on managerial ownership	
Ownership concentration	$\frac{\partial Mcr}{\partial Ocr} > 0$	Stock-based compensation preference
		Substitution-monitoring effect argument
Institutional ownership	$\frac{\partial Mcr}{\partial Icr} < 0$	Substitution-monitoring effect argument

Also for institutional ownership, the substitution effect of monitoring devices is based on spurious expectations. In order to explain the negative effect of institutional investments on managerial ownership, institutional ownership has to impact performance in a positive way. Then a high institutional shareholding would reduce the demand for managerial ownership as agency device and thus its cost-efficiency. Apart from the substitution effect based on false expectations, the negative relation may also originate from institutional investors' aversion to managerial ownership. This aversion might be explained by institutional investors' knowledge of the negative effect of managerial ownership on performance.

With the exception of the separate model of ownership concentration the divergence ratios of control and cash flow rights appear insignificant. Hence, the effects are mainly driven by the control rights and mediating effects of the cash flow rights are not observable.

In contrast, the share size of the second and third largest owners is highly significant. It enhances monitoring and thus performance. Institutional investors do also appreciate this positive effect on Tobin's Q. However, the controlling shareholder perceives the existence of a large second and third owner as less advantageous, as it may limit the private benefits of a large share. Nevertheless, in the managerial ownership equation its positive effect contradicts the assumption. This might originate from a preference of stock-based remuneration not only by the largest but also by the second and third largest owner leading to the positive relation with the managerial ownership.

6
Conclusion

In the course of the last decade corporate governance has become a key issue in academic discussion as well as the business world. This work has set out to analyze its basis, the assumed relation between ownership and performance. The literature examining this relationship theoretically has found many arguments for various effects running from ownership to performance and vice versa. The discussion has not reach a consensus though and even supports contradicting effects. Also the empirical studies trying to solve the dilemma by empirical evidence have rendered different versions of this relation and have not resulted in consistent findings.

Literature has also discussed reasons for these contradictions. One argument for a bias of the results leading to inconsistent estimates is the potential endogeneity of performance and ownership. Theory has found effects in both directions arguing for a simultaneous effect. Although this has been often assumed, performance and ownership were only modelled in a simultaneous setting by five studies. Yet, the error caused by the endogeneity bias is significant and questions the results of the studies not considering simultaneity.

Furthermore, researchers have tried to find a solution by closer examining the ownership structure and its different aspects. They started arguing that different types of owners have different utility functions and capabilities resulting in different effects of their ownership on performance. The identity first considered was the management as insiders to the firm. The differences in utility function and capabilities of managerial owners were already discussed in the early agency theoretic papers by Jensen/Meckling [1976] and Fama [1980]. A further identity coming into focus of research have been institutional investors as the importance of professional investments has risen drastically in the last 25 years. The professional occupation of the institutional investors with the firms and the market votes for a higher sophistication which impacts some of the assumed effects of ownership on performance.

While the difference of the owners identities and their effects are acknowledged, most studies focus on one single or rarely two types of owners. In real life, however, they exist conjointly and influence performance simultaneously. Furthermore, the interaction of different ownership variables was already hypothesized by Jensen/Meckling [1976] and Jensen [1986]. Thus, the estimated models may not only suffer from the endogeneity of the performance and ownership relation, but also by the simultaneity of effects of the different ownership types themselves. To cope with these problems, this study simultaneously analyzes performance and three ownership identities: general ownership concentration, managerial ownership, and institutional ownership. The usage of simultaneous equations methods allows ownership interactions and a clear separation of their effects on performance.

In addition, researcher also argued that the data selection would distort the results; especially, the national differences may result in inconsistency. Most studies are performed using USA and UK data. These data origins differ drastically from most other European and Asian countries in three ways. First, both the USA and UK have by far the lowest ownership concentration worldwide. Thus US and UK provide only little data of highly concentrated firms to estimate the effects of high concentration which are frequently found in other countries. Hence, the estimation quality and significance suffer from the low amount of data. Second, the US and UK ownership structures also differ in the distribution of owner types. Finally, complex ownership structures, such as control chains and crossholdings, are rarely used in the USA and the UK relative to other countries. These three differences make the results of US and UK studies questionable and less transferable to other countries. In contrast, the German ownership structures show high resemblance to the international average. This makes them a more promising research object and opens the prospect of more applicable results.

Recapitulating, the empirical analyses of this work promise more precise and unbiased results, since they model not only performance and ownership but also different ownership types simultaneously. Furthermore, they use a German data set which should be more representative for the international average ownership structure. The studies were performed in two parts. First, performance and each ownership type are estimated in a separate model. In the second part the resulting three models are combined to a four-equations system also including ownership interactions.

The results show a positive monitoring effect of the share size of the largest owner on performance. In contrast, institutional ownership has a negative impact on performance due to the strategic-alignment-conflict of interest and/or myopic investment goals. In addition, management entrenches by its shareholdings against sanctioning actions which results in more managerial actions harming corporate value. Furthermore, the share size of the largest owner has a positive effect on managerial stock holdings. This could indicate a preference of stock-base management remuneration and a spurious expectation of an interest alignment of the management due to the shareholdings. In contrast, institutional shareholdings reduce the managerial ownership, as they know about its negative effect on performance.

These results contradict some frequently assumed hypotheses on the effects of ownership on performance. Corporate governance actions on the basis of these spurious assumptions may be counterproductive and yield a loss of corporate value instead of an augmentation. The effects of different corporate governance mechanisms in such a simultaneous setting may serve as research objects for further studies.

The reverse effects of performance on ownership are mainly insignificant. Only for managerial ownership and high institutional ownership a negative effect can be found contradicting the insider-investment argument. In general, these weak results can be interpreted in four different ways. First, ownership structure is only marginally caused by performance. Second, other important factors of influence are not included in the equations, i.e. the liquidity situation and risk profile of shareholders. Thirdly, it may also be that no factors are missing but the system still suffers from endogeneity of further variables modelled as exogenous. For example this might be the case for the financial leverage, as the endogeneity of the capital structure to performance and ownership was implied by Jensen/Meckling [1976] and Jensen [1986]. Thus, additional research has to be performed on the determinants and their effects on ownership structure.

Finally, an event study of Mußler [2005] published in the Frankfurter Allgemeine Zeitung states a further reason for the mixed findings. It analyzed the rate of return of legal insider trading on the data of the BAFIN. Investors who copied the stock purchase of insiders yielded an average surplus of 2 to 4% over the market in 60% of the cases.[1] However, when considering the stock sales of insiders, the rate of return merely equalled the market's average. Consequently, stock sales of insiders are barely caused by bad company's prospects but may also stem from liquidity and portfolio reasons. This difference between stock purchases and sales is not considered in the models applied here. Thus, it could lessen the efficiency of the coefficients leading to the insignificant and partly negative effects.

Consequently, the course of the analysis has also opened research questions on ownership structure, such as the need to explain the negative effect of performance and to examine the timing issues. The determination of the ownership structure is an object for future research. The consideration of differences in behavior of stock sales versus purchases can clarify the development of ownership structures and their interaction with performance and corporate governance. Furthermore, there are plenty of factors also assumed to be endogenous on the relation of ownership and performance. Other corporate governance mechanisms and mediating factors, such as capital structure could be included as endogenous variables in the simultaneous equations system.

---

[1] The previous year's study resulted in a surplus in 50% of the cases with an average of 3 to 5%. See Mußler [2005, p. 25].

List of Abbreviations

2SLS	two-stage least squares
3SLS	three-stage least squares
BAFIN	Bundesanstalt für Finanzdienstleistungsaufsicht
CAPM	Capital Asset Pricing Model
CAR	cumulated abnormal return
CEO	Chief Executive Officer
CFO	Chief Financial Officer
CFR	cash flow rights
CR	control rights
DH	diffusely held
EA	entrenchment argument
EBIT	earnings before interest expenses and taxes
EC	externally controlled
EPS	earnings per share
FC	financially controlled
FCF	free cash flow
FIM	full information methods
FIML	full information maximum likelihood
I3SLS	iterated three-stage least squares
IAA	incentive alignment argument
ILS	indirect least squares
IQR	interquartile range
LIM	limited information methods
MC	management-controlled
MH	majority held
M/B	market-to-book ratio
MV	market value
NOPLAT	net operating profit less adjusted taxes
NWC	net working capital
OC	owner-controlled

OECD	Organisation for Economic Co-operation and Development
OLS	ordinary least squares
PV	present value
RMSEA	root mean square error of approximation
ROA	return on assets
ROE	return on equity
SIC	standard industrial classification
SOC	strong-owner-controlled
TPA	takeover premium argument
Q	Tobin's Q
WOC	weak-owner-controlled

List of Symbols

β	matrix of direct effects / coefficients of endogenous variables ($m \times m$), D_{yy}
β_{ij}	direct effect of y_j on y_i
Γ	matrix of direct effects / coefficients of endogenous variables ($m \times k$), D_{yx}
γ_{ij}	direct effect of x_j on y_i
μ_i	disturbance term of equation i
$\overline{R}^2$	adjusted R-square
τ_1	first threshold and turning point
τ_2	second threshold and turning point
Age	logarithm of years since foundation
$Beta$	beta of a firm
D_{yx}	matrix of direct effects of exogenous on endogenous variables
D_{yy}	matrix of direct effects of endogenous variables on themselves
Dcr	sum of the control rights of directors
$Debt$	long-term debt divided by total assets
Div	diversification measured by
$DRatio$	control rights of directors' shares divided by their cash flow rights
Eom	fixed assets divided by total assets
Gro	Annual growth rate of sales
I	identity matrix
I_{yx}	matrix of indirect effects of exogenous on endogenous variables
I_{yy}	matrix of indirect effects of endogenous variables on themselves
Icr	sum of the control rights of institutional investors
Ind_i	industry dummies
Inv	investment level
$IRatio$	control rights of institutional shares divided by their cash flow rights
k	number of exogenous variables
m	number of endogenous variables and number of equations in the equations system

List of Symbols

$Mbcr$	sum of the control rights of management and board
$MbRatio$	control rights of management and board shares divided by their cash flow rights
Mcr	sum of the control rights of management
$MRatio$	control rights of management shares divided by their cash flow rights
N	number of observations
N_{yx}	matrix of noncausal effects of exogenous on endogenous variables
N_{yy}	matrix of noncausal effects of endogenous variables on themselves
Nwc	net working capital
O	ownership
Ocr	control rights of the largest share
$OcST$	sum of the control rights of the second and third largest share
$ORatio$	control rights of the largest share divided by its cash flow rights
$Perf$	performance
Q	Tobin's Q ratio
ROE	return on equity
$Size$	logarithm of sales as measure for firm size
T_{ij}	tolerance of variable i on variable j
T_{yx}	matrix of total effects of exogenous on endogenous variables
T_{yy}	matrix of total effects of endogenous variables on themselves
$Time$	dummy for the year of observation
U	matrix of disturbance terms ($m \times 1$)
VIF_{ij}	variance inflation of variable i on variable j
X	matrix of exogenous variables ($k \times 1$)
x_i	i^{th} exogenous variable
Y	matrix of endogenous variables ($m \times 1$)
y_i	i^{th} endogenous variable

References

Achleitner, A.-C. and Wichels, D. (2000). Stock Option-Pläne als Bestandteil wertorientierter Entlohnungssysteme: Eine Einführung. In: Achleitner, A.-C. and Wollmert, P., editors, *Stock options*, pp. 1–21. Stuttgart.

Aggarwal, R. K. and Samwick, A. A. (2003). Why do managers diversify their firms? Agency reconsidered. *Journal of Finance*, Vol. 58(1), pp. 71–118.

Agrawal, A. and Knoeber, C. R. (1996). Firm performance and mechanisms to control agency problems between managers and shareholders. *Journal of Financial and Quantitative Analysis*, Vol. 31(3), pp. 377–397.

Agrawal, A. and Mandelker, G. N. (1990). Large shareholders and the monitoring of managers: The case of antitakeover charter amendments. *Journal of Financial and Quantitative Analysis*, Vol. 25(2), pp. 143–161.

Agrawal, A. and Nagarajan, N. J. (1990). Corporate capital structure, agency costs, and ownership control: The case of all-equity firms. *Journal of Finance*, Vol. 45(4), pp. 1325–1331.

Ahuja, G., Coff, R. W., and Lee, P. M. (2005). Managerial foresight and attempted rent appropriation: Insider trading on knowledge of imminent breakthroughs. *Strategic Management Journal*, Vol. 26(9), pp. 791–808.

Alchian, A. A. (1950). Uncertainty, evolution and economic theory. *Journal of Political Economy*, Vol. 58(3), pp. 211–221.

Amemiya, T. (1985). *Advanced Econometrics*. Cambridge (MA).

Amihud, Y. and Lev, B. (1981). Risk reduction as a managerial motive for conglomerate mergers. *Bell Journal of Economics (now: RAND Journal of Economics)*, Vol. 12(2), pp. 605–617.

Amihud, Y. and Lev, B. (1999). Does corporate ownership structure affect its strategy towards diversification? *Strategic Management Journal*, Vol. 20(11), pp. 1063–1069.

Amihud, Y., Lev, B., and Travlos, N. G. (1990). Corporate control and the choice of investment financing: The case of corporate acquisitions. *Journal of Finance*, Vol. 45(2), pp. 603–616.

Anand, V. (1991). Big and small companies are marketing their stock. *Investor's Daily*, Vol. 25/Jan/1991, pp. 8.

Anderson, R. C. (2000). Corporate governance and firm diversification. *Financial Management*, Vol. 29(1), pp. 5–23.

Anderson, R. C. and Reeb, D. M. (2003). Founding-family ownership, corporate diversification, and firm leverage. *Journal of Law and Economics*, Vol. 46(2), pp. 653–680.

Ang, J. S. and Cole, R. A. (2000). Agency costs and ownership structure. *Journal of Finance*, Vol. 55(1), pp. 81–106.

Arbuckle, J. L. (1999). *AMOS 4.0 User's Guide*. Chicago (IL).

Badrinath, S. G., Gay, G. D., and Kale, J. R. (1989). Patterns of institutional investment, prudence, and the managerial 'safety-net' hypothesis. *Journal of Risk and Insurance*, Vol. 56(4), pp. 605–629.

Baesel, J. B. and Stein, G. R. (1979). The value of information: Inferences from the profitability of insider trading. *Journal of Financial and Quantitative Analysis*, Vol. 14(3), pp. 553–571.

Baetge, J., Hüls, D., and Uthoff, C. (1996). Früherkennung der Unternehmenskrise. In: Corsten, H. v. and May, C., editors, *Neuronale Netze in der Betriebswissenschaft*, pp. 151–168. Wiesbaden.

Bagnani, E. S. and Milonas, N. T. (1994). Managers, owners, and the pricing of risky debt: An empirical analysis. *Journal of Finance*, Vol. 49(2), pp. 453.

Bahng, J. S. (2002). Nonlinear Effects of Insider Ownership on Corporate Value: Korean Evidence. *Social Science Research Network (SSRN)*, electronic paper collection edition.

Baker, G. P., Jensen, M. C., and Murphy, K. J. (1988). Compensation and incentives: Practice vs. theory. *Journal of Finance*, Vol. 43(3), pp. 593–616.

Banker, R. D., Lee, S.-Y., and Potter, G. (1996). A field study of the impact of a performance-based incentive plan. *Journal of Accounting and Economics*, Vol. 21(2), pp. 195–226.

Barclay, M. J. and Holderness, C. G. (1989). Private benefits from control of public corporations. *Journal of Financial Economics*, Vol. 25(2), pp. 371–395.

Barclay, M. J. and Holderness, C. G. (1991). Negotiated block trades and corporate control. *Journal of Finance*, Vol. 46(3), pp. 861–878.

Barclay, M. J., Holderness, C. G., and Pontiff, J. (1993). Private benefits from block ownership and discounts on closed-end funds. *Journal of Financial Economics*, Vol. 33(3), pp. 263–291.

Barnea, A., Haugen, R. A., and Senbet, L. W. (1981). Market imperfections, agency problems, and capital structure: A review. *Financial Management*, Vol. 10(3), pp. 7–22.

Barnhart, S. W. and Rosenstein, S. (1998). Board composition, managerial ownership, and firm performance: An empirical analysis. *Financial Review*, Vol. 33(4), pp. 1–16.

Barontini, R. and Caprio, L. (2005). The effect of ownership structure and family control on firm value and performance: Evidence from continental europe. *European Financial Management*, Vol. forthcoming, accepted in 2005.

Bassen, A., Böcking, H. J., Loistl, O., and Strenger, C. (2000). Die Analyse von Unternehmen mit der "Scorecard for German Corproate Governance". *Finanz Betrieb*, Vol. 2, pp. 693–698.

Bathala, C. (1996). Determinants of managerial stock ownership: The case of CEOs. *The Financial Review*, Vol. 31(1), pp. 127–147.

Bathala, C. and Moon, K. P. (1994). Managerial ownership, debt policy, and the impact of institutional holdings: An agency perspective. *Financial Management*, Vol. 23(3), pp. 38–50.

Beaver, W., Kettler, P., and Scholes, M. (1970). The association between market determined and accounting determined risk measures. *Accounting Review*, Vol. 45(4), pp. 654–682.

Bebchuk, L. A. (1999). A rent-protection theory of corporate ownership and control. *National Bureau of Economic Research (NBER)*, working paper series edition.

Bebchuk, L. A. and Fried, J. M. (2003). Executive compensation as an agency problem. *Journal of Economic Perspectives*, Vol. 17(3), pp. 71–92.

Bebchuk, L. A., Kraakman, R., and Triantis, G. (2000). Stock pyramids, cross-ownership, and dual-class equity: The mechanisms and agency costs of separating control from cash-flow rights. In: Mørck, R. K., editor, *Concentrated Corporate Ownership*, pp. 295–315.

Becht, M. (1999). European corporate governance: Trading off liquidity against control. *European Economic Review*, Vol. 43(4-6), pp. 1071–1083.

Becht, M., Bolton, P., and Röell, A. (2002). Corporate Governance and Control. *European Corporate Governance Institute (ECGI)*, finance working paper edition.

Becht, M. and Röell, A. (1999). Blockholdings in Europe: An international comparison. *European Economic Review*, Vol. 43(4-6), pp. 1049–1056.

Becker, G. S. (1962). Irrational behavior and economic theory. *Journal of Political Economy*, Vol. 70(1), pp. 1–13.

Beneish, M. D. and Vargus, M. E. (2002). Insider trading, earnings quality, and accrual mispricing. *Accounting Review*, Vol. 77(4), pp. 755–791.

Benston, G. J. (1985). The self-serving management hypothesis: Some evidence. *Journal of Accounting and Economics*, Vol. 7(1/2/3), pp. 67–84.

Berger, P. G. and Ofek, E. (1995). Diversification's effect on firm value. *Journal of Financial Economics*, Vol. 37(1), pp. 39–65.

Bergström, C. and Rydqvist, K. (1990a). The determinants of corporate ownership: An empirical study on Swedish data. *Journal of Banking and Finance*, Vol. 14(2/3), pp. 237–253.

Bergström, C. and Rydqvist, K. (1990b). Ownership of equity in dual-class firms. *Journal of Banking and Finance*, Vol. 14(2/3), pp. 255–269.

Berle, A. A. and Means, G. C. (1932). *The Modern Corporation and Private Property*. New York (NY).

Bernard, V. L., Thomas, J. K., and Abarbanell, J. S. (1993). How sophisticated is the market in interpreting earnings news? *Journal of Applied Corporate Finance*, Vol. 6(2), pp. 54–63.

Bertrand, M. and Mullainathan, S. (2000). Do CEOs Set Their Own Pay? The Ones without Principals Do. *National Bureau of Economic Research (NBER)*, Chicago (IL), working paper series edition.

Bertrand, M. and Mullainathan, S. (2001). Are CEOs rewarded for luck? The ones without principals are. *Quarterly Journal of Economics*, Vol. 116(3), pp. 901–932.

Bethel, J. E. and Liebeskind, J. P. (1993). The effects of ownership structure on corporate restructuring. *Strategic Management Journal*, Vol. 14(4), pp. 15–30.

Bethel, J. E., Liebeskind, J. P., and Opler, T. C. (1997). Block Share Purchases and Corporate Performance. *Ohio State University*, Colombia (OH), working paper edition.

Beyer, J. (1996). Governance structures: Unternehmensverflechtungen und Unternehmenserfolg in Deutschland. In: Albach, H., editor, *Zeitschrift für Betriebswirtschaft (ZfB): Governance Structures*. Supplement 3/96 edition.

Bøhren, O. and Ødegaard, B. A. (2003). Governance and Performance Revisited. *European Corporate Governance Institute (ECGI)*, Sandvika, finance working paper edition.

Bolton, P. and von Thadden, E.-L. (1998). Blocks, liquidity, and corporate control. *Journal of Finance*, Vol. 53(1), pp. 1–25.

Borokhovich, K. A., Brunarski, K., and Parrino, R. (1997). Heterogeneity in the Monitoring Incentives of Outside Blockholders. *University of Texas*, Austin (TX), working paper edition.

Bothwell, J. L. (1980). Profitability, risk, and the seperation of ownership from control. *Journal of Industrial Economics*, Vol. 28(3), pp. 303–311.

Boubaker, S. (2003). On the relationship between ownerhip-control structure and debt financing: new evidence from France. *Université Paris XII, Institut de Recherche en Gestion*, Paris, working paper edition.

Boudreaux, K. J. (1973). 'Managerialsm'and risk-return performance. *Southern Economic Journal*, Vol. 39(3), pp. 366–372.

Boyle, G. W., Carter, R. B., and Stove, R. D. (1998). Extraordinary anti-takeover provisions and insider ownership structure: The case of converting savings and loans. *Journal of Financial and Quantitative Analysis*, Vol. 33(2), pp. 291–304.

Bradley, M. and Wakeman, L. M. (1983). The wealth effects of trageted share repurchases. *Journal of Financial Economics*, Vol. 11(1-4), pp. 301–328.

Brailsford, T. J., Oliver, B. R., and Pua, S. L. H. (2002). On the relation between ownership structure and capital structure. *Accounting and Finance*, Vol. 42(1), pp. 1–26.

Brandhoff, J. (1999). Anreizkompartible Stock Option-Pläne. *Personal*, Vol. 51(5), pp. 222–227.

Brau, J. C. (2002). Do banks price owner-manager agency costs? An examination of small business borrowing. *Journal of Small Business Management*, Vol. 40(4), pp. 273–286.

Breid, V. (1995). Aussagefähigkeit agencytheoretischer Ansätze im Hinblick auf die Verhaltenssteuerung von Entscheidungsträgern. *Zeitschrift für betriebswirtschaftliche Forschung (ZfbF)*, Vol. 47(9), pp. 821–854.

Brickley, J. A., Lease, R. C., and Smith, C. W. (1988). Ownership structure and voting on antitakeover amendments. *Journal of Financial Economics*, Vol. 20(1/2), pp. 267–291.

Brown, K. C. and Brooke, B. A. (1993). Institutional demand and security price pressure: The case of corporate spinoffs. *Financial Analysts Journal*, Vol. 49(5), pp. 53–62.

Browne, M. W. and Cudeck, R. (1993). Alternative ways of assessing model fit. In: Bollen, K. A. and Long, J. S., editors, *Testing structural equation models.*, pp. 139–151. Newbury Park (CA).

Burkart, M., Gromb, D., and Panunzi, F. (1997). Large shareholders, monitoring, and the value of the firm. *Quarterly Journal of Economics*, Vol. 112(3), pp. 693–728.

Burton, B. M., Lonie, A. A., and Power, D. M. (2003). Insider trading, growth opportunities and the market reaction to new financing announcements. *European Journal of Finance*, Vol. 9(4), pp. 301–322.

Bushee, B. J. (1998). The influence of institutional investors on myopic R&D investment behavior. *The Accounting Review*, Vol. 73(3), pp. 305–333.

Bushee, B. J. (2001). Do institutional investors prefer near-term earnings over long-run value? *Contemporary Accounting Research*, Vol. 18(2), pp. 207–246.

Bushman, R. M., Indjejikian, R. J., and Smith, A. (1996). CEO compensation: The role of individual performance evaluation. *Journal of Accounting and Economics*, Vol. 21(2), pp. 161–193.

Bushman, R. M., Piotroski, J. D., and Smith, A. J. (2005). Insider trading restrictions and analysts' incentives to follow firms. *Journal of Finance*, Vol. 60(1), pp. 35–66.

Byrd, J., Parrino, R., and Pritsch, G. (1998). Stockholder-manager conflicts and firm value. *Financial Analysts Journal*, Vol. 54(3), pp. 14–30.

Carney, M. and Gedajlovic, E. R. (2002). The coupling of ownership and control and the allocation of financial resources: Evidence from Hong Kong. *Journal of Management Studies*, Vol. 39(1), pp. 123–146.

Carter, D. A., Simkins, B. J., and Simpson, W. G. (2003). Corporate governance, board diversity, and firm value. *The Financial Review*, Vol. 38(1), pp. 33–53.

Cebenoyan, A. S., Cooperman, E. S., and Register, C. A. (2000). Managerial Stock Ownership as a Corporate Control Device: When Is Enough, Enough? *Stern School of Business*, New York (NY), working paper edition.

Chaganti, R. and Damanpour, F. (1991). Institutional ownership, capital structure, and firm performance. *Strategic Management Journal*, Vol. 12(7), pp. 479–491.

References

Chalmers, J. M. R., Dann, L. Y., and Harford, J. (2002). Managerial opportunism? Evidence from directors and officers insurance purchases. *Journal of Finance*, Vol. 57(2), pp. 609–636.

Chan, S. H., Martin, J. D., and Kensinger, J. (1990). Corporate research and development expenditures and share value. *Journal of Financial Economics*, Vol. 26(2), pp. 255–276.

Chang, S. J. (2003). Ownership structure, expropriation, and performance of group-affiliated companies in Korea. *Academy of Management Journal*, Vol. 46(2), pp. 238–253.

Chapelle, A. (2005). Separation between ownership and control: Where do we stand? *Corporate Ownership and Control*, Vol. 2(2), pp. 91–101.

Chen, C. R. and Steiner, T. L. (1999). Managerial ownership and agency conflicts: A nonlinear simultaneous equation analysis of managerial ownership, risk taking, debt policy, and dividend policy. *Financial Review*, Vol. 34(1), pp. 119–136.

Chen, H., Hexter, L., and Hu, M. (1993). Management ownership and corporate value. *Managerial and Decision Economics*, Vol. 14(4), pp. 335–346.

Chen, S.-S. and Ho, K. W. (2000). Corporate diversification, ownership structure, and firm value. *International Review of Financial-Analysis*, Vol. 9(3), pp. 315–326.

Chevalier, J.-M. (1969). The problems of control in large American corporations. *Anti-Trust Bulletin*, Vol. 14, pp. 163–180.

Cho, M.-H. (1998). Ownership structure, investment, and the corporate value: An empirical analysis. *Journal of Financial Economics*, Vol. 47(1), pp. 103–121.

Chowdhury, S. D. and Geringer, J. M. (2001). Institutional ownership, strategic choices and corporate efficiency: Evidence from Japan. *Journal of Management Studies*, Vol. 38(2), pp. 271–292.

Chung, K. H. and Pruitt, S. W. (1994). A simple approximation of Tobin's q. *Financial Management*, Vol. 23(3), pp. 70–74.

Claessens, S., Djankov, S., Fan, J. P., and Lang, L. H. (2002). Disentangling the incentive and entrenchment effects of large shareholdings. *Journal of Finance*, Vol. 57(6), pp. 2741–2771.

Claessens, S., Djankov, S., and Lang, L. H. (2000). The separation of ownership and control in East Asian corporations. *Journal of Financial Economics*, Vol. 58(1/2), pp. 81–112.

Cleary, S. (2000). The sensitivity of canadian corporate investment to liquidity. *Canadian Journal of Administrative Sciences*, Vol. 17(3), pp. 217–232.

Coase, R. (1937). The nature of the firm. *Economica*, Vol. 4(16), pp. 386–405.

Coffee Jr., J. C. (1991). Liquidity versus control: The institutional investor as corporate monitor. *Columbia Law Review*, Vol. 91(6), pp. 1277–1368.

Comment, R. and Jarrell, G. A. (1995). Corporate focus and stock returns. *Journal of Financial Economics*, Vol. 37(1), pp. 67–87.

Cook, W. W. (1894). *A Treatise on Stock and Stockholders, Bonds, Mortgages, and General Corporation Law A*. New York (NY), 3rd edition.

Cotter, J. F., Shivdasani, A., and Zenner, M. (1994). How managerial wealth affects the tender offer process. *Journal of Financial Economics*, Vol. 35(1), pp. 63–97.

Crutchley, C. E. and Hansen, R. S. (1989). A test of the agency theory of managerial ownership, corporate leverage, and corporate dividends. *Financial Management*, Vol. 18(4), pp. 36–46.

Cubbin, J. and Leech, D. (1983). The effect of shareholding dispersion on the degree of control in British companies: Theory and measurement. *Economic Journal*, Vol. 93(370), pp. 351–369.

Cubbin, J. and Leech, D. (1986). Growth versus profit maximisation: A simultaneous-equations approach to testing the Marris model. *Managerial and Decision Economics*, Vol. 7(2), pp. 123–131.

Cui, H. and Mak, Y. T. (2002). The relationship between managerial ownership and firm performance in high R&D firms. *Journal of Corporate Finance*, Vol. 8(4), pp. 313–336.

DaDalt, P. J., Donaldson, J. R., and Garner, J. L. (2003). Will any q do? *Journal of Financial Research*, Vol. 26(4), pp. 535–551.

Dahya, J., Lonie, A. A., and Power, D. M. (1998). Ownership structure, firm performance and top executive change: An analysis of UK firms. *Journal of Business Finance and Accounting*, Vol. 25(9/10), pp. 1089.

Dann, L. Y. and DeAngelo, H. (1983). Standstill agreements, privately negotiated stock repurchases, and the market for corporate control. *Journal of Financial Economics*, Vol. 11(1-4), pp. 275–300.

Darrough, M. N. and Stoughton, N. M. (1986). Moral hazard and adverse selection: The question of financial structure. *Journal of Finance*, Vol. 41(2), pp. 501–513.

Davidson, R. and MacKinnon, J. G. (1993). *Estimation and Inference in Econometrics*. Oxford.

DeAngelo, H. and DeAngelo, L. (1985). Managerial ownership of voting rights: A study of public corporations with dual classes of common stock. *Journal of Financial Economics*, Vol. 14(1), pp. 33–70.

DeAngelo, H. and Rice, E. M. (1983). Antitakeover charter amendments and stockholder wealth. *Journal of Financial Economics*, Vol. 11(1-4), pp. 329–360.

Dechow, P. M. and Sloan, R. G. (1991). Executive incentives and the horizon problem: An empirical investigation. *Journal of Accounting and Economics*, Vol. 14(1), pp. 51–89.

Demsetz, H. (1986). Corporate control, insider trading, and rates of return. *American Economic Review*, Vol. 76(2), pp. 313–316.

Demsetz, H. and Lehn, K. (1985). The structure of corporate ownership: Causes and consequences. *Journal of Political Economy*, Vol. 93(6), pp. 1155–1177.

Demsetz, H. and Ricardo-Campbell, R. (1983). The structure of ownership and the theory of the firm. *Journal of Law and Economics*, Vol. 26(2), pp. 375–390.

Demsetz, H. and Villalonga, B. (2001). Ownership structure and corporate performance. *Journal of Corporate Finance*, Vol. 7(3), pp. 209–233.

Denis, D. J. and Denis, D. K. (1994). Majority owner-managers and organizational efficiency. *Journal of Corporate Finance*, Vol. 1(1), pp. 91–118.

Denis, D. J., Denis, D. K., and Sarin, A. (1997). Agency problems, equity ownership, and corporate diversification. *Journal of Finance*, Vol. 52(1), pp. 135–160.

Denis, D. J., Denis, D. K., and Sarin, A. (1999). Agency theory and the influence of equity ownership structure on corporate diversification strategies. *Strategic Management Journal*, Vol. 20(11), pp. 1071–1076.

Denis, D. J. and Serrano, J. M. (1996). Active investors and management turnover following unsuccessful control contests. *Journal of Financial Economics*, Vol. 40(2), pp. 239–266.

Dilling-Hansen, M., Madsen, E. S., and Smith, V. (2003). Efficiency, R&D and ownership: some empirical evidence. *International Journal of Production Economics*, Vol. 83(1), pp. 85–94.

Donaldson, G. (1961). Corporate Debt Capacity: A Study of the Corporate Debt Policy and the Determination of Corporate Debt Capacity. *Harvard Business School*, Cambridge (MA), working paper edition.

Duggal, R. and Millar, J. A. (1999). Institutional ownership and firm performance: The case of bidder returns. *Journal of Corporate Finance*, Vol. 5(2), pp. 103–117.

Durbin, J. (1954). Errors in variables. *Review of the International Statistical Institute*, Vol. 22, pp. 23–32.

Dyck, I. A. and Zingales, L. (2004). Private benefits of control: An international comparison. *Journal of Finance*, Vol. 59(2), pp. 537–600.

Eames, M. (1997). Institutional investor myopia, ownership, earnings, and returns. *Santa Clara University*, Santa Clara (CA), working paper edition.

Eckbo, B. E. and Smith, D. C. (1998). The conditional performance of insider trades. *Journal of Finance*, Vol. 53(2), pp. 467–498.

Edwards, J. S. and Nibler, M. (2000). Corporate governance in Germany: the role of banks and ownership concentration. *Economic Policy*, Vol. 15(31), pp. 237.

Edwards, J. S. and Weichenrieder, A. J. (1999). Ownership Concentration and Share Valuation: Evidence from Germany. *The Center for Economic Studies (CES)*, Munich, working paper edition.

Edwards, J. S. and Weichenrieder, A. J. (2004). Ownership concentration and share valuation: Evidence from Germany. *German Economic Review*, Vol. 5(2), pp. 143–171.

Elgin, P. R. (1992). Strategic pairings uncork the blessings for investors, issuers. *Corporate Cashflow*, Vol. 13(10), pp. 7–8.

Elliott, J. W. (1972). Control, size, growth, and financial performance in the firm. *Journal of Financial and Quantitative Analysis*, Vol. 7(1), pp. 1309–1320.

Elston, J. A. (2004). Bank influence, firm performance and survival: Empirical evidence from Germany 1970-1986. *Corporate Ownership and Control*, Vol. 1(2), pp. 65–70.

Elston, J. A., Hofler, R., and Lee, J. (2002). Institutional Ownership, Agency Costs and Dividend Policy. *University of Central Florida, Department of Economics*, Orlando (FL), working paper edition.

Elton, E. J. and Gruber, M. J. (1995). *Modern Portfolio Theory and Investment Analysis*. New York (NY), 5th edition.

Faccio, M. and Lang, L. H. (2002). The ultimate ownership of Western European corporations. *Journal of Financial Economics*, Vol. 65(3), pp. 365–395.

Fama, E. F. (1980). Agency problems and the theory of the firm. *Journal of Political Economy*, Vol. 88(2), pp. 288–307.

Fama, E. F. and Jensen, M. C. (1983a). Agency problems and residual claims. *Journal of Law and Economics*, Vol. 26(2), pp. 327–350.

Fama, E. F. and Jensen, M. C. (1983b). Separation of ownership and control. *Journal of Law and Economics*, Vol. 26(2), pp. 301–326.

Fama, E. F. and Jensen, M. C. (1985). Oragnizational forms and investment decisions. *Journal of Financial Economics*, Vol. 14(1), pp. 101–119.

Farinha, J. (2003). Divided policy, corporate governance and the managerial entrenchment hypothesis: An empirical analysis. *Journal of Business Finance and Accounting*, Vol. 30(9/10), pp. 1173–1209.

Fee, C. E. (2002). The costs of outside equity control: Evidence from motion picture financing decisions. *Journal of Business*, Vol. 75(4), pp. 681.

Finnerty, J. E. (1976). Insiders and marekt efficiency. *Journal of Finance*, Vol. 31(4), pp. 1141–1148.

Forbes (ed.) (1991). What 800 companies paid their bosses (cover story). *Forbes*, Vol. 147(11), pp. 237–289.

Fox, M. A. and Hamilton, R. T. (1994). Ownership and diversification: Agency theory or stewardship theory. *Journal of Management Studies*, Vol. 31(1), pp. 69–82.

Francis, J. and Smith, A. (1995). Agency costs and innovation: Some empirical evidence. *Journal of Accounting and Economics*, Vol. 19(2/3), pp. 383–409.

Franks, J. R. and Mayer, C. P. (2001). Ownership and control of German corporations. *Review of Financial Studies*, Vol. 14(4), pp. 943–977.

Franks, J. R., Mayer, C. P., and Renneboog, L. (1997). Capital Structure, Ownership and Board Restructuring in Poorly Performing Companies. *Catholic University of Leuven*, Leuven, working paper edition.

Friday, H. S. and Sirmans, G. S. (1999). Ownership structure and the value of the firm: The case of REITs. *Journal of Real Estate Research*, Vol. 17(1/2), pp. 71–90.

Friedman, M. (1953). The methodology of positive economics. *Essays in Positive Economics*, pp. 18–35.

Friend, I. and Lang, L. H. (1988). An empirical test of the impact of managerial self-interest on corporate capital structure. *Journal of Finance*, Vol. 43(2), pp. 271–281.

Froot, K. A., Perold, A. F., and Stein, J. C. (1992a). Shareholder trading practices and corporate investment horizons. *Journal of Applied Corporate Finance*, Vol. 5(2), pp. 42–58.

Froot, K. A., Scharfstein, D. S., and Stein, J. C. (1992b). Herd on the street: Informational inefficiencies in a market with short-term speculation. *Journal of Finance*, Vol. 47(4), pp. 1461–1484.

Fukuyama, F. (1995). *Trust: The Social Virtues and the Creation of Prosperity.* London.

Gaver, J. J. and Gaver, K. M. (1993). Additional evidence on the association between the investment opportunity set ad corporate financing, dividend, and compensation policies. *Journal of Accounting and Economics*, Vol. 16(1-3), pp. 125–160.

Gedajlovic, E. R. (1993). Ownership, strategy and performance: Is the dichotomy sufficient? *Organization Studies*, Vol. 14(5), pp. 731–752.

Gedajlovic, E. R. and Shapiro, D. M. (2002). Ownership structure and firm profitability in Japan. *Academy of Management Journal*, Vol. 45(3), pp. 565–575.

Gertler, M. and Hubbard, R. G. (1993). Corporate financial policy, taxation, and macroeconomic risk. *RAND Journal of Economics*, Vol. 24(2), pp. 286–303.

Gibbons, R. and Murphy, K. J. (1992). Optimal incentive contracts in the presence of career concerns: Theory and evidence. *Journal of Political Economy*, Vol. 100(3), pp. 468–505.

Gillan, S. L. and Starks, L. T. (1997). Corporate Governance Proposals and Shareholder Activism: The Role of Institutional Investors. *University of Texas*, Austin (TX), working paper edition.

Gillan, S. L. and Starks, L. T. (2000). Corporate governance proposals and shareholder activism: the role of institutional investors. *Journal of Financial Economics*, Vol. 57(2), pp. 275–305.

Gilson, S. (1989). Management turnover and financial distress. *Journal of Financial Economics*, Vol. 25(2), pp. 241–262.

Givoly, D. and Palmon, D. (1985). Insider trading and the exploitation of inside information: Some empirical evidence. *Journal of Business*, Vol. 58(1), pp. 69–87.

Goergen, M. and Renneboog, L. (2001). Investment policy, internal financing and ownership concentration in the UK. *Journal of Corporate Finance*, Vol. 7(3), pp. 257–284.

Goldfeld, S. M. and Quandt, R. E. (1968). Nonlinear simultaneous equations: Estimation and prediction. *International Economic Review*, Vol. 9(1), pp. 113–136.

Gombola, M. J., Lee, H. W., and Liu, F.-Y. (1999). Further evidence on insider selling prior to seasoned equity offering announcements: The role of growth opportunities. *Journal of Business Finance and Accounting*, Vol. 26(5/6), pp. 621–649.

Gordon, L. A. and Pound, J. (1993). Information, ownership structure, and shareholder voting: Evidence from shareholder-sponsored corporate governance proposals. *Journal of Finance*, Vol. 48(2), pp. 697–718.

Goshen, Z. (2003). The efficiency of controlling corporate self-dealing: Theory meets reality. *California Law Review*, Vol. 91(2), pp. 393–438.

Grant, J. and Kirchmaier, T. (2005). Corporate control in Europe. *Corporate Ownership and Control*, Vol. 2(2), pp. 65–76.

Graves, S. B. (1988). Institutional ownership and corporate R&D in the computer industry. *Academy of Management Journal*, Vol. 31(2), pp. 417–428.

Graves, S. B. and Waddock, S. A. (1990). Institutional ownership and control: Implications for long-term corporate strategy. *Academy of Management Excutive*, Vol. 4(1), pp. 75–83.

Greene, W. H. (1990). *Econometric analysis*. New York (NY), 3rd edition.

Grossman, S. J. (1976). On the efficiency of competitive stock markets where traders have diverse information. *Journal of Finance*, Vol. 31(2), pp. 573–585.

Grossman, S. J. (1995). Dynamic asset allocation and the informational efficiency of markets. *Journal of Finance*, Vol. 50(3), pp. 773–787.

Grossman, S. J. and Hart, O. D. (1980). Takeover bids, the free rider problem and the theory of the corporation. *Bell Journal of Economics (now: RAND Journal of Economics)*, Vol. 11(Spring), pp. 42–64.

Grossman, S. J. and Hart, O. D. (1986). The costs and benefits of ownership: a theory of vertical and lateral integration. *Journal of Political Economy*, Vol. 94(4), pp. 691–719.

Grossman, S. J. and Stiglitz, J. E. (1976). Information and competitive price systems. *American Economic Review*, Vol. 66(2), pp. 246–253.

Gugler, K. P., Müller, D. C., and Yurtoglu, B. B. (2003a). Corporate Governance and the Returns on Investment. *European Corporate Governance Institute (ECGI)*, finance working paper edition.

Gugler, K. P., Müller, D. C., and Yurtoglu, B. B. (2003b). Separating the Wealth and Entrenchment Effects of Insider Ownership on Investment Performance. *University Vienna*, Vienna, economic working papers edition.

Gugler, K. P., Müller, D. C., and Yurtoglu, B. B. (2004). Marginal q, Tobin's q, cash flow, and investment. *Southern Economic Journal*, Vol. 70(3), pp. 512–531.

Gupta, A. and Rosenthal, L. (1991). Ownership structure, leverage, and firm value: The case of leveraged recapitalizations. *Financial Management*, Vol. 20(3), pp. 69–83.

Hair, J. F., Anderson, R. E., Tatham, R. L., and Black, W. C. (1998). *Multivariate Data Analysis*. Upper Saddle River (NJ), 5th edition edition.

Hall, B. H. (1999). The manufacturing sector master file: 1959-1987. *National Bureau of Economic Research*, Chicago (IL), working paper series edition.

Han, K. C. and Suk, D. Y. (1998a). The effect of ownership structure on firm performance: Additional evidence. *Review of Financial Economics*, Vol. 7(2), pp. 143–155.

Han, K. C. and Suk, D. Y. (1998b). Insider ownership and signals: Evidence from stock split announcement effects. *Financial Review*, Vol. 33(2), pp. 1–18.

Hand, J. R. M. (1990). A test of the extended functional fixation hypothesis. *Accounting Review*, Vol. 65(4), pp. 740–763.

Hanson, R. C. and Song, M. H. (1995). Managerial ownership change and firm value: Evidence from dual-class recapitalizations and insider trading. *Journal of Financial Research*, Vol. 18(3), pp. 281–297.

Hanson, R. C. and Song, M. H. (2000). Managerial ownership, board structure, and the division of gains in divestitures. *Journal of Corporate Finance*, Vol. 6(1), pp. 55–70.

Harris, M. and Raviv, A. (1991). The theory of capital structure. *Journal of Finance*, Vol. 46(1), pp. 297–355.

Hart, O. D. (1983). The market mechanism as an incentive scheme. *Bell Journal of Economics (now: RAND Journal of Economics)*, Vol. 14(2), pp. 366–382.

Hartmann-Wendels, T. (1989). Principal-Agent-Theorie und asymmetrische Informationsverteilung. *Zeitschrift für Betriebswirtschaft (ZfB)*, Vol. 59(7), pp. 228–250.

Hartzell, J. C. and Starks, L. T. (2003). Institutional investors and executive compensation. *Journal of Finance*, Vol. 58(6), pp. 2351–2374.

Hausman, J. A. (1975). An instrumental variable approach to full information estimators for linear and certain nonlinear econometric models. *Econometrica*, Vol. 43(4), pp. 727–738.

Hausman, J. A. (1978). Specification tests in econometrics. *Econometrica*, Vol. 46(6), pp. 1251–1271.

Heiss, F. and Köke, J. (2004). Dynamics in ownership and firm survival: Evidence from corporate Germany. *European Financial Management*, Vol. 10(1), pp. 167–195.

Hermalin, B. E. and Weisbach, M. S. (1991). The effects of board composition and direct incentives on firm performance. *Financial Management*, Vol. 20(4), pp. 101–112.

Herman, E. S. (1981). *Corporate Control, Corporate Power*. Cambridge.

Hill, C. W. L. (1995). National institutional structures, transaction cost economizing and competitive advantage: The case of Japan. *Organization Science*, Vol. 6(1), pp. 119–131.

Hill, C. W. L. and Snell, S. A. (1988). External control, corporate strategy, and firm performance in research-intensive industries. *Strategic Management Journal*, Vol. 9(6), pp. 577–588.

Hill, C. W. L. and Snell, S. A. (1989). Effects of ownership structure and control on corporate productivity. *Academy of Management Journal*, Vol. 32(1), pp. 25–46.

Himmelberg, C. P., Hubbard, R. G., and Palia, D. (1999). Understanding the determinants of managerial ownership and the link between ownership and performance. *Journal of Financial Economics*, Vol. 53(3), pp. 353–384.

Hindley, B. (1970). Separation of ownership and control in the modern corporation. *Journal of Law and Economics*, Vol. 13(1), pp. 185–222.
Hüls, D. (1995). *Früherkennung insolvenzgefährdeter Unternehmen*. Düsseldorf.
Hofer, C. W. (1983). ROVA: A new measure for assessing organizational performance. In: Lamb, R., editor, *Advances in Strategic Management*, volume 2, pp. 43–55. New York.
Holderness, C. G. (2003). A survey of blockholders and corporate control. *FRBNY Economic Policy Review*, Vol. 9(1), pp. 51–64.
Holderness, C. G., Kroszner, R. S., and Sheehan, D. P. (1999). Were the good old days that good? Changes in managerial stock ownership since the Great Depression. *Journal of Finance*, Vol. 54(2), pp. 435–469.
Holderness, C. G. and Sheehan, D. P. (1985). Raiders or saviors? The evidence on six controversial investors. *Journal of Financial Economics*, Vol. 14(4), pp. 555–579.
Holderness, C. G. and Sheehan, D. P. (1988). The role of majority shareholders in publicly held corporations: an explanatory analysis. *Journal of Financial Economics*, Vol. 20(1/2), pp. 317–346.
Holl, P. (1975). Effect of control type on the performance of the firm in the UK. *Journal of Industrial Economics*, Vol. 23(4), pp. 257–371.
Holl, P. (1977). Control type and the market for corporate control in large U.S. corporations. *Journal of Industrial Economics*, Vol. 25(4), pp. 259–373.
Holthausen, R. W. and Larcker, D. F. (1993). Organizational Structure and Financial Performance. *The Wharton School, University of Pennsylvania*, Philadelphia (PA), working paper edition.
Holthausen, R. W. and Larcker, D. F. (1996). The financial performance of reverse leveraged buyouts. *Journal of Financial Economics*, Vol. 42(3), pp. 293–332.
Holthausen, R. W., Larcker, D. F., and Sloan, R. G. (1995a). Annual bonus schemes and the manipulation of earnings. *Journal of Accounting and Economics*, Vol. 19(1), pp. 29–74.
Holthausen, R. W., Larcker, D. F., and Sloan, R. G. (1995b). Business unit innovation and the structure of executive compensation. *Journal of Accounting and Economics*, Vol. 19(2/3), pp. 279–313.
Horwitz, M. J. (1985). Santa clara revisited: The development of corporate theory. *West Virginia Law Review*, Vol. 88, pp. 173–224.
Hu, J. and H., N. T. (2001). Insider trading and managerial incentives. *Journal of Banking and Finance*, Vol. 25(4), pp. 681–716.
Hubbard, R. G. and Palia, D. (1995). Benefits of control, managerial ownership, and the stock returns of acquiring firms. *RAND Journal of Economics*, Vol. 26(4), pp. 782–792.
Huddart, S. (1993). The effect of a large shareholder on corporate value. *Management Science*, Vol. 39(11), pp. 1407–1421.

Hudson, C. D., Jahera Jr., J. S., and Lloyd, W. P. (1992). Further evidence on the relationship between ownership and performance. *The Financial Review*, Vol. 27(2), pp. 227–239.

Huson, M. (1997). Does Governance Matter? Evidence from CalPERS Interventions. *University of Alberta*, Edmonton (AB), working paper edition.

Hyland, D. C. and Diltz, J. D. (2002). Why firms diversify: An empirical examination. *Financial Management*, Vol. 31(1), pp. 51–81.

Jacobs, M. (1991). *Short-Term America: The Causes and Cures of our Business Myopia*. Boston (MA).

Jacquemin, A. and De Ghellinck, E. (1980). Familial control, size and performance in the largest french firms. *European Economic Review*, Vol. 13(1), pp. 81–91.

Jaffe, J. P. (1974). Special information and insider trading. *Journal of Business*, Vol. 47(3), pp. 410–428.

Jain, B. A. and Kini, O. (1994). The post-issue operating performance of IPO firms. *Journal of Finance*, Vol. 49(5), pp. 1699–1726.

Jarrell, G. A. and Poulsen, A. B. (1987). Shark repellents and stock prices: The effects of antitakeover amendments since 1980. *Journal of Financial Economics*, Vol. 19(1), pp. 127–168.

Jarrell, G. A. and Poulsen, A. B. (1988). Dual-class recapitalization as antitakeover mechanisms: The recent evidence. *Journal of Financial Economics*, Vol. 20(1/2), pp. 129–152.

Jensen, G. R., Solberg, D. P., and Zorn, T. S. (1992). Simultaneous determination of insider ownership, debt and dividend policies. *Journal of Financial and Quantitative Analysis*, Vol. 27(2), pp. 247–263.

Jensen, M. C. (1986). Agency costs of free cash flow, corporate finance and takeovers. *American Economic Review*, Vol. 76(2), pp. 323–329.

Jensen, M. C. (1988). Takeovers their causes and consequences. *Journal of Economic Perspectives*, Vol. 2(1), pp. 21–48.

Jensen, M. C. and Meckling, W. H. (1976). Theory of the firm: Managerial behavior, agency costs and ownership structure. *Journal of Financial Economics*, Vol. 3(4), pp. 305–360.

Jensen, M. C. and Murphy, K. J. (1990). Performance pay and top-management incentives. *Journal of Political Economy*, Vol. 98(2), pp. 225–264.

Jensen, M. C. and Ruback, R. S. (1983). The market for corporate control: The scientific evidence. *Journal of Financial Economics*, Vol. 11(1-4), pp. 5–50.

Jensen, M. C. and Smith, C. W. (1985). Stockholder, manager and creditor interests: Applications of agency theory. In: Altman, E. and Subrahmanyam, M., editors, *Recent Advances in Corporate Finance*, pp. 95–131.

Jensen, M. C. and Warner, J. B. (1988). The distribution of power among corporate managers, shareholders, and directors. *Journal of Financial Economics*, Vol. 20(1/2), pp. 3–24.

Johnson, W. B., Magee, R. P., Nagarajan, N. J., and Newman, H. A. (1985). An analysis of the stock price reaction to sudden death: Implications for the management labor market. *Journal of Accounting and Economics*, Vol. 7(1-3), pp. 151–174.

Jones, M. and Morse, B. (1997). Institutional investors: Some reflections. *Management Accounting*, Vol. 75(11), pp. 44–45.

Kamerschen, D. R. (1968). The influence of ownership and control on profit rates. *American Economic Review*, Vol. 58(3), pp. 432–447.

Kamerschen, D. R. and Paul, R. J. (1971). A second look at ownership and management in the large U.S. firms. *Management International Review (MIR)*, Vol. 11(2/3), pp. 25–50.

Kania, J. J. and McKean, J. R. (1976). Ownership, control, and the contemporary corporation: a general behavior analysis. *Kyklos*, Vol. 29(2), pp. 272–291.

Kaplan, S. N. (1989). The effects on managemen buyouts on operation performance and value. *Journal of Financial Economics*, Vol. 24(2), pp. 217–254.

Kaplan, S. N. (1994). Top executives, turnover, and firm performance in Germany. *Journal of Law, Economics and Organization*, Vol. 10(1), pp. 142–159.

Karpoff, J. M., Malatesta, P. H., and Walkling, R. A. (1996). Corporate governance and shareholder initiatives: Empirical evidence. *Journal of Financial Economics*, Vol. 42(3), pp. 365–395.

Kesner, I. F. (1987). Director's stock ownership and organizational performance: An investigation of Fortune 500 companies. *Journal of Management*, Vol. 13(3), pp. 499–508.

Kim, J.-B., Krinsky, I., and Lee, J. (1997). Institutional holdings and trading volume reactions to quarterly earnings announcements. *Journal of Accounting, Auditing and Finance*, Vol. 12(1), pp. 1–14.

Kim, W. S., Lee, J. W., and Francis, J. C. (1988). Investment performance of common stocks in relation to inside ownership. *The Financial Review*, Vol. 23(1), pp. 53–64.

Kim, W. S. and Sorensen, E. (1986). Evidence on the agency costs of debt on corporate debt policy. *Journal of Financial and Quantitative Analysis*, Vol. 21(2), pp. 131–144.

Kleine, A. (1995). *Entscheidungstheoretische Aspekte der Principal-Agent-Theorie*. Heidelberg.

Kole, S. R. (1995). Measuring managerial equity ownership: a comparison of sources of ownership data. *Journal of Corporate Finance*, Vol. 1(3-4), pp. 413–435.

Kole, S. R. (1996). Managerial ownership and firm performance: Incentives or rewards? *Advances in Financial Economics*, Vol. 2, pp. 119–149.

Kole, S. R. and Lehn, K. (1997). Deregulation, the evolution of corporate governance structure, and survival. *American Economic Review*, Vol. 87(2), pp. 421–425.

La Porta, R., Lopez-de Silanes, F., and Shleifer, A. (1999). Corporate ownership around the world. *Journal of Finance*, Vol. 54(2), pp. 471–517.

La Porta, R., Lopez-De-Silanes, F., Shleifer, A., and Vishny, R. W. (1997). Legal determinants of external finance. *Journal of Finance*, Vol. 52(3), pp. 1131–1150.

La Porta, R., Lopez-de Silanes, F., Shleifer, A., and Vishny, R. W. (2000). Investor protection and corporate governance. *Journal of Financial Economics*, Vol. 58(1/2), pp. 3–27.

La Porta, R., Lopez-de Silanes, F., Shleifer, A., and Vishny, R. W. (2002). Investor protection and corporate valuation. *Journal of Finance*, Vol. 57(3), pp. 1147–1170.

Lambert, R. and Larcker, D. (1987). Analysis of the use of accounting and market measure of performance in executive compensation contracts. *Journal of Accounting Research*, Vol. 25(Supplement), pp. 85–129.

Lane, P. J., Cannella Jr., A. A., and Lubatkin, M. H. (1998). Agency problems as antecedents to unrelated mergers and diversification: Amihud and Lev reconsidered. *Strategic Management Journal*, Vol. 19(6), pp. 555.

Lane, P. J., Cannella Jr., A. A., and Lubatkin, M. H. (1999). Ownership structure and corporate strategy: one question viewed from two different worlds. *Strategic Management Journal*, Vol. 20(11), pp. 1077–1086.

Lang, L. H. and Stulz, R. M. (1994). Tobin's q, corporate diversification, and firm performance. *Journal of Political Economy*, Vol. 102(6), pp. 1248–1280.

Lang, L. H., Stulz, R. M., and Walkling, R. A. (1991). A test of the free cash flow hypothesis: The case of bidder returns. *Journal of Financial Economics*, Vol. 29(2), pp. 315–336.

Lang, M. and McNichols, M. (1997). Institutional Trading and Corporate Performance. *Stanford University*, Stanford (CA), working paper edition.

Larner, R. J. (1966). Ownership and control in the 200 largest nonfinancial corporations: 1929 and 1963. *American Economic Review*, Vol. 56(4), pp. 777–787.

Larner, R. J. (1970). *Management Control and the Large Corporation*. Port Washington (NY).

Lee, D. E. and Tompkins, J. G. (1999). A modified version of the Lewellen and Badrinath measure of Tobin's q. *Financial Management*, Vol. 28(1), pp. 20–31.

Lee, I. (2002). Insider trading and performance of seasoned equity offering firms after controlling for exogenous trading needs. *Quarterly Review of Economics and Finance*, Vol. 42(1), pp. 59–72.

Leech, D. (2001). Shareholder voting power and corporate governance: a study of large British companies. *Nordic Journal of Political Economy*, Vol. 27, pp. 33–54.

Leech, D. and Leahy, J. (1991). Ownership structure, control type classifications and the performance of large British companies. *The Economic Journal*, Vol. 101(409), pp. 1418–1437.

Lehmann, E. and Weigand, J. (2000). Does the governed corporation perform better? Governance structures and corporate performance in Germany. *Review of Finance*, Vol. 4(2), pp. 157–195.

Leland, H. E. and Pyle, D. H. (1977). Informational asymmetries, financial structure, and financial intermediation. *Journal of Finance*, Vol. 32(2), pp. 371–386.

Lemmon, M. L. and Lins, K. V. (2003). Ownership structure, corporate governance, and firm value: Evidence from the East Asian financial crisis. *Journal of Finance*, Vol. 58(4), pp. 1445–1468.

Lenz, R. T. (1981). "determinants" of organizational performance: An interdisciplinary review. *Strategic Management Journal*, Vol. 2(2), pp. 131–154.

Levin, S. G. and Levin, S. L. (1982). Ownership and control of large industrial firms: Some new evidence. *Review of Business and Economic Research*, (Spring), pp. 37–49.

Lewellen, W. G. and Badrinath, S. G. (1997). On the measurement of Tobin's q. *Journal of Financial Economics*, Vol. 44(1), pp. 77–122.

Lewellen, W. G., Loderer, C., and Rosenfeld, A. (1985). Merger decisions and executive stock ownership in acquiring firms. *Journal of Accounting and Economics*, Vol. 7(1-3), pp. 209–231.

Liebeskind, J. P. and Opler, T. C. (1994). Corporate diversification and agency costs: Evidence from privately held firms, working paper edition.

Lindenberg, E. B. and Ross, S. A. (1981). Tobin's q ratio and industrial organization. *Journal of Business*, Vol. 54(1), pp. 1–32.

Lins, K. V. (2003). Equity ownership and firm value in emerging markets. *Journal of Financial and Quantitative Analysis*, Vol. 38(1), pp. 159–184.

Lintner, J. (1965). The valuation of risk assets and the selection of risky investments in stock portfolios and capital budgets. *Review of Economics and Statistics*, Vol. 47(1), pp. 13–37.

Liu, T.-C. (1960). Underidentication, structural estimation, and forecasting. *Econometrica*, Vol. 28(4), pp. 855–865.

Lloyd, W. P., Jahera Jr., J. S., and Goldstein, S. J. (1986). The relation between returns, ownership structure, and market value. *Journal of Financial Research*, Vol. 9(2), pp. 171–177.

Loderer, C. and Martin, K. (1997). Executive stock ownership and performance: Tracking faint traces. *Journal of Financial Economics*, Vol. 45(2), pp. 223–255.

Loderer, C. F. and Sheehan, D. P. (1989). Corporate bankruptcy and managers' self-serving behavior. *Journal of Finance*, Vol. 44(4), pp. 1059–1075.

Lorie, J. H. and Niederhoffer, V. (1968). Predictive and statistical properties of insider trading. *Journal of Law and Economics*, Vol. 11(1), pp. 35–51.

Lucas, R. E. (1976). Economic policy evaluation: A critique. In: Brunner, K. L., editor, *The Philips Curve and Labor Markets*, supplement to The Journal of Monetary Economics, pp. 19–46.

Machen Jr., A. W. (1908). *A Treatise on the Modern Law of Corporations with Reference to Formation and Operation under General Laws*. Boston (MA).

Machlup, F. (1967). Theories of the firm: Marginalist, behavioral, managerial. *American Economic Review*, Vol. 57(1), pp. 1–33.

Maddala, G. S. (1992). *Introduction to Econometrics*. Englewood Cliffs (NJ), 2nd edition.

Madden, G. P. (1982). The separation of ownership from control and investment performance. *Journal of Economics and Business*, Vol. 34(2), pp. 149–152.

Mak, Y. T. and Li, Y. (2001). Determinants of corporate ownership and board structure: Evidence from Singapore. *Journal of Corporate Finance*, Vol. 7(3), pp. 235–256.

Malatesta, P. H. and Walkling, R. A. (1988). Poison pill securities: Stockholder wealth, profitability, and ownership structure. *Journal of Financial Economics*, Vol. 20(1-4), pp. 347–376.

Masson, R. T. (1971). Executive motivations, earnings, and consequent equity performance. *Journal of Political Economy*, Vol. 79(6), pp. 1278–1292.

Mathiesen, H. (2002). *Managerial ownership and Financial Performance*. PhD thesis, Department of International Economics and Management, Copenhagen Business School, Copenhagen.

Maug, E. (1998). Large shareholders as monitors: Is there a trade-off between liquidity and control? *Journal of Finance*, Vol. 53(1), pp. 65–98.

McConnell, J. J. and Muscarella, C. J. (1985). Corporate capital expenditure decisions and the market value of the firm. *Journal of Financial Economics*, Vol. 14(3), pp. 399–422.

McConnell, J. J. and Servaes, H. (1990). Additional evidence on equity ownership and corporate value. *Journal of Financial Economics*, Vol. 27(2), pp. 595–612.

McConnell, J. J. and Servaes, H. (1995). Equity ownership and the two faces of debt. *Journal of Financial Economics*, Vol. 39(1), pp. 131–157.

McEachern, W. A. (1975). *Corporate Control and Performance*. Lexington (MA).

McEachern, W. A. (1978). Corporate control and growth: An alternative approach. *Journal of Industrial Economics*, Vol. 26(3), pp. 257–266.

McEachern, W. A. and Romeo, A. A. (1978). Stockholder control, uncertainty and the allocation of resources to research and development. *Journal of Industrial Economics*, Vol. 26(4), pp. 349–360.

McKean, J. R. and Kania, J. J. (1978). An industry approach to owner-manager control and profit performance. *Journal of Business*, Vol. 51(2).

McKinsey & Company (ed.) (2002). Global investor opinion survey 2002.

Mehran, H. (1995). Executive compensation structure, ownership, and firm performance. *Journal of Financial Economics*, Vol. 38(2), pp. 163.

Mikkelson, W. H. and Partch, M. M. (1989). Managers' voting rights and corporate control. *Journal of Financial Economics*, Vol. 25(2), pp. 263–290.

Mikkelson, W. H., Partch, M. M., and Shah, K. (1997). Ownership and operating performance of companies that go public. *Journal of Financial Economics*, Vol. 44(3), pp. 281–307.

Mikkelson, W. H. and Regassa, H. (1991). Premiums paid in block transactions. *Managerial and Decision Economics*, Vol. 12(6), pp. 511–517.

Mikkelson, W. H. and Ruback, R. S. (1985). An empirical analysis of the interfirm equity investment process. *Journal of Financial Economics*, Vol. 14(4), pp. 523–553.

Mikkelson, W. H. and Ruback, R. S. (1991). Targeted repurchases and common stock returns. *RAND Journal of Economics*, Vol. 22(4), pp. 544–561.

Müller, D. C. (1972). A life cycle theory of the firm. *Journal of Industrial Economics*, Vol. 10(3), pp. 198–219.

Monks, R. and Minow, N. (1995). *Corporate Governance*. Cambridge.

Monsen, R. J., Chiu, J. S., and Cooley, D. E. (1968). The effect of separation of ownership and control on the performance of the large firm. *Quarterly Journal of Economics*, Vol. 82(3), pp. 435–451.

Mørck, R. K., Shleifer, A., and Vishny, R. W. (1988). Management ownership an market valuation: An empirical analysis. *Journal of Financial Economics*, Vol. 20(1/2), pp. 293–315.

Moyer, R. C., Rao, R., and Sisneros, P. M. (1992). Substitutes for voting rights evidence from dual class recapitalizations. *Financial Management*, Vol. 21(3), pp. 35–47.

Mudambi, R. and Nicosia, C. (1998). Ownership structure and firm performance: evidence from the UK financial services industry. *Applied Financial Economics*, Vol. 8(2), pp. 175–180.

Mußler, H. (2005). Investieren wie die Insider. *Frankfurter Allgemeine Zeitung (FAZ)*, Vol. 256, pp. 25.

Murali, R. and Welch, J. B. (1989). Agents, owners, control and performance. *Journal of Business Finance and Accounting*, Vol. 16(3), pp. 385–398.

Murphy, K. J. (1985). Corporate performance and managerial remuneration: An empirical analysis. *Journal of Accounting and Economics*, Vol. 7(1/2/3), pp. 11–43.

Murphy, K. J. and Zimmerman, J. L. (1993). Financial performance surrounding CEO turnover. *Journal of Accounting and Economics*, Vol. 16(1-3), pp. 273–315.

Myers, S. C. (1984). The capital structure puzzle. *Journal of Finance*, Vol. 39(3), pp. 575–592.

Myers, S. C. and Majluf, N. S. (1984). Corporate financing and investment decisions when firms have information that investors do not have. *Journal of Financial Economics*, Vol. 13(2), pp. 187–221.

Nakamura, A. and Nakamura, M. (1981). On the relationships among several specification error tests presented by Durbin, Wu, and Hausman. *Econometrica*, Vol. 49(6), pp. 1583–1588.

Nesbitt, S. L. (1994). Long-term rewards from shareholder activism: A study of the CalPERS effect. *Journal of Applied Corporate Finance*, Vol. 6(4), pp. 75–49.

Nickell, S., Nicolitsas, D., and Dryden, N. (1997). What makes firms perform well? *European Economic Review*, Vol. 41(3-5), pp. 783–796.

Nyman, S. and Silberstan, A. (1978). The ownership and control of industry. *Oxford Economic Papers*, Vol. 30(March), pp. 74–101.

OECD (ed.) (2001). OECD statistics on institutional investors: Data from 1980 onwards.

Opler, T. C. and Sokobin, J. (1997). Does coordinated institutional shareholder activism work? An analysis of the activities of the Council of Institutional Investors. *Ohio State University*, Columbus (OH), working paper edition.

Oswald, S. L. and Jahera Jr., J. S. (1991). The influence of ownership on performance: An empirical study. *Strategic Management Journal*, Vol. 12(4), pp. 321–326.

Pagano, M. and Röell, A. (1998). The choice of stock ownership structure: agency costs, monitoring and the decision to go public. *Quarterly Journal of Economics*, Vol. 113(1), pp. 187–225.

Palia, D. and Lichtenberg, F. (1999). Managerial ownership and firm performance: A re-examination using productivity measurement. *Journal of Corporate Finance*, Vol. 5(4), pp. 323–339.

Palmer, J. P. (1973a). Abstracts of doctoral dissertations: The profit-performance effects of the separation of ownership from control in large U.S. industrial corporations. *Journal of Finance*, Vol. 28(5), pp. 1377–1378.

Palmer, J. P. (1973b). The profit-performance effects of the separation of ownership from control in large U.S. industrial corporations. *Bell Journal of Economics and Management Science (now: RAND Journal of Economics)*, Vol. 4(1), pp. 293–303.

Peck, S. W. (1996). The influence of professional investors on the failure of management buyout attempts. *Journal of Financial Economics*, Vol. 40(2), pp. 267–294.

Pedersen, T. and Thomsen, S. (1996). Nationality and ownership structures: The 100 largest companies in six European nations. *Management International Review (MIR)*, Vol. 36(2), pp. 149–166.

Pedersen, T. and Thomsen, S. (1997). European patterns of corporate ownership. *Journal of International Business Studies*, Vol. 28(4), pp. 759–778.

Pedersen, T. and Thomsen, S. (1998). Industry and ownership structure. *International Review of Law and Economics*, Vol. 18(4), pp. 385–402.

Pedersen, T. and Thomsen, S. (1999). Economic and systemic explanations of ownership concentration among Europe's largest companies. *International Journal of the Economics of Business*, Vol. 6(3), pp. 367–381.

Perfect, S. B. and Wiles, K. W. (1994). Alternative constructions of Tobin's q: An empirical comparison. *Journal of Empirical Finance*, Vol. 1(3-4), pp. 313–341.

Pescatrice, D., Calluzzo, V., and Fragola, M. (1992). Insider trading characteristics offering superior investment returns. *American Business Review*, Vol. 10(2), pp. 73–77.

Pope, P. F., Morris, R. C., and Peel, D. A. (1990). Insider trading: Some evidence on market efficiency and directors' share dealings in Great Britain. *Journal of Business Finance and Accounting*, Vol. 17(3), pp. 359–380.

Porter, M. (1992). *Capital Choices: Changing the Way America Invests in Industry*. Boston (MA).

Potter, G. (1992). Accounting earnings announcements, institutional investor concentration, and common stock returns. *Journal of Accounting Research*, Vol. 30(1), pp. 146–155.

Pound, J. (1988a). The information effects of takeover bids and resistance. *Journal of Financial Economics*, Vol. 22(2), pp. 207–227.

Pound, J. (1988b). Proxy contests and the efficiency of shareholder oversight. *Journal of Financial Economics*, Vol. 20(1/2), pp. 237–265.

Prowse, S. D. (1990). Institutional ownership patterns and corporate financial behavior in the United States and Japan. *Journal of Financial Economics*, Vol. 27(1), pp. 43–66.

Radice, H. K. (1971). Control type, profitability and growth in large firms: An empirical study. *Economic Journal*, Vol. 81(323), pp. 547–563.

Rappaport, A. (1995). *Shareholder Value: Wertsteigerung als Maßstab für die Unternehmensführung*. Stuttgart.

Redding, S. G. (1990). *The Spirit of Chinese Capitalism*. New York (NY).

Redding, S. G. (1994). Competitive advantage in the context of Hong Kong. *Journal of Far Eastern Business*, Vol. 1(1), pp. 71–89.

Renneboog, L. (2000). Ownership, corporate control and large shareholder monitoring in companies listed on the Brussels stock exchange. *Journal of Banking and Finance*, Vol. 24(12), pp. 1959–95.

Richter, R. and Furubotn, E. G. (1999). *Institutions and Economic Theory: The Contribution of the New Institutional Economics*. Ann Arbor (USA).

Rosenberg, B. and Guy, J. (1976). Prediction of beta from investment fundamentals. *Financial Analysts Journal*, Vol. 32(3), pp. 60–75.

Ross, S. A. (1977). The determination of financial structure: The incentive-signalling approach. *Bell Journal of Economics (now: RAND Journal of Economics)*, Vol. 8(1), pp. 23–40.

Round, D. K. (1976). The effect of the separation of ownership and control on large firm profit rates in Australia: An exploratory investigation. *Rivista Internazionale Di Scienze Economiche e Commercial*, Vol. 23, pp. 426–436.

Rozeff, M. S. and Zaman, M. A. (1988). Market efficiency and insider trading: New evidence. *Journal of Business*, Vol. 61(1), pp. 25–44.

Rozeff, M. S. and Zaman, M. A. (1998). Overreaction and insider trading: Evidence from growth and value portfolios. *Journal of Finance*, Vol. 53(2), pp. 701–716.

Ryan, L. V. and Schneider, M. (2002). The antecedents of institutional investor activism. *Academy of Management Review*, Vol. 27(4), pp. 554.

Savvides, A. (1998). Inflation and monetary policy in selected West and Central African countries. *World Development*, Vol. 26(5), pp. 809–827.

Schellenger, M. H., Wood, D. D., and Tashakori, A. (1989). Board of director composition, shareholder wealth, and dividend policy. *Journal of Management*, Vol. 15(3), pp. 457–467.

Schipper, K. (1989). Commentary on earnings management. *Accounting Horizons*, Vol. 3(4), pp. 91–102.

Schulze, W. S., Lubatkin, M. H., and Dino, R. N. (2003). Exploring the agency consequences of ownership dispersion among the directors of private family firms. *Academy of Management Journal*, Vol. 46(2), pp. 179–194.

Servaes, H. (1996). The value of diversification during the conglomerate merger wave. *Journal of Finance*, Vol. 51(4), pp. 1201–1225.

Seyhun, H. N. (1986). Insiders' profits, costs of trading, and market efficiency. *Journal of Financial Economics*, Vol. 16(2), pp. 189–212.

Sharpe, W. F. (1963). A simplified model for portfolio analysis. *Management Science*, Vol. 9(2), pp. 277–293.

Sharpe, W. F. (1964). Capital asset prices: A theory of market equilibrium under conditions of risk. *Journal of Finance*, Vol. 19(3), pp. 425–442.

Shin, H.-H. and Kim, Y. H. (2002). Agency costs and efficiency of business capital investment: Evidence from quarterly capital expenditures. *Journal of Corporate Finance*, Vol. 8(2), pp. 139–158.

Shivdasani, A. (1993). Board composition, ownership structure, and hostile takeovers. *Journal of Accounting and Economics*, Vol. 16(1-3), pp. 167–198.

Shleifer, A. and Vishny, R. W. (1986). Large stakeholders and corporate control. *Journal of Political Economy*, Vol. 94(3), pp. 461–488.

Shleifer, A. and Vishny, R. W. (1989). Management entrenchment: The case of manager-specific investments. *Journal of Financial Economics*, Vol. 25(1), pp. 123–139.

Shleifer, A. and Vishny, R. W. (1997). A survey of corporate governance. *Journal of Finance*, Vol. 52(2), pp. 737–783.

Shome, D. K. and Singh, S. (1995). Firm value and external blockholders. *Financial Management*, Vol. 24(4), pp. 3–14.

Short, H. (1994). Ownership, control, financial structure and the performance of firms. *Journal of Economic Surveys*, Vol. 8(3), pp. 203.

Short, H. and Keasey, K. (1999). Managerial ownership and the performance of firms: Evidence from the UK. *Journal of Corporate Finance*, Vol. 5(1), pp. 79–101.

Short, H., Keasey, K., and Duxbury, D. (2002a). Capital structure, management ownership and large external shareholders: A UK analysis. *International Journal of the Economics of Business*, Vol. 9(3), pp. 375–399.

Short, H., Keasey, K., and Watson, R. (1994). Directors' ownership and the performance of small and medium sized firms in the U.K. *Small Business Economics*, Vol. 6(3), pp. 225–36.

Short, H., Zhang, H., and Keasey, K. (2002b). The link between dividend policy and institutional ownership. *Journal of Corporate Finance*, Vol. 8(2), pp. 105–122.

Sloan, R. (1993). Accounting earnings and top executive compensation. *Journal of Accounting and Economics*, Vol. 16(1-3), pp. 55–100.

Slovin, M. B. and Sushka, M. E. (1993). Ownership concentration, corporate control activity, and firm value: Evidence from the death of inside blockholders. *Journal of Finance*, Vol. 48(4), pp. 1293–1321.

Smith, A. J. (1990). Corporate ownership structure and performance: The case of management buyouts. *Journal of Financial Economics*, Vol. 27(1), pp. 143–164.

Smith, C. W. and Watts, R. L. (1992). The investment opportunity set and corporate financing, dividend, and compensation policies. *Journal of Financial Economics*, Vol. 32(2), pp. 263–292.

Smith, M. P. (1996). Shareholder activism by institutional investors: Evidence from CalPERS. *Journal of Finance*, Vol. 51(1), pp. 227–252.

Smithers, A. and Wright, S. (2000). *Valuing Wall Street: Protecting Wealth in Turbuluent Markets*. Blacklick (OH).

Song, M. H. and Walkling, R. A. (1993). The impact of managerial ownership on acquisition attempts and target shareholder wealth. *Journal of Financial and Quantitative Analysis*, Vol. 28(4), pp. 439–457.

Sorensen, R. (1974). The separation of ownership and control and firm performance: an empirical analysis. *Southern Economic Journal*, Vol. 41(1), pp. 145–149.

Spremann, K. (1987). Zur Reduktion von Agency-Kosten. In: Scheider, D., editor, *Kapitalmarkt und Finanzierung*, pp. 341–350. Berlin.

Spremann, K. (1988). Reputation, Garantie, Information. *Zeitschrift für Betriebswirtschaft (ZfB)*, Vol. 58(5-6), pp. 613–629.

Stano, M. (1975). Executive ownership, interests and corporate performance. *Southern Economic Journal*, Vol. 42(2), pp. 272–278.

Stano, M. (1976). Monopoly power, ownership control, and corporate performance. *Bell Journal of Economics (now: RAND Journal of Economics)*, Vol. 7(2), pp. 672–679.

Steer, P. and Cable, J. (1978). Internal organization and profit: An empirical analysis of large U.K. companies. *Journal of Industrial Economics*, Vol. 27(1), pp. 13–30.

Steiger, J. H. (1990). Structural model evaluation and modification: An interval estimation approach. *Multivariate Behavioural Research*, Vol. 25, pp. 173–180.

Stein, J. C. (1988). Takeover threats and managerial myopia. *Journal of Political Economy*, Vol. 96(1), pp. 61–80.

Stein, J. C. (1989). Efficient capital markets, inefficient firms: A model of mypopic corporate behavior. *Quarterly Journal of Economics*, Vol. 104(4), pp. 655–669.

Stekler, H. O. (1964). The variability of profitability with size of firm, 1947-1958. *American Statistical Association Journal*, Vol. 59(308), pp. 1183–1193.

Strickland, D., Wiles, K. W., and Zenner, M. (1996). A requiem for the USA: Is small shareholder monitoring effective? *Journal of Financial Economics*, Vol. 40(2), pp. 319–338.

Stulz, R. M. (1988). Managerial control of voting rights: Financing policies and the market for corporate control. *Journal of Financial Economics*, Vol. 20(1/2), pp. 25–54.

Stulz, R. M. (1990). Managerial discretion and optimal financing policies. *Journal of Financial Economics*, Vol. 26(1), pp. 3–27.

Stulz, R. M., Walkling, R. A., and Song, M. H. (1990). The distribution of target ownership and the division of gains in successful takeovers. *Journal of Finance*, Vol. 45(3), pp. 817–833.

Swoboda, P. (1982). Heterogene Information und Kapitalstruktur der Unternehmung. *Zeitschrift für betriebswirtschaftliche Forschung (ZfbF)*, Vol. 34(2), pp. 549–561.

Taylor, W. (1990). Can big owners make a big difference? *Harvard Business Review*, Vol. 68(5), pp. 70–82.

Thompson II, D. J. (1976). Sources of systematic risk in common stocks. *Journal of Business*, Vol. 49(2), pp. 173–188.

Thomsen, S. (2005). Blockholder Ownership, Dividends and Firm Value In Continental Europe. Leeds, european financial management symposium 2005 edition.

Thonet, P. J. and Poensgen, O. H. (1979). Managerial control and economic performance in Western Germany. *Journal of Industrial Economics*, Vol. 28(1), pp. 23–37.

Tobin, J. (1969). A general equilibrium approach to monetary theory. *Journal of Money, Credit and Banking*, Vol. 1(1), pp. 15–19.

Tobin, J. (1978). Monetary policies and the economy: The transmission mechanism. *Southern Economic Journal*, Vol. 44(3), pp. 421–431.

Upton, N., Teal, E. J., and Seaman, S. L. (2003). Growth goals, strategies and compensation practices of US family and non-family high-growth firms. *International Journal of Entrepreneurship and Innovation*, Vol. 4(2), pp. 113–120.

Villajero, D. (1962). Stock ownership and the control of corporations. *New University Thought*, Vol. 2, pp. 33–77.

Wahal, S. (1996). Pension fund activism and firm performance. *Journal of Financial and Quantitative Analysis*, Vol. 31(1), pp. 1–23.

Wahal, S. and McConnell, J. J. (2000). Do institutional investors exacerbate managerial myopia? *Journal of Corporate Finance*, Vol. 6(3), pp. 307–329.

Walkling, R. A. and Long, M. S. (1984). Agency theory, managerial welfare, and takeover bid rescue. *RAND Journal of Economics*, Vol. 15(1), pp. 54–67.

Ware, R. F. (1975). Performance of manager- versus owner-controlled firms in the food and beverage industry. *Quarterly Review of Economics and Business*, Vol. 15(Summer), pp. 81–92.

Warner, J. B., Watts, R. L., and Wruck, K. H. (1988). Stock prices and top management changes. *Journal of Financial Economics*, Vol. 20(1-2), pp. 461–492.

Weber, M. and Dudney, D. (2003). A reduced form coefficients analysis of executive ownership, corporate value, and executive compensation. *The Financial Review*, Vol. 38(3), pp. 399–413.

Welch, E. (2003). The relationship between ownership structure and performance in listed Australian companies. *Australian Journal of Management*, Vol. 28(3), pp. 287–305.

Weston, J. F. (1979). The tender takeover. *Mergers and Acquisitions*, Vol. 14, pp. 74–82.

Williamson, O. E. (1975). *Markets and Hierarchies: Analysis and Anti-Trust Implications*. New York (NY).

Williamson, O. E. (1985). *The Economic Institutions of Capitalism*. New York (NY).

Winkler, A. (2004). Corporate law or the law of business?: stakeholders and corporate governance at the end of history. *Law and Contemporary Problems*, Vol. 67, pp. 109–133.

Witte, E. (1981). Der Einfluß der Anteilseigner auf die Unternehmenspolitik. *Zeitschrift für Betriebswirtschaft (ZfB)*, Vol. 51, pp. 733–779.

Wruck, K. H. (1989). Equity ownership concentration and firm value: Evidence from private equity financings. *Journal of Financial Economics*, Vol. 23(1), pp. 3–28.

Wu, D. M. (1973). Alternative tests of independence between stochastic regressors and disturbances. *Econometrica*, Vol. 41(4), pp. 733–750.

Yafeh, Y. and Yosha, O. (1995). Large Shareholders and Banks: Who Monitors and How? *Center for Economic Policy Research (CEPR)*, discussion paper edition.

Yeo, G. H., Tan, P. M., Ho, K. W., and Chen, S.-S. (2002). Corporate ownership structure and the informativeness of earnings. *Journal of Business Finance and Accounting*, Vol. 29-52(7-8), pp. 1023–1046.

Yermack, D. (1995). Do corporations award CEO stock options effectively? *Journal of Financial Economics*, Vol. 39(2-3), pp. 237–269.

Yermack, D. (1996). Higher market valuation of companies with a small board of directors. *Journal of Financial Economics*, Vol. 40(2), pp. 185–211.

Yermack, D. (1997). Good timing: CEO stock option awards and company news announcements. *Journal of Finance*, Vol. 52(2), pp. 449–476.

Yoshihara, K. (1988). *The Rise of Ersatz Capitalism in Southeast Asia*. Oxford.

Zeckhauser, R. J. and Pound, J. (1990). Are large shareholders effective monitors: An investigation of share ownership and corporate performance. In: Hubbard, R. G., editor, *Asymmetric Information, Corporate Finance, and Investment*, pp. 149–180. Chicago (IL).

Zellner, A. and Theil, H. (1962). Three-stage least squares: Simultaneous estimation of simultaneous equations. *Econometrica*, Vol. 30(1), pp. 54–78.

Zhang, G. (1998). Ownership concentration, risk aversion and the effect of financial structure on investment decisions. *European Economic Review*, Vol. 42(9), pp. 1751–1778.

Zhang, S. (2005). Underpricing, share overhang, and insider selling in follow-on offerings. *Financial Review*, Vol. 40(3), pp. 409–428.

Zingales, L. (1994). The value of the voting right: a study of the Milan Stock Exchange experience. *Review of Financial Studies*, Vol. 7(1), pp. 125–148.

Zwiebel, J. (1995). Block investment and partial benefits of corporate control. *Review of Economic Studies*, Vol. 62(211), pp. 161–185.

A

Appendices

A.1 Results of "Global Investor Opinion Survey 2002" by McKinsey

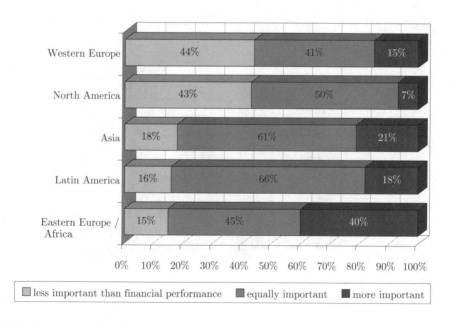

Fig. A.1: Respondents rating of the importance of corporate governance compared to financial performance

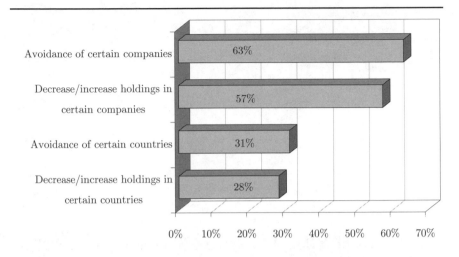

Fig. A.2: Impact of bad corporate governance on the investment decision

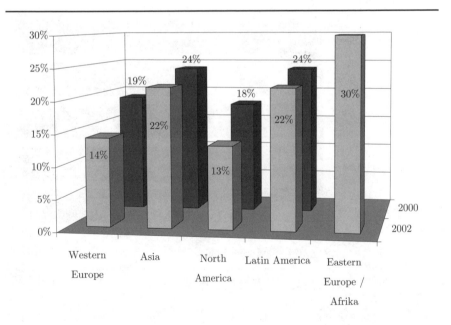

Fig. A.3: Willingness to pay a premium for good corporate governance

A.1 Results of "Global Investor Opinion Survey 2002" by McKinsey 219

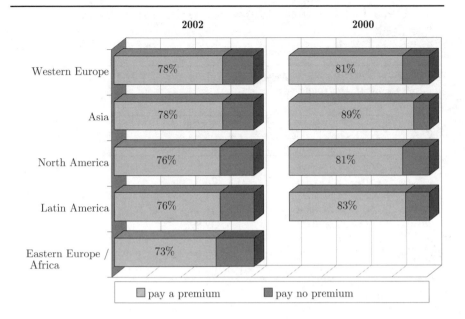

Fig. A.4: Size of the premium for good corporate governance

A.2 Detailed Data on National Ownership Structures

Table A.1: Distribution of the largest voting stock in Germany and the USA
Source: Becht/Röell [1999]

	Germany %	cumulated %	NYSE %	cumulated %	NASDAQ %	cumulated %
0-5%	1.1	1.1	52.8	52.8	54.4	54.4
5-10%	1.9	3.0	21.1	73.9	17.4	71.9
10-25%	14.5	17.5	20.9	94.8	20.6	92.4
25-50%	18.3	35.8	3.5	98.3	5.5	98.0
50-75%	25.5	61.3	1.5	99.8	1.5	99.4
75-90%	17.5	78.8	0.2	100.0	0.5	99.9
90-95%	5.7	84.4	0.0	100.0	0.0	99.9
95-100%	15.6	100.0	0.0	100.0	0.1	100.0

Table A.2: Median of the largest voting stock by different countries
[1] a random sample of 250 firms *Source: Becht/Röell [1999]*

	Number of companies	Median in %
Austria	50	52.0
Belgium	121	50.6
- BEL20	20	45.1
Germany	374	52.1
- DAX30	30	11.0
Spain	193	34.2
France - CAC40	40	20.0
Italy	216	54.5
Netherlands	137	43.5
UK[1]	250	9.9
US - NYSE	1309	below 5.0
- NASDAQ	2831	below 5.0

A.2 Detailed Data on National Ownership Structures

Table A.3: Distribution of controlling shareholders' identities for different countries Widely held if no combined share exceeds 10% of the control rights, else classification by the largest owner *Source: La Porta et al. [1999]*

	Widely Held	Family	State	Widely Held Financial	Widely Held Corporation	Misc.
Argentina	0.00	0.65	0.20	0.10	0.05	0.00
Australia	0.55	0.10	0.05	0.05	0.25	0.00
Austria	0.05	0.15	0.70	0.00	0.00	0.10
Belgium	0.00	0.50	0.05	0.35	0.00	0.10
Canada	0.50	0.30	0.00	0.00	0.15	0.05
Denmark	0.10	0.35	0.20	0.05	0.00	0.30
Finland	0.15	0.10	0.35	0.25	0.00	0.15
France	0.30	0.20	0.20	0.20	0.10	0.00
Germany	0.35	0.10	0.30	0.25	0.00	0.00
Greece	0.05	0.65	0.30	0.00	0.00	0.00
Hong Kong	0.10	0.70	0.05	0.05	0.00	0.10
Ireland	0.45	0.15	0.00	0.05	0.05	0.30
Israel	0.05	0.50	0.40	0.00	0.05	0.00
Italy	0.15	0.20	0.50	0.00	0.00	0.15
Japan	0.50	0.10	0.05	0.00	0.00	0.35
Mexico	0.00	1.00	0.00	0.00	0.00	0.00
Netherlands	0.30	0.20	0.05	0.00	0.10	0.35
New Zealand	0.05	0.45	0.25	0.05	0.20	0.00
Norway	0.05	0.25	0.40	0.10	0.00	0.20
Portugal	0.00	0.50	0.25	0.20	0.00	0.05
Singapore	0.05	0.45	0.45	0.00	0.00	0.05
South Korea	0.40	0.35	0.15	0.00	0.05	0.05
Spain	0.15	0.25	0.45	0.15	0.00	0.00
Sweden	0.00	0.55	0.10	0.30	0.00	0.05
Switzerland	0.50	0.40	0.00	0.05	0.00	0.05
UK	0.90	0.05	0.00	0.05	0.00	0.00
US	0.80	0.20	0.00	0.00	0.00	0.00
Sample average	0.24	0.35	0.20	0.08	0.04	0.09

Table A.4: Cash flow and control right stake of the ultimate owner over European countries

Source: Faccio/Lang [2002]

	Number of firms	Mean	Standard deviation	Median	First quartile	Third quartile
Cash flow rights						
Austria	95	47.16	23.52	50.00	25.50	65.00
Belgium	120	35.14	24.96	36.10	14.98	51.81
France	604	46.68	26.69	48.98	24.69	66.00
Germany	690	48.54	31.46	48.89	21.05	75.00
Italy	204	38.33	25.13	39.68	16.61	56.83
Norway	149	24.39	21.26	19.42	8.91	36.12
Portugal	86	38.42	20.45	39.31	19.83	52.00
Spain	610	42.72	30.46	32.55	18.50	64.91
Sweden	244	25.15	23.06	17.30	9.45	33.55
Switzerland	189	34.66	24.69	29.00	12.85	51.00
UK	1,628	22.94	17.87	16.21	10.96	29.66
Total	4,806	34.64	26.76	25.90	13.02	51.00
Control rights						
Austria	95	53.52	22.77	54.70	34.00	75.00
Belgium	120	40.09	23.20	39.56	19.49	55.86
France	604	48.32	25.55	50.00	28.70	66.00
Germany	690	54.50	28.70	50.76	27.00	76.91
Italy	204	48.26	21.00	50.11	31.39	63.15
Norway	149	31.47	20.18	27.78	15.10	43.59
Portugal	86	41.00	19.18	44.95	22.28	52.30
Spain	610	44.24	29.59	35.73	20.00	65.03
Sweden	244	30.96	22.37	24.90	14.50	40.55
Switzerland	189	46.68	25.97	50.00	22.50	63.00
UK	1,628	25.13	17.87	18.02	13.28	30.19
Total	4,806	38.48	26.10	30.01	15.96	53.98
Ratio of cash flow rights to control rights						
Austria	95	0.85	0.22	1.00	0.70	1.00
Belgium	120	0.78	0.36	1.00	0.60	1.00
France	604	0.93	0.19	1.00	1.00	1.00
Germany	690	0.84	0.27	1.00	0.71	1.00
Italy	204	0.74	0.34	0.97	0.55	1.00
Norway	149	0.78	0.34	1.00	0.53	1.00
Portugal	86	0.92	0.22	1.00	1.00	1.00
Spain	610	0.94	0.18	1.00	1.00	1.00
Sweden	244	0.79	0.34	1.00	0.53	1.00
Switzerland	189	0.74	0.29	0.83	0.47	1.00
UK	1,628	0.89	0.23	1.00	0.91	1.00
Total	4,806	0.87	0.26	1.00	0.85	1.00

A.3 Example on Argument of Constant Market Return

The following scenario clarifies the argument of Demsetz/Lehn [1985] of the inadequacy of the market return as a performance measures. It has following case assumptions:

1. Firm A and Firma B earn at the beginning a free cash flow (FCF) of €1 per year. In 2001, Firm A unexpectedly invents something that increases the FCF to €1.2 per year.
2. Both firms have a weighted average cost of capital of 10% per year and are for simplicity reasons 100% equity-financed.
3. For both firms the going concern is assumed.
4. All stock market investors are perfectly informed; thus the present value (PV) equals the market value (MV).
5. All FCF is paid to the shareholder as dividends at the end of the year.
6. Both firms make an initial investment of €10 at the beginning of 1999.
7. Both firms have zero growth and total reinvestments equals total depreciations of €2 per year.[1]
8. For simplicity reasons there is a tax rate of 0%.
9. Each firm has ten shares outstanding.
10. There is zero inflation and no technological progress; the replacement value of invested capital equals its book value.

Given these assumptions the performance measures are calculated as follows:

- EPS = NOPLAT / number of shares outstanding;
- PV = FCF / weighted average cost of capital, especially under second, third, and seventh assumption;
- MV = PV;
- Market return = $(PV_t + \text{dividends}_t - PV_{t-1})/ PV_{t-1}$;
- Q = market value / replacement costs of invested capital.

Both Table A.5 and Figure A.5 demonstrate that, unless an unexpected event happens, the market return can not distinguish the two firms.

---

[1] As consequence, the FCF equals the net operating profit less adjusted taxes (NOPLAT) and the invested capital equals the initial investment.

Table A.5: Calculated Performance Measures for Firm A and Firm B

	FCF		EPS		MV = PV		Market return		Q	
Year	A	B	A	B	A	B	A	B	A	B
1999	1.0	1.0	0.10	0.10	10	10	10%	10%	1.0	1.0
2000	1.0	1.0	0.10	0.10	10	10	10%	10%	1.0	1.0
2001	1.2	1.0	0.12	0.10	12	10	32%	10%	1.2	1.0
2002	1.2	1.0	0.12	0.10	12	10	10%	10%	1.2	1.0
2003	1.2	1.0	0.12	0.10	12	10	10%	10%	1.2	1.0

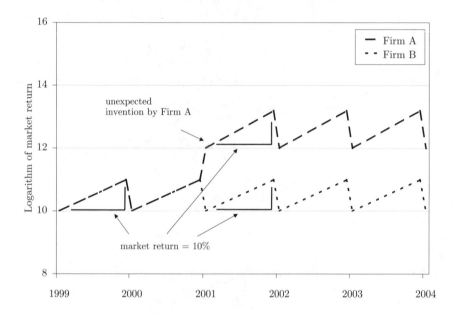

Fig. A.5: Market return and its reaction on an unexpected event

A.4 Historic Tobin's Qs

The Federal Reserve of the United States provides aggregated and historical replacement costs for United States businesses in its Flow of Funds Reports. It contains data for both, public and private companies. Smithers/Wright [2000] did extensive research on the levels of Tobin's Q from 1925 to 1997. Due to the need for market values and possible biases, they calculate the Tobin's Q data referring to public, non-farm, corporate, and non-financial businesses.

Table A.6 contains the Federal Reserve data and Tobin's Q calculation by Smithers/Wright [2000] from 1900 through 2004. The mean Tobin's Q for this period is .63. This low average, as opposed to 1.0, is primarily attributed to the lack of market value information for private businesses. Thus, Smithers/Wright [2000] also stated the relative value of Q to its mean as proxy for the Tobin's Q of private and public companies. Further, the degree of under- and overvaluation is measured by the logarithm of the relative value of Tobin's Q, which is also demonstrate by Figure A.6.

Table A.6: Historic Tobin's Qs from 1900 to 2004 for the United States
Where "abs. Q" stands for absolute value of Q, "rel. Q" for relative value of Q to its mean, and "Ln(Q/μ_Q)" for logarithm of the ratio of Q and its mean
The geometrical mean of Tobin's Q for 1990 to 2004 lies at approximately .63; Data source: Smithers/Wright [2000] and the Flow of Funds Accounts of the Federal Reserve of the United States

Year	abs. Q	rel. Q	Ln(Q/μ_Q)	Year	abs. Q	rel. Q	Ln(Q/μ_Q)
1900	0.80	1.27	0.24	1910	0.87	1.38	0.32
1901	0.94	1.49	0.40	1911	0.87	1.38	0.32
1902	1.00	1.58	0.46	1912	0.88	1.40	0.34
1903	0.77	1.23	0.20	1913	0.78	1.25	0.22
1904	1.02	1.63	0.49	1914	0.66	1.06	0.05
1905	1.12	1.77	0.57	1915	0.81	1.29	0.25
1906	1.02	1.62	0.48	1916	0.65	1.03	0.03
1907	0.64	1.02	0.02	1917	0.34	0.53	-0.63
1908	0.91	1.45	0.37	1918	0.33	0.53	-0.64
1909	0.99	1.57	0.45	1919	0.34	0.53	-0.63

Table continues at the following page

Table A.6: Historic Tobin's Qs ... (continued)

Year	abs. Q	rel. Q	$\operatorname{Ln}(Q/\mu_Q)$	Year	abs. Q	rel. Q	$\operatorname{Ln}(Q/\mu_Q)$
1920	0.27	0.43	-0.85	1960	0.70	1.10	0.10
1921	0.35	0.55	-0.60	1961	0.81	1.28	0.25
1922	0.40	0.64	-0.45	1962	0.76	1.21	0.19
1923	0.40	0.63	-0.46	1963	0.81	1.29	0.25
1924	0.46	0.73	-0.32	1964	0.91	1.44	0.37
1925	0.56	0.89	-0.11	1965	0.97	1.55	0.44
1926	0.58	0.93	-0.07	1966	0.80	1.26	0.23
1927	0.74	1.17	0.16	1967	0.96	1.53	0.43
1928	0.97	1.54	0.43	1968	1.06	1.68	0.52
1929	1.35	2.15	0.76	1969	0.82	1.29	0.26
1930	0.73	1.16	0.15	1970	0.75	1.19	0.17
1931	0.45	0.72	-0.34	1971	0.81	1.28	0.25
1932	0.43	0.68	-0.38	1972	0.92	1.47	0.38
1933	0.61	0.97	-0.03	1973	0.65	1.02	0.02
1934	0.57	0.91	-0.10	1974	0.36	0.57	-0.55
1935	0.78	1.24	0.22	1975	0.45	0.71	-0.34
1936	0.98	1.55	0.44	1976	0.49	0.78	-0.25
1937	0.56	0.89	-0.11	1977	0.39	0.62	-0.47
1938	0.66	1.04	0.04	1978	0.36	0.58	-0.55
1939	0.63	1.00	0.00	1979	0.38	0.60	-0.52
1940	0.49	0.78	-0.25	1980	0.43	0.68	-0.39
1941	0.35	0.56	-0.58	1981	0.35	0.55	-0.59
1942	0.37	0.59	-0.52	1982	0.38	0.60	-0.51
1943	0.44	0.69	-0.37	1983	0.43	0.68	-0.39
1944	0.48	0.76	-0.28	1984	0.38	0.61	-0.50
1945	0.55	0.87	-0.14	1985	0.46	0.73	-0.32
1946	0.44	0.70	-0.36	1986	0.52	0.82	-0.19
1947	0.37	0.58	-0.54	1987	0.51	0.80	-0.22
1948	0.34	0.53	-0.63	1988	0.53	0.84	-0.17
1949	0.36	0.57	-0.57	1989	0.62	0.99	-0.01

Table continues at the following page

Table A.6: Historic Tobin's Qs ... (continued)

Year	abs. Q	rel. Q	Ln(Q/μ_Q)	Year	abs. Q	rel. Q	Ln(Q/μ_Q)
1950	0.40	0.63	-0.46	1990	0.59	0.94	-0.07
1951	0.42	0.67	-0.40	1991	0.84	1.33	0.29
1952	0.40	0.63	-0.46	1992	0.94	1.50	0.40
1953	0.38	0.60	-0.51	1993	0.99	1.57	0.45
1954	0.50	0.79	-0.24	1994	0.92	1.45	0.37
1955	0.58	0.91	-0.09	1995	1.12	1.78	0.58
1956	0.58	0.91	-0.09	1996	1.20	1.90	0.64
1957	0.50	0.79	-0.23	1997	1.37	2.17	0.78
1958	0.65	1.03	0.03	1998	1.50	2.38	0.87
1959	0.70	1.10	0.10	1999	1.83	2.91	1.07
2000	1.34	2.13	0.76	2003	0.99	1.47	0.38
2001	1.15	1.83	0.60	2004	0.97	1.45	0.37
2002	0.83	1.32	0.28				

Smithers/Wright [2000] find the Tobin's Q as a remarkably useful gauge of aggregated stock market levels. In the late 1920s and middle 1930s, the Tobin's Q reached levels that were similar to the late 1990s, but not quite as high. Both periods were followed by serious market declines based on Tobin's Q. In the late 1940s and early 1950s it correctly signaled undervaluation, marking the period as an excellent entry point. This was followed by a significant overvaluation in the late 1960's and early 1970s, which was also reflected in high Tobin's Qs. The significant market break of 1973-74 let the Tobin's Q drop and made the late 1970's and early 1980s again a good entry point. In 1999 Tobin's Q was at its all time high of 1.83 and signaling massive overvaluation. With the normalization of valuation the Tobin's Q fell under one.

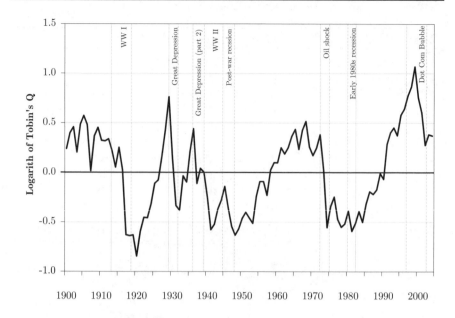

Fig. A.6: Historic logarithmical ratios of Tobin's Q to its average value. The geometrical mean of Tobin's Q for 1990 to 2004 lies at approximately .63. Data source: Smithers/Wright [2000] and the Flow of Funds Accounts of the Federal Reserve of the United States .

A.5 Overview over Selected Studies

Table A.7: Selected studies assuming the incentive alignment

Study	Result
Bøhren/Ødegaard [2003]	supported
Bothwell [1980]	no effect
Boudreaux [1973]	supported
Cebenoyan et al. [2000]	supported
Chaganti/Damanpour [1991]	supported
Cotter et al. [1994]	supported
Elliott [1972]	no effect
Francis/Smith [1995]	supported
Gupta/Rosenthal [1991]	supported
Han/Suk [1998a]	supported
Han/Suk [1998b]	supported
Hanson/Song [2000]	supported
Hermalin/Weisbach [1991]	supported
Holl [1975]	no effect
Holl [1977]	no effect
Holthausen et al. [1995b]	supported
Jacquemin/De Ghellinck [1980]	no effect
Jain/Kini [1994]	supported
Kamerschen [1968]	no effect
Kaplan [1989]	supported
Larner [1970]	supported
Leech/Leahy [1991]	supported
Lewellen et al. [1985]	supported
McConnell/Servaes [1990]	supported
McEachern [1975]	supported
Mehran [1995]	supported
Mikkelson/Partch [1989]	supported
Monsen et al. [1968]	supported
Mørck et al. [1988]	supported
Oswald/Jahera Jr. [1991]	supported
Palia/Lichtenberg [1999]	supported
Radice [1971]	supported
Smith [1990]	supported
Song/Walkling [1993]	supported
Sorensen [1974]	no effect
Stano [1975]	supported
Stano [1976]	supported
Steer/Cable [1978]	supported
Stulz [1988]	supported
Thonet/Poensgen [1979]	no effect
Ware [1975]	rejected
Zeckhauser/Pound [1990]	no effect

Table A.8: Selected studies assuming the entrenchment argument

Study	Result
Agrawal/Mandelker [1990]	supported
Brailsford et al. [2002]	supported
Cho [1998]	*no effect*
Dahya et al. [1998]	supported
Dann/DeAngelo [1983]	supported
DeAngelo/Rice [1983]	supported
Denis/Denis [1994]	*no effect*
Eckbo/Smith [1998]	*no effect*
Gugler et al. [2003b]	supported
Hermalin/Weisbach [1991]	supported
Holderness/Sheehan [1988]	*no effect*
Holderness et al. [1999]	supported
Jarrell/Poulsen [1987]	supported
Jarrell/Poulsen [1988]	supported
Johnson et al. [1985]	supported
Short et al. [1994]	supported
Leech/Leahy [1991]	*rejected*
Malatesta/Walkling [1988]	supported
McConnell/Servaes [1990]	supported
McConnell/Servaes [1995]	supported
Mørck et al. [1988]	supported
Mudambi/Nicosia [1998]	supported
Shivdasani [1993]	supported
Short/Keasey [1999]	supported
Slovin/Sushka [1993]	supported
Song/Walkling [1993]	*rejected*
Wruck [1989]	supported
Yeo et al. [2002]	supported

Table A.9: Overview over the main empirical studies

	Sample	Ownership var.	Performance var.	Statistical methods	Main results
Aggarwal/Samwick [2003]	US, 1993-98	% MO also containing grants of options.	Q.	Model. Panel	Diversification is positively related to managerial incentives. The link of performance and managerial ownership is weaker for firms that experienced changes in diversification. Consequently, managers diversify their firm in response to private benefits than to reduce their risk.

	Sample	Ownership var.	Performance var.	Statistical methods	Main results
Agrawal/Knoeber [1996]	US, 1987	1) % MBO. 2) Dummy for presence of founding CEO. 3) % blockholders (>5%).	Q.	OLS and 2SLS regression. Test for a roof-shaped relation by including the squared insider ownership. Dependents: 1) IO. 2) Blockholder ownership. 3) IO. 4) Fraction of non-officers in the board. 5) Years of CEO employment. 6) Leverage by dept to firm value.	OLS on Q: Q decreases significantly with board outsiders, leverage, and corporate control activity. It increases significantly with insider ownership. 2SLS on Q: Q decreases significantly with board outsiders. 2SLS without Q: Shareholdings by blockholders and institutional investors increases significantly by corporate control activity. Institutional ownership decreases significantly with blockholder ownership and vice versa. Leverage increases significantly with insider ownership and outside board membership but not vice versa. Years of CEO employment decreases significantly with institutional and blockholder ownership, but not vice versa.

A.5 Overview over Selected Studies

	Sample	Ownership var.	Performance var.	Statistical methods	Main results
Agrawal/Mandelker [1990]	US, 1979-85	1) % IO. 2) Herfindahl index of IO. 3) % two largest blockholders (>5%). 4) MBO.	41-days CAR	Event-study. OLS regression. Checks for simultaneous effect of type of amendment and % IO by including interaction terms.	CAR decreases significantly with the adoption of anti-takeover amendments. CAR increases for increasing IO, concentration of IO, and ownership by 5% blockholders. However, no evidence of a difference in CAR for different levels of insider ownership. The OLS regression confirms the above results regarding institutional and insider ownership. It also shows a higher decrease in CAR the more entrenching the amendments.
Agrawal/Nagarajan [1990]	US, 1979-83	% and $ value of ownership by senior management.	None.	Matched samples of all-equtiy and leveraged firms.	Finds evidence that all-equity firms exhibit greater levels of managerial stockholding, more extensive family relationships among top management, and higher liquidity positions than a matched sample of levered firms. Top managers with family involvement have greater control rights than without involvement.

	Sample	Ownership var.	Performance var.	Statistical methods	Main results
Ang/Cole [2000]	US, 1992	1) Ocr. 2) Dummy if a single family controls more than 50%. 3) # of nonmanager shareholders. 4) Dummy if firm is managed by a shareholder rather than an outsider.	Measure of agency costs.	Comparison of subsamples grouped by ownership structure.	Agency costs: 1) are significantly higher when an outsider manages the firm; 2) are inversely related to MO; 3) increase with the # of non-manager shareholders; 4) to a lesser extent, are lower with greater monitoring by banks.
Baesel/Stein [1979]	Canada, 1968-72	Insider trades.	CAR.	Event study comparing insider trades with others.	Find that managers make abnormal returns when trading in their firm's stock.
Bagnani/Milonas [1994]	US, 1977-85	% MBO.	Return premia on corporate bonds	OLS of MBO on the bond return premium.	Positive relation between managerial ownership and bond return premium in the low to medium ownership range (5-25%); weak evidence for a nonpositive relation in the large ownership range (>25%).

	Sample	Ownership var.	Performance var.	Statistical methods	Main results
Bahng [2002]	Korea, 1992-94	% of insider ownership including top-officers, directors, the firm's auditor, investment advisor, and their family members of these.	Price-to-book value ratio.	OLS of insider ownership on corporate value.	No evidence for linear, quadartic or cubic relation; supports natural selection argument.

	Sample	Ownership var.	Performance var.	Statistical methods	Main results
Barclay/Holderness [1989]	US, 1978-82	Block trades involving at least 5% of the common stock.	CAR.	Event study.	These blocks are typically priced at substantial premiums to the post-announcement exchange price. They argue that the premiums, which average 20%, reflect private benefits that accrue exclusively to the blockholder because of his voting power. The premiums paid by both individual and corporate block purchasers increase with firm size, fractional ownership, and firm performance. Individuals pay larger premiums for firms with greater leverage, lower stock-return variance, and larger cash holdings.

A.5 Overview over Selected Studies

	Sample	Ownership var.	Performance var.	Statistical methods	Main results
Barclay/Holderness [1991]	US, 1978-82	Presence of large-block equity holder or not.	CAR.	Event study.	Significant and positive performance on announcement of outsider's acquisition of a large equity position, but only persistent if takeover or other corporate restructure follows.

	Sample	Ownership var.	Performance var.	Statistical methods	Main results
Barclay et al. [1993]	US, 1979 & 1984 & 1989	% of block ownership.	CAR.	Event study.	The greater the managerial stock ownership in closed-end funds, the larger are the discounts to net asset value. The average discount for funds with blockholders is 14%, whereas the average discount for funds without blockholders is only 4%. This relation is robust over time and to various model specifications that control for other factors that affect discounts. They argue that blockholders receive private benefits that do not accrue to other shareholders and that they veto open-ending proposals to preserve these benefits. They support this argument by documenting a range of potential private benefits received by blockholders in closed-end funds.

	Sample	Ownership var.	Performance var.	Statistical methods	Main results
Barnhart/Rosenstein [1998]	US, 1990	% MO.	Q.	IV approach with dependents: 1) Q; 2) board composition; 3) MO.	Variables are jointly determined. However, results depend strongly on the specification of model and instruments. They conclude that results using simultaneous equations methods must be interpreted cautiously, OLS estimates should not be casually dismissed, and that sensitivity analysis is essential when estimating an empirical model whose structure is uncertain.
Bathala/Moon [1994]	US, 1988	1) % MO. 2) % IO.	None.	2SLS with the dependents debt and MO; IO as exogenous.	Debt and managerial ownership are reversely related to institutional ownership.

	Sample	Ownership var.	Performance var.	Statistical methods	Main results
Bethel/Liebeskind [1993]	US, 1981-87	Block ownership.	None.	OLS of ownership on restructuring.	The results show that blockholder ownership is associated significantly with corporate restructuring, suggesting that many managers restructured their corporations during the 1980s only when pressured to do so by large shareholders.
Bøhren/Ødegaard [2003]	Norway, 1989-97	1) % MBO. 2) % Ocr. 3) Classification in state, individuals (persons), financials (institutions), non-financials, and international.	1) Q. 2) ROA over 5 years. 3) Return on Sales over 5 years. 4) ROA. 5) Return on Sales.	OLS regressions. Simultaneous equations system with performance, concentration and insider ownership.	Insider ownership matters the most for economic performance. Outside ownership concentration destroys market value. Direct ownership is superior to indirect. Performance decreases with increasing board size, leverage, dividend payout, and the fraction of non-voting shares.

A.5 Overview over Selected Studies

	Sample	Ownership var.	Performance var.	Statistical methods	Main results
Bothwell [1980]	Australia, 1962-64	As Palmer [1973]: MC - $\leq 10\%$ single block of common stock; $30\% >$ WOC $> 10\%$; SOC $> 30\%$; AOC=WOC+SOC	1) A risk adjusted return on sales. 2) ROE	Use binary regression equivalent of a two-way analysis of variance with interactions. The sample is classified in order to control for monopoly power.	Among firms with a large degree of monopoly power WOC and AOC firms are significantly more profitable than MC firms if the risk adjusted measure of return is used. Otherwise not.
Boudreaux [1973]	US, 1952-63	MC $\leq 5\%$ single block of voting control; OC $\geq 10\%$ and evidence of active control, or $\geq 20\%$.	As Monsen et al [1968]: ROE.	Analysis of variance and covariance analysis.	The results are similar to Monsen et al. [1968] since their studies are almost identical. Boudreaux, however, is also interested in risk issues.

	Sample	Ownership var.	Performance var.	Statistical methods	Main results
Boyle et al. [1998]	US, 1985-86	Natural log of percentage of offering shares subscribed by management and directors.	None.	Event study.	Find that insider ownership is weakly (10% level) negatively related to the number of anti-takeover provisions at levels of ownership below 10,3%. This is evidence of substitution between two entrenchment mechanism.
Bradley/Wakeman [1983]	US, 1978-80			Event study.	For repurchases marking the termination of a takeover bid the non-participating shareholders take a highly significant loss of 13%.
Brickley et al. [1988]	US, 1984	1) IO. 2) MBO. 3) ownership of individual or blockholding (>5%).	None.	Event study.	Institutional shareholders vote more actively on antitakeover amendments than other shareholders and they more actively oppose proposals that seem harmful to shareholders. This could hint a positive relation between IO and corporate performance.

A.5 Overview over Selected Studies 243

	Sample	Ownership var.	Performance var.	Statistical methods	Main results
Bushee [1998]	US, 1983-94	% IO	None.	OLS of IO on R&D expenses.	Managers are less likely to cut R&D to reverse an earnings decline when institutional own. is high, implying that institutions are sophisticated investors who typically serve a monitoring role in reducing pressures for myopic behavior. However, the study finds that a large proportion of own. by institutions that have high portfolio turnover and engage in momentum trading significantly increases the probability that managers reduce R&D to reverse an earnings decline. High turnover and momentum trading by institutional investors encourages myopic investment behavior when such institutional investors have extremely high levels of own. in a firm;...

	Sample	Ownership var.	Performance var.	Statistical methods	Main results
Bushee [1998] (continued)					... otherwise, institutional own. serves to reduce pressures on managers for myopic investment behavior.
Bushee [2001]	US, 1980-92	% IO.	CAR.	Event study.	The results provide no evidence that high levels of ownership by banks translate into myopic mispricing. However, high levels of transient ownership are associated with an over- (under-) weighting of near-term (long-term) expected earnings, and a trading strategy based on this finding generates significant abnormal returns. This finding supports the concerns that many corporate managers have about the adverse effects of an ownership base dominated by short-term-focused institutional investors.

	Sample	Ownership var.	Performance var.	Statistical methods	Main results
Cebenoyan et al. [2000]	US, 1989-94	1) MO and its squared measure. 2) IO.	1) Estimation of stochastic cost and profit frontiers. 2) ROA	Cross-sectional regressions.	Managerial stock own. provides an effective corporate control device. However, this device is only effective as managerial holdings surpass about 33% of outstanding shares for improvements in cost efficiency and 40% for profit efficiency.
Chaganti/-Damanpour [1991]	US, 1983-85	1) IO. 2) MO. 3) Family ownership.	1) ROE. 2) ROA. 3) Price-earnings ratio	Pairwise analysis.	IO has a significant effect on capital structure. IO and MO have a negative effect on performance.

	Sample	Ownership var.	Performance var.	Statistical methods	Main results
Chen/Steiner [1999]	US, 1994	1) MO. 2) Blockholdings (>5%). 3) IO.	None.	Nonlinear simultaneous equation methodology to examine how managerial own. relates to risk taking, debt policy, and dividend policy.	Find risk to be a significant and positive determinant of the level of managerial own. while managerial own. is also a significant and positive determinant of the level of risk. The result supports the argument that managerial own. helps to resolve the agency conflicts between external stockholders and managers but at the expense of exacerbating the agency conflict between stockholders and bondholders. They further observe evidence of substitution-monitoring effects between managerial own. and debt policy, between managerial own. and dividend policy, and between managerial own. and institutional own..

A.5 Overview over Selected Studies   247

	Sample	Ownership var.	Performance var.	Statistical methods	Main results
Chen et al. [1993]	US, 1976 & 1980 & 1984	MO.	Q.	OLS of MO on Q.	Find that Q increases for management ownership in the range [0-7%] and decreases in the range [7-12%]. For the 1976 sample it continues to fall in the [12-100%] range, but increases for the 1980 and 1984 sample.

	Sample	Ownership var.	Performance var.	Statistical methods	Main results
Chen/Ho [2000]	Singapore, 1995	1) % and $ MO. 2) Outside block ownership. 3) MBO: 0-5%, 5-25%, and 25-100%.	Q.	Cross-sectional regression on Q.	Find that the level of diversification is positively related to firm size and negatively related to the equity ownership of outside blockholders. However, no evidence that insider ownership has a significant impact on the level of diversification. They find significant value loss from diversification only for those firms with low managerial ownership, suggesting that value-reducing diversification stems from agency problems. Outside block ownership does not have a significant impact on the value of diversification. Thus, while outside blockholders may act as a deterrent on the level of diversification, there is no evidence that they can effectively reduce the agency problems for those firms with low managerial ownership.

	Sample	Ownership var.	Performance var.	Statistical methods	Main results
Cho [1998]	US, 1991	1) MBO. 2) MBO in the ranges: 0-7%, 7-38%, and 28-100%.	Q.	OLS regression. Test for non-monotonic relation by piecewise linear regression and fix the breakpoints by a grid search technique that maximizes significance.	In two separate OLS regressions Q and capital expenditure is significantly increasing for inside ownership in the [0,7%] range and significantly decreasing in the [7%, 38%] range. The 2SLS regression reveals that inside ownership increases significantly with Q, and Q increases insignificantly with inside ownership. Performance increases significantly by capital expenditure and also so the other way around. Significant controls: Market value of equity, and liquidity.
Cotter et al. [1994]	US, 1989-90	Managerial wealth change of three years.	None.	Event study.	Finds that the likelihood of a successful tender offer increases with managerial ownership and that successful tender offers are associated with significant abnormal returns.

	Sample	Ownership var.	Performance var.	Statistical methods	Main results
Cubbin/Leech [1986]	UK, 1969-74	1) Dummy for external control that is control by non-directors and managers. 2) Ocr	Average profit rate.	OLS and 2SLS regressions. Dependent variables are growth and profits. Checks for simultaneous effect of internal vs external control and degree of control by including interaction terms.	It is more a study on the relation between growth and profits than on ownership and performance. Positive relation between asset growth and profits but none for ownership and profits. Significant controls: 1) Industry sub-group average profit; 2) Beta risk.
Cui/Mak [2002]	US, 1994-98	1) MBO. 2) Average ownership of managers and directors. 3) CEO ownership. 4) Piecewise MO with 10%, 30% and 50% as thresholds.	1) Q. 2) ROA	Correlation analysis. OLS regression.	It finds that Q initially declines with managerial ownership, then increases, then declines again and, finally, increases again - a W-shaped relationship. The findings from our study point to the importance of industry effects in the relationship between managerial ownership and firm performance.

	Sample	Ownership var.	Performance var.	Statistical methods	Main results
Cui/Mak [2002]	US, 1994-98	1) MBO. 2) Average ownership of managers and directors. 3) CEO ownership. 4) Piecewise MO with 10%, 30% and 50% as thresholds.	1) Q. 2) ROA	Correlation analysis. OLS regression.	It finds that Q initially declines with managerial ownership, then increases, then declines again and, finally, increases again - a W-shaped relationship. The findings from our study point to the importance of industry effects in the relationship between managerial ownership and firm performance.
Dahya et al. [1998]	UK, 1989-92	1) % by top management. 2) % by directors. 3) # of blockholders (>3%). 4) # of blockholders (>10%). 5) % of blockholdings.	None.	Logit regression on top management change.	UK managers become entrenched at very low levels of equity ownership, hence limit the management change.

	Sample	Ownership var.	Performance var.	Statistical methods	Main results
Dahya et al. [1998]	UK, 1989-92	1) % by top mgmt. 2) % by directors. 3) & 4) # of blockholders (>3% / >10%). 5) % of blockholdings.	None.	Logit regression on top management change.	UK managers become entrenched at very low levels of equity ownership, hence limit the management change.

	Sample	Ownership var.	Performance var.	Statistical methods	Main results
Dann/DeAngelo [1983]	US, 1977-80	Standstill agreements limiting a substantial stockholder's ownership interest in a corporation for a specified number of years.	Cumulative average prediction errors of returns to stockholders.	Event study on the announcement of standstill agreements.	Support of the entrenchment argument. Standstill agreements are often accompanied by repurchase of the substantial stockholder's shares at a premium above the market price. Standstills and premium buybacks reduce competition for corporate control and provide differential treatment of large blockholders. Statistically significant negative average effect on non-participating stockholder wealth associated with standstill agreements. Negotiated premium repurchases are also associated with negative, but less significant, stockholder returns.

	Sample	Ownership var.	Performance var.	Statistical methods	Main results
DeAngelo/DeAngelo [1985]	US, 1980	% MO.	None.	Comparison of subsamples grouped by ownership structure.	Find week evidence in support of entrenchment. In firms with dual classes of common stock, managerial vote ownership is an important element of the corporate ownership structure. Corporate officers and their families hold a larger percentage of the superior voting stock than of the inferior voting stock.
DeAngelo/Rice [1983]	US, 1974-79	% MO.	Two-day CAR.	Event study on antitakeover amendment proposal.	The preponderance of observed negative returns at the time of amendment proposal is viewed as weak preliminary support for the managerial entrenchment hypothesis.

A.5 Overview over Selected Studies

	Sample	Ownership var.	Performance var.	Statistical methods	Main results
Demsetz [1986]	US, 1980	1) MBO. 2) Insider trading volume.	Insider trading involvement as insider trading volume to insider ownership.	Descriptive.	Insider trading involvement is 7 times higher for firms with high insider ownership.
Demsetz/Lehn [1985]	US, 1976-80	1) Log of an Herfindal index. 2) Log of combined holding by 5 largest shareholders. 3) Log of holding by 20 largest shareholders. 4) Holdings by 5 largest families and individuals. 5) Holdings by 5 largest institutional investors.	1) ROE. 2) Standard error of market model regressing firm return on market return.	OLS regression.	Performance by accounting return is insignificantly decreasing with ownership by 5 or 20 largest shareholders or the Herfindal index. Ownership by 5 or 20 largest shareholders (or Herfindal or ownership by family and individuals or institutional investors) increases significantly by standard error of market return. Significant controls: Market value and all measures of industry and standard deviation.

	Sample	Ownership var.	Performance var.	Statistical methods	Main results
Demsetz/Villalonga [2001]	US, 1976–80	1) % MO. 2) % of the five largest shareholders.	Q.	2SLS with the dependents: 1) Q; 2) % MO.	Find no statistically significant relation between ownership structure and firm performance. This finding is consistent with the view that diffuse ownership, while it may exacerbate some agency problems, also yields compensating advantages that generally offset such problems. Consequently, for data that reflect market-mediated ownership structures, no systematic relation between ownership structure and firm performance is to be expected.

A.5 Overview over Selected Studies

	Sample	Ownership var.	Performance var.	Statistical methods	Main results
Denis/Denis [1994]	US, 1985	1) Majority ownership - $\geq 50\%$ insider ownership by managers and directors. 2) IO. 3) Dummy for outside blockholder ownership. 4) Dummy for family or founder involvement in management or board of directors.	1) ROE. 2) ROA. 3) Operating income to assets. 4) Q. 5) M/B.	Standard t-tests are applied to test for differences between the main sample and an industry paired control sample.	No difference in performance between majority controlled firms and other firms. The likelihood of majority control increases significantly with family or founder involvement Indeed, 80% of majority controlled firms have substantial family or founder involvement Indeed, 80% of majority controlled firms have substantial family or founder involvement. Majority controlled firms have significantly: 1) less outside directors, 2) less outside blockholdings, 3) less institutional shareholdings, 4) pay less dividends, 5) Dual class shares. Other controls are insignificant.

	Sample	Ownership var.	Performance var.	Statistical methods	Main results
Denis/Serrano [1996]	US, 1983-89	1) Presence of a blockholder (>5%). 2) Change in management.	Cumulative market-adjusted returns.	Event Study.	Find that 34% of targets of unsuccessful control contents experience a change in top manager within two years following the contest. Management turnover is concentrated among poorly performing firms in which outside blockholders acquire an ownership stake. These blockholders improve operating performance. In the absence of an outsider blockholder, managers typically retain their positions despite poor pre-contest performance and the use of value-reducing defensive tactics during the control contest.
Dilling-Hansen et al. [2003]	Denmark, 1995-97	# of blockholder (>5%).	Value added.	Fixed-effects panel analysis on efficiency.	Find no significant increase of efficiency due to blockholdings.

A.5 Overview over Selected Studies 259

Sample	Ownership var.	Performance var.	Statistical methods	Main results
Duggal/Millar [1999] US, 1985-90	1) % IO of bidder common stock. 2) % MO of bidder common stock. 3) % IO of target common stock.	1) CAR over 22-days. 2) Q.	OLS regression on IO, 2SLS of IO and bidder gains.	Find a positive relation between bidder gains and IO in the OLS model. IO is significantly determined by firm size, MO and the firm's presence in the S&P 500 index. Thus, when bidder gains are regressed on the predicted values of institutional ownership in 2SLS regressions, the recursive estimates do not confirm the relationship shown by the OLS regressions. Furthermore, the study finds no evidence that active institutional investors as a group enhance efficiency in the market for corporate control. These findings cast doubt on the superior selection/monitoring abilities of institutional investors.

Sample	Ownership var.	Performance var.	Statistical methods	Main results
Dyck/Zingales [2004] International, 1990-2000	1) Presence of a majority shareholder (>50%). 2) Presence of a second dominant shareholder (>20%).	None.	Event study on the premium of block sales.	Find private benefits with an average value of control of 14% and a maximum of 65%.

	Sample	Ownership var.	Performance var.	Statistical methods	Main results
Eckbo/Smith [1998]	Norway, 1985-92	Insiders are top-officers and directors, the firm's auditor and investment advisor, and close family members of these.	1) AMAR1, average monthly abnormal return using equal weighted CAPM. 2) AMAR2, using conditional multifactor model with value weights. 3) AMAR3, using conditional multifactor model with ownership weights.	Event / portfolio-study. Compare various measures of AMAR on various definitions of insider portfolios.	AMAR1 produce conflicting evidence on insider earnings. AMAR2 and 3 does not produce any significant evidence on insider trading. No systematic evidence on insider profits could be found on insider portfolios sorted after: 1) Size of trades, 2) % size of insider ownership, 3) Value of insider ownership. Finally, insider portfolios are found unable to outperform mutual funds.
Edwards/Nibler [2000]	Germany, 1992	1) Exercised votes of the largest blockholder. 2) % of proxy vote holdings by first and second largest bank.	M/B.	OLS regression on M/B.	Banks influences is insignificant and ownership concentration is only partly significant depending on the owner's identity. The effect is only slightly positive for families with a minority stake, foreign firms and banks, belonging to the top 3 banks.

	Sample	Ownership var.	Performance var.	Statistical methods	Main results
Edwards/-Weichenrieder [2004]	Germany, 1992	1) Exercised votes of the largest shareholder. 2) CFR of the largest shareholder 3) Exercised votes of the second largest owner. 4) Classification of bank, non-bank, family, public and foreign investors.	M/B.	OLS regression on M/B.	Find that, for most types of largest shareholder, the beneficial effects on minority shareholders of increased ownership (greater monitoring of management, and reduced incentives to exploit minority shareholders due to greater cash-flow rights) outweigh the harmful effect (greater private benefits of control due to greater control rights).
Elliott [1972]	US, 1964-67	MC $\leq 5\%$ single block of voting control; OC $\geq 10\%$ and evidence of active control, or, $\geq 20\%$.	1) Change in sales. 2) Change in assets. 3) Dividends. 4) Return on stocks. 5) Profits. 6) ROE. 7) Growth in spending.	Variance analysis.	No significant effects between OC and MC except with regard to change in cash flow.
Elston et al. [2002]	Germany, 1970-86	1) % IO. 2) % bank ownership.	None.	Propensity score matching (PSM) method on dividend pay-out.	Find evidence that neither institutional ownership nor bank control is statistically significant in determining dividend payouts.

	Sample	Ownership var.	Performance var.	Statistical methods	Main results
Elston [2004]	Germany, 1970-86	1) Ownership concentration. 2) Bank ownership.	M/B.	OLS and survival analysis.	Find that bank influenced firms have higher survival rates than independent firms. However, firm growth appears to be independent of bank influence and negatively related to firm size. Ownership concentration has no effect.
Farinha [2003]	UK, 1991 % 1996	% MO.	None.	OLS regression on dividend pay-out structure.	Consistent with entrenchment argument, a significant U-shaped relationship between dividend payout ratios and insider ownership is observed for a large sample and two distinct periods. These results strongly suggest the possibility of managerial entrenchment when insider ownership reaches a threshold of around 30%.
Fee [2002]	US, 1992-93	% of the highest artistic stake.	None.	Predictive regression and comparison.	Find evidence of over-monitoring in the film industry.

	Sample	Ownership var.	Performance var.	Statistical methods	Main results
Finnerty [1976]	US, 1969-72	Insider trades.	CAR.	Event study.	Find that managers make abnormal returns when trading in their firm's stock.
Francis/Smith [1995]	US, 1980-89	CEO-held - CEO ownerhsip $\geq$ 30%; Insider-held - CEO < 5% and MO $\geq$ 20%; Outsider-held - CEO < 5% and outsider ownership $\geq$ 20%; Diffusely-held - otherwise.	None.	OLS regression.	The evidence indicates that diffusely-held firms are less innovative along patent activity, growth by acquisition versus internal development, and timing of long-term investment spending. These results are consistent with the conjecture that concentrated ownership and shareholder monitoring are effective at alleviating the high agency and contracting costs associated with innovation.
Friday/Sirmans [1999]	US, 1980-94	1) % MO. 2) % of outside blockholding.	M/B.	Piecewise regression.	Find negative effect for insider ownership above 5% and a general negative effect of outside blockholdings.

A.5 Overview over Selected Studies

	Sample	Ownership var.	Performance var.	Statistical methods	Main results
Friend/Lang [1988]	US, 1979-83	1) % by largest managerial owner. 2) % by largest non-managerial owner. 3) Classification in closely held and publicly held with and without managerial owner.	M/B.	Comparison of regressions on debt of subsamples grouped by ownership structure.	Support for a substitution hypothesis between debt, managerial ownership and external ownership. Debt ratio decreases significantly for higher managerial ownership and it increases significantly for more concentrated external ownership.
Gillan/Starks [2000]	US, 1987-94	% IO.	None.	Analysis of voting outcomes of proposals by OLS.	Proposals sponsored by institutions or coordinated groups appear to act as substitutes gaining substantially more support than proposals sponsored by individuals.
Givoly/Palmon [1985]	US, 1973-75	Insider transactions.	CAR.	Event study.	Find that insiders make abnormal return on their trading but that this return does not appear to be related to news other than information about insider trading.

	Sample	Ownership var.	Performance var.	Statistical methods	Main results
Goergen/Renneboog [2001]	UK, 1988-93	1) Directors' shareholdings. 2) Blockholdings (>5%). 3) Classification of individuals, family, institutionals, other companies, executive and non-executive directors.	None.	Euler-equation model for a panel.	When industrial companies control large shareholdings, there is evidence of increased overinvestment. In contrast, large institutional holdings reduce the positive link between investment spending and cash flow relation and, hence, suboptimal investing. Whereas there is no evidence of over- or underinvesting at low levels of insider shareholding, a high concentration of control in the hands of executive directors reduces the underinvestment problem.
Gordon/Pound [1993]	US, 1990	1) % IO. 2) % MO. 3) % of directors' ownership. 4) % ownership of outsiders. 5) # of shareholders.	None.	OLS regression.	Find evidence that insider and directors' ownership has a negative effect on the approvals of a proposal and institutional and outsider investors have a positive effect.

A.5 Overview over Selected Studies

	Sample	Ownership var.	Performance var.	Statistical methods	Main results
Graves [1988]	US, 1976-85	% IO.	None.	OLS regression on R&D spending.	Support the argument of myopic behavior of institutional investors.
Gugler et al. [2003a]	International, 1985-2000	% MO.	Return on investment.	Comparison and OLS regression on return on investment.	Differences in investment performance related to a country's legal system dominate differences related to ownership structure. Furthermore, managerial entrenchment worsens a company's investment performance.
Gugler et al. [2003b]	North America, 1996-2000	1) % MO. 2) % IO.	1) Q. 2) Marginal Q.	OLS regression on Q.	MO increases Q if lower than 50%. Passing the threshold the impact is negative. Furthermore, IO has positive effect on performance.
Gupta/Rosenthal [1991]	US, 1984-88	Insider gains.	CAR.	Event study.	Find that the abnormal returns of a leveraged recapitalization increases marginally (10% level) with changes in managerial ownership and increases significantly with the level of distributable cash flow.

	Sample	Ownership var.	Performance var.	Statistical methods	Main results
Han/Suk [1998a]	US, 1988-92	1) % MO and MO^2. 2) % IO.	Stock return.	OLS regression on stock return.	MO is positively related to performance for low levels. Excessive MO has a negative entrenchment effect. IO has a positive monitoring effect.
Han/Suk [1998b]	US, 1983-90	% MO.	CAR.	Event study.	Find Abnormal returns at the announcement of stock splits to be positively related to MO. The effect only exists for small firms, hence informational asymmetry is also important.
Hanson/Song [1995]	US, 1961-90	1) % MO before and after recapitalization. 2) Insider trading.	CAR.	Event study.	Find support for the entrenchment argument.

	Sample	Ownership var.	Performance var.	Statistical methods	Main results
Hanson/Song [2000]	US, 1981-95	1) % MBO. 2) % ownership of CEO. 3) % ownership of different directors' types.	Two-days' CAR.	Event study on mergers.	Gains are significantly related to MBO when the divestiture produces positive total dollar gains. Higher levels of ownership give managers the incentive to sell assets that create negative synergies, the incentive to negotiate the best price for shareholders, and that outside directors fulfill their responsibilities as effective monitors and advisors to management.
Heiss/Köke [2004]	Germany, 1986–95	1) Herfindahl index of concentration. 2) Level of pyramiding.	ROA.	Multinominal logit model with ownership change, no change and failure.	The Herfindahl index has a negative effect on the probability of change; the level of pyramiding is increasing it.

	Sample	Ownership var.	Performance var.	Statistical methods	Main results
Hermalin/Weisbach [1991]	US, 1971 & 1974 & 1977 & 1980 & 1983	Combined stock ownership by present CEO and all former CEOs still on the board in the ranges 0-1%, 1-5%, 5-20%, and 20-100%.	1) Q. 2) ROA.	OLS regression pooling the data on all five periods. IV regression using lagged values of stock ownership as instruments. Use piecewise linear regression on CEO ownership, outside director proportion of board, and CEO tenure.	Performance increases significantly with CEO ownership in the [0-1%] range and decreases significantly in the [1-5%] range. Significant controls: R&D to size, and advertising to size. Otherwise the different regressions present insignificant or contradicting evidence. The Hausman test rejects the hypothesis that there is no simultaneity at the five percent level.
Hill/Snell [1988]	US, 1980	1) % blockholdings. 2) % MO. 3) % of outside directors. 4) % of inside directors.	ROA.	OLS regression.	Ownership concentration positively effects performance. But MO has no effect on productivity.
Hill/Snell [1989]	US, 1978-80	1) Herfindahl index of concentration. 2) % MO.	Value added.	OLS regression.	Ownership concentration positively effects productivity and MO. Find no effect for MO and directors ownership.

A.5 Overview over Selected Studies   271

	Sample	Ownership var.	Performance var.	Statistical methods	Main results
Himmelberg et al. [1999]	US, 1982-84	1) % of common equity holdings by all top-level managers. This value, say m, is transformed using $\log(m/(m-1))$. 2) Average % of equity ownership per top-level managers. Use log of this value.	1) Q. 2) ROA.	OLS and IV regressions. Use panel data to obtain a fixed-effects estimator to avoid inconsistent estimates because of endogeneity of managerial ownership caused by unobserved common determinants of ownership and performance as opposed to reverse causality	Find evidence of endogeneity of managerial ownership caused by unobserved heterogeneity as opposed to reverse causality. This is supported by Hausman specification test. Performance regression: Find some evidence of a roof-shaped relation. But after controlling for firm characteristics and firm fixed effects they find no relation between managerial ownership and performance even for sub-samples of large and small firms. Significant controls: Size, squared size, return variation, income to sales, capital exp to capital. Ownership regression: Do not test the effect of performance. ...

	Sample	Ownership var.	Performance var.	Statistical methods	Main results
Himmelberg et al. [1999] (continued)					... Significant 'controls': Size, capital to sales ratio, returns variability (only for sample of small firms). Almost similar results for both ownership measures.
Hindley [1970]	US, 1952-56	Classification into majority, minority interest and others.	Q.	Comparisons of groups by ownership structure.	Ownership concentration has a negative effect on performance.
Holderness/Sheehan [1985]	US, 1977-82	Presence of large-block equity holder or not.	Abnormal returns.	Event study.	Significant and positive performance on announcement of outsider's acquisition of a large equity position, but only persistent if takeover or other corporate restructure follows.
Holderness/Sheehan [1988]	US, 1979-84	95% > MH > 50,1%, ownership by any single individual or entity (other corporation, or fund); DH < 20% ownership by any shareholder.	1) Q. 2) ROE.	Standard t-tests are applied. The sample is further classified in order to control for identity of MH control: MH by individuals and OC by entities.	Finds no significant difference in performance between MH and DH firms.

	Sample	Ownership var.	Performance var.	Statistical methods	Main results
Holderness et al. [1999]	US, 1935 &1995	1) % and $ MBO. 2) % and $ ownership by CEO. 3) MBO: 0-5%, 5-25%, and 25-100%.	Q.	Descriptive statistics and OLS regressions. Test for roof-shaped relation by using piecewise linear regression.	Mean (median) own. by managers and directors increased from 13% (7%) in 1935 to 21% (14%) in 1995. In $ millions it increased from $18 ($3) to $73 ($16). For any given firm size own. is higher in 1995 than in 1935. However, using the value-weighted mean, own. increases insignificantly and median own. of the 10% largest firms falls from 2.1% to 1.5%. OLS regressions: Profitability is significantly increasing for management own. in the [0-5%] range and significantly decreasing in the [5-25%] range in the 1935. For 1995 Q is significantly increasing for management own. in the [0-5%] range. Mean (median) own. by CEO is 1.25% (0.09%) in 1935 and 1.25% (0.06%) in 1995.

	Sample	Ownership var.	Performance var.	Statistical methods	Main results
Holl [1975]	UK, 1948-60	MC all non-OC firms. OC if ≤ 50% of vote carrying shares are held by individual or if 20-50% of the votes are held by an individual, or if at least 20% of the votes are held by largest 20 vote holders subject to certain constraints.	Pre-tax profit / Net worth.	Discriminant analysis and generalized Mahalanobis distance analysis. The sample is classified in order to control for industry.	No significant difference between MC and OC when industry bias is accounted for.
Holl [1977]	US, 1960-72	Same as Palmer [1973]. However, in the final test: MC ≤10% single block of common stock. OC >10%.	Return on stocks calculated as average stock returns observed from 1962 to 72 assuming that dividends are reinvested.	Standard t-tests are applied. The sample is classified in order to control for 'efficiency of market for corporate control', monopoly and size.	OC firms are only significantly more profitable than MC firms with regard to MC firms who lack an efficient market for corporate control.
Holthausen/Larcker [1996]	US, 1976-88	1) % Insider ownership. 2) % MO. 3) % outsider ownership.	1) Operating income / total assets. 2) Operating cash flow / total assets.	OLS regression on performance.	Operating performance declines following a reversed leveraged buy-out and so does insider ownership.

A.5 Overview over Selected Studies

	Sample	Ownership var.	Performance var.	Statistical methods	Main results
Hubbard/Palia [1995]	US, 1985-91	% MO in the ranges: 0-5%, 5-25%, and 25-100%.	CAR.	Event study.	Evidence of a roof-shaped relation.
Hudson et al. [1992]	US, 1982-85	% MO in the ranges: 0-5%, 5-25%, and 25-100%.	Earnings / price ratio.	OLS regression.	Find a positive relationship between the degree of insider ownership and performance.
Jacquemin/-De Ghellinck [1980]	France	1) Majority control $\geq 50\%$; $5\% \leq$ Minority control $< 50\%$; Internal control $< 5\%$. 2) Case by case classification of firms into family and non-family control.	1) Net cash flow / Book value of equity and reserves. 2) ROE.	OLS regression. Checks for simultaneous effect of size and ownership by including interaction terms.	For none of the ownership definitions are there any significant differences in performance. Significant controls: Size, industry, and family*size.
Jaffe [1974]	US, 1962-68	Insider trades by management and directors.	CAR.	Event study.	Find that managers make abnormal returns when trading in their firm's stock.
Jain/Kini [1994]	US, 1976-88	Ownership retained by managers after IPO.	1) M/B. 2) Price / earnings ratio. 3) Earnings per share.	Comparisons of subsamples. OLS regression.	Operating profitability declines after going public and so does insider ownership.

	Sample	Ownership var.	Performance var.	Statistical methods	Main results
Jarrell/Poulsen [1987]	US, 1979-85	1) % MBO. 2) % IO.	30-days' CAR, by the firm over the interval (AD-20, AD+10) where AD is the announcement date.	Event-study. OLS and logit regressions on the probability of adopting a 'fair price' amendment.	CAR decreases significantly with the adoption of anti-takeover amendments. The more entrenching the type of amendment the larger the decrease in CAR. This amendment is the least entrenching of five types of amendments. OLS regression finds no significant relation between ownership and CAR. Logit regression finds that the probability of 'fair price' adoption increases significantly with IO.
Jarrell/Poulsen [1988]	US, 1976-87	% MBO.	Four-days' CAR	Event-study. OLS-regressions.	CAR decreases significantly at the announcement of the introduction of dual-class stocks with differential voting rights. CAR decreases with insider ownership. Significant controls: Net of market increase.
Jensen et al. [1992]	US, 1982-87	% MO.	None.	Structural equations with dependents: 1) MO; 2) Debt; 3) Dividend policy.	Higher MO has a negative effect on debt and dividends.

A.5 Overview over Selected Studies

	Sample	Ownership var.	Performance var.	Statistical methods	Main results
Jensen/Murphy [1990]	US, 1938 & 1974 & 1984	% ownership by highest paid executive, typically the CEO.	None.	OLS regression on shareholder wealth.	CEO mean (median) ownership declined from 1.7% (0.3%) in 1938 to 1.5% (0.05%) in 1974 to 1% (0.03%) in 1984. MBOs have increased from \$1,2 billion in 1979 to \$77 billion in 1987. Franchising accounts for 12% of GDP in 1986, page 245.
Johnson et al. [1985]	US, 1971-82	Dummy for executive being a corporate founder.	Three-days' standardized CAR	Event-study. OLS regression in the final model.	No general effect of executive death. However, significant positive returns if executive is the founder. Significant controls: Lower returns for higher executive position.
Kamerschen [1968]	US, 1959-64	1) MC $\leq$ 10% single block of voting control; OC >10%. Dummy for change in control from 1929 to 1963.	ROE.	OLS regression.	OC firms are insignificantly more profitable than MC firms. The ownership dummy is significant and positive. Significant controls: Barriers to entry, sales, assets, and growth.

	Sample	Ownership var.	Performance var.	Statistical methods	Main results
Kania/McKean [1976]	US, 1972	OC - $\geq$ 10% of 500 largest companies or $\geq$ 15% of the 500 second largest companies or $\geq$ 20% of next 800 largest companies ; MC - otherwise.	Various measures among those ROA, ROE and earnings per share.	ANOVA.	No relation.
Kaplan [1989]	US, 1980-86	1) % pre- and post-buyout ownership by all buyout managers not including directors. 2) $ pre- and post-buyout ownership by all buyout managers not including directors.	Market adjusted stock return in the ranges: 1) From two month before buyout to buyout date. 2) From buyout date to first post buyout valuation date. 3) From two month before buyout to first post-buyout valuation date.	No regressions. Primarily a descriptive study. However, in this study the changes are so profound that the demand for statistics is less.	Kaplan obtains a post-buyout market valuation for 25 of the 76 buyouts. For these firms the three measures of market adjusted stock return increased respectively by 38%, 42%, and 96%. Managerial ownership increases from 9% to 31%, but the value of the new ownership stake is less than the old stake. Other results: Leverage increases from 21% to 86%.

A.5 Overview over Selected Studies

	Sample	Ownership var.	Performance var.	Statistical methods	Main results
Karpoff et al. [1996]	US, 1986-90	1) % MO. 2) % IO.	1) M/B. 2) Return on sales. 3) CAR.	Matched pairs. Logit regression on shareholder corporate governance proposal outcome. Event study.	MO has a negative effect on the proposal, while IO has a positive effect.
Kim et al. [1988]	US, 1975-78	% MO.	Risk-adjusted returns.	Two-way test and regression.	Insider ownership effects performance significantly positive.
Kole [1995]	US, 1980-81	% MBO in the ranges: 0- 5%, 5-25%, and 25-100%.	Q.	Pairwise analysis and regression on Q.	This paper demonstrates that differences in managerial ownership data cannot explain contradictory empirical evidence on the relation between equity ownership and the entrenchment of managers.

	Sample	Ownership var.	Performance var.	Statistical methods	Main results
Kole [1996]	US, 1980	% MBO in the ranges: 0-5%, 5-25%, and 25-100%.	1) Q. 2) ROA. 3) Change in Q. 4) Change in ROA.	OLS regression. Use piecewise linear regression. Use sub-samples of high and low R&D firms to check directly for Q bias due to R&D. Finally, he uses lagged performance variables to test for causality.	Starts reproducing the model of Morck et al. [1988]. When that model is run on a sub-sample of low R&D firms [a better way to correct for Q bias due to R&D) profitability is only significantly increasing for board ownership in the [0, 5%] range. Same result is produced running a full sample less outliers [Q >4,5] and including two more controls: Firm growth and stock performance. In this model all controls [1-6] become significant and the adjusted R reaches 55%. Finally, Kole runs a series of lagged OLS regressions indicating that ownership is endogenous.
Larner [1966]	US, 1929 & 1963	MC ≤ 10% single block of voting control; OC > 10%.	None.	Comparison of the 200 largest firms.	Finds that 44% of the firms in the 1929 sample were management controlled compared to 85% in the 1963 sample.

A.5 Overview over Selected Studies

	Sample	Ownership var.	Performance var.	Statistical methods	Main results
Larner [1970]	US, 1956-62	MC $\leq$ 10% single block of voting control. OC > 10%.	ROE.	OLS regression. Corrects for heteroscedasticity by weighted regressions.	OC firms are significantly (weak) more profitable than MC firms. Significant controls: General state and industry state.
Leech/Leahy [1991]	UK, 1983-85	1) Five ownership concentration indices: Herfindahl index and combined holding of largest 1, 5, 10, and 20 shareholders. 2) Six control type indices for MC or OC: OC > 5%, 10%, and 20% of cohesive stock ownership or OC if largest cohesive stockholding has 90%, 95% or 99% chance of winning a majority vote; MC otherwise.	1) Historic market value / ordinary share capital. 2) Return on sales. 3) ROE.	Multivariate regression. Also apply simultaneous equations but without significant results. Multiple regression analysis. Each performance variable is regressed individually. Dependents: 1) Sales growth. 2) Asset growth. 3) Salary of highest paid director.	OC firms are significantly (weak) more 'profitable' than MC firms with regard to ROE, return on sales, growth of sales and growth of net assets. Rules based on OC $\geq$ 5%, 10%, and 20% were never significant. More concentration caused significantly less performance in terms of historic market value / ordinary share capital and return on sales. Significant controls: Size, export intensity of sales, beta risk and standard risk.

	Sample	Ownership var.	Performance var.	Statistical methods	Main results
Lehmann/Weigand [2000]	Germany, 1991-96	1) Herfindahl index. 2) Ocr. 3) Dummy: family, bank, industrial firm, foreign investor and mixed.	1) ROA. 2) ROE.	Panel analysis with fixed and random effects.	Find ownership concentration to affect profitability significantly negatively. However, a financial institution as largest shareholder enhances performance.
Levin/Levin [1982]	US, 1967-76	MC ≤ 10% block of common stock and not FC; OC >10% and not FC; FC > 10% of cohesive ownership by financial institutions and > 10% of ownership by non-financial, or > 5% and ≤ 10% of ownership by non-financial, or financial institution is a leading creditor and ≤ 10% of ownership by non-financial.	1) ROE. 2) Return on stocks. Observed 1967-76.	Covariance analysis. The sample is classified in order to control for corporate diversification. Firms with substantial production in unrelated areas are classified as diversified. Dependents: 1) Standard deviation of earnings; 2) Dispersion of earnings; 3) Growth of sales; 4) Difference between growth of sales and ROE; 5) Capital structure; 6) Dividends to earnings.	With regard to ROE and return on stocks MC, OC and FC firms have significantly different returns if they are non-diversified. Otherwise not. The direction of the performance difference is not reported and neither is the significance or direction of the control variables.

	Sample	Ownership var.	Performance var.	Statistical methods	Main results
Lewellen et al. [1985]	US, 1963-81	1) % ownership of bidder by bidder's officers and directors. 2) % ownership of bidder by bidder's highest paid executive. 3) % ownership of bidder by two highest paid executives.	CAR by the bidding firm over the interval (A-5, R0) where A is the announcement date of the acquisition activity and R is the merger approval date.	Event study. Initially Z-tests are applied to test for significance of CAR in the total sample. Finally, they run univariate OLS regressions for bidder CAR on the various ownership variables.	Bidder CAR increases significantly with bidder management's ownership of the bidder company for all the three definitions of ownership.
Lloyd et al. [1986]	US, 1978-81	Ocr.	Monthly return.	Comparison of portfolios constructed on ownership concentration.	The results indicate no significant relationship between ownership and return.

	Sample	Ownership var.	Performance var.	Statistical methods	Main results
Loderer/Martin [1997]	US, 1978-88	1) % MBO prior to the acquisition announcement. 2) % IO. 3) % blockholders (> 5%).	1) Q prior to announcement. 2) Six-day's CAR	Event-study. OLS regression. Test for roof-shaped relation by including the squared insider ownership. Two-stage least squares regression.	In two separate OLS regressions with market value of equity as the only control variable Q and CAR are significantly increasing with inside ownership. The 2SLS regression reveals that inside ownership increases significantly with CAR, and CAR decreases significantly with inside ownership. Further, inside ownership decreases significantly with Q, and Q decreases insignificantly with inside ownership. All controls are significant. For both OLS and 2SLS there are none significant non-linear effects.

A.5 Overview over Selected Studies

	Sample	Ownership var.	Performance var.	Statistical methods	Main results
Loderer/Sheehan [1989]	US, 1971-85	1) % of highest paid officer. 2) Ocr. 3) Largest outside blockholder. 4) % of directors.	None.	Time-series analysis.	During the five years leading up to bankruptcy, the stockholdings of officers and directors in NYSE and AMEX bankrupt firms are no different from those observed in non-bankrupt firms.
Lorie/Niederhoffer [1968]	US	Insider trading.	CAR.	Event study.	Find that managers make abnormal returns when trading in their firm's stock.
Madden [1982]	US, 1964-73	% MO.	Performance measures from a naive arbitrage model.	OLS regression on market model.	No difference in performance.
Mak/Li [2001]	Singapore, 1991-95	1) % MO. 2) % blockholdings (>5%).	1) ROE. 2) Q.	2SLS with the dependents: 1) MO; 2) blockholdings; 3) # of outside directors; 4) dual leadership; 5) board size.	Find that corporate ownership and board structures are related. MO and blockholdings are not influenced by performance. The proportion of outside directors is negatively related to managerial ownership, board size and government ownership.

	Sample	Ownership var.	Performance var.	Statistical methods	Main results
Malatesta/Walkling [1988]	US, 1982-86	% MBO.	Two-days' CAR	Event-study. Standard t-test for differences in means between two industry-paired samples.	The adoption of poison pill securities significantly reduces shareholder wealth. Abandoning them significantly increases shareholder wealth. Firms with poison pills have significantly less managerial ownership and are more subject to takeover attempts than firms in the same industries without poison pills.
Masson [1971]	US, 1947-66	% MO.	PV of dividends plus capital gains.	OLS regression.	Find evidence for managerial interest alignment.
Mathiesen [2002]	US, 1997-2000	% MO.	1) M/B. 2) ROA.	3SLS with dependents: 1) Performance; 2) Expected performance; 3) MO.	Find only for the 0-.5% range of MO a positive effect. Outside this range the results are not stable.

	Sample	Ownership var.	Performance var.	Statistical methods	Main results
McConnell/Servaes [1990]	US, 1976 & 1986	1) MBO. 2) IO. 3) Blockholdering by non-insiders ($\geq 5\%$). 4) Ocr. 5) Dummy for presence of blockholders. 6) MBO plus blockholders. 7) MBO in the ranges: 0-5%, 5-25%, and 25-100%. 8) MBO plus blockholders in the ranges: 0-5%, 5-25%, and 25-100%.	1) Q. 2) ROA	OLS regression. Test for roof-shaped relation by including the squared insider (or insiders plus all blockholders) and by using piecewise linear regression.	Both measures of profitability is significantly increasing with ownership by managers and directors, and this relation is significantly roof-shaped with a performance peek for 69% ownership in 1976 and 41% in 1986. Defining ownership as insiders plus all blockholders, Performance increases significantly with IO, but no measure of blockholder ownership seems to have any effect. All control variables are significant. Using piecewise linear regression profitability is significantly increasing for insider [or insider plus all blockholders] ownership in the [0-5%] range.

	Sample	Ownership var.	Performance var.	Statistical methods	Main results
McConnell/Servaes [1995]	US, 1976 & 1986 & 1988	1) Insider stock ownership by managers and directors. 2) IO. 3) Blockholders as combined ownership by non-insiders who have more than 5% ownership.	Q	OLS regression. Test for roof-shaped relation by including the squared insider ownership. The sample is classified in order to control for growth opportunities.	Using the new 1988 sample reproduces the results from McConnell and Servaes [1990]. Only difference is that Q now is significantly increasing with blockholder ownership. For all sample periods the relation between Q and all ownership variables is insignificant for high-growth firms and significantly positive and roof-shaped for low-growth firms. Significant controls: Q increases with leverage in low-growth firms and decreases for high-growth firms.
McEachern [1975]	US, 1963-72	MC ≤ 4%; OM > 4% and management representation; EC >4% and no management representation.	Return on stocks calculated as average price increases from 1963 to 72 assuming dividends are reinvested.	OLS regression.	OM and EC firms are significantly more profitable (weak) than MC firms. Industry type is significant as well. Also interested in remuneration.

	Sample	Ownership var.	Performance var.	Statistical methods	Main results
McEachern/Romeo [1978]	US	MC ≤ 4%; OM > 4% and management representation; EC >4% and no management representation.	None.	OLS regression on R&D.	Firms controlled by dominant outside stockholder interest tend to allocate relatively more of their resources to R&D than either owner-managed or manager-controlled firms.
McKean/Kania [1978]	US, 1963-72	OC - ≥ 10% of 500 largest companies or ≥ 15% of the 500 second largest companies or ≥ 20% of next 800 largest companies ; MC - otherwise.	Net worth.	Analysis-of-variance.	Find no relation between performance and control type.
Mehran [1995]	US, 1979-80	1) % of shares and stock options held by CEOs and their immediate families. 2) % MBO. 3) % of shares held by outside directors. 4) % of shares held by all outside 5% blockholders. 5) Various definitions of outside blockholders.	1) Q. 2) ROA.	OLS regression. Test for heteroskedasticity, but finds none.	Both performance measures increase significantly with CEO ownership. No significant effect of ownership by all officers and directors or ownership by outside directors. Blockholder ownership is not significant in any sence.

	Sample	Ownership var.	Performance var.	Statistical methods	Main results
Mikkelson/Partch [1989]	US, 1975-84	% MO.	None.	Event study.	Find that the likelihood of a successful acquisition is unrelated to managerial shareholdings. It covers that lower managerial shareholding increase the likelihood of receiving a takeover offer but decreases the likelihood that it will succeed.
Mikkelson/Regassa [1991]	US, 1980-83	Block trades by managers	None.	OLS regression on premium paid.	Find no significant difference between the premiums paid by managers in block repurchases and the premiums paid by outsiders in block purchases.
Mikkelson/Ruback [1991]	US, 1978-83		CAR, by the repurchasing firm over the intervals (A-1, A0) and (R-1, R0) where A is the date of the 5% block acquisition and R is the date of the targeted repurchase.	Event study.	Look at targeted repurchases from the time of block investment. At that initial stage stock prices rises significantly whereas they fall significantly at the time of repurchase. For the entire period it increased significantly.

A.5 Overview over Selected Studies

	Sample	Ownership var.	Performance var.	Statistical methods	Main results
Mikkelson/Ruback [1985]	US, 1952-63	MC ≤ 5% single block of voting control; OC ≥ 10% and evidence of active control, or, ≥ 20%.	ROE. Observed 1952-63.	Variance analysis and a balanced fixed model of three-way analysis of covariance with one concomitant variable.	OC firms are significantly (strong) more profitable than MC firms. Time and industry type are also significant. Size is not.
Mikkelson et al. [1997]	US, 1980-83	% MBO before and after IPO.	None.	Event study on the IPO.	Find no significant decline in operating performance of firms that go public. Insider ownership falls from 68% to 18% after 10 years of the IPO.
Monsen et al. [1968]	US, 1952-63	OC - ≥ 10% of one person or ≥ 20% of a party; MC - ≤ 5% and no evidence of owner control.	1) Q. 2) ROE.	ANOVA.	Find significant higher performance for owner controlled firms.
Bebchuk et al. [2000]	Japan, 1981-87	Bank holdings and linkage.	Q.		No relation between bank oversight and performance.

	Sample	Ownership var.	Performance var.	Statistical methods	Main results
Morck et al. [1988]	US, 1980	1) Combined shareholding by all members of the board in the ranges: 0-5%, 5-25%, and 25-100%. 2) Combined shareholding by top two officers. 3) Dummy for presence of founder on board.	1) Q. 2) Profit rate by net cash flow to replacement cost of capital.	OLS regression. Use piecewise linear regression.	Profitability is significantly increasing for board ownership in the [0-5%] range and significantly decreasing in the [5-25%] range and if the founder is present on the board of old firms. Significant controls: R&D to size and debt to size. Similar results for top two officers.
Mudambi/Nicosia [1998]	UK, 1992-94	1) Herfindahl index of concentration. 2) MBO.	Abnormal returns.	OLS and WLS regression on performance.	Provide evidence supporting the entrenchment and interest alignment effects. Ownership concentration has a negative effect on performance. MBO is positive in the linear and cubic measure, but negative in the quadratic variable.
Mußler [2005]	Germany, 2004	Insider trades.	CAR.	Event study.	Insiders achieve abnormal returns with purchases, but not with sales.

	Sample	Ownership var.	Performance var.	Statistical methods	Main results
Murali/Welch [1989]	US, 1977-81	Closely held firms- > 50% by small group or individual; widely held firms - All other firms.	1) Adjusted stock market return. 2) ROA. 3) ROE.	OLS regression on performance.	No significant difference in performance between closely held and widely held firms. Significant controls: Standard variation on ROA and equity, and R&D to sales.
Nickell et al. [1997]	UK, 1985-94	Dummies SC1, SC2, and SC3 equal to 1 if as largest shareholder has 90% or 95% chance of winning a majority vote; SC1 = financial firm; SC2 = person, a family, a group of linked individuals, a company pension fund or charity; SC3 = non-financial company.	Productivity growth as change in log of real sales.	Regression technique by Arellano and Bond 1991 for dynamic panel data models. Checks for substitution effects between financial pressure, monopoly power and shareholder control by including interaction terms.	Productivity increases significantly with SC1 and decreases significantly with SC3. Significant substitution effect between financial pressure and monopoly power, and SC1 and monopoly power. Significant controls: Employment. Index of industry overtime hours. Market share. Rent / value added.
Nyman/Silberstan [1978]	UK, 1975-76	1) Ocr. 2) Classification for financial institutions, directors, industrial company, charitable trust, government, mixed and others.	Turnover.	Comparison.	Ownership interest especially of financial institutions has increased in the UK. Most firms are controled in one way or another.

	Sample	Ownership var.	Performance var.	Statistical methods	Main results
Oswald/Jahera Jr. [1991]	US, 1982-87	% MBO.	Excess stock return.	ANOVA.	Ownership is significantly related to firm perfomance even after controlling for size.
Palia/Lichtenberg [1999]	US, 1981-93	% MO.	Q.	OLS regression on productiviy.	Find that managerial ownership changes are positively related to changes in productivity. Also find a higher sensitivity of changes in managerial ownership to changes in productivity for firms who experience greater than the median change in managerial ownership.
Palmer [1973a]	US, 1961-69	$MC \leq 10\%$ single block of common stock; $30\% > WOC > 10\%$; $SOC > 30\%$; AOC=WOC+SOC.	ROE.	Use Satterthwaite's approximation. Corrects for heteroscedasticity by statistical comparisons. The sample is classified in order to control for monopoly power.	Among firms with a large degree of monopoly power AOL and SOC firms are significantly more profitable than MC firms. Otherwise not.

A.5 Overview over Selected Studies

	Sample	Ownership var.	Performance var.	Statistical methods	Main results
Peck [1996]	US, 1984-87		None.	Event study on Management-Buy Outs.	Evidence that new blockholders help to increase the performance of Management-Buy Outs and that old institutional blockholders has no effect.
Pedersen/Thomsen [1996]	Europe, 1990	Ownership concentration by logistic transformation of % voting ownership by largest owner.	ROE.	OLS regression.	ROE is insignificantly decreasing with ownership concentration. Significant controls: Capital intensity and return variability.
Pedersen/Thomsen [1997]	Europe, 1990	Disperced - $\leq 20\%$; Dominant - $20\% <$ share $< 50\%$; Majority ownership distinguished by family, government, foreign company and cooperative.	None.	Cochran-Mantel-Haenszel statistics. Multinominal logit regression.	Ownership structure differs among nations and also depends on the corporate governance rules.

	Sample	Ownership var.	Performance var.	Statistical methods	Main results
Pedersen/Thomsen [1998]	Europe, 1990	Disperced - ≤ 20%; Dominant - 20% < share < 50%; Majority ownership distinguished by family, government, foreign company and cooperative.	None.	Cochran-Mantel-Haenszel statistics. Multinominal logit regression.	Industry is effecting ownership even after nations control.
Pedersen/Thomsen [1999]	Europe, 1990	1) Ocr. 2) Ownership concentration by logistic transformation of % voting ownership by largest owner.	ROE.	OLS regression on ownership concentration.	Ownership concentration is found to have an insignificant effect on accounting profitability.
Pope et al. [1990]	UK, 1977-84	Insider trading.	CAR.	Event study.	Find that managers make abnormal returns when trading in their firm's stock.
Pound [1988b]	US, 1981-85		None.	Logit regression. Dependent variable is one if management wins the proxy contest and zero if dissident wins.	The probability that management will prevail in a proxy contest is increasing with the fraction of shares held by institutional investors. This could hint a negative relation between IO and corporate performance.

A.5 Overview over Selected Studies 297

	Sample	Ownership var.	Performance var.	Statistical methods	Main results
Pound [1988a]	US, 1976-84		2 years earnings forcasts.	OLS regression.	The management entrenchment in the takeover is negatively related to performance.
Radice [1971]	UK, 1957-67	MC $\leq$ 5% single block of voting control; OC $\geq$ 15%.	ROE.	OLS regression.	OC firms are significantly (weak) more profitable than MC firms. Growth is significant. Size and industry are not significant.
Renneboog [2000]	Belgium, 1989-94	Classification of largest owner in holding companies, banks, investment companies, insurance companies, industrial and commercial companies, families and individual investors, federal or regional authorities, and realty investment companies.	1) Market adjusted returns. 2) Earnings after tax. 3) ROE. 4) ROA	Multinominal logit model of turnover of management, CEO or management committee.	Find little relation between ownership and managerial replacement. When industrial companies increase their share stake or acquire a new stake in a poorly performing company, there is evidence of an increase in executive board turnover, which suggests a partial market for control. There is little relation between changes in ownership concentration held by institutions and holding companies, and disciplining.

	Sample	Ownership var.	Performance var.	Statistical methods	Main results
Round [1976]	Australia, 1962-64	1) Control types: MC ≤ 5% held by person; OC ≥ 10% held by person; Company control ≥ 15% held by other company. 2) % shares held by top 20 shareholders. 3) Dummy for overseas ownership and control.	ROA.	OLS regression.	MC firms have insignificantly lower returns than OC and company controlled firms. Significant controls: Number of directors among top 20 shareholders is positive.
Rozeff/Zaman [1988]	US, 1973-82	1) Insiders trading by officers and directors. 2) Outsiders trading on public but delayed information on insiders' trades from SEC's Official Summery.	1) Standard CAR (12 months). 2) CAR adjusted for predictable firm size and earnings / price effects (12 months).	Event-study. The sample is selected to sort out insider trades that relate to portfolio rearrangement. CAR is calculated on portfolios maintained by particular trading rules.	Standard CAR with or without transaction costs is significant and positive for both insiders and outsiders. Size and e/p adjusted CAR with or without transaction costs is significant and positive for insiders but not for outsiders.

A.5 Overview over Selected Studies

	Sample	Ownership var.	Performance var.	Statistical methods	Main results
Rozeff/Zaman [1998]	US, 1978-91	Insiders are defined as officers and directors: 1) The proportion of insider buying as the number of insider purchases to number of insider purchases and sales. 2) % of stocks by insiders.	1) Stock return prior to insider sales. 2) Ratio of cash flow to stock price. 3) Ratio of book value to price.	Event-study. OLS regressions.	The proportion of insider buying is significantly decreasing with prior stock returns. No significant effect of regressing insider holdings against cash flow to stock price. The proportion of insider buying is significantly increasing with the ratio of cash flow to stock price (as well as book value to stock price).

	Sample	Ownership var.	Performance var.	Statistical methods	Main results
Seyhun [1986]	US, 1975-81	1) Insider sales by officers, directors and above 10% blockholders. 2) Insider purchases by officers, directors and above 10% blockholders. 3) Outsider trading on public but delayed information on insider trades from the Security Exchange Committee. 4) Outsider trading on publicly available but delayed informantion on insider trades form SEC's official Summary.	1) CAR (adjusted for size effects) over the intervals (TD0, TD+100) and (TD-100, TD0) where TD is the insider trading date. 2) CAR further adjusted for transaction costs and the bid-ask spread.	Event-study. GLS regression. For sales CAR is multiplied by -1 in order for CAR to represent insider gains on trading.	CAR increases significantly after insider purchases and it decreases significantly after insider sales. CAR decreases significantly before insider purchases and it increases significantly before insider sales. CAR increases significantly after outsider trading at both announcement dates, but vanish when transaction costs are added. GLS regressions: CAR increases significantly for: 1) Insiders that are both officers and directors. 2) Insider being the chairman. 3) Log value of trade. 4) % of firm traded. CAR decreases significantly for log of firm value.

A.5 Overview over Selected Studies

	Sample	Ownership var.	Performance var.	Statistical methods	Main results
Short/Keasey [1999]	UK, 1988-92	1) % of shares held by directors. 2) % IO (>5%). 3) % external ownership.	1) ROE. 2) Q.	Heteroskedasticity corrected OLS regression. Performance is regressed as a 3rd degree polynomial of director ownership.	Director ownership and cubic ownership is significantly positive and squared ownership is significantly negative. The polynomial reach its maximum at 16% and its minimum at 42% ownership. Significant controls: Size, growth, and R&D.
Short et al. [1994]	UK, 1986-88	1) Directors' ownership. 2) MC ≤ X% of directors' ownership, X=[10, 20,..., 90]; OC > X% of directors' ownership. 3) Directors' ownership in the ranges 0-68%, and 68-100%.	ROA.	OLS regression and the Halbert-White technique to correct for heteroscedasticity. Test for roof-shaped relation by squaring board ownership and use piecewise linear regression.	Performance is significantly increasing with board ownership and this relation is significantly roof-shaped. This is also confirmed using piecewise linear regression. Performance also increases if directors are represented in other firm's boards. Significant controls: Need for management systems and director remuneration.

	Sample	Ownership var.	Performance var.	Statistical methods	Main results
Short et al. [2002a]	UK, 1988-92	1) % MO. 2) % of largest outside owner.	Operating profit / total assets of 5 years.	OLS regression on leverage.	The debt ratio is positively related to management ownership and negatively related to ownership by large external shareholders. Furthermore, the presence of a large external shareholder acts to negate the positive relationship between debt ratios and management ownership; in the presence of a large external shareholder, no significant relationship between debt ratios and management ownership exists.
Short et al. [2002b]	UK, 1988-92	1) % IO (>5%). 2) % MBO.	Net profit derived from normal trading activities after depreciation and other operating provisions.	Dividend models FAM, PAM and ETM.	A positive association exists between dividend payout policy and institutional ownership. In addition, there is some evidence in support of the hypothesis that a negative association exists between dividend payout policy and managerial ownership.

	Sample	Ownership var.	Performance var.	Statistical methods	Main results
Slovin/Sushka [1993]	US, 1973-89	1) % shareholding by the deceased. 2) % shareholdings by non-deceased officers and directors. 3) % MBO before and after the event. 4) % IO. 5) Dummy for deceased being a foun	Two-day CAR	Event-study. Control for variables by sample classification. WLS regression in order to correct for heteroscedasticity.	Sample 1: 60% of the events leads to decreased ownership by insiders and 52% receive bids for control within 10 years of the event. Using classified samples CAR increases significantly if the shareholding of the deceased is above 10%. The rise in CAR is larger if ownership by the deceased is between 20 and 30%, if the deceased is the founder, a non-CEO, or if ownership by insiders dec WLS regressions show a significant bell-shaped relation between CAR and the deceased shareholdings. However, none of the other ownership or control variables are significant although they have the expected sign.

	Sample	Ownership var.	Performance var.	Statistical methods	Main results
Smith [1990]	US, 1977-86		Operating cash flows (before interest and taxes) per employee and per dollar of operating assets.	Comparison of pre- and post-Management-Buy out performance.	Operating returns increase significantly from the year before to the year after buyouts. Subsequent changes in operating returns suggest that this increase is sustained.
Song/Walkling [1993]	US, 1977-86	1) % MBO. 2) Interaction effect for contested and managerial ownership. 3) Interaction effect of successful and managerial ownership. 4) Interaction effect for contested, successful, and managerial ownership. 5) IO.	CAR, by the target firm over the interval (A-5, R+5) where A is the announcement date of the acquisition activity and R is the announcement date of the final outcome.	Event study. Initially standard t-tests are applied to test for differences in the three samples. Logistic regression with probability of acquisition attempt as the dependent variable. OLS regression with CAR as dependent variable.	CAR increases significantly with managerial ownership in contested cases that are ultimately successful. Significant controls: Dummy for successfully acquired. Other results: The probability of acquisition attempts is significantly decreasing with managerial ownership at the target firm, and the result is due to variance among contested targets. Finally, managerial ownership is significantly lower in contested compared to uncontested acquisitions and in unsuccessful compared to successful cases.

A.5 Overview over Selected Studies 305

	Sample	Ownership var.	Performance var.	Statistical methods	Main results
Sorensen [1974]	US, 1948-66	MC ≤ 5% single block of ownership; OC ≥ 20%.	1) ROE. 2) Stock return assuming dividends are reinvested. 3) Dividends / earnings. 4) Growth in sales. 5) Growth in equity.	Variance analysis.	No average difference between MC and OC firms, but a few significant differences between industry groups.
Stano [1975]	US, 1956-62	% ownership by top five executives.	After-tax rate of return on equity.	OLS regression.	Find a positive relationship between managerial ownership and profit rate.
Stano [1976]	US, 1963-72	MC ≤ 10% single block of common stock; 30% > WOC > 10%; SOC ≥ 30%; AOC=WOC+SOC.	Stock return assuming dividends are reinvested, observed 1965-72.	Multiple regression analysis. Check for model specification error due to dependence between sales growth and ownership type.	SOC firms are significantly more profitable than MC firms. WOC are not. The final regression that this conclusion is based upon does only control for industry type.

	Sample	Ownership var.	Performance var.	Statistical methods	Main results
Steer/Cable [1978]	UK, 1967-71	OC ≥ 15% of cohesive ownership or ≥ 3% ownership by managers; MC otherwise.	1) ROE. 2) ROA. 3) Return on sales.	OLS regression. Test for multicollinearity.	OC firms are significantly more profitable (weak) than MC firms. Organizational form and change are significant (the main interest of Steer and Cable). Growth is significant. Other variables are insignificant.
Strickland et al. [1996]	US, 1990-93,		CAR.	Event study on the effect of monitor actions by small shareholders.	Evidence that united small shareholder activism enhances shareholder value.
Stulz et al. [1990]	US, 1968-86	Target ownership: 1) % managerial ownership by officers, directors and other insiders prior to announcement. 2) % IO prior to announcement. 3) % ownership by bidder prior to announcement. 4) Bidder acquiring %.	CAR by the target firm over the interval (A-5, R+5) where A is the announcement date of the acquisition activity and R is the announcement date of the final outcome.	Event study. Initially standard t-tests are applied to test for significance of CAR in the total sample and the two sub-samples both with regard to bidder CAR, target CAR and combined firm CAR. Then OLS regression with CAR as dependent variable.	Target CAR increases significantly with target managerial ownership in successful, multiple bids. Target CAR decreases significantly with IO in multiple bids and in total sample. Target CAR decreases significantly with bidder ownershi Significant controls: CAR if positive in all samples; market value of target equity for multiple bids.

	Sample	Ownership var.	Performance var.	Statistical methods	Main results
Thomsen [2005]	US and Europe, 1992	% blockholdings (>5%).	Q.	OLS regression.	Find a negative effect of blockholder ownership on firm value in continental Europe. No similar effect is found in the US/UK.
Thonet/Poensgen [1979]	Germany, 1961-70	MC $\leq$ 25% of cohesive stock ownership; OC > 25% of cohesive stock ownership and no other part with 25% of cohesive stock ownership.	1) ROE. 2) Stock return assuming dividends are reinvested. 3) Market value to book value.	Multiple regression: OLS, and GLS. Corrects for heteroscedasticity due to size. Dependents: 1) Sales growth; 2) Variance of ROE; 3) Beta risk.	OC firms are significantly less profitable than MC firms in terms of ROE and market value to book value. Size and concentration are not significant. No significant difference between MC and OC with regard to return on stocks, growth, variance on equity and beta risk.
Wahal/McConnell [2000]	US, 1988-94	1) % IO. 2) % MO.	M/B.	2SLS on R%D.	Find no support for the contention that institutional investors cause corporate managers to behave myopically.
Walkling/Long [1984]	US, 1972-77			Logistic regression.	Find that managerial ownership is significantly higher in uncontested tender offers than in contested ones.

	Sample	Ownership var.	Performance var.	Statistical methods	Main results
Ware [1975]	US, 1960-70	MC $\leq$ 5% single block of voting stock and no evidence of owner control. OC $\geq$ 15% of cohesive voting stock and board or management representation or $\geq$ 25%.	ROE.	Covariance analysis with 1) Net sales / #of employees; 2) Retained earnings / net income; 3) Debt / Assets.	OC firms are significantly less profitable (weak) than MC firms with regard to ROE. OC firms have significantly (weak) higher net sales / # of employees and retained earnings / net income. Other variables are insignificant.
Welch [2003]	Australia, 1999-2000	1) % MO. 2) % by top five executives.	Q.	GLS regression on ownership of top five executive and Q.	Results provide limited evidence of a nonlinear relationship between managerial share ownership and firm performance.
Witte [1981]	Germany, 1974-76	1) Ocr. 2) MO.	None.	OLS regression.	Find no evidence for influence of ownership concentration and managerial ownership on performance.

	Sample	Ownership var.	Performance var.	Statistical methods	Main results
Wruck [1989]	US, 1979-85	1) Changes in ownership concentration (due to a private sale) in the ranges 0-5%, 5-25%, and 25-100% using either board voting stock or combined voting stock by managers, directors and $\geq$ 5% block holders. 2) Purchaser is management controlled or not.	Five-day CAR	Event-study of private sales of equity. OLS regression. Use piecewise linear regression.	Profitability is significantly increasing for changes in board voting stock in the [0-5%] range and significantly decreasing in the [5-25%] range. Considering the model using changes in combined voting stock by managers, directors and$\geq$ 5% block holders, profitability is significantly decreasing in the [5-25%] range and significantly increasing in the [25-100%] range. If the purchaser wants control the profit decreases.

	Sample	Ownership var.	Performance var.	Statistical methods	Main results
Yeo et al. [2002]	Singapore, 1990-92	1) % MBO. 2) Blockholdings.	12-month stock returns.	OLS regressions.	Nonlinear relation between managerial own. and earnings informativeness. Earnings informativeness rises with managerial own. at low levels but not at higher levels of managerial own. where the entrenchment effect sets in. The evidence shows a strong positive relationship between external unrelated blockholdings and earnings informativeness.

	Sample	Ownership var.	Performance var.	Statistical methods	Main results
Yermack [1997]	US, 1992-94	Stock option award.	149-day's CAR, by the bidding firm over the interval (AD-20, AD+120) where AD is the award date.	Event-study. The sample is classified in order to control for different things.	CAR increases significantly after the award of CEO stock options. CAR is lower for grants at predictable times. CAR is four times higher than average if the CEO is represented in the remuneration committee. Awards are more often made before good news announcements.
Zeckhauser/Pound [1990]	US, 1988-89	MC - ≤ 15% of cohesive voting stock ownership; OC - > 15% of cohesive voting stock ownership.	Earnings / price ratio.	Standard t-tests are applied. The sample is classified in order to control for 'asset specificity'. Dependents: 1) Dividend payout by dividend / earnings; 2) Leverage by debt / debt plus market value of equity.	Among firms with high asset-specificity OC firms have significantly lower E/P ratios than MC firms do. Firms with low asset specificity have no significant E/P difference. No significant difference in dividend or leverage between OC and MC.
Zingales [1994]	Italy, 1987-90	1) Ocr. 2) % of second largest shareholder.		Event study on premiums of block sales.	Find large private benefits.

A.6 Decomposition of Effects in Simultaneous Equation Models

A.6.1 Decomposition of Total Association in Causal and Noncausal Effects

Considering the example given in Figure A.7, the composition of the total association and the emergence of noncausal effects can be clarified.

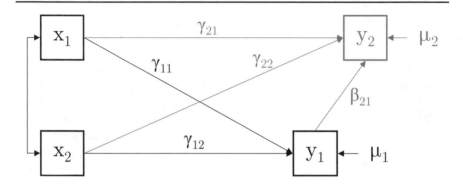

Fig. A.7: Example of noncausal effects

The covariance of x_1 and y_1 gives the total association and can be calculated and decomposed as follows:

$$\begin{aligned}
cov(x_1, y_1) &= cov(x_1, \gamma_{11}x_1 + \gamma_{12}x_2 + \mu_1) \\
&= cov(x_1, \gamma_{11}x_1) + cov(x_1, \gamma_{12}x_2) + cov(x_1, \mu_1) \\
&= \gamma_{11}\phi_{11} + \gamma_{12}\phi_{12} + 0 \\
&= T_{x_1 y_1} + N_{x_1 y_1}
\end{aligned}$$

x_1 is per definition uncorrelated to the disturbances; thus the covariance of x_1 and μ_1 is 0.

The final result shows that one part of the association is due to the direct effect (γ_{11}), which equals in this case the total causal effects. However, the second part of the association is not due to a direct or indirect effect, but to the covariance of x_1 and x_2.

A.6.2 Decomposition into Direct and Indirect Effects

Figure A.8 explains the decomposition of the total association into direct and indirect effects on the example of the effect of x_1 on y_2.

A.6 Decomposition of Effects in Simultaneous Equation Models

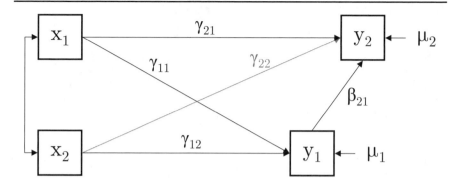

Fig. A.8: Example of noncausal effects

The total association equals the covariance of x_1 and y_2 and can be transformed the following way:

$$\begin{aligned}
cov(x_1, y_2) &= cov(x_1, \beta_{21}y_1 + \gamma_{21}x_1 + \gamma_{22} + \mu_2) \\
&= cov(x_1, \beta_{21}(\gamma_{11}x_1 + \gamma_{12}x_2 + \mu_1) + \gamma_{21}x_1 + \gamma_{22} + \mu_2) \\
&= \beta_{21}\gamma_{11}\phi_{11} + \beta_{21}\gamma_{12}\phi_{12} + \gamma_{21}\phi_{11} + \gamma_{22}\phi_{12} \\
&= I_{x_1\,y_2} + N_{x_1\,y_2} + D_{x_1\,y_2} + N_{x_1\,y_2}
\end{aligned}$$

x_1 is per definition uncorrelated to the disturbances; thus the covariance of x_1 and μ_2 is 0.

While the direct effect is given by third term (γ_{21}), the first term states the indirect effect ($\beta_{21}\gamma_{11}$). The second and forth terms represent noncausal effects through the correlation of x_1 and x_2, where the first affect through the indirect effect and the latter through the direct effect.

A.7 Detailed Skewness and Kurtosis

Table A.10: Detailed skewness and percentiles of variables

	Mean	Skewness	Kurtosis	Min.	1%	10%	25%	50%	75%	90%	99%	Max.
Ownership Variables												
Ocr	0.444	0.409	2.406	0.004	0.050	0.133	0.251	0.426	0.600	0.772	1.000	1.000
ORatio	1.151	9.581	117.075	0.415	0.648	1.000	1.000	1.000	1.000	1.335	3.376	11.494
Oc2	0.177	1.034	3.542	0.000	0.000	0.000	0.000	0.046	0.118	0.173	0.356	0.412
Mcr	0.231	1.007	2.736	0.000	0.000	0.000	0.000	0.000	0.500	0.674	1.000	1.000
MRatio	1.020	9.616	108.086	0.648	1.000	1.000	1.000	1.000	1.000	1.000	1.983	3.220
Mbcr	0.271	0.803	2.321	0.000	0.000	0.000	0.000	0.073	0.533	0.747	1.000	1.000
MbRatio	1.024	9.021	92.363	0.648	0.998	1.000	1.000	1.000	1.000	1.000	2.012	3.220
Icr	0.129	2.076	6.389	0.000	0.000	0.000	0.000	0.000	0.147	0.532	1.000	1.000
IRatio	2.719	8.752	99.001	0.521	0.939	1.000	1.000	1.000	1.000	5.491	33.440	100.647
Performance Variables												
Q	0.566	−0.659	3.053	0.000	0.033	0.276	0.448	0.588	0.714	0.796	0.928	0.979
Roe	−0.127	0.084	4.885	−2.664	−2.664	−1.102	−0.519	−0.102	0.205	0.807	2.314	2.314
Control Variables												
Size	19.466	0.534	3.933	13.143	14.592	16.791	17.971	19.128	20.882	22.531	25.172	29.618
Debt	0.123	1.610	6.069	0.000	0.000	0.000	0.014	0.074	0.191	0.298	0.669	0.714
Inv	0.076	0.526	4.868	−0.784	−0.736	−0.252	−0.059	0.057	0.183	0.408	0.908	0.908
Nwc	0.373	0.551	1.580	0.026	0.041	0.110	0.151	0.241	0.766	0.766	0.766	0.766
Eom	0.475	1.613	4.702	0.010	0.019	0.103	0.193	0.328	0.558	1.257	1.642	1.642
Beta	0.770	0.946	4.258	−0.626	−0.119	0.152	0.333	0.642	1.126	1.601	2.319	3.505
Gro	1.080	0.734	4.753	0.224	0.318	0.809	0.935	1.033	1.175	1.467	1.883	1.883
Div	1.996	1.061	3.473	1.000	1.000	1.000	1.000	2.000	3.000	4.000	5.000	6.000
Age	3.347	−0.232	1.974	0.000	0.693	1.609	2.398	3.296	4.477	4.868	5.226	5.541

A.8 Detailed and Additional Results of Empirical Analyses

A.8.1 Simultaneous Equations Model of General Ownership

Endogeneity Tests of roe

Table A.11: Wu-Hausman F-test and Durbin-Wu-Hausman χ^2-test for different relationships of ownership concentration and ROE

		ROE			Ocr		
ROE	Ocr	value	distr.	p-value	value	distr.	p-value
Linear	Linear	28.194	F(1, 496)	(0.000)	11.481	F(1, 499)	(0.001)
		28.022	$\chi^2(1)$	(0.000)	11.717	$\chi^2(1)$	(0.001)
	Squared	14.159	F(2, 494)	(0.000)	11.448	F(1, 499)	(0.001)
		28.246	$\chi^2(2)$	(0.000)	11.685	$\chi^2(1)$	(0.001)
	Piecewise	0.346	F(3, 494)	(0.792)	0.217	F(1, 499)	(0.642)
		1.092	$\chi^2(3)$	(0.779)	0.226	$\chi^2(1)$	(0.634)
Squared	Linear	68.085	F(1, 496)	(0.000)	10.028	F(2, 497)	(0.000)
		62.885	$\chi^2(1)$	(0.000)	20.210	$\chi^2(2)$	(0.000)
	Squared	12.009	F(2, 494)	(0.000)	9.913	F(2, 497)	(0.000)
		24.157	$\chi^2(2)$	(0.000)	19.987	$\chi^2(2)$	(0.000)
	Piecewise	0.596	F(3, 494)	(0.618)	0.703	F(2, 497)	(0.496)
		1.878	$\chi^2(3)$	(0.598)	1.470	$\chi^2(2)$	(0.480)

Table A.12: Comparison of I3SLS and OLS estimates for ownership concentration and Tobin's Q

	I3SLS		OLS		Difference	
	Q	Ocr	Q	Ocr	Q	Ocr
Ocr $_{x \leq 39\%}$	−0.192		−0.061		−0.086	
	(0.002)		(0.476)		−0.464	
Ocr $_{39\% \leq x \leq 80\%}$	0.445		0.010		0.435	
	(0.000)		(0.893)		−0.893	
Ocr $_{80\% \leq x}$	1.275		−0.096		1.371	
	(0.000)		(0.564)		−0.564	
Q $_{x \leq .22}$		−1.584		−0.101		−1.973
		(0.000)		(0.861)		−0.861

Table continues at the following page

Table A.12: Comparison of I3SLS and OLS estimates (continued)

	I3SLS		OLS		Difference	
	Q	Ocr	Q	Ocr	Q	Ocr
$Q_{.22 \leq x \leq .72}$	0.416 (0.000)		0.135 (0.123)		0.281 −0.123	
$Q_{.72 \leq x}$	2.901 (0.000)		0.536 (0.211)		2.365 −0.211	
ORatio	−0.015 (0.023)		−0.003 (0.692)		−0.012 −0.669	
OcST	0.239 (0.000)	−0.392 (0.000)	0.062 (0.106)	−0.388 (0.000)	0.177 −0.106	−0.004 0.000
Size	0.159 (0.006)	−0.010 (0.914)	0.242 (0.000)	0.204 (0.037)	−0.083 0.006	−0.215 0.877
$Size^2$	−0.004 (0.008)	0.000 (0.939)	−0.006 (0.000)	−0.005 (0.023)	0.002 0.008	0.005 0.916
Debt	0.268 (0.008)	−0.078 (0.393)	0.345 (0.002)	−0.008 (0.925)	−0.077 0.006	−0.070 −0.532
$Debt^2$	−0.234 (0.060)		−0.392 (0.008)		0.158 0.052	
Inv	0.060 (0.125)	−0.040 (0.459)	0.052 (0.169)	−0.039 (0.456)	0.008 −0.044	−0.001 0.003
Inv^2	−0.044 (0.088)		−0.057 (0.065)		0.013 0.023	
Nwc	−0.766 (0.000)	0.044 (0.266)	−0.714 (0.000)	0.053 (0.163)	0.166 0.000	−0.009 0.103
Nwc^2	0.808 (0.000)		0.611 (0.000)		−0.167 0.000	
Eom	0.315 (0.000)	−0.151 (0.061)	0.301 (0.000)	−0.019 (0.815)	0.014 0.000	−0.132 −0.754
Eom^2	−0.051 (0.006)	0.009 (0.755)	−0.045 (0.007)	0.012 (0.686)	−0.006 −0.001	
Beta	−0.018 (0.281)	−0.067 (0.015)	−0.043 (0.004)	−0.062 (0.024)	0.025 0.277	−0.005 −0.009
Gro	0.020 (0.324)	−0.008 (0.793)	0.017 (0.330)	−0.011 (0.712)	0.002 −0.006	0.003 0.081

Table continues at the following page

Table A.12: Comparison of 3SLS and OLS estimates (continued)

	I3SLS		OLS		Difference	
	Q	Ocr	Q	Ocr	Q	Ocr
Div	0.008	−0.034	−0.003	−0.034	0.011	0.001
	(0.287)	(0.003)	(0.603)	(0.002)	−0.316	0.001
Age		0.020		0.030		−0.011
		(0.051)		(0.022)		0.029
Ind_2	0.105	−0.013	0.118	0.027	−0.012	−0.040
	(0.025)	(0.858)	(0.005)	(0.715)	0.020	0.143
Ind_3	0.128	−0.088	0.112	−0.059	0.016	−0.030
	(0.004)	(0.219)	(0.005)	(0.400)	−0.001	−0.181
Ind_4	−0.016	0.097	−0.004	0.054	−0.013	0.042
	(0.766)	(0.284)	(0.941)	(0.541)	−0.175	−0.257
Ind_5	0.139	−0.040	0.131	0.028	0.008	−0.068
	(0.005)	(0.613)	(0.003)	(0.722)	0.002	−0.109
Ind_7	0.002	0.017	0.000	0.007	0.002	0.010
	(0.977)	(0.836)	(0.995)	(0.926)	−0.018	−0.090
Ind_8	−0.014	0.068	−0.033	−0.014	0.019	0.083
	(0.824)	(0.495)	(0.542)	(0.885)	0.282	−0.390
Time	−0.001	0.006	0.001	0.011	−0.002	−0.005
	(0.966)	(0.830)	(0.945)	(0.669)	0.021	0.161
constant	−1.322	0.804	−1.982	−1.429	0.660	2.233
	(0.027)	(0.421)	(0.000)	(0.154)	0.027	0.267
RMSE	0.147	0.225	0.133	0.219		
pseudo $\bar{R}^2$	0.463	0.182	0.586	0.263		
χ^2 / F	759.670	282.640	28.010	8.100		
Prob.$_{\chi^2/F}$	(0.000)	(0.000)	(0.000)	(0.000)		

Simultaneous Equations Results

Table A.13: Detailed 3SLS estimates for ownership concentration and Tobin's Q

	Model 3		Model 4		Model 5	
	Q	Ocr	Q	Ocr	Q	Ocr
Ocr_a	−1.002 (0.000)	— —			−0.907 (0.000)	
Ocr_b	−0.183 (0.143)		−0.192 (0.002)		−0.300 (0.028)	
Ocr_c	0.752 (0.000)		0.445 (0.000)		0.512 (0.000)	
Ocr_d	— —		1.275 (0.000)		1.579 (0.000)	
$Q_{0 \leq x \leq .22}$		−1.944 (0.000)		−1.584 (0.000)		−2.134 (0.000)
$Q_{.22 \leq x \leq .72}$		0.362 (0.000)		0.416 (0.000)		0.413 (0.000)
$Q_{.72 \leq x}$		2.737 (0.000)		2.901 (0.000)		3.008 (0.000)
ORatio	−0.015 (0.012)		−0.015 (0.023)		−0.016 (0.011)	
OcST	0.355 (0.000)	−0.395 (0.000)	0.239 (0.000)	−0.392 (0.000)	0.267 (0.000)	−0.394 (0.000)
Size	0.045 (0.546)	0.026 (0.780)	0.159 (0.000)	−0.010 (0.914)	0.094 (0.140)	−0.011 (0.910)
$Size^2$	−0.001 (0.655)	−0.001 (0.652)	−0.004 (0.000)	0.000 (0.939)	−0.002 (0.193)	0.000 (0.948)
Debt	0.258 (0.014)	−0.083 (0.357)	0.268 (0.008)	−0.078 (0.393)	0.245 (0.015)	−0.085 (0.354)
$Debt^2$	−0.201 (0.074)		−0.234 (0.060)		−0.173 (0.144)	
Inv	0.056 (0.231)	−0.038 (0.470)	0.060 (0.125)	−0.040 (0.459)	0.056 (0.177)	−0.040 (0.458)

Table continues at the following page

Table A.13: Results for ownership concentration and Tobin's Q (continued)

	Model 3		Model 4		Model 5	
	Q	Ocr	Q	Ocr	Q	Ocr
Inv^2	−0.041 (0.083)		−0.044 (0.088)		−0.044 (0.072)	
Nwc	−0.506 (0.000)	0.046 (0.239)	−0.766 (0.000)	0.044 (0.266)	−0.521 (0.000)	0.044 (0.265)
Nwc^2	0.390 (0.000)		0.808 (0.000)		0.413 (0.000)	
Eom	0.308 (0.000)	−0.139 (0.078)	0.315 (0.000)	−0.151 (0.061)	0.303 (0.000)	−0.156 (0.053)
Eom^2	−0.056 (0.018)	0.008 (0.779)	−0.051 (0.006)	0.009 (0.755)	−0.051 (0.012)	0.009 (0.771)
Beta	0.011 (0.598)	−0.076 (0.004)	−0.018 (0.281)	−0.067 (0.015)	−0.008 (0.661)	−0.070 (0.010)
Gro	0.026 (0.302)	−0.011 (0.702)	0.020 (0.324)	−0.008 (0.793)	0.024 (0.274)	−0.009 (0.765)
Div	0.017 (0.069)	−0.034 (0.003)	0.008 (0.287)	−0.034 (0.003)	0.011 (0.154)	−0.034 (0.003)
Age		0.009 (0.199)		0.020 (0.051)		0.015 (0.076)
Ind_2	0.088 (0.142)	−0.015 (0.841)	0.105 (0.025)	−0.013 (0.858)	0.096 (0.062)	−0.016 (0.830)
Ind_3	0.136 (0.019)	−0.088 (0.212)	0.128 (0.004)	−0.088 (0.219)	0.133 (0.007)	−0.090 (0.213)
Ind_4	−0.046 (0.516)	0.082 (0.355)	−0.016 (0.766)	0.097 (0.284)	−0.029 (0.640)	0.095 (0.293)
Ind_5	0.126 (0.048)	−0.047 (0.546)	0.139 (0.005)	−0.040 (0.613)	0.136 (0.013)	−0.047 (0.554)
Ind_7	0.001 (0.987)	0.013 (0.880)	0.002 (0.977)	0.017 (0.836)	0.002 (0.969)	0.016 (0.844)
Ind_8	0.003 (0.974)	0.051 (0.606)	−0.014 (0.824)	0.068 (0.495)	−0.003 (0.961)	0.068 (0.499)
Time	−0.013 (0.540)	0.006 (0.822)	−0.001 (0.966)	0.006 (0.830)	−0.004 (0.846)	0.005 (0.840)

Table continues at the following page

Table A.13: Results for ownership concentration and Tobin's Q (continued)

	Model 3		Model 4		Model 5	
	Q	Ocr	Q	Ocr	Q	Ocr
constant	−0.302	0.476	−1.322	0.804	−0.721	0.827
	(0.695)	(0.623)	(0.027)	(0.421)	(0.275)	(0.405)
RMSE	0.186	0.230	0.144	0.231	0.160	0.232
pseudo $\bar{R}^2$	−0.093	0.172	0.463	0.182	0.200	0.151
χ^2	954.660	327.830	487.580	234.810	623.260	282.880
Prob.$_{\chi^2}$	(0.000)	(0.000)	(0.000)	(0.000)	(0.000)	(0.000)
RMSEA	0.073	0.000	0.036	0.000	0.050	0.000

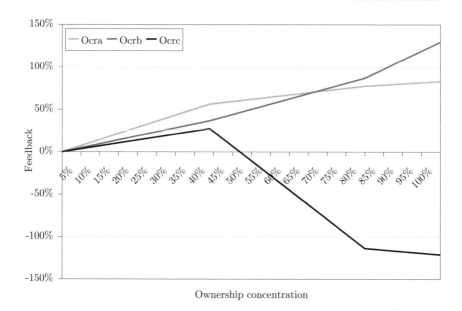

Fig. A.9: Feedback effects of ownership concentration on itself

A.8 Detailed and Additional Results of Empirical Analyses

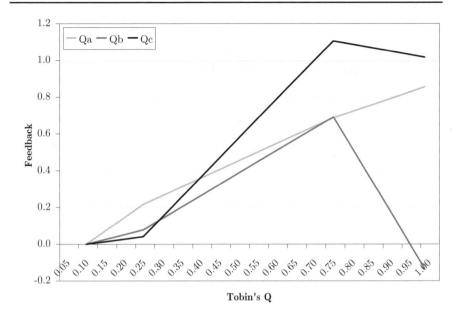

Fig. A.10: Feedback effects of Tobin's Q on itself

Table A.14: Frequency table of the different ownership concentration and Tobin's Q categories

	Ocr_a	Ocr_b	Ocr_c	
Q_a	25	10	2	37
Q_b	176	151	34	361
Q_c	57	56	10	123
	258	217	46	521

Table A.15: Detailed effects of the control variables on Tobin's Q

	D_{Qx}	Ocr_a		Ocr_b		Ocr_c	
		I_{Qx}	T_{Qx}	I_{Qx}	T_{Qx}	I_{Qx}	T_{Qx}
ORatio	−0.015	0.008	−0.007	−0.025	−0.040	−0.070	−0.085
OcST	0.239	0.263	0.502	−0.791	−0.552	−2.266	−2.027
Size	0.159	−0.086	0.073	0.260	0.419	0.744	0.903
Size^2	−0.004	0.002	−0.002	−0.007	−0.011	−0.019	−0.023
Debt	0.268	−0.146	0.122	0.438	0.706	1.255	1.523
Debt^2	−0.234	0.127	−0.107	−0.382	−0.616	−1.095	−1.329
Inv	0.000	0.000	0.000	0.000	0.000	0.000	0.000
Inv^2	−0.044	0.024	−0.020	−0.072	−0.116	−0.206	−0.250
Nwc	−0.548	0.298	−0.250	−0.895	−1.443	−2.565	−3.113
Nwc^2	0.443	−0.241	0.202	0.724	1.167	2.074	2.517
Eom	0.315	−0.020	0.295	0.060	0.375	0.171	0.486
Eom^2	−0.051	0.028	−0.023	−0.083	−0.134	−0.239	−0.290
Beta	0.000	0.067	0.067	−0.202	−0.202	−0.579	−0.579
Gro	0.000	0.000	0.000	0.000	0.000	0.000	0.000
Div	0.000	0.034	0.034	−0.102	−0.102	−0.294	−0.294
Age	0.000	−0.020	−0.020	0.060	0.060	0.173	0.173
Ind$_2$	0.105	−0.057	0.048	0.172	0.277	0.492	0.597
Ind$_3$	0.128	−0.070	0.058	0.209	0.337	0.599	0.727
Ind$_4$	0.000	0.000	0.000	0.000	0.000	0.000	0.000
Ind$_5$	0.139	−0.076	0.063	0.227	0.366	0.651	0.790
Ind$_7$	0.000	0.000	0.000	0.000	0.000	0.000	0.000
Ind$_8$	0.000	0.000	0.000	0.000	0.000	0.000	0.000
Time	0.000	0.000	0.000	0.000	0.000	0.000	0.000
constant	−1.322	0.718	−0.604	−2.160	−3.482	−6.189	−7.511

Table A.16: Detailed effects of the control variables on ownership concentration

	$D_{Ocr\,x}$	Q_a		Q_b		Q_c	
		$I_{Ocr\,x}$	$T_{Ocr\,x}$	$I_{Ocr\,x}$	$T_{Ocr\,x}$	$I_{Ocr\,x}$	$T_{Ocr\,x}$
ORatio	0.000	0.211	0.211	−0.042	−0.042	−0.295	−0.295
OcST	−0.392	0.419	0.027	−0.084	−0.476	−0.585	−0.977
Size	0.000	−2.233	−2.233	0.448	0.448	3.124	3.124
Size^2	0.000	0.056	0.056	−0.011	−0.011	−0.079	−0.079
Debt	0.000	−3.764	−3.764	0.755	0.755	5.265	5.265
Debt^2	0.000	3.287	3.287	−0.659	−0.659	−4.597	−4.597
Inv	0.000	0.000	0.000	0.000	0.000	0.000	0.000
Inv^2	0.000	0.618	0.618	−0.124	−0.124	−0.864	−0.864
Nwc	0.000	7.697	7.697	−1.544	−1.544	−10.766	−10.766
Nwc^2	0.000	−6.222	−6.222	1.248	1.248	8.703	8.703
Eom	−0.151	−2.970	−3.121	0.596	0.445	4.154	4.003
Eom^2	0.000	0.716	0.716	−0.144	−0.144	−1.002	−1.002
Beta	−0.067	0.645	0.578	−0.129	−0.196	−0.903	−0.970
Gro	0.000	0.000	0.000	0.000	0.000	0.000	0.000
Div	−0.034	0.327	0.293	−0.066	−0.100	−0.458	−0.492
Age	0.020	−0.193	−0.173	0.039	0.059	0.269	0.289
Ind$_2$	0.000	−1.475	−1.475	0.296	0.296	2.063	2.063
Ind$_3$	0.000	−1.798	−1.798	0.361	0.361	2.515	2.515
Ind$_4$	0.000	0.000	0.000	0.000	0.000	0.000	0.000
Ind$_5$	0.000	−1.952	−1.952	0.392	0.392	2.731	2.731
Ind$_7$	0.000	0.000	0.000	0.000	0.000	0.000	0.000
Ind$_8$	0.000	0.000	0.000	0.000	0.000	0.000	0.000
Time	0.000	0.000	0.000	0.000	0.000	0.000	0.000
constant	0.000	18.568	18.568	−3.724	−3.724	−25.972	−25.972

Table A.17: 3SLS estimates for ownership concentration and Tobin's Q with nonlinear and linear ease of monitoring measure

	linear & squared		linear		difference	
	Q	Ocr	Q	Ocr	Q	Ocr
Ocr$_a$	−0.192		−0.172		0.020	
	(0.002)		(0.003)		−0.001	
Ocr$_b$	0.445		0.424		0.021	
	(0.000)		(0.000)		0.000	
Ocr$_c$	1.275		1.246		0.030	
	(0.000)		(0.000)		0.000	

Table continues at the following page

Table A.17: Results with nonlinear and linear ease of monitoring measure (continued)

	linear & squared		linear		difference	
	Q	Ocr	Q	Ocr	Q	Ocr
$Q_{0 \leq x \leq .22}$	−1.584		−2.039		−0.455	
	(0.000)		(0.000)		0.000	
$Q_{.22 \leq x \leq .72}$	0.416		0.417		−0.001	
	(0.000)		(0.000)		0.000	
$Q_{.72 \leq x}$	2.901		2.898		0.003	
	(0.000)		(0.000)		0.000	
ORatio	−0.015		−0.015		0.000	
	(0.023)		(0.023)		0.000	
OcST	0.239	−0.392	0.240	−0.394	−0.002	0.002
	(0.000)	(0.000)	(0.000)	(0.000)	0.000	0.000
Size	0.159	−0.010	0.160	−0.006	0.000	−0.004
	(0.006)	(0.914)	(0.005)	(0.951)	0.001	−0.037
$Size^2$	−0.004	0.000	−0.004	0.000	0.000	0.000
	(0.008)	(0.939)	(0.007)	(0.901)	0.001	0.038
Debt	0.268	−0.078	0.266	−0.084	0.002	0.006
	(0.008)	(0.393)	(0.008)	(0.345)	0.000	0.048
$Debt^2$	−0.234		−0.232		−0.003	
	(0.060)		(0.062)		−0.002	
Inv	0.060	−0.040	0.056	−0.040	0.003	0.000
	(0.125)	(0.459)	(0.145)	(0.454)	−0.020	0.005
Inv^2	−0.044		−0.042		−0.002	
	(0.088)		(0.106)		−0.018	
Nwc	−0.766	0.044	−0.553	0.044	0.005	−0.001
	(0.000)	(0.266)	(0.000)	(0.260)	0.000	0.006
Nwc^2	0.808		0.447		−0.004	
	(0.000)		(0.000)		0.000	
Eom	0.315	−0.151	0.307	−0.128	0.007	−0.023
	(0.000)	(0.061)	(0.000)	(0.000)	0.000	0.061
Eom^2	−0.051	0.009	−0.048		−0.003	
	(0.006)	(0.755)	(0.000)		0.006	

Table continues at the following page

Table A.17: Results with nonlinear and linear ease of monitoring measure (continued)

	linear & squared		linear		difference	
	Q	Ocr	Q	Ocr	Q	Ocr
Beta	−0.018	−0.067	−0.018	−0.066	0.000	0.000
	(0.281)	(0.015)	(0.279)	(0.015)	0.002	0.000
Gro	0.020	−0.008	0.019	−0.008	0.001	0.000
	(0.324)	(0.793)	(0.344)	(0.790)	−0.020	0.003
Div	0.008	−0.034	0.008	−0.034	0.000	0.000
	(0.287)	(0.003)	(0.285)	(0.003)	0.002	0.000
Age		0.020		0.019		0.000
		(0.051)		(0.053)		−0.002
Ind_2	0.105	−0.013	0.107	−0.016	−0.001	0.003
	(0.025)	(0.858)	(0.022)	(0.830)	0.003	0.028
Ind_3	0.128	−0.088	0.129	−0.089	0.000	0.001
	(0.004)	(0.219)	(0.004)	(0.214)	0.000	0.005
Ind_4	−0.016	0.097	−0.016	0.095	0.000	0.002
	(0.766)	(0.284)	(0.767)	(0.293)	−0.001	−0.009
Ind_5	0.139	−0.040	0.139	−0.040	0.001	−0.001
	(0.005)	(0.613)	(0.005)	(0.619)	0.000	−0.006
Ind_7	0.002	0.017	0.003	0.016	−0.001	0.001
	(0.977)	(0.836)	(0.955)	(0.846)	0.022	−0.010
Ind_8	−0.014	0.068	−0.012	0.063	−0.002	0.005
	(0.824)	(0.495)	(0.851)	(0.524)	−0.027	−0.029
Time	−0.001	0.006	−0.001	0.005	0.000	0.001
	(0.966)	(0.830)	(0.965)	(0.848)	0.001	−0.018
constant	−1.322	0.804	−1.315	0.756	−0.007	0.048
	(0.027)	(0.421)	(0.027)	(0.447)	0.000	−0.026
RMSE	0.144	0.231	0.144	0.231	0.001	0.000
pseudo $\bar{R}^2$	0.344	0.161	0.351	0.162	−0.007	−0.001
χ^2	487.580	234.810	499.270	232.930	−11.690	1.880
Prob.$_{\chi^2}$	(0.000)	(0.000)	(0.000)	(0.000)	(0.000)	(0.000)
RMSEA	0.036	0.000	0.036	0.000	0.000	0.000

Table A.18: Noncausal effects of the control variables on Tobin's Q

	$cov(x,Q)$	Ocr_a		Ocr_b		Ocr_c	
		T_{Qx}	N_{Qx}	T_{Qx}	N_{Qx}	T_{Qx}	N_{Qx}
ORatio	−0.027	−0.007	−0.020	−0.040	0.012	−0.085	0.058
OcST	−0.301	0.502	−0.803	−0.552	0.251	−2.027	1.726
Size	0.320	0.073	0.247	0.419	−0.099	0.903	−0.584
Size^2	0.315	−0.002	0.317	−0.011	0.325	−0.023	0.337
Debt	0.196	0.122	0.073	0.706	−0.510	1.523	−1.327
Debt^2	0.030	−0.107	0.137	−0.616	0.646	−1.329	1.359
Inv	−0.054	0.000	−0.054	0.000	−0.054	0.000	−0.054
Inv^2	−0.088	−0.020	−0.068	−0.116	0.027	−0.250	0.162
Nwc	−0.766	−0.250	0.210	−1.443	1.403	−3.113	3.073
Nwc^2	0.808	0.202	−0.032	1.167	−0.997	2.517	−2.347
Eom	0.135	0.295	−0.160	0.375	−0.239	0.486	−0.351
Eom^2	−0.012	−0.023	0.011	−0.134	0.122	−0.290	0.277
Beta	−0.332	0.067	−0.399	−0.202	−0.130	−0.579	0.246
Gro	−0.044	0.000	−0.044	0.000	−0.044	0.000	−0.044
Div	−0.034	0.034	−0.068	−0.102	0.069	−0.294	0.260
Age	0.448	−0.020	0.468	0.060	0.388	0.173	0.275
Ind$_2$	0.193	0.048	0.145	0.277	−0.083	0.597	−0.403
Ind$_3$	−0.157	0.058	−0.216	0.337	−0.494	0.727	−0.884
Ind$_4$	−0.056	0.000	−0.056	0.000	−0.056	0.000	−0.056
Ind$_5$	0.004	0.063	−0.060	0.366	−0.363	0.790	−0.786
Ind$_7$	−0.065	0.000	−0.065	0.000	−0.065	0.000	−0.065
Ind$_8$	−0.050	0.000	−0.050	0.000	−0.050	0.000	−0.050
Time	0.048	0.000	0.048	0.000	0.048	0.000	0.048

A.8 Detailed and Additional Results of Empirical Analyses

Table A.19: Noncausal effects of the control variables on ownership concentration

	$cov(x, Ocr)$	Q_a		Q_b		Q_c	
		$T_{Ocr\,x}$	$N_{Ocr\,x}$	$T_{Ocr\,x}$	$N_{Ocr\,x}$	$T_{Ocr\,x}$	$N_{Ocr\,x}$
ORatio	0.129	0.211	−0.081	−0.042	0.172	−0.295	0.424
OcST	0.305	0.027	0.279	−0.476	0.781	−0.977	1.283
Size	0.166	−2.233	2.399	0.448	−0.282	3.124	−2.958
Size^2	0.156	0.056	0.100	−0.011	0.167	−0.079	0.234
Debt	0.403	−3.764	4.167	0.755	−0.352	5.265	−4.862
Debt^2	0.148	3.287	−3.139	−0.659	0.807	−4.597	4.745
Inv	−0.279	0.000	−0.279	0.000	−0.279	0.000	−0.279
Inv^2	−0.157	0.618	−0.775	−0.124	−0.033	−0.864	0.708
Nwc	−0.261	7.697	−7.958	−1.544	1.282	−10.766	10.505
Nwc^2	−0.039	−6.222	6.183	1.248	−1.287	8.703	−8.742
Eom	0.405	−3.121	3.526	0.445	−0.040	4.003	−3.598
Eom^2	0.267	0.716	−0.449	−0.144	0.411	−1.002	1.269
Beta	−0.300	0.578	−0.879	−0.196	−0.104	−0.970	0.669
Gro	−0.113	0.000	−0.113	0.000	−0.113	0.000	−0.113
Div	−0.087	0.293	−0.381	−0.100	0.012	−0.492	0.405
Age	0.255	−0.173	0.427	0.059	0.196	0.289	−0.035
Ind$_2$	0.236	−1.475	1.711	0.296	−0.060	2.063	−1.827
Ind$_3$	0.141	−1.798	1.939	0.361	−0.219	2.515	−2.373
Ind$_4$	0.046	0.000	0.046	0.000	0.046	0.000	0.046
Ind$_5$	0.066	−1.952	2.019	0.392	−0.325	2.731	−2.665
Ind$_7$	−0.514	0.000	−0.514	0.000	−0.514	0.000	−0.514
Ind$_8$	−0.177	0.000	−0.177	0.000	−0.177	0.000	−0.177
Time	0.064	0.000	0.064	0.000	0.064	0.000	0.064

Robustness Checks

Table A.20: Correlation and tolerance of piecewise variables of Q and previous year's Q

	Correlation			Tolerance		
	Q_a	Q_b	Q_c	Q_a	Q_b	Q_c
Q_a^{t-1}	0.427	−0.268	−0.100	0.820	0.930	0.992
Q_b^{t-1}	−0.148	0.285	−0.260	0.980	0.921	0.935
Q_c^{t-1}	−0.149	−0.302	0.687	0.980	0.910	0.529

Table A.21: Robustness checks on lagged measures of Q

	Alternation 1		Alternation 2		Original	
	Q	Ocr	Q	Ocr	Q	Ocr
Ocr_a	−0.117		−0.100		−0.148	
	(0.019)		(0.047)		(0.012)	
Ocr_b	0.573		0.564		0.445	
	(0.000)		(0.000)		(0.000)	
Ocr_c	1.581		1.526		1.275	
	(0.000)		(0.000)		(0.000)	
Q_a		−1.041		−0.868		−2.074
		(0.000)		(0.001)		(0.000)
Q_b		0.385		0.376		0.416
		(0.000)		(0.000)		(0.000)
Q_c		2.133		1.762		2.901
		(0.000)		(0.000)		(0.000)
Q_a^{t-1}		−0.301		−0.475		
		(0.050)		(0.002)		
Q_b^{t-1}		−0.086		0.080		
		(0.636)		(0.407)		
Q_c^{t-1}		0.514		0.864		
		(0.000)		(0.000)		
Oratio	−0.015		−0.015		−0.015	
	(0.024)		(0.028)		(0.023)	
OcST	0.256	−0.432	0.246	−0.423	0.239	−0.392
	(0.000)	(0.000)	(0.000)	(0.000)	(0.000)	(0.000)
Size	0.169	0.070	0.190	0.009	0.159	−0.010
	(0.000)	(0.243)	(0.000)	(0.872)	(0.006)	(0.914)
$Size^2$	−0.004	−0.002	−0.005	0.000	−0.004	0.000
	(0.000)	(0.183)	(0.000)	(0.845)	(0.008)	(0.939)
Debt	0.352	−0.218	0.336	−0.137	0.268	−0.078
	(0.001)	(0.013)	(0.001)	(0.082)	(0.008)	(0.393)
$Debt^2$	−0.289		−0.334		−0.234	
	(0.108)		(0.066)		(0.060)	
Inv	0.074	−0.011	0.119	0.015	0.060	−0.040
	(0.021)	(0.817)	(0.000)	(0.520)	(0.125)	(0.459)

Table continues at the following page

Table A.21: Robustness checks on lagged measures of Q (continued)

	Alternation 1		Alternation 2		Original	
	Q	Ocr	Q	Ocr	Q	Ocr
Inv^2	−0.044		−0.077		−0.044	
	(0.177)		(0.021)		(0.088)	
Nwc	−0.774	0.072	−0.807	0.079	−0.548	0.044
	(0.000)	(0.087)	(0.000)	(0.032)	(0.000)	(0.266)
Nwc^2	0.757		0.791		0.443	
	(0.000)		(0.000)		(0.000)	
Eom	0.531	−0.314	0.524	−0.313	0.315	−0.151
	(0.000)	(0.003)	(0.000)	(0.000)	(0.000)	(0.061)
Eom^2	−0.172	0.106	−0.166	0.077	−0.051	0.009
	(0.000)	(0.087)	(0.000)	(0.118)	(0.006)	(0.755)
Beta	−0.014	−0.051	−0.015	−0.056	−0.018	−0.067
	(0.314)	(0.018)	(0.267)	(0.008)	(0.281)	(0.015)
Gro	0.039	−0.011	0.058	0.093	0.020	−0.008
	(0.184)	(0.812)	(0.008)	(0.000)	(0.324)	(0.793)
Div	0.011	−0.026	0.012	−0.029	0.008	−0.034
	(0.081)	(0.009)	(0.065)	(0.003)	(0.287)	(0.003)
Age		0.000		0.005		0.020
		(0.972)		(0.557)		(0.051)
Ind_2	0.084	−0.030	0.086	−0.010	0.105	−0.013
	(0.084)	(0.691)	(0.071)	(0.891)	(0.025)	(0.858)
Ind_3	0.131	−0.121	0.132	−0.103	0.128	−0.088
	(0.005)	(0.090)	(0.004)	(0.142)	(0.004)	(0.219)
Ind_4	−0.028	0.000	−0.021	0.004	−0.016	0.097
	(0.594)	(0.997)	(0.689)	(0.956)	(0.766)	(0.284)
Ind_5	0.137	−0.098	0.138	−0.091	0.139	−0.040
	(0.006)	(0.204)	(0.005)	(0.234)	(0.005)	(0.613)
Ind_7	0.032	−0.049	0.025	−0.023	0.002	0.017
	(0.524)	(0.522)	(0.606)	(0.762)	(0.977)	(0.836)
Ind_8	0.035	−0.056	0.032	−0.039	−0.014	0.068
	(0.517)	(0.508)	(0.546)	(0.634)	(0.824)	(0.495)
Time	−0.009	−0.005	−0.013	0.034	−0.001	0.006
	(0.601)	(0.848)	(0.401)	(0.162)	(0.966)	(0.830)

Table continues at the following page

Table A.21: Robustness checks on lagged measures of Q (continued)

	Alternation 1		Alternation 2		Original	
	Q	Ocr	Q	Ocr	Q	Ocr
constant	−1.485	0.009	−1.678	0.391	−1.322	0.804
	(0.000)	(0.989)	(0.000)	(0.511)	(0.027)	(0.421)
RMSE	0.156	0.239	0.155	0.237	0.144	0.231
pseudo $\bar{R}^2$	0.398	0.078	0.409	0.096	0.344	0.161
Prob.$_{\chi^2}$	(0.000)	(0.000)	(0.000)	(0.000)	0.000	0.000
RMSEA	0.037	0.000	0.039	0.000	0.036	0.000

Table A.22: Robustness checks on ROE

	ROE		Q	
	Q	Ocr	ROE	Ocr
Ocr$_a$	0.171		−0.148	
	(0.034)		(0.012)	
Ocr$_b$	−2.124		0.445	
	(0.000)		(0.000)	
Ocr$_c$	−5.832		1.275	
	(0.000)		(0.000)	
ROE$_a$ / Q$_a$		−0.588		−2.074
		(0.000)		(0.000)
ROE$_b$ / Q$_b$		0.133		0.416
		(0.051)		(0.000)
ROE$_c$ / Q$_c$		−0.652		2.901
		(0.000)		(0.000)
Oratio	0.029		−0.015	
	(0.009)		(0.023)	
OcST	−1.047	−0.641	0.239	−0.392
	(0.000)	(0.000)	(0.000)	(0.000)
Size	−0.102	0.047	0.159	−0.010
	(0.629)	(0.723)	(0.006)	(0.914)
Size^2	0.003	−0.001	−0.004	0.000
	(0.496)	(0.856)	(0.008)	(0.939)

Table continues at the following page

Table A.22: Robustness checks on ROE (continued)

	ROE		Q	
	Q	Ocr	ROE	Ocr
Debt	0.069	−0.016	0.268	−0.078
	(0.842)	(0.936)	(0.008)	(0.393)
Debt^2	−0.332		−0.234	
	(0.267)		(0.060)	
Inv	−1.249	−0.780	0.060	−0.040
	(0.000)	(0.000)	(0.125)	(0.459)
Inv^2	−0.139		−0.044	
	(0.011)		(0.088)	
Nwc	0.932	0.368	−0.548	0.044
	(0.000)	(0.000)	(0.000)	(0.266)
Nwc^2	−0.368		0.443	
	(0.087)		(0.000)	
Eom	−0.931	−0.579	0.315	−0.151
	(0.012)	(0.013)	(0.000)	(0.061)
Eom^2	0.370	0.254	−0.051	0.009
	(0.088)	(0.064)	(0.006)	(0.755)
Beta	−0.236	−0.182	−0.018	−0.067
	(0.002)	(0.000)	(0.281)	(0.015)
Gro	−0.054	−0.030	0.020	−0.008
	(0.736)	(0.766)	(0.324)	(0.793)
Div	−0.100	−0.069	0.008	−0.034
	(0.006)	(0.002)	(0.287)	(0.003)
Age		−0.006		0.020
		(0.234)		(0.051)
Ind$_2$	−0.342	−0.193	0.105	−0.013
	(0.200)	(0.251)	(0.025)	(0.858)
Ind$_3$	−0.430	−0.274	0.128	−0.088
	(0.090)	(0.087)	(0.004)	(0.219)
Ind$_4$	−0.493	−0.326	−0.016	0.097
	(0.090)	(0.075)	(0.766)	(0.284)
Ind$_5$	−0.566	−0.319	0.139	−0.040
	(0.039)	(0.066)	(0.005)	(0.613)

Table continues at the following page

Table A.22: Robustness checks on ROE (continued)

	ROE		Q	
	Q	Ocr	ROE	Ocr
Ind_7	−0.261	−0.142	0.002	0.017
	(0.336)	(0.409)	(0.977)	(0.836)
Ind_8	−0.522	−0.331	−0.014	0.068
	(0.079)	(0.078)	(0.824)	(0.495)
Time	0.026	0.021	−0.001	0.006
	(0.781)	(0.719)	(0.966)	(0.830)
constant	1.838	0.460	−1.322	0.804
	(0.405)	(0.741)	(0.027)	(0.421)
RMSE	0.864	0.545	0.144	0.231
pseudo $\bar{R}^2$	0.157	−3.793	0.344	0.161
$Prob._{\chi^2}$	(0.000)	(0.000)	(0.000)	(0.000)
RMSEA	0.066	0.194	0.036	0.000

A.8.2 Simultaneous Equations Model of Insider Ownership

Endogeneity Tests of ROE

Table A.23: Wu-Hausman F-test and Durbin-Wu-Hausman χ^2-test for different relationships of managerial ownership and ROE

		ROE			Mcr		
		value	distr.	p-value	value	distr.	p-value
Linear	Linear	45.472	$F(1, 496)$	(0.000)	4.374	$F(1, 499)$	(0.037)
		43.753	$\chi^2(1)$	(0.000)	4.527	$\chi^2(1)$	(0.033)
	Squared	.	$F(2, 494)$	.	4.372	$F(1, 499)$	(0.037)
		521.000	$\chi^2(2)$	(0.000)	4.525	$\chi^2(1)$	(0.033)
	Piecewise	.	$F(3, 493)$	.	2.267	$F(1, 499)$	(0.133)
		521.000	$\chi^2(3)$	(0.000)	2.356	$\chi^2(1)$	(0.125)
Squared	Linear	16.101	$F(1, 496)$	(0.000)	11.905	$F(2, 497)$	(0.000)
		16.381	$\chi^2(1)$	(0.000)	23.818	$\chi^2(2)$	(0.000)
	Squared	8.105	$F(2, 494)$	(0.000)	11.831	$F(2, 497)$	(0.000)
		16.552	$\chi^2(2)$	(0.000)	23.677	$\chi^2(2)$	(0.000)
	Piecewise	29.097	$F(3, 493)$	(0.000)	13.584	$F(2, 497)$	(0.000)
		78.373	$\chi^2(3)$	(0.000)	27.004	$\chi^2(2)$	(0.000)

Simultaneous Equations Results

Table A.24: Detailed i3SLS estimates for managerial ownership and Q

	Model 2		Model 5	
	Q	Mcr	Q	Mcr
Mcr	−5.484		−7.990	
	(0.101)		(0.045)	
Mcr^2			8.582	
			(0.049)	
Q^2		−4.260		10.648
		(0.170)		(0.023)
Q^2		3.678		−9.783
		(0.190)		(0.021)
MRatio	0.813		−0.661	
	(0.517)		(0.082)	

Table continues at the following page

Table A.24: Results for managerial ownership and Q (continued)

	Model 2		Model 5	
	Q	Mcr	Q	Mcr
OcST	−0.499	−0.142	0.109	0.068
	(0.336)	(0.114)	(0.555)	(0.628)
Size	0.705	0.282	0.096	−0.336
	(0.110)	(0.067)	(0.649)	(0.154)
Size^2	−0.020	−0.007	−0.005	0.007
	(0.086)	(0.044)	(0.350)	(0.205)
Debt	0.782	−0.101	0.551	0.604
	(0.499)	(0.603)	(0.448)	(0.045)
Debt^2	−0.537		−0.729	
	(0.766)		(0.579)	
Inv	−0.505	−0.005	−0.261	−0.222
	(0.246)	(0.953)	(0.295)	(0.080)
Inv^2	0.494		−0.112	
	(0.267)		(0.643)	
Nwc	−0.196	−0.021	0.086	0.036
	(0.835)	(0.741)	(0.932)	(0.713)
Nwc^2	0.211		−0.109	
	(0.834)		(0.921)	
Eom	1.282	0.677	0.771	−0.932
	(0.091)	(0.066)	(0.040)	(0.096)
Eom^2	−0.676	−0.348	−0.355	0.477
	(0.154)	(0.070)	(0.117)	(0.104)
Beta	−0.094	−0.053	0.173	0.095
	(0.478)	(0.211)	(0.174)	(0.154)
Gro	−0.007	0.034	0.098	−0.069
	(0.981)	(0.624)	(0.522)	(0.526)
Div	−0.046	−0.001	0.001	−0.031
	(0.507)	(0.968)	(0.978)	(0.210)
Age		−0.004		0.024
		(0.723)		(0.359)
Ind_2	1.070	0.191	0.384	0.227
	(0.153)	(0.080)	(0.164)	(0.186)

Table continues at the following page

Table A.24: Results for managerial ownership and Q (continued)

	Model 2		Model 5	
	Q	Mcr	Q	Mcr
Ind_3	0.653	0.186	0.442	−0.039
	(0.237)	(0.105)	(0.115)	(0.829)
Ind_4	0.210	−0.043	0.186	0.291
	(0.698)	(0.749)	(0.515)	(0.171)
Ind_5	0.673	0.117	0.490	0.190
	(0.232)	(0.308)	(0.107)	(0.295)
Ind_7	0.823	0.114	0.392	0.268
	(0.232)	(0.318)	(0.205)	(0.137)
Ind_8	0.190	0.020	0.285	0.109
	(0.725)	(0.872)	(0.350)	(0.575)
Time	−0.108	−0.036	0.043	0.015
	(0.547)	(0.344)	(0.635)	(0.809)
constant	−5.570	−1.580	0.845	1.575
	(0.224)	(0.158)	(0.737)	(0.367)
RMSE	1.517	0.348	0.800	0.550
pseudo $\bar{R}^2$	−55.909	−0.396	−14.819	−2.482
χ^2	42.450	40.870	24.710	20.460
Prob.$_{\chi^2}$	(0.008)	(0.006)	(0.421)	(0.492)
RMSEA	0.000	0.000	0.000	0.000

Table A.25: Detailed effects of the control variables on Tobin's Q and managerial ownership

	Q			Mcr		
	D_{Qx}	I_{Qx}	T_{Qx}	D_{Mcrx}	I_{Mcrx}	T_{Mcrx}
MRatio	0.000	0.000	0.000	0.000	0.000	0.000
OcST	0.000	0.000	0.000	0.000	0.000	0.000
Size	0.000	0.000	0.000	0.282	0.000	0.282
Size^2	−0.020	0.000	−0.020	−0.007	0.000	−0.007
Debt	0.000	0.000	0.000	0.000	0.000	0.000
Debt^2	0.000	0.000	0.000	0.000	0.000	0.000
Inv	0.000	0.000	0.000	0.000	0.000	0.000
Inv^2	0.000	0.000	0.000	0.000	0.000	0.000
Nwc	0.000	0.000	0.000	0.000	0.000	0.000
Nwc^2	0.000	0.000	0.000	0.000	0.000	0.000
Eom	1.282	0.000	1.282	0.677	0.000	0.677
Eom^2	0.000	0.000	0.000	−0.348	0.000	−0.348
Beta	0.000	0.000	0.000	0.000	0.000	0.000
Gro	0.000	0.000	0.000	0.000	0.000	0.000
Div	0.000	0.000	0.000	0.000	0.000	0.000
Age	0.000	0.000	0.000	0.000	0.000	0.000
Ind$_2$	0.000	0.000	0.000	0.000	0.000	0.000
Ind$_3$	0.000	0.000	0.000	0.000	0.000	0.000
Ind$_4$	0.000	0.000	0.000	0.000	0.000	0.000
Ind$_5$	0.000	0.000	0.000	0.000	0.000	0.000
Ind$_7$	0.000	0.000	0.000	0.000	0.000	0.000
Ind$_8$	0.000	0.000	0.000	0.000	0.000	0.000
Time	0.000	0.000	0.000	0.000	0.000	0.000
constant	0.000	0.000	0.000	0.000	0.000	0.000

Table A.26: Noncausal effects of the control variables on Tobin's Q and managerial ownership

	Q			Mcr		
	$cov(x,Q)$	T_{Qx}	N_{Qx}	$cov(x,Mcr)$	$T_{Mcr\,x}$	$N_{Mcr\,x}$
MRatio	0.073	0.000	0.073	0.102	0.000	0.102
OcST	0.046	0.000	0.046	−0.237	0.000	−0.237
Size	0.139	0.000	0.139	0.109	0.282	−0.173
Size^2	0.121	−0.020	0.141	0.094	−0.007	0.101
Debt	0.475	0.000	0.475	0.069	0.000	0.069
Debt^2	0.354	0.000	0.354	0.040	0.000	0.040
Inv	−0.107	0.000	−0.107	−0.028	0.000	−0.028
Inv^2	−0.091	0.000	−0.091	−0.068	0.000	−0.068
Nwc	−0.183	0.000	−0.183	0.171	0.000	0.171
Nwc^2	−0.139	0.000	−0.139	0.179	0.000	0.179
Eom	0.428	1.282	−0.854	0.038	0.677	−0.639
Eom^2	0.329	0.000	0.329	−0.029	−0.348	0.320
Beta	−0.191	0.000	−0.191	−0.290	0.000	−0.290
Gro	−0.035	0.000	−0.035	0.034	0.000	0.034
Div	−0.013	0.000	−0.013	−0.192	0.000	−0.192
Age	0.128	0.000	0.128	0.377	0.000	0.377
Ind$_2$	0.194	0.000	0.194	0.272	0.000	0.272
Ind$_3$	0.183	0.000	0.183	−0.055	0.000	−0.055
Ind$_4$	0.058	0.000	0.058	−0.121	0.000	−0.121
Ind$_5$	−0.035	0.000	−0.035	−0.026	0.000	−0.026
Ind$_7$	−0.346	0.000	−0.346	−0.079	0.000	−0.079
Ind$_8$	−0.195	0.000	−0.195	−0.214	0.000	−0.214
Time	−0.056	0.000	−0.056	−0.108	0.000	−0.108

Table A.27: Wu-Hausman F-test and Durbin-Wu-Hausman χ^2-test for different relationships of managerial and board ownership and Tobin's Q

Q	Mbcr	Q value	Q distr.	Q p-value	Mbcr value	Mbcr distr.	Mbcr p-value
Linear	Linear	74.880	F(1, 499)	(0.000)	3660.000	F(1, 497)	(0.000)
		67.980	$\chi^2(1)$	(0.000)	458.738	$\chi^2(1)$	(0.000)
	Squared	74.599	F(1, 499)	(0.000)	.	F(2, 495)	.
		67.758	$\chi^2(1)$	(0.000)	521.000	$\chi^2(2)$	(0.000)
	Piecewise	1.597	F(1, 499)	(0.207)	.	F(3, 494)	.
		1.662	$\chi^2(1)$	(0.197)	521.000	$\chi^2(3)$	(0.000)
Squared	Linear	44.906	F(2, 497)	(0.000)	1460.000	F(1, 497)	(0.000)
		79.739	$\chi^2(2)$	(0.000)	388.725	$\chi^2(1)$	(0.000)
	Squared	44.856	F(2, 497)	(0.000)	1600.000	F(2, 495)	(0.000)
		79.664	$\chi^2(2)$	(0.000)	451.325	$\chi^2(2)$	(0.000)
	Piecewise	0.961	F(2, 497)	(0.383)	879.685	F(3, 494)	(0.000)
		2.008	$\chi^2(2)$	(0.366)	438.852	$\chi^2(3)$	(0.000)
Piecewise	Linear	255.524	F(3, 495)	(0.000)	103.865	F(1, 497)	(0.000)
		316.576	$\chi^2(3)$	(0.000)	90.059	$\chi^2(1)$	(0.000)
	Squared	252.233	F(3, 495)	(0.000)	94.508	F(2, 495)	(0.000)
		314.964	$\chi^2(3)$	(0.000)	143.970	$\chi^2(2)$	(0.000)
	Piecewise	0.094	F(3, 495)	(0.963)	166.731	F(3, 494)	(0.000)
		0.296	$\chi^2(3)$	(0.961)	262.123	$\chi^2(3)$	(0.000)

Robustness regarding the Insider Definition

Table A.28: Wu-Hausman F-test and Durbin-Wu-Hausman χ^2-test for different relationships of managerial and board ownership and ROE

ROE	Mbcr	ROE value	ROE distr.	ROE p-value	Mbcr value	Mbcr distr.	Mbcr p-value
Linear	Linear	732.948	F(1, 497)	(0.000)	10.168	F(1, 499)	(0.002)
		310.473	$\chi^2(1)$	(0.000)	10.404	$\chi^2(1)$	(0.001)
	Squared	$1.450e^{13}$	F(2, 495)	(0.000)	6.693	F(1, 499)	(0.010)
		521.000	$\chi^2(2)$	(0.000)	6.896	$\chi^2(1)$	(0.009)
	Piecewise	.	F(3, 494)	.	14.074	F(1, 499)	(0.000)
		521.000	$\chi^2(3)$	(0.000)	14.291	$\chi^2(1)$	(0.000)
Squared	Linear	120.105	F(1, 497)	(0.000)	19.818	F(2, 497)	(0.000)
		101.400	$\chi^2(1)$	(0.000)	38.480	$\chi^2(2)$	(0.000)
	Squared	259.899	F(2, 495)	(0.000)	18.975	F(2, 497)	(0.000)
		266.866	$\chi^2(2)$	(0.000)	36.961	$\chi^2(2)$	(0.000)
	Piecewise	738.890	F(3, 494)	(0.000)	16.128	F(2, 497)	(0.000)
		426.052	$\chi^2(3)$	(0.000)	31.753	$\chi^2(2)$	(0.000)

A.8 Detailed and Additional Results of Empirical Analyses   339

Table A.29: Detailed 3SLS estimates for managerial and board ownership and Q

	Mbcr - Model 5			Mcr - Model 2	
	Q	Mbcr		Q	Mcr
Mbcr	−9.541		Mcr	−5.484	
	(0.057)			(0.101)	
Mbcr^2	8.671		Mcr^2		
	(0.087)				
Q^2		7.056			−4.260
		(0.082)			(0.170)
Q^2		−6.662			3.678
		(0.070)			(0.190)
MbRatio	−1.784		MRatio	0.813	
	(0.088)			(0.517)	
OcST	−0.053	0.074		−0.499	−0.142
	(0.834)	(0.519)		(0.336)	(0.114)
Size	0.145	−0.158		0.705	0.282
	(0.611)	(0.427)		(0.110)	(0.067)
Size^2	−0.007	0.003		−0.020	−0.007
	(0.306)	(0.546)		(0.086)	(0.044)
Debt	0.717	0.451		0.782	−0.101
	(0.455)	(0.072)		(0.499)	(0.603)
Debt^2	−0.711			−0.537	
	(0.675)			(0.766)	
Inv	−0.162	−0.177		−0.505	−0.005
	(0.554)	(0.086)		(0.246)	(0.953)
Inv^2	−0.365			0.494	
	(0.274)			(0.267)	
Nwc	0.301	0.025		−0.196	−0.021
	(0.809)	(0.749)		(0.835)	(0.741)
Nwc^2	−0.181			0.211	
	(0.890)			(0.834)	
Eom	0.787	−0.540		1.282	0.677
	(0.116)	(0.258)		(0.091)	(0.066)

Table continues at the following page

Table A.29: Results for managerial ownership and Q (continued)

	Mbcr - Model 5		Mcr - Model 2	
	Q	Mbcr	Q	Mcr
Eom^2	−0.426	0.281	−0.676	−0.348
	(0.165)	(0.259)	(0.154)	(0.070)
Beta	0.229	0.069	−0.094	−0.053
	(0.196)	(0.205)	(0.478)	(0.211)
Gro	0.164	−0.040	−0.007	0.034
	(0.453)	(0.646)	(0.981)	(0.624)
Div	−0.059	−0.032	−0.046	−0.001
	(0.264)	(0.109)	(0.507)	(0.968)
Age		0.024		−0.004
		(0.229)		(0.723)
Ind_2	0.726	0.268	1.070	0.191
	(0.081)	(0.049)	(0.153)	(0.080)
Ind_3	0.655	0.068	0.653	0.186
	(0.102)	(0.637)	(0.237)	(0.105)
Ind_4	0.354	0.244	0.210	−0.043
	(0.384)	(0.155)	(0.698)	(0.749)
Ind_5	0.672	0.257	0.673	0.117
	(0.102)	(0.072)	(0.232)	(0.308)
Ind_7	0.681	0.262	0.823	0.114
	(0.133)	(0.068)	(0.232)	(0.318)
Ind_8	0.589	0.154	0.190	0.020
	(0.209)	(0.316)	(0.725)	(0.872)
Time	−0.092	−0.006	−0.108	−0.036
	(0.448)	(0.897)	(0.547)	(0.344)
constant	2.224	0.546	−5.570	−1.580
	(0.556)	(0.701)	(0.224)	(0.158)
RMSE	1.103	0.435	1.517	0.348
pseudo $\bar{R}^2$	−29.109	−0.930	−55.909	−0.396
$Prob._{\chi^2}$	(0.002)	(0.036)	(0.008)	(0.006)
RMSEA	0.000	0.000	0.000	0.000

Robustness Checks

A.8 Detailed and Additional Results of Empirical Analyses

Table A.30: Robustness checks on lagged measures of Q

	Alternation 1		Alternation 2		Original	
	Q	Mcr	Q	Mcr	Q	Mcr
Mcr	−2.973		−0.661		−5.484	
	(0.043)		(0.000)		(0.101)	
Q		−1.926		3.033		−4.260
		(0.373)		(0.001)		(0.170)
Q^2		1.437		−3.641		3.678
		(0.464)		(0.000)		(0.190)
Q^{t-1}		1.214		−3.527			
		(0.469)		(0.000)			
$Q^{2\,t-1}$		−1.111		2.873			
		(0.472)		(0.000)			
Mratio		0.061		−0.001		0.813
		(0.911)		(0.991)		(0.517)
OcST	−0.227	−0.078	−0.019	−0.041	−0.499	−0.142
	(0.374)	(0.230)	(0.720)	(0.601)	(0.336)	(0.114)
Size	0.481	0.188	0.213	0.231	0.705	0.282
	(0.036)	(0.027)	(0.000)	(0.002)	(0.110)	(0.067)
$Size^2$	−0.014	−0.005	−0.005	−0.006	−0.020	−0.007
	(0.025)	(0.012)	(0.000)	(0.001)	(0.086)	(0.044)
Debt	0.460	0.103	0.143	0.244	0.782	−0.101
	(0.321)	(0.356)	(0.177)	(0.003)	(0.499)	(0.603)
$Debt^2$	−0.185		−0.035		−0.537	
	(0.753)		(0.827)		(0.766)	
Inv	−0.210	−0.024	0.174	−0.020	−0.505	−0.005
	(0.332)	(0.720)	(0.000)	(0.356)	(0.246)	(0.953)
Inv^2	0.164		−0.156		0.494	
	(0.471)		(0.000)		(0.267)	
Nwc	−0.287	−0.002	−0.091	−0.030	−0.196	−0.021
	(0.436)	(0.974)	(0.408)	(0.436)	(0.835)	(0.741)
Nwc^2	0.275		0.090		0.211	
	(0.478)		(0.440)		(0.834)	
Eom	0.951	0.415	0.591	0.646	1.282	0.677
	(0.016)	(0.019)	(0.000)	(0.000)	(0.091)	(0.066)

Table continues at the following page

Table A.30: Robustness checks on lagged measures of Q (continued)

	Alternation 1		Alternation 2		Original	
	Q	Mcr	Q	Mcr	Q	Mcr
Eom^2	−0.445	−0.189	−0.222	−0.237	−0.676	−0.348
	(0.068)	(0.035)	(0.000)	(0.000)	(0.154)	(0.070)
Beta	−0.070	−0.034	−0.036	−0.021	−0.094	−0.053
	(0.339)	(0.264)	(0.065)	(0.478)	(0.478)	(0.211)
Gro	0.011	0.023	0.087	−0.043	−0.007	0.034
	(0.944)	(0.697)	(0.000)	(0.086)	(0.981)	(0.624)
Div	−0.025	−0.008	−0.003	−0.006	−0.046	−0.001
	(0.489)	(0.488)	(0.726)	(0.699)	(0.507)	(0.968)
Age		−0.002		0.004		−0.004
		(0.776)		(0.559)		(0.723)
Ind_2	0.635	0.218	0.248	0.341	1.070	0.191
	(0.081)	(0.016)	(0.001)	(0.001)	(0.153)	(0.080)
Ind_3	0.412	0.153	0.201	0.240	0.653	0.186
	(0.149)	(0.082)	(0.003)	(0.019)	(0.237)	(0.105)
Ind_4	0.106	0.029	0.027	0.058	0.210	−0.043
	(0.717)	(0.767)	(0.721)	(0.615)	(0.698)	(0.749)
Ind_5	0.450	0.170	0.236	0.300	0.673	0.117
	(0.128)	(0.080)	(0.001)	(0.006)	(0.232)	(0.308)
Ind_7	0.455	0.158	0.123	0.165	0.823	0.114
	(0.183)	(0.086)	(0.095)	(0.128)	(0.232)	(0.318)
Ind_8	0.108	0.043	0.044	0.035	0.190	0.020
	(0.715)	(0.670)	(0.567)	(0.764)	(0.725)	(0.872)
Time	−0.065	−0.029	−0.036	−0.042	−0.108	−0.036
	(0.495)	(0.358)	(0.117)	(0.233)	(0.547)	(0.344)
constant	−3.488	−1.377	−1.803	−1.799	−5.570	−1.580
	(0.141)	(0.107)	(0.000)	(0.017)	(0.224)	(0.158)
RMSE	0.837	0.290	0.229	0.347	1.517	0.348
pseudo $\bar{R}^2$	−16.329	0.032	−0.294	−0.384	−55.909	−0.396
Prob.$_{\chi^2}$	(0.000)	(0.000)	(0.000)	(0.000)	(0.008)	(0.006)
RMSEA	0.034	0.000	0.000	0.037	0.000	0.000

Table A.31: Robustness checks on ROE

	ROE		Q	
	Q	Mcr	ROE	Mcr
Mcr	−2.538 (0.370)		−5.484 (0.101)	
ROE		0.128 Q (0.006)		−4.260 (0.170)
ROE^2		0.018 Q^2 (0.022)		3.678 (0.190)
Mratio	1.824 (0.091)		0.813 (0.517)	
OcST	−0.706 (0.081)	−0.050 (0.466)	−0.499 (0.336)	−0.142 (0.114)
Size	−0.234 (0.465)	0.109 (0.141)	0.705 (0.110)	0.282 (0.067)
Size^2	0.005 (0.547)	−0.004 (0.053)	−0.020 (0.086)	−0.007 (0.044)
Debt	−2.684 (0.014)	0.021 (0.843)	0.782 (0.499)	−0.101 (0.603)
Debt^2	5.852 (0.002)		−0.537 (0.766)	
Inv	−1.282 (0.000)	0.066 (0.429)	−0.505 (0.246)	−0.005 (0.953)
Inv^2	−0.664 (0.027)		0.494 (0.267)	
Nwc	3.319 (0.002)	−0.066 (0.251)	−0.196 (0.835)	−0.021 (0.741)
Nwc^2	−3.200 (0.007)		0.211 (0.834)	
Eom	−0.133 (0.814)	0.276 (0.041)	1.282 (0.091)	0.677 (0.066)
Eom^2	−0.110 (0.758)	−0.155 (0.044)	−0.676 (0.154)	−0.348 (0.070)
Beta	−0.126 (0.166)	0.014 (0.614)	−0.094 (0.478)	−0.053 (0.211)

Table continues at the following page

Table A.31: Robustness checks on ROE (continued)

	ROE		Q	
	Q	Mcr	ROE	Mcr
Gro	−0.027 (0.888)	−0.001 (0.979)	−0.007 (0.981)	0.034 (0.624)
Div	−0.076 (0.122)	0.002 (0.879)	−0.046 (0.507)	−0.001 (0.968)
Age		0.004 (0.778)		−0.004 (0.723)
Ind_2	0.041 (0.945)	0.231 (0.013)	1.070 (0.153)	0.191 (0.080)
Ind_3	−0.127 (0.756)	0.154 (0.082)	0.653 (0.237)	0.186 (0.105)
Ind_4	−0.407 (0.283)	0.129 (0.216)	0.210 (0.698)	−0.043 (0.749)
Ind_5	−0.260 (0.529)	0.191 (0.053)	0.673 (0.232)	0.117 (0.308)
Ind_7	0.180 (0.734)	0.181 (0.054)	0.823 (0.232)	0.114 (0.318)
Ind_8	−0.241 (0.521)	0.108 (0.304)	0.190 (0.725)	0.020 (0.872)
Time	−0.025 (0.843)	−0.028 (0.379)	−0.108 (0.547)	−0.036 (0.344)
constant	1.418 (0.671)	−0.767 (0.321)	−5.570 (0.224)	−1.580 (0.158)
RMSE	1.036	0.295	1.517	0.348
pseudo $\bar{R}^2$	−0.210	−0.001	−55.909	−0.396
$Prob._{\chi^2}$	(0.000)	(0.000)	(0.008)	(0.006)
RMSEA	0.000	0.000	0.000	0.000

A.8.3 Simultaneous Equations Model of Institutional Ownership

Endogeneity Tests of roe

Table A.32: Wu-Hausman F-test and Durbin-Wu-Hausman χ^2-test for different relationships of institutional ownership and ROE

		ROE			Icr		
ROE	Icr	value	distr.	p-value	value	distr.	p-value
Linear	Linear	89.606	F(1, 497)	(0.000)	5.203	F(1, 499)	(0.023)
		79.585	$\chi^2(1)$	(0.000)	5.377	$\chi^2(1)$	(0.020)
	Squared	$7.000e^{14}$	F(2, 495)	(0.000)	5.074	F(1, 499)	(0.025)
		521.000	$\chi^2(2)$	(0.000)	5.244	$\chi^2(1)$	(0.022)
	Piecewise	78.705	F(3, 495)	(0.000)	8.274	F(1, 499)	(0.004)
		168.258	$\chi^2(3)$	(0.000)	8.498	$\chi^2(1)$	(0.004)
Squared	Linear	37.311	F(1, 497)	(0.000)	8.274	F(1, 499)	(0.004)
		36.382	$\chi^2(1)$	(0.000)	8.498	$\chi^2(1)$	(0.004)
	Squared	116.176	F(2, 495)	(0.000)	14.328	F(2, 497)	(0.000)
		166.433	$\chi^2(2)$	(0.000)	28.402	$\chi^2(2)$	(0.000)
	Piecewise	70.854	F(3, 495)	(0.000)	18.508	F(2, 497)	(0.000)
		156.516	$\chi^2(3)$	(0.000)	36.113	$\chi^2(2)$	(0.000)

Simultaneous Equations Results

Table A.33: Detailed I3SLS estimates for institutional ownership and Q

	Model 1		Model 2		Model 3	
	Q	Icr	Q	Icr	Q	Icr
Icr	−1.051				−2.467	
	(0.001)				(0.005)	
Icr $_{0\leq x\leq 10\%}$			−1.337			
			(0.005)			
Icr $_{10\%\leq x\leq 20\%}$			−0.552			
			(0.001)			
Icr $_{20\%\leq x\leq 40\%}$			−0.297			
			(0.000)			
Icr $_{40\%\leq x}$			−0.917			
			(0.000)			

Table continues at the following page

Table A.33: Results for institutional ownership and Q (continued)

	Model 1		Model 2		Model 3	
	Q	Icr	Q	Icr	Q	Icr
$Q_{0 \leq x \leq .5}$		0.365		0.412		0.099
		(0.003)		(0.000)		(0.000)
$Q_{.5 \leq x \leq .7}$		−0.302		−0.394		−0.257
		(0.021)		(0.010)		(0.000)
$Q_{.7 \leq x}$		−1.277		−1.491		−0.746
		(0.000)		(0.000)		(0.001)
IRatio	0.000		−0.001			
	(0.775)		(0.495)			
OcST	0.952	0.831	0.810	0.837	1.700	0.688
	(0.001)	(0.000)	(0.000)	(0.000)	(0.005)	(0.000)
Size	0.509	0.283	0.490	0.291	0.312	0.049
	(0.002)	(0.034)	(0.000)	(0.029)	(0.071)	(0.459)
$Size^2$	−0.012	−0.006	−0.011	−0.007	−0.006	−0.001
	(0.002)	(0.041)	(0.000)	(0.035)	(0.117)	(0.631)
Debt	0.097	0.128	0.093	0.148	0.162	0.026
	(0.710)	(0.519)	(0.690)	(0.452)	(0.553)	(0.771)
$Debt^2$	−0.003		−0.057		−0.208	
	(0.992)		(0.842)		(0.411)	
Inv	−0.054	−0.046	−0.036	−0.046	0.129	0.053
	(0.632)	(0.650)	(0.703)	(0.650)	(0.394)	(0.363)
Inv^2	−0.252		−0.235		−0.126	
	(0.001)		(0.002)		(0.015)	
Nwc	−0.389	0.154	−0.420	0.148	−0.196	0.040
	(0.191)	(0.140)	(0.106)	(0.154)	(0.333)	(0.435)
Nwc^2	0.601		0.599		0.295	
	(0.056)		(0.045)		(0.179)	
Eom	0.538	0.160	0.554	0.201	0.479	0.070
	(0.045)	(0.519)	(0.016)	(0.410)	(0.112)	(0.556)
Eom^2	−0.247	−0.065	−0.249	−0.083	−0.152	−0.010
	(0.143)	(0.674)	(0.085)	(0.588)	(0.430)	(0.898)
Beta	−0.070	−0.023	−0.075	−0.024	0.005	0.016
	(0.118)	(0.574)	(0.050)	(0.563)	(0.933)	(0.468)

Table continues at the following page

Table A.33: Results for institutional ownership and Q (continued)

	Model 1		Model 2		Model 3	
	Q	Icr	Q	Icr	Q	Icr
Gro	−0.220	−0.226	−0.181	−0.234	−0.082	−0.024
	(0.083)	(0.026)	(0.061)	(0.022)	(0.559)	(0.660)
Div	−0.060	−0.049	−0.052	−0.049	−0.036	−0.015
	(0.015)	(0.007)	(0.003)	(0.008)	(0.185)	(0.133)
Age		0.010		0.013		0.003
		(0.451)		(0.198)		(0.639)
Ind_2	0.086	0.033	0.097	0.050	−0.071	−0.040
	(0.509)	(0.784)	(0.369)	(0.661)	(0.688)	(0.537)
Ind_3	0.115	0.021	0.131	0.037	−0.089	−0.060
	(0.321)	(0.843)	(0.174)	(0.719)	(0.600)	(0.335)
Ind_4	−0.058	−0.083	−0.032	−0.064	−0.319	−0.124
	(0.714)	(0.536)	(0.790)	(0.621)	(0.163)	(0.107)
Ind_5	0.161	0.085	0.173	0.109	−0.007	−0.015
	(0.194)	(0.478)	(0.098)	(0.329)	(0.970)	(0.827)
Ind_7	0.033	0.046	0.041	0.061	−0.295	−0.115
	(0.827)	(0.744)	(0.751)	(0.655)	(0.161)	(0.110)
Ind_8	0.003	0.016	0.008	0.030	−0.182	−0.072
	(0.985)	(0.922)	(0.956)	(0.849)	(0.415)	(0.396)
Time	0.060	0.054	0.045	0.052	0.118	0.051
	(0.298)	(0.266)	(0.327)	(0.280)	(0.121)	(0.034)
constant	−4.678	−2.826	−4.511	−2.933	−2.967	−0.628
	(0.007)	(0.045)	(0.001)	(0.039)	(0.102)	(0.369)
RMSE	0.508	0.199	0.342	0.200	0.506	0.199
pseudo $\bar{R}^2$	−6.756	0.363	−2.514	0.353	−6.695	0.363
χ^2	98.950	310.600	4408.050	505.890	79.480	313.040
Prob.$_{\chi^2}$	(0.000)	(0.000)	(0.000)	(0.000)	(0.000)	(0.000)
RMSEA	0.000	0.000	0.185	0.038	0.000	0.000

Table A.34: Detailed effects of the control variables on Tobin's Q

	D_{Qx}	Icr_a		Icr_b		Icr_c	
		I_{Qx}	T_{Qx}	I_{Qx}	T_{Qx}	I_{Qx}	T_{Qx}
IRatio	0.000	0.000	0.000	0.000	0.000	0.000	0.000
OcST	0.831	0.495	1.326	−0.410	0.421	−1.732	−0.901
Size	0.283	0.338	0.621	−0.280	0.003	−1.182	−0.900
Size^2	−0.006	−0.008	−0.015	0.007	0.000	0.029	0.023
Debt	0.000	0.000	0.000	0.000	0.000	0.000	0.000
Debt^2	0.000	0.000	0.000	0.000	0.000	0.000	0.000
Inv	0.000	0.000	0.000	0.000	0.000	0.000	0.000
Inv^2	0.000	−0.231	−0.231	0.191	0.191	0.808	0.808
Nwc	0.000	0.000	0.000	0.000	0.000	0.000	0.000
Nwc^2	0.000	0.551	0.551	−0.456	−0.456	−1.927	−1.927
Eom	0.000	0.493	0.493	−0.408	−0.408	−1.725	−1.725
Eom^2	0.000	0.000	0.000	0.000	0.000	0.000	0.000
Beta	0.000	0.000	0.000	0.000	0.000	0.000	0.000
Gro	−0.226	−0.099	−0.325	0.082	−0.144	0.346	0.120
Div	−0.049	−0.033	−0.082	0.027	−0.022	0.115	0.065
Age	0.000	0.000	0.000	0.000	0.000	0.000	0.000
Ind$_2$	0.000	0.000	0.000	0.000	0.000	0.000	0.000
Ind$_3$	0.000	0.000	0.000	0.000	0.000	0.000	0.000
Ind$_4$	0.000	0.000	0.000	0.000	0.000	0.000	0.000
Ind$_5$	0.000	0.000	0.000	0.000	0.000	0.000	0.000
Ind$_7$	0.000	0.000	0.000	0.000	0.000	0.000	0.000
Ind$_8$	0.000	0.000	0.000	0.000	0.000	0.000	0.000
Time	0.000	0.000	0.000	0.000	0.000	0.000	0.000
constant	−2.826	−3.004	−5.830	2.485	−0.341	10.510	7.684

Table A.35: Detailed effects of the control variables on institutional ownership

	$D_{Icr\,x}$	$I_{Icr\,x}$	$T_{Icr\,x}$
IRatio	0.000	0.000	0.000
OcST	0.952	−1.159	−0.207
Size	0.509	−0.116	0.393
Size^2	−0.012	0.001	−0.011
Debt	0.000	0.000	0.000
Debt^2	0.000	0.000	0.000
Inv	0.000	0.000	0.000
Inv^2	−0.252	−0.381	−0.633
Nwc	0.000	0.000	0.000
Nwc^2	0.601	0.908	1.509
Eom	0.538	0.813	1.351
Eom^2	0.000	0.000	0.000
Beta	0.000	0.000	0.000
Gro	−0.220	0.374	0.154
Div	−0.060	0.063	0.003
Age	0.000	0.000	0.000
Ind$_2$	0.000	0.000	0.000
Ind$_3$	0.000	0.000	0.000
Ind$_4$	0.000	0.000	0.000
Ind$_5$	0.000	0.000	0.000
Ind$_7$	0.000	0.000	0.000
Ind$_8$	0.000	0.000	0.000
Time	0.000	0.000	0.000
constant	−4.678	1.766	−2.913

Table A.36: Noncausal effects of the control variables on Tobin's Q

	$cov(x,Q)$	Icr$_a$		Icr$_b$		Icr$_c$	
		T_{Qx}	N_{Qx}	T_{Qx}	N_{Qx}	T_{Qx}	N_{Qx}
ORatio	−0.049	0.000	−0.049	0.000	−0.049	0.000	−0.049
OcST	0.219	1.326	−1.106	0.421	−0.202	−0.901	1.121
Size	0.132	0.621	−0.489	0.003	0.128	−0.900	1.031
Size^2	0.109	−0.015	0.124	0.000	0.109	0.023	0.086
Debt	0.419	0.000	0.419	0.000	0.419	0.000	0.419
Debt^2	0.280	0.000	0.280	0.000	0.280	0.000	0.280
Inv	−0.108	0.000	−0.108	0.000	−0.108	0.000	−0.108
Inv^2	−0.351	−0.231	−0.120	0.191	−0.542	0.808	−1.159
Nwc	−0.182	0.000	−0.182	0.000	−0.182	0.000	−0.182
Nwc^2	−0.131	0.551	−0.682	−0.456	0.325	−1.927	1.797
Eom	0.402	0.493	−0.092	−0.408	0.810	−1.725	2.127
Eom^2	0.290	0.000	0.290	0.000	0.290	0.000	0.290
Beta	−0.295	0.000	−0.295	0.000	−0.295	0.000	−0.295
Gro	0.033	−0.325	0.359	−0.144	0.178	0.120	−0.087
Div	−0.057	−0.082	0.025	−0.022	−0.035	0.065	−0.122
Age	0.162	0.000	0.162	0.000	0.162	0.000	0.162
Ind$_2$	0.220	0.000	0.220	0.000	0.220	0.000	0.220
Ind$_3$	0.057	0.000	0.057	0.000	0.057	0.000	0.057
Ind$_4$	0.028	0.000	0.028	0.000	0.028	0.000	0.028
Ind$_5$	−0.007	0.000	−0.007	0.000	−0.007	0.000	−0.007
Ind$_7$	−0.248	0.000	−0.248	0.000	−0.248	0.000	−0.248
Ind$_8$	−0.094	0.000	−0.094	0.000	−0.094	0.000	−0.094
Time	−0.042	0.000	−0.042	0.000	−0.042	0.000	−0.042

A.8 Detailed and Additional Results of Empirical Analyses

Table A.37: Noncausal effects of the control variables on institutional ownership

	$cov(x, Icr)$	$T_{Ocr\,x}$	$N_{Ocr\,x}$
ORatio	−0.117	0.000	−0.117
OcST	0.515	−0.207	0.722
Size	0.032	0.393	−0.361
Size^2	0.023	−0.011	0.034
Debt	−0.049	0.000	−0.049
Debt^2	−0.025	0.000	−0.025
Inv	0.067	0.000	0.067
Inv^2	−0.128	−0.633	0.505
Nwc	0.110	0.000	0.110
Nwc^2	0.101	1.509	−1.408
Eom	−0.018	1.351	−1.369
Eom^2	−0.013	0.000	−0.013
Beta	−0.056	0.000	−0.056
Gro	−0.150	0.154	−0.304
Div	−0.134	0.003	−0.137
Age	0.181	0.000	0.181
Ind$_2$	0.041	0.000	0.041
Ind$_3$	0.055	0.000	0.055
Ind$_4$	−0.046	0.000	−0.046
Ind$_5$	−0.072	0.000	−0.072
Ind$_7$	−0.078	0.000	−0.078
Ind$_8$	0.031	0.000	0.031
Time	0.058	0.000	0.058

Robustness Checks

Table A.38: Correlation and tolerance of piecewise variables of Q and previous year's Q

	Correlation			Tolerance		
	Q_a	Q_b	Q_c	Q_a	Q_b	Q_c
Q_a^{t-1}	0.559	−0.269	−0.212	0.689	0.929	0.957
Q_b^{t-1}	−0.085	0.115	−0.202	0.995	0.989	0.961
Q_c^{t-1}	−0.407	−0.090	0.726	0.836	0.994	0.473

Table A.39: Robustness checks on lagged measures of Q

	Alternation 1		Alternation 2		Original	
	Q	Icr	Q	Icr	Q	Icr
Icr	−2.357 (0.010)		−0.861 (0.000)		−1.051 (0.001)	
Q_a		0.028 (0.051)		0.060 (0.076)		0.365 (0.003)
Q_b		−0.315 (0.000)		−0.627 (0.000)		−0.302 (0.021)
Q_c		−0.567 (0.010)		−0.988 (0.000)		−1.277 (0.000)
Q_a^{t-1}		0.063 (0.001)		0.145 (0.000)		
Q_b^{t-1}		−0.100 (0.402)		−0.275 (0.053)		
Q_c^{t-1}		−0.168 (0.011)		−0.531 (0.000)		
Iratio	−0.001 (0.422)		−0.001 (0.175)		0.000 (0.775)	
OcST	1.433 (0.008)	0.601 (0.000)	0.559 (0.000)	0.617 (0.000)	0.952 (0.001)	0.831 (0.000)
Size	0.293 (0.014)	0.060 (0.212)	0.246 (0.000)	0.091 (0.061)	0.509 (0.002)	0.283 (0.034)
Size^2	−0.006 (0.037)	−0.001 (0.407)	−0.006 (0.000)	−0.002 (0.102)	−0.012 (0.002)	−0.006 (0.041)
Debt	0.351 (0.074)	0.088 (0.219)	0.304 (0.002)	0.138 (0.010)	0.097 (0.710)	0.128 (0.519)
Debt^2	−0.263 (0.160)		−0.328 (0.046)		−0.003 (0.992)	
Inv	0.132 (0.156)	0.023 (0.541)	0.143 (0.000)	−0.011 (0.446)	−0.054 (0.632)	−0.046 (0.650)
Inv^2	−0.073 (0.040)		−0.120 (0.000)		−0.252 (0.001)	
Nwc	−0.292 (0.145)	0.026 (0.438)	−0.503 (0.000)	−0.026 (0.298)	−0.389 (0.191)	0.154 (0.140)

Table continues at the following page

A.8 Detailed and Additional Results of Empirical Analyses

Table A.39: Robustness checks on lagged measures of Q (continued)

	Alternation 1		Alternation 2		Original	
	Q	Icr	Q	Icr	Q	Icr
Nwc^2	0.340		0.471		0.601	
	(0.148)		(0.000)		(0.056)	
Eom	0.609	0.106	0.534	0.196	0.538	0.160
	(0.003)	(0.205)	(0.000)	(0.001)	(0.045)	(0.519)
Eom^2	−0.225	−0.038	−0.184	−0.056	−0.247	−0.065
	(0.065)	(0.439)	(0.000)	(0.082)	(0.143)	(0.674)
Beta	−0.003	0.007	−0.031	−0.007	−0.070	−0.023
	(0.944)	(0.679)	(0.091)	(0.711)	(0.118)	(0.574)
Gro	−0.026	−0.030	0.055	−0.052	−0.220	−0.226
	(0.776)	(0.412)	(0.013)	(0.001)	(0.083)	(0.026)
Div	−0.018	−0.009	−0.003	−0.007	−0.060	−0.049
	(0.397)	(0.247)	(0.750)	(0.428)	(0.015)	(0.007)
Age		0.002		0.004		0.010
		(0.705)		(0.383)		(0.451)
Ind_2	−0.032	−0.024	0.073	0.043	0.086	0.033
	(0.834)	(0.695)	(0.271)	(0.497)	(0.509)	(0.784)
Ind_3	−0.041	−0.039	0.066	0.008	0.115	0.021
	(0.785)	(0.496)	(0.302)	(0.898)	(0.321)	(0.843)
Ind_4	−0.354	−0.132	−0.107	−0.069	−0.058	−0.083
	(0.086)	(0.045)	(0.167)	(0.315)	(0.714)	(0.536)
Ind_5	−0.027	−0.026	0.087	0.051	0.161	0.085
	(0.869)	(0.678)	(0.211)	(0.438)	(0.194)	(0.478)
Ind_7	−0.256	−0.100	−0.092	−0.081	0.033	0.046
	(0.156)	(0.102)	(0.196)	(0.212)	(0.827)	(0.744)
Ind_8	−0.153	−0.058	−0.041	−0.024	0.003	0.016
	(0.377)	(0.384)	(0.581)	(0.729)	(0.985)	(0.922)
Time	0.099	0.048	0.029	0.039	0.060	0.054
	(0.134)	(0.019)	(0.217)	(0.057)	(0.298)	(0.266)
constant	−2.930	−0.744	−2.221	−0.974	−4.678	−2.826
	(0.021)	(0.137)	(0.000)	(0.046)	(0.007)	(0.045)

Table continues at the following page

Table A.39: Robustness checks on lagged measures of Q (continued)

	Alternation 1		Alternation 2		Original	
	Q	Icr	Q	Icr	Q	Icr
RMSE	0.474	0.194	0.213	0.206	0.508	0.199
pseudo $\bar{R}^2$	−4.554	0.302	−0.120	0.214	−6.756	0.363
Prob.$_{\chi^2}$	(0.000)	(0.000)	(0.000)	(0.000)	(0.000)	(0.000)
RMSEA	0.000	0.012	0.000	0.011	0.000	0.000

Table A.40: Robustness checks on ROE

	ROE		Q	
	Q	Icr	ROE	Icr
Ocr$_a$	−0.209		−1.051	
	(0.547)		(0.001)	
ROE$_a$ / Q$_a$			−0.022	0.365
			(0.177)	(0.003)
ROE$_b$ / Q$_b$			−0.068	−0.302
			(0.542)	(0.021)
ROE$_c$ / Q$_c$			0.024	−1.277
			(0.157)	(0.000)
Iratio	−0.001		0.000	
	(0.131)		(0.775)	
OcST	0.178		0.582	0.952	0.831
	(0.383)		(0.000)	(0.001)	(0.000)
Size	0.234		0.017	0.509	0.283
	(0.000)		(0.723)	(0.002)	(0.034)
Size^2	−0.006		0.000	−0.012	−0.006
	(0.000)		(1.000)	(0.002)	(0.041)
Debt	0.393		−0.004	0.097	0.128
	(0.001)		(0.953)	(0.710)	(0.519)
Debt^2	−0.440		−0.003		
	(0.043)		(0.992)		
Inv	0.092		−0.002	−0.054	−0.046
	(0.002)		(0.968)	(0.632)	(0.650)

Table continues at the following page

Table A.40: Robustness checks on ROE (continued)

	ROE		Q	
	Q	Icr	ROE	Icr
Inv^2	−0.089		−0.252	
	(0.025)		(0.001)	
Nwc	−0.938	0.030	−0.389	0.154
	(0.000)	(0.371)	(0.191)	(0.140)
Nwc^2	0.969		0.601	
	(0.000)		(0.056)	
Eom	0.524	0.038	0.538	0.160
	(0.000)	(0.645)	(0.045)	(0.519)
Eom^2	−0.168	−0.032	−0.247	−0.065
	(0.000)	(0.510)	(0.143)	(0.674)
Beta	−0.034	0.021	−0.070	−0.023
	(0.008)	(0.236)	(0.118)	(0.574)
Gro	0.028	−0.024	−0.220	−0.226
	(0.306)	(0.502)	(0.083)	(0.026)
Div	0.002	−0.008	−0.060	−0.049
	(0.714)	(0.325)	(0.015)	(0.007)
Age		0.010		0.010
		(0.288)		(0.451)
Ind_2	0.097	−0.054	0.086	0.033
	(0.036)	(0.365)	(0.509)	(0.784)
Ind_3	0.107	−0.057	0.115	0.021
	(0.018)	(0.320)	(0.321)	(0.843)
Ind_4	−0.044	−0.122	−0.058	−0.083
	(0.511)	(0.067)	(0.714)	(0.536)
Ind_5	0.123	−0.055	0.161	0.085
	(0.013)	(0.380)	(0.194)	(0.478)
Ind_7	−0.014	−0.100	0.033	0.046
	(0.804)	(0.105)	(0.827)	(0.744)
Ind_8	−0.003	−0.049	0.003	0.016
	(0.959)	(0.467)	(0.985)	(0.922)
Time	−0.002	0.048	0.060	0.054
	(0.913)	(0.020)	(0.298)	(0.266)

Table continues at the following page

Table A.40: Robustness checks on ROE (continued)

	ROE		Q	
	Q	Icr	ROE	Icr
constant	−2.014	−0.312	−4.678	−2.826
	(0.000)	(0.528)	(0.007)	(0.045)
RMSE	0.135	0.192	0.508	0.199
pseudo $\bar{R}^2$	0.546	0.317	−6.756	0.363
Prob.$_{\chi^2}$	(0.000)	(0.000)	(0.000)	(0.000)
RMSEA	0.026	0.000	0.000	0.000

A.8.4 Combined Simultaneous Equations Model

Simultaneous Equations Results

Table A.41: Detailed 3SLS estimates for ownership and Q

	Q	Ocr	Icr		Mcr
Ocr $_{0 \leq x \leq 39\%}$	−0.089			Ocr^2	0.359
	(0.202)				(0.000)
Ocr $_{39\% \leq x \leq 80\%}$	0.233				
	(0.012)				
Ocr $_{80\% \leq x}$	0.890				
	(0.000)				
Icr^2	−0.119			Icr^2	−0.165
	(0.014)				(0.010)
Mcr	−0.613				
	(0.000)				
Q_a		0.043	−0.031 Q		−0.826
		(0.807)	(0.621)		(0.000)
Q_b		0.011	−0.266 Q^2		−0.168
		(0.926)	(0.117)		(0.388)
Q_c		0.010	−0.483		
		(0.957)	(0.044)		
Oratio	−0.002				
	(0.854)				
Iratio	−0.001				
	(0.239)				
Mratio	0.006				
	(0.906)				
Oc2	0.154	−0.433	0.589		0.208
	(0.004)	(0.000)	(0.000)		(0.003)
Size	0.251	0.239	0.040		0.239
	(0.000)	(0.000)	(0.407)		(0.000)
Size^2	−0.006	−0.006	−0.001		−0.006
	(0.000)	(0.000)	(0.651)		(0.000)
Debt	0.345	−0.031	0.046		0.310
	(0.007)	(0.695)	(0.524)		(0.001)

Table continues at the following page

Table A.41: Results for ownership and Q (continued)

	Q	Ocr	Icr	Mcr
Debt^2	−0.213 (0.320)			
Inv	0.033 (0.394)	0.011 (0.801)	0.020 (0.599)	−0.011 (0.837)
Inv^2	−0.043 (0.274)			
Nwc	−0.509 (0.001)	0.028 (0.458)	0.034 (0.311)	−0.075 (0.100)
Nwc^2	0.482 (0.003)			
Eom	0.621 (0.000)	−0.003 (0.973)	0.040 (0.636)	0.681 (0.000)
Eom^2	−0.228 (0.000)	0.035 (0.521)	−0.015 (0.760)	−0.270 (0.000)
Beta	−0.030 (0.064)	−0.071 (0.000)	0.020 (0.246)	−0.017 (0.478)
Gro	0.029 (0.393)	0.003 (0.947)	−0.017 (0.646)	0.022 (0.659)
Div	0.000 (0.956)	−0.022 (0.013)	−0.009 (0.253)	−0.003 (0.817)
Age		0.015 (0.131)	0.010 (0.272)	0.002 (0.830)
Ind_2	0.200 (0.001)	0.083 (0.210)	−0.044 (0.462)	0.254 (0.002)
Ind_3	0.180 (0.001)	−0.025 (0.699)	−0.053 (0.355)	0.216 (0.005)
Ind_4	−0.009 (0.883)	0.037 (0.620)	−0.129 (0.052)	−0.002 (0.983)
Ind_5	0.200 (0.001)	0.053 (0.449)	−0.043 (0.490)	0.240 (0.004)
Ind_7	0.103 (0.086)	−0.011 (0.875)	−0.100 (0.104)	0.162 (0.050)

Table continues at the following page

Table A.41: Results for ownership and Q (continued)

	Q	Ocr	Icr	Mcr
Ind_8	0.041	−0.044	−0.057	0.063
	(0.512)	(0.563)	(0.405)	(0.484)
Time	−0.019	0.005	0.048	−0.028
	(0.326)	(0.826)	(0.019)	(0.317)
constant	−2.056	−1.801	−0.556	−1.985
	(0.000)	(0.001)	(0.270)	(0.004)
RMSE	0.202	0.214	0.192	0.288
pseudo $\bar{R}^2$	−0.009	0.259	0.318	0.042
χ^2	425.480	182.460	243.810	358.210
Prob.$_{\chi^2}$	(0.000)	(0.000)	(0.000)	(0.000)
RMSEA	0.000	0.000	0.000	0.000

Table A.42: Direct effects of the control variables on Tobin's Q and ownership

	$D_{Q\,x}$	$D_{Ocr\,x}$	$D_{Icr\,x}$	$D_{Mcr\,x}$
ORatio	0.000	0.000	0.000	0.000
IRatio	0.000	0.000	0.000	0.000
MRatio	0.000	0.000	0.000	0.000
OcST	0.154	−0.433	0.589	0.208
Size	0.251	0.239	0.000	0.239
Size^2	−0.006	−0.006	0.000	−0.006
Debt	0.345	0.000	0.000	0.310
Debt^2	0.000	0.000	0.000	0.000
Inv	0.000	0.000	0.000	0.000
Inv^2	0.000	0.000	0.000	0.000
Nwc	−0.509	0.000	0.000	−0.075
Nwc^2	0.482	0.000	0.000	0.000
Eom	0.621	0.000	0.000	0.681
Eom^2	−0.228	0.000	0.000	−0.270
Beta	−0.030	−0.071	0.000	0.000
Gro	0.000	0.000	0.000	0.000
Div	0.000	−0.022	0.000	0.000
Age	0.000	0.000	0.000	0.000
Ind$_2$	0.200	0.000	0.000	0.254
Ind$_3$	0.180	0.000	0.000	0.216
Ind$_4$	0.000	0.000	−0.129	0.000
Ind$_5$	0.200	0.000	0.000	0.240
Ind$_7$	0.103	0.000	0.000	0.162
Ind$_8$	0.000	0.000	0.000	0.000
Time	0.000	0.000	0.048	0.000
constant	−2.056	−1.801	0.000	−1.985

A.8 Detailed and Additional Results of Empirical Analyses

Calculation of the Effects

Direct effects:

$$D_{Q\,Ocr} = \begin{cases} .000 & \text{if Ocr} < 39\% \\ .233 & \text{if } 39\% \leq \text{Ocr} < 80\% \\ .890 & \text{if Ocr} \geq 80\% \end{cases}$$

$$\begin{aligned} D_{Q\,Icr} &= 2 * -.119 * Icr \\ &= -.238 * Icr \end{aligned}$$

$$D_{Q\,Mcr} = -.613$$

$$D_{Ocr\,Q} = .000$$

$$D_{Icr\,Q} = \begin{cases} .000 & \text{if Q} < .7 \\ -.483 & \text{if Q} \geq .7 \end{cases}$$

$$D_{Mcr\,Q} = -.826$$

$$\begin{aligned} D_{Mcr\,Ocr} &= 2 * .359 * Ocr \\ &= .718 * Ocr \end{aligned}$$

$$\begin{aligned} D_{Mcr\,Icr} &= 2 * -.165 * Ocr \\ &= -.330 * Icr \end{aligned}$$

Feedback loops of the direct effects:

$$\begin{aligned} TF_{Q\,Icr} &= \frac{D_{Q\,Icr}}{1-(D_{Q\,Icr}*D_{Icr\,Q})} \\ &= \begin{cases} \frac{-.238*Icr}{1-(-.238*Icr*0)} = -.238 * Icr & \text{if Q} < .7 \\ \frac{-.238*Icr}{1-(-.238*Icr*-.483)} = \frac{-.238*Icr}{1-.115*Icr} & \text{if Q} \geq .7 \end{cases} \end{aligned}$$

$$\begin{aligned} TF_{Q\,Mcr} &= \frac{D_{Q\,Mcr}}{1-(D_{Q\,Mcr}*D_{Mcr\,Q})} \\ &= \frac{-.613}{1-(-.613*-.826)} \\ &= -1.242 \end{aligned}$$

$$\begin{aligned} TF_{Icr\,Q} &= \frac{D_{Icr\,Q}}{1-(D_{Q\,Icr}*D_{Icr\,Q})} \\ &= \begin{cases} 0 & \text{if Q} < .7 \\ \frac{-.483*Icr}{1-(-.238*Icr*-.483)} = \frac{-.483*Icr}{1-.115*Icr} & \text{if Q} \geq .7 \end{cases} \end{aligned}$$

$$\begin{aligned} TF_{Mcr\,Q} &= \frac{D_{Mcr\,Q}}{1-(D_{Q\,Mcr}*D_{Mcr\,Q})} \\ &= \frac{-.826}{1-(-.613*-.826)} \\ &= -1.673 \end{aligned}$$

Total effects on Tobin's Q:

$$T_{Q\,Ocr} = D_{Q\,Ocr} + D_{Mcr\,Ocr} * T_{Q\,Mcr}$$

$$= \begin{cases} D_{Q\,Ocr} + .718 * Ocr * -1.242 & \text{if } Q < .7 \\ D_{Q\,Ocr} + .718 * Ocr * \frac{.242+.143*Icr}{1-.115*Icr} & \text{if } Q \geq .7 \end{cases}$$

$$= \begin{cases} D_{Q\,Ocr} - .892 * Ocr & \text{if } Q < .7 \\ D_{QOcr} + \frac{.174*Ocr+.103*Icr*Ocr}{1-.115*Icr} & \text{if } Q \geq .7 \end{cases}$$

$$= \begin{cases} -.892 * Ocr & \text{if } Q < .7 \text{ and } Ocr < 39\% \\ \frac{.174*Ocr+.103*Icr*Ocr}{1-.115*Icr} & \text{if } Q \geq .7 \text{ and } Ocr < 39\% \\ .233 - .892 * Ocr & \text{if } Q < .7 \text{ and } 39\% \leq Ocr < 80\% \\ .233 + \frac{.174*Ocr+.103*Icr*Ocr}{1-.115*Icr} & \text{if } Q \geq .7 \text{ and } 39\% \leq Ocr < 80\% \\ .890 - .892 * Ocr & \text{if } Q < .7 \text{ and } Ocr \geq 80\% \\ -.794 + \frac{.174*Ocr+.103*Icr*Ocr}{1-.115*Icr} & \text{if } Q \geq .7 \text{ and } Ocr \geq 80\% \end{cases}$$

$$T_{Q\,Icr} = TF_{Q\,Icr} + D_{Mcr\,Icr} * TF_{Q\,Mcr}$$
$$= TF_{Q\,Icr} + -.330 * Icr * -1.242 = TF_{Q\,Icr} + = .410 * Icr$$

$$= \begin{cases} -.238 * Icr + .410 * Icr = .172 * Icr & \text{if } Q < .7 \\ \frac{-.238*Icr}{1-.115*Icr} + .410 * Icr = \frac{.172*Icr - .047*Icr^2}{1-.115*Icr} & \text{if } Q \geq .7 \end{cases}$$

$$T_{Q\,Mcr} = TF_{Q\,Mcr} + \frac{1}{1-D_{Q\,Icr}*D_{Icr\,Q}}$$

$$= \begin{cases} -1.242 + 0 = -1.242 & \text{if } Q < .7 \\ -1.242 + \frac{1}{1-(-.238*Icr*-.483)} = \frac{-.242+.143*Icr}{1-.115*Icr} & \text{if } Q \geq .7 \end{cases}$$

Total effects of Tobin's Q:

$$T_{Ocr\,Q} = .000$$

$$T_{Icr\,Q} = TF_{Icr\,Q}$$

$$= \begin{cases} 0 & \text{if } Q < .7 \\ \frac{-.483*Icr}{1-(-.238*Icr*-.483)} = \frac{-.483*Icr}{1-.115*Icr} & \text{if } Q \geq .7 \end{cases}$$

$$T_{Mcr\,Q} = \frac{D_{Mcr\,Q} + TF_{Icr\,Q} * D_{Mcr\,Icr}}{1-((D_{Mcr\,Q} + TF_{Icr\,Q} * D_{Mcr\,Icr}) * D_{Q\,Mcr})}$$

$$= \begin{cases} \frac{-.826}{1-(-.826*-.613)} & \text{if } Q < .7 \\ \frac{-.826 + \frac{-.483*Icr}{1-.115*Icr}*-.330*Icr}{1-((-.826 + \frac{-.483*Icr}{1-.115*Icr}*-.330*Icr)*-.613)} & \text{if } Q \geq .7 \end{cases}$$

$$= \begin{cases} = -1.673 & \text{if } Q < .7 \\ = \frac{-.826+.095*Icr-.159*Icr^2}{1.506-.173*Icr+.097*Icr^2} & \text{if } Q \geq .7 \end{cases}$$

A.8 Detailed and Additional Results of Empirical Analyses

Total effects of the ownership interactions:

$$T_{McrOcr} = D_{McrOcr} + D_{QOcr} * T_{McrQ}$$

$$= \begin{cases} \text{if Ocr} < 39\% \\ \text{if Q} < .7 \ \& \ 39\% \le \text{Ocr} < 80\% \\ \text{if Q} \ge .7 \ \& \ 39\% \le \text{Ocr} < 80\% \\ \text{if Q} < .7 \ \& \ \text{Ocr} \ge 80\% \\ \text{if Q} \ge .7 \ \& \ \text{Ocr} \ge 80\% \end{cases}$$

$$= \begin{cases} -.718 * Ocr \\ -.718 * Ocr + .233 * -1.673 \\ -.718 * Ocr + .233 * \frac{-.826+.095*Icr-.159*Icr^2}{1.506-.173*Icr+.097*Icr^2} \\ -.718 * Ocr + .890 * -1.673 \\ -.718 * Ocr + .890 * \frac{-.826+.095*Icr-.159*Icr^2}{1.506-.173*Icr+.097*Icr^2} \end{cases}$$

$$= \begin{cases} -.718 * Ocr \\ -.718 * Ocr - .390 \\ -.718 * Ocr + .890 * \frac{-.735+.085*Icr-.142*Icr^2}{1.506-.173*Icr+.097*Icr^2} \\ -.718 * Ocr - 1.489 \\ -.718 * Ocr + .890 * \frac{-.192+.022*Icr-.037*Icr^2}{1.506-.173*Icr+.097*Icr^2} \end{cases}$$

$$T_{McrIcr} = D_{McrIcr} + TF_{QIcr} * TF_{McrQ}$$

$$= \begin{cases} -.330 * Icr - .238 * Icr * -1.673 = .068 * Icr & \text{if Q} < .7 \\ -.330 * Icr - \frac{.238*Icr}{1-.115*Icr} * -1.673 = \frac{.068*Icr+.038*Icr^2}{1-.115*Icr} & \text{if Q} \ge .7 \end{cases}$$

Robustness Checks

Table A.43: Robustness checks on the insider definition

	Q	Ocr	Icr	Mbcr
Ocr $_{0 \le x \le 39\%}$	−0.040		Ocr^2	0.261
	(0.510)			(0.000)
Ocr $_{39\% \le x \le 80\%}$	0.259			
	(0.004)			
Ocr $_{80\% \le x}$	1.052			
	(0.000)			
Icr^2	−0.064			−0.077
	(0.372)			(0.257)
Mbcr	−0.982			
	(0.000)			

Table continues at the following page

Table A.43: Robustness checks on the insider definition (continued)

	Q	Ocr	Icr	Mbcr
Q_a		0.045	−0.032 Q	−0.827
		(0.798)	(0.616)	(0.000)
Q_b		0.016	−0.232 Q^2	−0.074
		(0.897)	(0.172)	(0.545)
Q_c			0.031 −0.421	
			(0.862) (0.079)	
Oratio	−0.002			
	(0.777)			
Iratio	0.000			
	(0.745)			
Mbratio	−0.017			
	(0.704)			
OcST	0.144	−0.434	0.588	0.164
	(0.065)	(0.000)	(0.000)	(0.027)
Size	0.284	0.237	0.037	0.242
	(0.000)	(0.000)	(0.444)	(0.000)
$Size^2$	−0.007	−0.006	0.000	−0.006
	(0.000)	(0.000)	(0.697)	(0.000)
Debt	0.271	−0.034	0.040	0.253
	(0.061)	(0.670)	(0.574)	(0.013)
$Debt^2$	−0.020			
	(0.918)			
Inv	−0.018	0.010	0.019	−0.029
	(0.755)	(0.810)	(0.610)	(0.590)
Inv^2	−0.009			
	(0.805)			
Nwc	−0.195	0.029	0.035	−0.053
	(0.177)	(0.448)	(0.305)	(0.275)
Nwc^2	0.148			
	(0.325)			
Eom	0.633	−0.006	0.036	0.581
	(0.000)	(0.953)	(0.665)	(0.000)

Table continues at the following page

Table A.43: Robustness checks on the insider definition (continued)

	Q	Ocr	Icr	Mbcr
Eom^2	−0.249 (0.001)	0.035 (0.519)	−0.015 (0.759)	−0.237 (0.001)
Beta	−0.023 (0.359)	−0.071 (0.000)	0.021 (0.237)	−0.012 (0.634)
Gro	0.025 (0.641)	0.002 (0.954)	−0.016 (0.651)	0.020 (0.695)
Div	−0.013 (0.306)	−0.022 (0.013)	−0.009 (0.254)	−0.012 (0.304)
Age		0.015 (0.137)	0.010 (0.258)	0.001 (0.799)
Ind_2	0.295 (0.001)	0.083 (0.214)	−0.046 (0.446)	0.283 (0.001)
Ind_3	0.249 (0.004)	−0.025 (0.694)	−0.054 (0.345)	0.241 (0.003)
Ind_4	0.029 (0.772)	0.037 (0.621)	−0.129 (0.053)	0.033 (0.725)
Ind_5	0.300 (0.001)	0.052 (0.461)	−0.046 (0.468)	0.286 (0.001)
Ind_7	0.183 (0.051)	−0.011 (0.872)	−0.100 (0.103)	0.184 (0.036)
Ind_8	0.108 (0.286)	−0.044 (0.562)	−0.056 (0.409)	0.114 (0.235)
Time	−0.036 (0.245)	0.005 (0.830)	0.048 (0.019)	−0.038 (0.198)
constant	−2.222 (0.003)	−1.786 (0.002)	−0.525 (0.297)	−1.922 (0.008)
RMSE	0.296	0.214	0.192	0.294
pseudo $\bar{R}^2$	−1.163	0.259	0.318	0.117
χ^2	352.870	182.420	242.680	473.270
Prob.$_{\chi^2}$	(0.000)	(0.000)	(0.000)	(0.000)
RMSEA	0.000	0.000	0.000	0.000

Table A.44: Robustness checks on ROE

	Q	Ocr	Icr		Mcr
Ocr $_{0\leq x\leq 39\%}$	−0.012 (0.863)			Ocr^2	0.394 (0.000)
Ocr $_{39\%\leq x\leq 80\%}$	−0.202 (0.037)				
Ocr $_{80\%\leq x}$	−0.746 (0.004)				
Icr^2	0.032 (0.448)				−0.077 (0.257)
Mcr	0.368 (0.004)				
Roe$_a$		0.010 (0.599)	−0.024 (0.142)	Roe	0.003 (0.793)
Roe$_b$		−0.011 (0.934)	−0.071 (0.560)	Roe^2	0.009 (0.148)
Roe$_c$		−0.030 (0.124)	0.016 (0.361)		
Oratio	0.004 (0.631)				
Iratio	−0.001 (0.113)				
Mratio	−0.073 (0.181)				
OcST		0.008 (0.859)	−0.436 (0.000)	0.580 (0.000)	0.167 (0.018)
Size		0.227 (0.000)	0.236 (0.000)	0.012 (0.802)	−0.014 (0.825)
Size^2		−0.005 (0.000)	−0.006 (0.000)	0.000 (0.922)	0.000 (0.863)
Debt		0.381 (0.002)	−0.019 (0.802)	−0.006 (0.932)	0.050 (0.593)
Debt^2	−0.480 (0.027)				

Table continues at the following page

Table A.44: Results checks on ROE (continued)

	Q	Ocr	Icr	Mcr
Inv	0.124	0.010	−0.009	−0.089
	(0.000)	(0.829)	(0.827)	(0.101)
Inv^2	−0.107			
	(0.007)			
Nwc	−0.958	0.037	0.033	−0.007
	(0.000)	(0.329)	(0.337)	(0.884)
Nwc^2	0.985			
	(0.000)			
Eom	0.468	−0.025	0.031	0.145
	(0.000)	(0.790)	(0.713)	(0.198)
Eom^2	−0.128	0.048	−0.029	−0.109
	(0.001)	(0.375)	(0.558)	(0.100)
Beta	−0.045	−0.072	0.022	0.032
	(0.001)	(0.000)	(0.217)	(0.184)
Gro	0.031	0.006	−0.022	0.002
	(0.256)	(0.881)	(0.541)	(0.960)
Div	0.006	−0.024	−0.008	−0.003
	(0.339)	(0.008)	(0.324)	(0.765)
Age		0.015	0.013	0.008
		(0.139)	(0.174)	(0.490)
Ind$_2$	0.060	0.079	−0.054	0.139
	(0.214)	(0.234)	(0.362)	(0.085)
Ind$_3$	0.085	−0.032	−0.057	0.110
	(0.059)	(0.615)	(0.320)	(0.152)
Ind$_4$	−0.017	0.026	−0.120	0.030
	(0.723)	(0.728)	(0.071)	(0.742)
Ind$_5$	0.109	0.042	−0.056	0.097
	(0.023)	(0.547)	(0.366)	(0.248)
Ind$_7$	−0.045	−0.016	−0.098	0.155
	(0.369)	(0.816)	(0.111)	(0.061)
Ind$_8$	−0.006	−0.053	−0.049	0.071
	(0.914)	(0.480)	(0.472)	(0.436)

Table continues at the following page

Table A.44: Results checks on ROE (continued)

	Q	Ocr	Icr	Mcr
Time	−0.006	0.006	0.048	−0.022
	(0.707)	(0.777)	(0.018)	(0.419)
constant	−1.932	−1.773	−0.270	0.325
	(0.000)	(0.001)	(0.586)	(0.629)
RMSE	0.164	0.214	0.192	0.261
pseudo $\bar{R}^2$	0.337	0.263	0.318	0.217
χ^2	618.270	185.870	243.110	126.950
Prob.$_{\chi^2}$	(0.000)	(0.000)	(0.000)	(0.000)
RMSEA	0.022	0.000	0.000	0.000

Table A.45: Robustness checks on timing issues (Alternation 1)

	Q	Ocr	Icr	Mcr
Ocr $_{0 \leq x \leq 39\%}$	−0.108		Ocr^2	0.370
	(0.103)			(0.000)
Ocr $_{39\% \leq x \leq 80\%}$	0.216			
	(0.012)			
Ocr $_{80\% \leq x}$	0.807			
	(0.000)			
Icr^2	−0.121			−0.171
	(0.005)			(0.008)
Mbcr	−0.555			
	(0.000)			
Q_a		−0.017	−0.029 Q	−0.723
		(0.931)	(0.691)	(0.030)
Q_b		0.004	−0.211 Q^2	−0.232
		(0.973)	(0.234)	(0.467)
Q_c		0.298	−0.403	
		(0.205)	(0.196)	
Q_a^{t-1}		0.139	−0.028 Q^{t-1}	−0.113
		(0.478)	(0.702)	(0.730)
Q_b^{t-1}		0.030	−0.245 Q$^{t-1\,2}$	0.090
		(0.812)	(0.184)	(0.772)

Table continues at the following page

Table A.45: Robustness checks on timing issues 1 (continued)

	Q	Ocr	Icr	Mcr
Q_c^{t-1}		−0.344	−0.220	
		(0.107)	(0.449)	
Oratio	−0.002			
	(0.862)			
Iratio	−0.001			
	(0.149)			
Mratio	0.018			
	(0.697)			
OcST	0.157	−0.432	0.591	0.214
	(0.001)	(0.000)	(0.000)	(0.003)
Size	0.247	0.233	0.042	0.230
	(0.000)	(0.000)	(0.392)	(0.001)
Size^2	−0.006	−0.006	−0.001	−0.006
	(0.000)	(0.000)	(0.630)	(0.000)
Debt	0.363	−0.024	0.059	0.305
	(0.003)	(0.766)	(0.416)	(0.002)
Debt^2	−0.271			
	(0.200)			
Inv	0.040	0.003	0.018	−0.014
	(0.246)	(0.937)	(0.628)	(0.780)
Inv^2	−0.054			
	(0.171)			
Nwc	−0.591	0.032	0.035	−0.075
	(0.000)	(0.394)	(0.300)	(0.102)
Nwc^2	0.572			
	(0.000)			
Eom	0.609	0.020	0.045	0.669
	(0.000)	(0.834)	(0.591)	(0.000)
Eom^2	−0.221	0.022	−0.016	−0.268
	(0.000)	(0.694)	(0.743)	(0.000)
Beta	−0.029	−0.075	0.018	−0.015
	(0.042)	(0.000)	(0.316)	(0.540)

Table continues at the following page

Table A.45: Robustness checks on timing issues 1 (continued)

	Q	Ocr	Icr	Mcr
Gro	0.030	−0.005	−0.019	0.019
	(0.322)	(0.909)	(0.611)	(0.693)
Div	0.000	−0.023	−0.009	−0.002
	(0.970)	(0.011)	(0.293)	(0.825)
Age		0.019	0.010	0.002
		(0.073)	(0.293)	(0.811)
Ind_2	0.191	0.085	−0.038	0.250
	(0.000)	(0.203)	(0.533)	(0.002)
Ind_3	0.175	−0.025	−0.049	0.214
	(0.000)	(0.697)	(0.392)	(0.006)
Ind_4	−0.009	0.042	−0.125	−0.002
	(0.864)	(0.566)	(0.061)	(0.982)
Ind_5	0.192	0.058	−0.038	0.235
	(0.000)	(0.402)	(0.543)	(0.006)
Ind_7	0.094	−0.010	−0.098	0.160
	(0.080)	(0.889)	(0.112)	(0.053)
Ind_8	0.040	−0.043	−0.055	0.064
	(0.483)	(0.567)	(0.421)	(0.484)
Time	−0.018	0.010	0.049	−0.027
	(0.295)	(0.656)	(0.017)	(0.338)
constant	−2.036	−1.758	−0.560	−1.897
	(0.000)	(0.002)	(0.266)	(0.006)
RMSE	0.190	0.214	0.192	0.287
pseudo $\bar{R}^2$	0.109	0.265	0.320	0.051
χ^2	511.510	187.930	247.230	316.760
Prob.$_{\chi^2}$	(0.000)	(0.000)	(0.000)	(0.000)
RMSEA	0.009	0.000	0.000	0.000

Table A.46: Robustness checks on timing issues (Alternation 2)

	Q	Ocr	Icr	Mcr
Ocr $_{0 \leq x \leq 39\%}$	−0.129		Ocr^2	0.408
	(0.089)			(0.000)

Table continues at the following page

Table A.46: Robustness checks on timing issues 2 (continued)

	Q	Ocr	Icr	Mcr
Ocr $_{39\% \leq x \leq 80\%}$	0.122 (0.205)			
Ocr $_{80\% \leq x}$	0.509 (0.041)			
Icr^2	−0.109 (0.011)			−0.180 (0.005)
Mbcr	−0.292 (0.009)			
Q_a		−0.062 (0.745)	−0.024 Q (0.738)	−0.006 (0.988)
Q_b		0.038 (0.772)	−0.243 Q^2 (0.171)	−0.504 (0.176)
Q_c		0.491 (0.024)	−0.602 (0.039)	
Q_a^{t-1}		0.100 (0.614)	−0.011 Q^{t-1}Q (0.883)	−0.249 (0.522)
Q_b^{t-1}		0.012 (0.927)	−0.215 Q$^{t-1}{}^2$ (0.254)	0.237 (0.523)
Q_c^{t-1}		−0.422 (0.063)	−0.034 (0.913)	
Oratio	0.000 (0.979)			
Iratio	−0.002 (0.017)			
Mratio	−0.009 (0.868)			
OcST	0.153 (0.001)	−0.433 (0.000)	0.588 (0.000)	0.213 (0.003)
Size	0.195 (0.000)	0.211 (0.000)	−0.011 (0.831)	0.117 (0.095)
Size^2	−0.005 (0.000)	−0.005 (0.000)	0.001 (0.586)	−0.003 (0.047)

Table continues at the following page

Table A.46: Robustness checks on timing issues 2 (continued)

	Q	Ocr	Icr	Mcr
Debt	0.465 (0.001)	−0.008 (0.921)	0.066 (0.378)	0.182 (0.073)
Debt^2	−0.525 (0.041)			
Inv	−0.035 (0.207)	−0.012 (0.685)	−0.020 (0.463)	−0.059 (0.105)
Inv^2	−0.015 (0.693)			
Nwc	−0.547 (0.001)	0.039 (0.303)	0.024 (0.482)	−0.022 (0.634)
Nwc^2	0.564 (0.002)			
Eom	0.490 (0.000)	−0.029 (0.756)	0.077 (0.343)	0.340 (0.004)
Eom^2	−0.175 (0.000)	0.027 (0.612)	−0.039 (0.426)	−0.168 (0.011)
Beta	−0.017 (0.226)	−0.076 (0.000)	0.018 (0.322)	0.021 (0.400)
Gro	0.002 (0.952)	0.017 (0.662)	−0.025 (0.475)	0.013 (0.780)
Div	0.001 (0.926)	−0.024 (0.008)	−0.008 (0.320)	−0.004 (0.728)
Age		0.018 (0.090)	0.012 (0.191)	0.004 (0.752)
Ind$_2$	0.159 (0.002)	0.088 (0.190)	−0.032 (0.593)	0.206 (0.011)
Ind$_3$	0.149 (0.002)	−0.023 (0.714)	−0.044 (0.444)	0.162 (0.037)
Ind$_4$	0.007 (0.900)	0.052 (0.485)	−0.105 (0.112)	0.035 (0.698)
Ind$_5$	0.170 (0.001)	0.055 (0.431)	−0.029 (0.641)	0.168 (0.049)

Table continues at the following page

Table A.46: Robustness checks on timing issues 2 (continued)

	Q	Ocr	Icr	Mcr
Ind_7	0.069 (0.186)	0.004 (0.958)	−0.094 (0.125)	0.157 (0.059)
Ind_8	0.034 (0.532)	−0.027 (0.721)	−0.054 (0.424)	0.070 (0.444)
Time	−0.032 (0.073)	0.018 (0.452)	0.049 (0.020)	−0.027 (0.341)
constant	−1.509 (0.000)	−1.554 (0.009)	−0.023 (0.965)	−0.894 (0.213)
RMSE	0.164	0.215	0.192	0.270
pseudo $\bar{R}^2$	0.336	0.259	0.319	0.158
χ^2	424.340	181.510	249.990	178.450
Prob.$_{\chi^2}$	(0.000)	(0.000)	(0.000)	(0.000)
RMSEA	0.000	0.000	0.000	0.000